MONETARY POLICY OPERATIONS AND THE FINANCIAL SYSTEM

Monetary Policy Operations and the Financial System

ULRICH BINDSEIL

OXFORD
UNIVERSITY PRESS

OXFORD
UNIVERSITY PRESS

Great Clarendon Street, Oxford, OX2 6DP,
United Kingdom

Oxford University Press is a department of the University of Oxford.
It furthers the University's objective of excellence in research, scholarship,
and education by publishing worldwide. Oxford is a registered trade mark of
Oxford University Press in the UK and in certain other countries

First Edition published in 2014
Impression: 2

Published in the United States of America by Oxford University Press
198 Madison Avenue, New York, NY 10016, United States of America

British Library Cataloguing in Publication Data
Data available

Library of Congress Control Number: 2014939133

ISBN 978–0–19–871690–7

Printed and bound by
CPI Group (UK) Ltd, Croydon, CR0 4YY

Contents

Part II: Monetary Policy Operations in Times of Crisis

List of Figures

List of Tables

List of Abbreviations

ABS	Asset Backed Securities
CDO	collateralized debt obligation
CVPH	collateral value post-haircut
DTI	distance to illiquidity
ECB	European Central Bank
ELA	emergency liquidity assistance
EONIA	Euro overnight interest average
FLS	'Funding for Lending' Scheme
FOMC	Federal Open Market Committee
HKMA	Hong Kong Monetary Authority
IMF	International Monetary Fund
LCR	Liquidity Coverage Ratio
LOLR	lender of last resort
LSAP	large scale asset purchase programme
MFI	Monetary Financial Institutions
OMOs	open market operations
OTC	over-the-counter
RMBS	retail mortgage-backed securities
SLP	securities lending programme
SOMA	system open market account
SONIA	Sterling overnight index average
TAF	Term Auction Facility
VaR	Value-at-Risk

Introduction and Overview

Implementing monetary policy normally means controlling through central bank market operations the short-term interbank interest rate. The target level of the short-term interbank rate to be achieved can be considered as the key 'exogenous' input to monetary policy implementation, i.e. the short-term interest rate target is what needs to be 'implemented'. The target is derived on the basis of a macroeconomic model of the transmission mechanism between short-term interest rates and the ultimate target of monetary policy. In times of financial crisis, the usual dichotomy (the 'separation principle') between monetary macroeconomics being the basis for deriving the short-term interest rate target, and the implementation of this short-term rate target through market operations, breaks down: as the monetary policy transmission is impaired and as banks and other indebted entities struggle for funding to prevent default (and the associated additional economic damage), the way central bank market operations are conducted becomes directly relevant for the stance of monetary policy.

Central bank monetary policy operations have traditionally been considered as a matter of practice, while the macroeconomic modelling of the transmission mechanism is regarded as a discipline relying on substantial theory ('monetary economics'). However, monetary policy operations can equally benefit from a theory and from a normative framework to guide policy choices. Part I of the text contains an introduction to a theory of monetary policy operations in normal times, while part II covers monetary policy operations in times of crisis. Part II also discusses the role of monetary policy implementation for banks' funding liquidity, for financial stability, and for central bank risk management.

Chapter 1 introduces the basic terminology of monetary policy implementation and its relationship to monetary macroeconomics in normal times. Chapter 2 proposes a representation of the quantity side (in contrast to the interest rate side) of monetary policy operations in a closed system of financial accounts. This approach clarifies the impact of any central bank financial transaction on the balance sheets of other economic agents as well as the impact of other agents' transactions on the central bank balance sheet. Chapter 3 discusses the choice of the operational target of monetary policy and the role of interest rates in this context. Chapter 4 presents a basic model of interest rate control and three different approaches to it. Chapter 5 extends this basic model to the case of several subsequent liquidity shocks and market sessions, and illustrates the martingale property of overnight rates. Chapters 6, 7, and 8 each deepen the analysis of one monetary policy instrument, namely, standing facilities, open market operations, and reserve requirements, respectively. Chapter 9 treats a much under-researched topic, namely central bank collateral. Chapter 10 concludes part I with some examples of monetary policy implementation frameworks and some general reflections on optimal monetary policy operations in normal times.

Part II reviews the specific role, tools, and challenges of monetary policy implementation in times of a liquidity crisis. Chapter 11 analyses the mechanics, contagion channels, and feedback loops of liquidity crises. Chapters 12 and 13 look into the role of monetary policy instruments to maintain an effective monetary policy transmission in a crisis environment: Chapter 12 focuses on collateral, while chapter 13 goes on to cover standing facilities, central bank credit operations, and outright purchase programmes. Chapter 14 introduces the role of the central bank as lender of last resort (LOLR). Chapter 15 focuses on the liquidity-support/risk-taking trade-off that the central bank faces in its LOLR role, while chapter 16 covers moral hazard and incentive aspects, and the role of liquidity regulation. Chapter 17 turns to the role of an *international* lender of last resort and provides a simple financial accounts representation of relating liquidity flows. Chapter 18 draws conclusions on central bank operations in crisis times.

Throughout the book, liquidity flows and the way the financial system copes with them (or fails to do so) will be presented in financial account systems, with typically the following sectors: (i) households/real money investors; (ii) corporates/governments; (iii) banks; (iv) the central bank. Often, the banking sector is represented in these models by two banks, and in chapter 17 accounts of a foreign country will be added. Representing liquidity flows in closed systems of financial accounts ensures that both legs of every transaction are recorded, and that the transmission of shocks through the financial system and the interrelations across the economy are comprehensively captured.

Models are always kept as simple as possible, and they are never calibrated with actual data. Instead, comparative static output is often provided to illustrate key effects and to allow them to be compared with patterns observed during normal or crisis times.

It is important to highlight what this book does *not* pretend to cover, and why.

First, this book does not attempt to provide a comprehensive review of the academic monetary economics literature touching on monetary policy operations. Pre-crisis monetary economics was not really saying much about practical monetary policy implementation issues, and in fact has even been misleading for many decades during the twentieth century (see the section 3.3 for a critique, in line with Moore, 1988, of the money supply view of monetary policy implementation). For part II of the book, there is a lot of relevant academic literature to consider. In particular, the modelling of financial market impairment and of the implied credit constraints and hence disturbances of monetary policy transmission has contributed numerous valid insights (e.g. Stiglitz and Weiss, 1981, or Diamond and Dybvig, 1983). This microeconomic/finance literature also rapidly found its reflection in monetary macroeconomics (e.g. Bernanke and Gertler, 1989). However, this older monetary macroeconomic literature did not develop a meaningful link to central bank monetary policy operations, i.e. it remained focused on the more remote parts of the transmission mechanism. The financial crisis starting in 2007 has triggered a significant new wave of attempts to integrate the role of financial markets and institutions in monetary transmission, and this time also included relevant models to integrate 'non-conventional' monetary policy operations. This literature, which is still rapidly evolving, aims at capturing the role of central bank operations and the central bank balance sheet within comprehensive macroeconomic equilibrium models. Illing (2007) provides a (pre-crisis) model of the interaction between monetary policy, leverage and financial stability. Woodford (2010), Curdia and Woodford (2010), and Friedman (2013) aim at developing new Keynesian macroeconomic models integrating the crucial role of the spread between the risk-free and the actual financing rates of the real economy. Gertler and Kiyotaki (2010) provide an overview of the literature on how the impairment of financial intermediation affects real economic activity. Curdia and Woodford (2011), Gertler and Karadi (2011), Gertler and Karadi (2013), and Ashcraft et al. (2011) focus explicitly also on central bank monetary policy operations when modelling the role of non-conventional monetary policies in disturbed financial market conditions. Brunnermeier et al. (2012) provides a comprehensive overview of monetary macroeconomics with financial frictions. The present book does not aim at providing a general equilibrium perspective on monetary policy operations, in order to (i) keep the focus more clearly on central bank operations and the various relevant issues in practice; (ii) provide a broad and easily understandable introduction to the topic with various partial models and examples; (iii) avoid the complexity and unavoidable simplification and narrowing down of the problem that is associated with any general-equilibrium macroeconomic approach.

Second, this book does not provide a systematic and comprehensive survey of central bank monetary policy implementation practice. For a historical account of the nineteenth- and twentieth-century operations of the Bank of England, Fed, and German Reichsbank, see Bindseil (2005a). For a survey of practice at the end of the twentieth century see Borio (1997). Other surveys are Bindseil and Nyborg (2008), Markets Committee (2009), or Sellin and Sommar (2013). On collateral, recent comparative studies are Cheun et al. (2009), Tabakis and Weller (2009), European Central Bank (2013b), and Markets Committee (2013). For descriptions of operational frameworks as provided by the central banks themselves, see for example European Central Bank (2011a), (2011b), or Bank of England (2013). Moreover, part II on the role of central banks in financial crisis does not attempt to provide a review of the central bank measures during the subprime (and in the case of the ECB, during the euro area sovereign debt) crisis. On the ECB's measures, see for instance European Central Bank (2010), Papadia and Valimäki (2011), Bindseil and König (2011), González-Páramo (2011), Coeuré (2012), Shambaugh (2012), Allen and Moessner (2013), Cour-Thimann and Winkler (2013), Cour-Thimann (2013), or the critical review of Sinn and Wollmershäuser (2011). A comprehensive history of the various measures taken would be a book on its own. The present book may be considered to take an intermediate perspective between the verbal accounts of actual central bank monetary policy implementation and crisis measures on one side, and the highly sophisticated and general attempts to capture monetary policy operations in general-equilibrium macro models on the other side.

I wish to thank students at the Technical University of Berlin and audience members at a lecture at the Fields Institute in Toronto for feedback on previous versions of this text. I also want to thank my co-authors Juliusz Jablecki, Philipp König, Jeroen Lamoot, Adalbert Winkler, and Flemming Würtz for the inspiring collaboration, without which this material would be much poorer. I would like to thank Peter Sellin for providing me interest rate data he compiled for Sellin and Sommar (2013). For helpful comments, I would like to thank Andrew Fillardo, Matheus Graselli, Ken Nyholm, Francesco Papadia, Dan Rosen, Benjamin Sahel, Miklos Vari, and Thomas Werner, as well as two anonymous referees. I wish to thank Adam Swallow and Aimee Wright of OUP for their kind support throughout the entire process of finalizing the book. It has been a great experience to work with Malcolm Todd and Saipriya Kannan on the copy-editing and setting of the book. Last but not least, I would like to thank colleagues in the Directorate

General Market Operations of the ECB for the common work on many of the topics touched upon in the current text. Remaining errors in the book are mine. Opinions expressed are those of the author, and not necessarily those of the European Central Bank.

Part I

Monetary Policy Operations in Normal Times

1

Basic Terminology and Relationship to Monetary Macroeconomics

1.1 KEY CONCEPTS AND TERMINOLOGY

Monetary policy operations have normally little to do with monetary macroeconomics. Monetary macroeconomics in central bank practice aims in normal times at identifying the level of the short-term interest rate that should best contribute to achieving the central bank's ultimate objectives, like price stability and/or full employment. For this, the central bank has to understand the transmission mechanism, i.e. how the operational target, indicator variables, intermediate targets, and exogenous shocks are dynamically linked to the ultimate objective. The monetary policy strategy also specifies how, given the transmission mechanism, the central bank adjusts across time its operational target on the basis of new information and communicates on this with the public.

Monetary policy instruments are the tools used by the central bank to reach its operational target. Central banks use mainly three such tools: open market operations, standing facilities, and reserve requirements. Unfortunately, the term 'instrument' was understood in an ambiguous way for many decades, as illustrated by the influential article of Poole (1970).

Open market operations may be defined as central bank transactions with banks at the central bank's initiative. Two subtypes can be distinguished: (i) outright purchases or sales of assets (normally debt securities); (ii) lending (or 'credit', 'reverse', or 'temporary') operations, conducted for instance through an auction (or 'tender').

Standing facilities are central bank operations at the initiative of banks, on the basis of a commitment of the central bank to allow such operations under certain conditions. Three variants have to be distinguished, of which the first two are liquidity-providing and the third liquidity-absorbing:

(i) A discount facility: banks can sell certain short-term paper to the central bank at any time, whereby the discount rate specified by the central bank is applied to calculate the price on the basis of the securities' cash-flows.[1]

(ii) An overnight borrowing facility: banks can borrow at any time against the provision of eligible collateral at some rate specified by the central bank.

(iii) A deposit facility: banks can deposit at any time funds with the central bank on a specific account where it gets remunerated at a specific rate.

Reserve requirements oblige banks to hold a certain minimum level of sight deposits on their account with the central bank ('current accounts', 'reserves', and 'central bank liquidity' are used as synonyms for banks' sight deposits with central banks in monetary policy implementation jargon). The fulfilment of reserve requirements is measured only on the basis of end-of-day snapshots (i.e. intra-day levels of reserves are not relevant). The requirement may apply to single day-ends, or to an average over e.g. a one-month period. The size of the reserve requirement of a specific bank is normally set as a function of specific items of its balance sheet which need to be reported on a monthly basis. For example, in the case of the European Central Bank, the requirement for each bank amounts to 1% of its liabilities to non-banks with a maturity below two years.

The **operational target of monetary policy** is a variable with the following characteristics: (i) it can sufficiently be controlled by the central bank; (ii) it is economically relevant, in the sense that it effectively influences the ultimate target of monetary policy (e.g. price stability); (iii) it defines the stance of monetary policy, in the sense that it is set by the policy decision-making body of the central bank (e.g. the Federal Open Market Committee for the Federal Reserve or the Governing Council for the European Central Bank); (iv) it gives the necessary and sufficient guidance to the monetary policy implementation officers in the central bank on what to do. In a financial crisis, policy decision-makers will likely have to give guidance on more than one operational target variable, which makes policy decisions, communication, and implementation much more difficult (see section 11.8). In the chain of monetary policy action, implementation through market operations follows monetary macroeconomics in the sense that it starts from the chosen level of the operational target and via actual market operations ('open mouth' operations are not sufficient, contrary to what has sometimes been suggested in academic literature, e.g. Guthrie and Wright, 2000) ensures that this prevails in financial markets.

[1] Discount facilities were the predominant tool of central banks until at least the middle of the twentieth century. Today, they are no longer used in industrialized countries, although their name is still used by some central banks (e.g. the Federal Reserve) for their borrowing facility. (Borrowing facilities were called in the past 'Lombard' or 'advance' facilities.)

Monetary policy implementation consists, first, in establishing an operational framework to control the selected operational target (e.g. setting up the instruments including legal documentation, selecting counterparties, defining a list of eligible collateral). The second element of implementation is the use on a day-by-day basis of open market operations and standing facilities to influence the scarcity of sight deposits of banks with the central bank, to achieve the operational target of monetary policy. This second element is often called *central bank liquidity management.*

1.2 DICHOTOMY BETWEEN MONETARY MACROECONOMICS AND MONETARY POLICY IMPLEMENTATION IN NORMAL TIMES

Monetary policy can be said to have a *Sollbruchstelle* (a predetermined breaking point), which is where the monetary macroeconomists hand over the short-term interest level, identified as optimal to achieve the ultimate target, to the implementation experts. While the first function belongs to the area of 'white-collar' central banking and is usually performed by the economics department, the second function belongs more to the 'blue-collar' areas; for instance, in the European Central Bank it is carried out by a department called 'Market Operations'. In principle, monetary macroeconomists in central banks do not need to understand monetary policy implementation and, symmetrically, implementation experts do not need to understand much about monetary policy strategy and the transmission mechanism. Actually, the resulting potential for specialization and associated efficiency gains are normally realized in central banks, i.e. there are no attempts to make implementation experts at the same time macro-monetary economics specialists, and vice versa. This segregation between the two functions may be called a 'dichotomy' between monetary macroeconomics and monetary policy implementation. Others have referred to it as the 'separation principle' of monetary policy implementation. One may also speak about a 'hierarchy' organizing monetary policy, with the choice of the ultimate target at the top, followed by the analysis of the transmission mechanism and the associated identification of the optimal level of the operational target of monetary policy, and with monetary policy implementation finally achieving this target through monetary policy operations.

It should be noted that this dichotomy was blurred for quite a while during the twentieth century. The United States' 1920–1985 official monetary policy doctrine was characterized by the idea of a control of the monetary base through open market operations, which would feed via the money multiplier into intermediate targets (some broad monetary aggregate) and eventually to ultimate targets. Another example of a violation of the dichotomy was the practice of the Deutsche Bundesbank during the 1990s to signal the evolution of the monetary policy stance through a change in marginal allotment rates in its open market operations. Generally, in the years before the crisis, central banks had converged towards 'dichotomic' monetary policies. It was recognized that defining the stance of monetary policy (i.e. the target level of the short-term interest rates) is one issue, achieving it through operations another one. The transmission mechanism, according to this view, works through interest rates and, as long as the central bank sufficiently controls short-term interest rates, it does not matter, from a macroeconomic perspective, how it does so. In a financial crisis, when the usual arbitrage relationships between various financial instruments break down, and funding constraints become pervasive, the short-term rate loses its property as sufficient operational target of monetary policy and the central bank therefore takes so-called non-standard monetary policy measures to directly impact upon different elements of the transmission mechanism of monetary policy. A special case is when the level of nominal short-term rates reaches the zero lower bound and cannot be reduced further—again, in this case it is no longer sufficient to keep the short-term rate at zero, and the central bank may apply non-standard operations, e.g. to try to lower directly long-term interest rates or rates of less liquid or more credit-risky financial assets.

Figure 1.1 summarizes the logic of monetary policy in normal times, and the assignment of responsibilities to an 'economics' and a 'markets' department within the central bank. The economics department defines the monetary policy strategy and maintains a macroeconomic model including a model of the transmission of monetary policy. From this model, and its knowledge about the state of the economy and its forecast of exogenous variables, it derives the adequate level of the operational target of monetary policy (e.g. an overnight interest rate target). After approval by the decision-making body, the market operations department implements this target through its instruments. The rest is left to the financial system and to the real economy. The transmission mechanism can be conceived as consisting in three sub-elements:

- From the operational target variable of the central bank, i.e. the short-term interest rate, to the entire matrix of interest rates and quantities across maturities and financial instruments.
- From the financial system to the real economy. (There is also feedback from the latter to the former. For example, demand of the real economy for funding is influenced by factors exogenous to the financial system, or defaults of real-economy firms can create losses to financial institutions and impair their balance sheets, etc.)
- From the real economy to the ultimate targets of monetary policy, including in particular price stability.

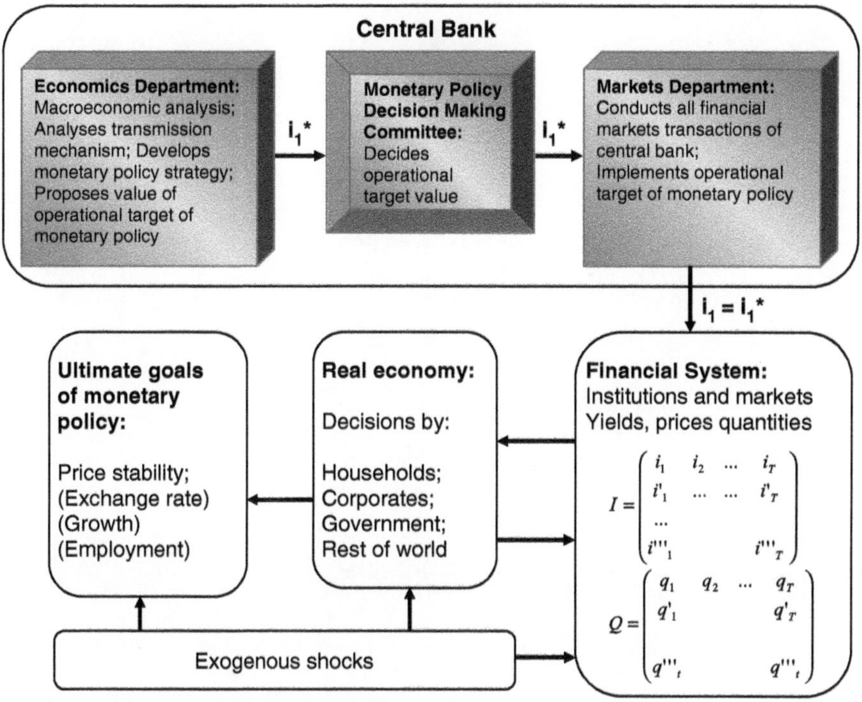

Fig. 1.1. Schematic representation of monetary policy operations in normal times, that is under the separation principle

It is assumed in normal times that the transmission from the short-term interbank rate to the matrix of all other interest rates and quantities is sufficiently predictable and stable, and that quantitative constraints are not too relevant, i.e. a 'normal' creditor who is willing to pay the market rate will be able to find a bank or an investor that will fund him.

Only for reasons of presentational simplicity, figure 1.1 does not mention other key central bank functions, such as Financial Stability, Payment Systems, Statistics, Legal, and Financial Risk Management, which are mostly independent from the Economics and Market Operations departments. These functions interact with the two functions shown and provide key input to the decision making bodies, also in relation to monetary policy.

2

Representing Monetary Policy Operations in Financial Accounts

2.1 INTRODUCTION TO THE FINANCIAL ACCOUNTS MODEL

A proper accounts representation of financial flows is essential to understanding central bank monetary policy operations in normal and crisis times.[1] This chapter introduces a system of financial accounts to allow for a representation of monetary policy implementation at the basic level of economic transactions. Transactions are represented within a closed economy consisting of the following sectors: (i) households; (ii) banks; (iii) corporations and the government; (iv) the central bank. These sectors have claims and liabilities towards each other. The basic types of assets and liabilities are: banknotes, deposits, bonds, loans, and in a few model variants also equity. It is assumed that at the origin of the economy stands the household sector. In the beginning, this sector only holds real assets of value E ('equity'). The household then diversifies into three financial assets, namely deposits with banks D, banknotes B, and debt instruments issued by corporates and the government S. To the extent that the household diversifies into financial assets, it sells real assets to the corporate and government sectors. However, households do not transact directly with corporates or governments and the central bank but use the intermediary services of banks. For the sake of presentational simplicity, households are strictly non-leveraged in the proposed financial accounts system, i.e. their balance sheet length always remains E.

Corporates and the government finance themselves via bank loans and debt securities issuance, whereby the debt securities can be held by the household

[1] See e.g. Keister and McAndrews, 2009, who discuss one widespread monetary policy misunderstanding resulting from the absence of a thorough financial accounts approach. The use of comprehensive financial accounts for a macroeconomic stock and flow analysis has been a topic in economics since the 1940s. Godley and Lavoie (2012) is the most ambitious recent attempt to base monetary economics on such an approach.

(S_{HH}) or by the central bank (S_{CB}). We treat the government and the corporates most of the time as one sector, which is an adequate parsimonious treatment for our purposes. The real resources that the corporate and the government sector can appropriate correspond to what the household wants to diversify into banknotes, deposits, and securities. The corporate and the government sector use the real assets for idiosyncratic illiquid projects (machines, schools, etc.). If the corporate and government sector can no longer roll over the loans obtained from banks and the debt securities issued, they would have to try to deleverage rapidly by selling their assets at loss-making prices (e.g. a sophisticated machine being sold as old metal), and would possibly default due to illiquidity or insolvency (or both). This will be the focus of part II of the book.

The provision of credit based on the diversification of household assets into banknotes and bank deposits runs via banks. The banking sector is the intermediary between the other sectors (except for the central bank's and the household's outright holdings of securities, S_{CB} and S_{HH}). First, it offers deposits D to households and invests them in loans to corporates. Second, the bank is an intermediary to the operation between the households, the corporates/government, and the central bank encompassing the issuance of banknotes B. Banks can be considered to use banknotes to purchase real assets from households, which they sell on to corporates who finance them through a loan from the bank. Thus, total funding and hence total assets held by banks amount to $B + D - S_{CB}$. Finally, banknotes are issued by the *central bank*, which provides them initially to banks through collateralized credit operations.

The resulting financial structure of the economy can be reflected in the form of a flow chart (figure 2.1) or in the form of financial accounts (figure 2.2). In the flow chart, the origin of an arrow is with the entity that has a claim and the peak with the entity that has a liability. Note that there are two sectors in this model who actually make choices: first, the household chooses to diversify its real assets into three financial assets D, S_{HH}, and B; second, the central bank decides on the split of its monetary policy operations between outright securities holdings S_{CB} and credit operations with banks (as residual, $B\text{-}S_{CB}$). All other balance-sheet positions are expressed in terms of these four choice variables and the initial level of household equity.

Figure 2.3 reflects that, typically, the accounts as presented above are not static in time. Instead, the household demand for financial assets is unstable, and households may want to rebalance their financial asset portfolio, e.g. for reasons of credit-risk fears or speculative position-taking. In particular, households may withdraw deposits from banks out of fear over the stability of banks, and hold more banknotes, like in a classical bank run (flow d). Moreover, they may be unwilling to roll over (or they may sell) debt securities out of credit fears regarding issuers, and instead hold more deposits (flows).

It is important to understand how these flows filter through the entire financial system. This depends inter alia on whether the central bank is ready or not to buffer out the impact of the shifts in household demand for financial assets.

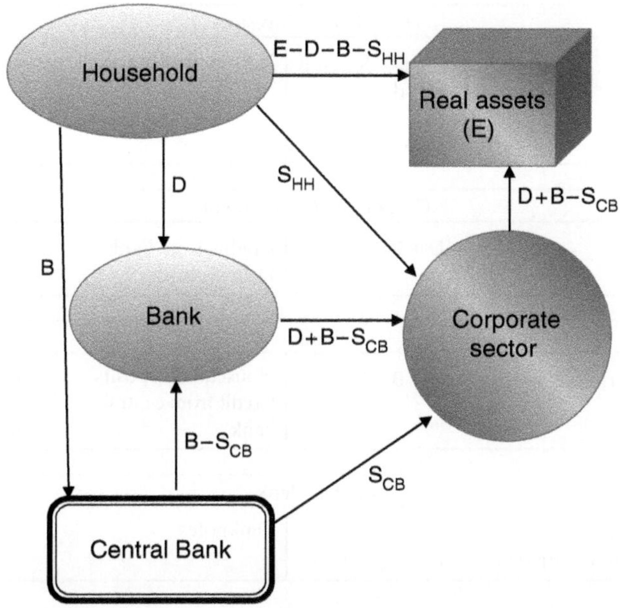

Fig. 2.1. A simple financial system—chart representation

Households / Investors			
Real Assets	$E - D - S_{HH} - B$	Household Equity	E
Deposits Bank	D		
Debt securities	S_{HH}		
Banknotes	B		

Corporate / Government			
Real assets	$D + B + S_{HH}$	Credits from banks	$D + B - S_{CB}$
		Debt securities	$S_{HH} + S_{CB}$

Bank			
Lending to corporates	$D + B - S_{CB}$	Household deposits	D
		Credit from central bank	$B - S_{CB}$

Central Bank			
Debt securities	S_{CB}	Banknotes	B
Credit operations with banks	$B - S_{CB}$		

Fig. 2.2. A simple system of financial accounts with one bank

Households / Investors			
Real Assets	$E - D - S_{HH} - B$	Household Equity	E
Deposits Bank	$D - d + s$		
Debt securities	$S_{HH} - s$		
Banknotes	$B + d$		

Corporate / Government			
Real assets	$D + B + S_{HH}$	Credits from banks	$D + B - S_{CB}$
		Debt securities	$S_{CB} + S_{HH}$

Bank			
Lending to corporates	$D + B - S_{CB}$	Household deposits	$D - d + s$
		Credit from central bank	$B - S_{CB} + d - s$

Central Bank			
Debt securities	$S_{CB} + s$	Banknotes	$B + d$
Credit operations with banks	$B - S_{CB} + d - s$		

Fig. 2.3. A simple system of financial accounts with two types of liquidity shocks

In the system of financial accounts shown in figure 2.3, it is assumed that the central bank is willing to react to flow d by tolerating more lending to banks, and to flow s by substituting lending to banks by outright holdings of securities. While the former has been best practice for central banks for a long time, the latter is more controversial. If the central bank refuses to react in this way to flow s, then the corporates must try to substitute debt securities issued with additional bank funding.

In this specification, the central bank is the key *built-in liquidity stabilizer* of the financial system. The central bank is able to issue banknotes demanded by households/investors and to compose its assets in line with the possible need to stabilize the demand for different financial assets (assuming illiquidity of real assets).

It should be noted that in the system of accounts presented here, none of the financial shocks relating to the instability of household demand for the various financial assets reaches the corporate/government sector. This is a 'positive' assumption, as funding shocks reaching the real sector imply forced deleveraging or defaults, both of which are costly for society. An effective financial system is one which allows efficient channelling of funds (and hence real assets) from households/investors to corporates and governments, and at the same time to absorb most changes in the financial asset allocation of households.

2.2 DEPOSIT SHIFTS BETWEEN INDIVIDUAL BANKS AND THE INTERBANK MARKET

Households also shift their deposits across financial institutions. Accordingly, we have to extend the model depicted in figure 2.2 by introducing a second bank. This will also be the precondition for representing interbank markets. We assume that the banks are identical *ex ante* and each represent one-half of the banking system.

The interbank market position between the two types of banks is set initially to Y, with bank 1 lending to bank 2. This could be the case because bank 1 has comparative advantages in deposit collection, while bank 2 has comparative advantages in originating and managing loans to corporates (see e.g. Bindseil and Jablecki, 2011a). To simplify, we no longer consider securities issuance as a funding source for corporates. However, we introduce two new flows to the model. Flow k reflects a deposit shift between banks initiated by households and may be triggered e.g. by one bank suddenly offering a higher remuneration rate for household deposits, or by rumours about one bank having problems. Flow y represents a change to the interbank lending volume, and may reflect a change of business strategy by the lending bank, or that the lending bank hears rumours about the borrowing banks having problems. Flows *k* and *y* both imply funding losses for bank 2, which consequently has to extend its central bank borrowing as far as it can (possibly until it hits its collateral constraints—see equation 2.1). Note that if $k + y > B/2 + d/2$, bank 1 will be in excess liquidity; i.e. without any recourse to central bank credit, bank 1 will have a claim on the central bank of $k + y - B/2 - d/2$. In this case, the central bank balance sheet expands by the latter amount. Figure 2.4 presents the financial accounts system with two banks as a chart, while figure 2.5 provides a financial account representation including the flows d, k, y. Figure 2.5 allows us to define three concepts that will also be important in particular in part II of the book.

- By allowing liquidity flows k, y, d to be compensated by heterogeneous changes of the recourse by individual banks to central bank credit, without this being yet visible in a lengthening of the central bank balance sheet (as $B/2 - k - y + d/2 \geq 0$, to speak in terms of the specific financial accounts system of figure 2.5), the central bank provides *relative intermediation to the banking system.*
- Once liquidity flows are such that some banks deposit excess funds with the central bank, thereby lengthening the central bank balance sheet, (which happens in the financial accounts system of figure 2.5 when $B/2 - k - y + d/2 < 0$), while other banks are particularly dependent on the central bank, we speak of *absolute central bank intermediation of the banking system.* Normally, absolute central bank intermediation can be avoided by setting a sufficient spread between the (higher) rate at which banks can borrow from the central bank and the (lower) rate of remuneration

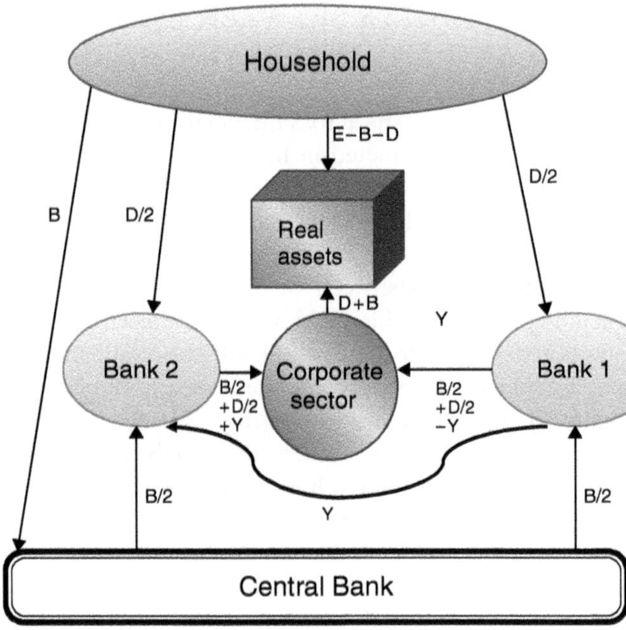

Fig. 2.4. Household deposit and interbank lending in chart representation—with two separate banks

Households / Investors			
Real Assets	E – D – B	Household Equity	E
Deposits Bank 1	D/2 – d/2 + k		
Deposits Bank 2	D/2 – d /2 – k		
Banknotes	B + d		

Bank 1			
Lending to corporates	D/2 + B/2 – Y	Household deposits / debt	D/2 + k – d/2
Deposits with CB	max(0,–B/2+k+y–d/2)	Credit from central bank	max(0,B/2 – k – y + d/2)
Lending to Bank 2	Y – y		

Bank 2			
Lending to corporates	D/2 + B/2 + Y	Household deposits / debt	D/2 – k – d/2
		Credit from central bank	B/2 + k + y + d/2
		Liabilities to Bank 1	Y – y

Central Bank			
Credit oper.	B/2 + k + y + d/2 + max(0, B/2 – k – y + d/2)	Banknotes	B + d
		Deposits banks	max(0, – B/2 + k + y – d/2)

Fig. 2.5. Financial accounts with household deposit and interbank lending shifts—with two separate banks

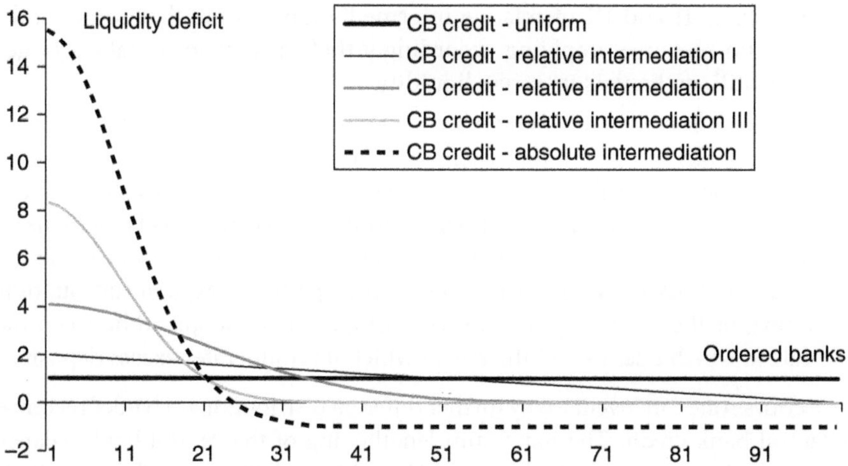

Fig. 2.6. Relative recourse to central bank credit of a population of 100 banks (with D = 900 and B = 100). Uniform distribution, three examples of relative central bank intermediation, and one example of absolute central bank intermediation

of excess deposits. Interbank lending allows the banks to avoid the costs associated with this spread.

- The central bank can provide these intermediation services *passively*, i.e. they can result from bank action alone. However, a natural limit to intermediation is normally collateral availability. Widening the collateral set in a crisis specifically for the sake of allowing for more intermediation, or for providing confidence to markets that banks have large liquidity buffers, would be examples of *active* intermediation measures.

Figure 2.6 illustrates different possible distributions of the recourse to central bank credit, for an assumed population of 100 banks with each having deposits of 9 (implying total deposits of 900), and with total banknotes of 100.

The different cases in figure 2.6 can be interpreted as follows.

- 'CB credit—uniform' assumes that the total recourse to central bank credit of 100 is shared equally across banks. This is an ideal case from the perspective of central bank exposure as it is as granular and diversified as it could be. In reality, this will rarely occur as it would require that banks are homogeneous in every respect.
- 'CB credit—relative intermediation I' assumes that almost all banks have some recourse to the central bank, but that this is not homogeneous. Instead, recourse is linearly distributed between 2 and 0. The distribution of central bank credit is still broad. In fact in practice it is more normal that quite a share of banks have no recourse to central bank credit at all, as assumed under the following two cases.

- The cases II and III of relative intermediation assume that some banks take no recourse, implying accordingly that those who do take a larger one. Still, no bank is in excess liquidity.
- Finally, 'CB credit—absolute intermediation' shows one example in which some banks are over-liquid (here 70 banks each have a surplus of 1 that they deposit with the central bank), while the first 24 banks share all the recourse to central bank credit. The central bank balance sheet lengthens by around 73 as this is the total amount of excess deposits. Obviously, capital and interbank markets must be seriously impaired to explain such an outcome, or the central bank must have set a too narrow spread between the rate at which it lends and the rate at which it remunerates excess deposits.

Of course one can invent many further different distributions of banks' recourse to central bank credit. The maximum lengthening of the central bank balance sheet under the assumptions taken would be achieved if 99 banks all finance their entire balance sheet through the central bank, while the hundredth bank runs a liquidity surplus of 890. Obviously in this case the financial system would be totally disrupted and the allocation of finance to the economy would in fact be controlled fully by the central bank—a miserable outcome. The case is anyway not fully realistic in particular for two reasons: first, the banks cannot finance their entire balance sheet with the central bank because of collateral constraints. If, for instance, the central bank imposes a 50% haircut on bank assets when accepting them as collateral, then only one-half of the bank balance sheets could be financed by the central bank, and the maximum lengthening of the central bank balance sheet would not be 890 but only around one-half of that. Second, the financial account systems here are assuming that bank assets are totally illiquid. In the medium term, banks can certainly sell assets, or entire banks can be taken over.

2.3 COLLATERAL CONSTRAINTS

Chapter 9 will develop further the role of collateral for central bank credit operations. The quantity and quality of eligible collateral limits the borrowing potential of banks from the central bank. Limits arise from (i) restricted eligibility (e.g. excluding particularly non-liquid and non-transparent asset classes and setting a minimum credit quality for the collateral obligor), (ii) conservative collateral valuation (to reduce the risk of assuming too-high collateral values), (iii) haircuts (to cater for losses in value during the liquidation period after a counterparty default), or (iv) quantitative collateral limits (to address concentration and correlation risks).

To simplify, assume that all loans of banks to corporates are eligible collateral and are subject to a haircut of h%, implying that for one unit of collateral value, the bank can obtain a maximum of (1 – h%) units of central bank funding. Assuming the bank balance sheet as depicted in figure 2.2, the maximum lending of the central bank to a homogeneous banking sector is determined as $(1 - h)(D + B - S_{CB})$. The actual borrowing from the central bank, $B - S_{CB} + d - s$, must not exceed this, i.e.:

$$B - S_{CB} + d - s \leq (1 - h)(D + B - S_{CB}) \tag{2.1}$$

Equation (2.1) implies that if the flow $(d - s)$ in figure 2.3 exceeds $(1 - h)D - h(B - S_{CB})$, the banking sector hits the collateral constraint, and banks may become illiquid and default, unless the central bank is willing to extend collateral availability (e.g. by reducing haircuts), or e.g. to lend further to banks against a government guarantee.

Apart from collateral constraints, the central bank could in principle impose additional *central bank borrowing limits* on banks. It could for instance set (i) an identical limit across all banks; (ii) a proportional limit, i.e. that each bank can only finance a share of *q*% of its balance sheet through borrowing from the central bank.

2.4 RESERVES OF BANKS WITH THE CENTRAL BANK AND REQUIRED RESERVES

Reserve requirements will be treated in chapter 8. From the perspective of monetary policy implementation, the money market is the interbank market for deposits ('reserves', 'current accounts'—all synonyms) with the central bank. Banks have to maintain a non-negative reserve position. In case of positive reserve requirements, banks have to hold a certain positive level of reserves, say RR ('reserve requirements'). In figure 2.7, we present the financial sector with positive reserve requirements RR. We simplify the presentation by ignoring the case of a liquidity surplus of bank 1 and we set interbank lending to zero.

It should be noted that in the representation in figure 2.7 it is assumed that banks hold as reserves precisely the required reserves RR. Often, banks also hold excess reserves XSR, which could be reflected in the financial accounts system in figure 2.7 by replacing 'RR' by 'RR+XSR'. Explanations of why banks hold voluntarily excess reserves can be found e.g. in Dow (2001) and Bindseil et al. (2006). These explanations have to be clearly distinguished from the case where excess reserves are injected by the central bank on aggregate into the system through an outright securities purchase programme (see sections 2.6 and 13.3), and are hence not voluntary (see also Keister and McAndrews, 2009).

Often (e.g. in the case of the US Fed and the ECB) reserve requirements have to be fulfilled *on average* over a reserve maintenance period. Assume that the reserve maintenance period has two days, and that the flows d and k have each independent realizations on day 1 and day 2 (d_1, d_2, k_1, k_2). Fulfilling reserve requirements precisely each day is then only one option for banks. Alternatively, banks can decide to let liquidity flows affect reserve holdings on day 1 (i.e. not

Bank 1			
Lending to corporates	D/2 + B/2	Household deposits / debt	D/2 + k − d/2
Deposits with CB	RR/2	Credit from central bank	B/2 + RR/2 − k + d/2

Bank 2			
Lending to corporates	D/2 + B/2	Household deposits / debt	D/2 − k − d/2
Deposits with CB	RR/2	Credit from central bank	B/2 + RR/2 + k + d/2

Central Bank			
Credit operations with banks	B + RR + d	Banknotes	B + d
		Deposits of banks	RR

Fig. 2.7. A financial accounts system with reserve requirements

Bank 1 – at end of day 1			
Lending to corporates	D/2 + B/2	Household deposits / debt	$D/2 + k_1 - d_1/2$
Deposits with CB	$RR/2 + k_1 - d_1/2$	Credit from central bank	B/2 + RR/2

Bank 1 – at end of day 2			
Lending to corporates	D/2 + B/2	Household deposits / debt	$D/2 + k_2 - d_2/2$
Deposits with CB	$RR/2 - k_1 + d_1/2$	Credit from central bank	$B/2 + RR/2 - k_1 + d_1/2 - k_2 + d_2/2$

Fig. 2.8. Financial accounts of a bank on two days with reserve requirements and a two-day averaging period and adjustments to address liquidity shocks only on day 2

neutralize them on day 1 through adjustments of the recourse to central bank lending), and to ensure precise fulfilment only on day 2. In this case, for example, bank 1's account in period 1 and 2 would be as shown in figure 2.8.

This averaging mechanism can stabilize the overnight interbank rate and can be the basis for the *martingale property* of overnight rates within the reserve maintenance period (see chapter 5).

2.5 OTHER AUTONOMOUS FACTORS AND TYPES OF MONETARY POLICY OPERATIONS

The central bank balance sheets shown so far were simplifications with regards to two important aspects that now need to be developed further.

First, so far the banknote item was the only balance sheet item outside monetary policy operations and the banks' sight deposits with the central bank. However, in reality, banknotes are only one amongst various so-called 'autonomous' central bank balance sheet factors. Autonomous factors may be defined as all those central bank balance sheet items which are neither monetary policy operations nor the deposits of banks with the central bank. They are factors that are not under direct control of the monetary policy implementation function, although they may have an impact on the amount of deposits of banks with the central bank, and hence on the money market. In the central bank balance sheets above, banknotes were the only autonomous factor. In reality, there are a number of other autonomous factors, which can all be integrated into the financial account model (essentially by introducing other sectors who interact with the central bank). For example: (i) governments may be allowed to use the central bank for their (volatile) cash holdings—when the Government collects taxes on a certain day, its deposits with the central bank will increase accordingly; (ii) the central bank may intervene in foreign exchange markets and increase or decrease its foreign reserves holdings; (iii) the central bank may purchase financial assets not for monetary policy, but for investment purposes; (iv) the IMF may draw on credit lines it has with the central bank.

Second, the different types of monetary policy operations, as briefly introduced in chapter 1, need to be shown separately in the central bank balance sheet. When the control of short-term interest rates is modelled in chapter 4, the differentiation between (i) outright open market operations, (ii) credit open market operations, and (iii) standing facilities will be necessary.

Figure 2.9 reflects this slightly more differentiated representation of the central bank balance sheet, ordered according to the three main types of balance sheet items.

What was labelled B (originally for 'banknotes') in the financial account models of sections 2.1–2.4, would now be defined as 'net autonomous actors', with:

Net autonomous factors = Banknotes + Government deposits
– Foreign reserves – Investment portfolios

Defined in this way, autonomous factors are netted as a central bank *liability* item. If we define 'monetary policy operations' as the sum of all monetary policy operations netted as a central bank balance sheet *asset* item, we can write the balance sheet identity as follows:

Deposits of banks = Monetary policy operations – Net autonomous factors

If the central bank imposes reserve requirements, then deposits of banks have to be equal to (at least) those reserve requirements. This implies that

Central bank	
Autonomous factors: liquidity providing Net Foreign assets Investment portfolios	**Autonomous factor: liquidity absorbing** Banknotes Government deposits
Monetary policy operations: liquidity providing Outright purchases (OMO) Credit operations (OMO) Borrowing facility	**Monetary policy operations: liquidity absorbing** Term deposit collection / repo Issuance of debt certificates Deposit facility
	Deposits of banks

Fig. 2.9. A central bank balance sheet ordered according to the types of balance sheet items

central banks have to adjust in principle their monetary policy operations to the fluctuations of autonomous factors such that:

$$\text{Monetary policy operations} = \text{Reserve requirements} + \text{Net autonomous factors}$$

One can call the left hand side of this equation 'supply' and the right hand side of this equation 'demand' for central bank reserves of banks. Accordingly, the liquidity supply by the central bank has to be such as to suffice both for reserve requirements and the liquidity absorption through autonomous factors.

Moving again down to the level of the individual central bank balance sheet items, one can call 'liquidity absorbing' all central bank balance sheet *liability* items (except bank deposits), and 'liquidity providing' all central bank balance sheet *asset* items. This is because bank deposits with the central bank are a central bank liability item, and therefore any increase of another central bank liability item leads—all other items being assumed unchanged—to a decrease of bank deposits, while any increase of a central bank asset item leads—again all other items being assumed unchanged—to an increase in central bank deposits. Consider now as an example the Eurosystem balance sheet as of February 2012, as shown in Figure 2.10.

Net autonomous factors were liquidity-absorbing for EUR 310 billion. Required reserves amounted approximately to the actual current accounts of banks, i.e. EUR 94 billion. Monetary policy operations injected (in net terms) EUR 404 billion. Reflecting impaired money markets, banks in fact took much higher recourse to Eurosystem credit operations, namely for a total of EUR 818 billion. The excess liquidity was either taken back by the Eurosystem through the collection of fixed-term deposits (EUR 220 billion), or was placed by the cash rich banks in the Eurosystem deposit facility (remunerated at 25 basis

Eurosystem, 24 February 2012 (in billion euro)			
Autonomous factors		**Autonomous factor**	
Net Foreign assets	633	Banknotes	867
Domestic investment assets	374	Government deposits	142
		Net other autonomous factors	308
Monetary policy operations			
Outright holdings	283		
Short term credit operations	166		
Longer term credit operations	652	Collection of fixed term deposits	220
Borrowing facility	0	Deposit facility	477
		Current accounts of banks	**94**
Sum	**2108**	**Sum**	**2108**

Fig. 2.10. Stylized Eurosystem balance sheet, February 2012, in million euro

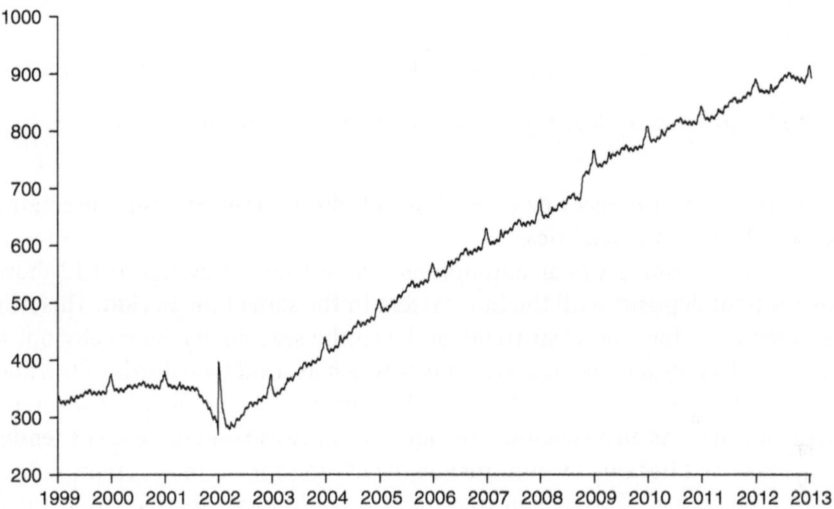

Fig. 2.11. Banknotes in circulation, Eurosystem, 1999–2013, in million euro
Source: ECB

points at that time, against a zero remuneration of excess reserves held on the current accounts).

Consider now two examples of autonomous factor developments across time. Figure 2.11 shows the *daily time series* of euro banknotes in circulation since 1999. One recognizes a clear trend and monthly and annual seasonality. There are some exceptional movements around 2002 explained by the introduction of the euro banknotes. To set the size of their open market operations, the central banks rely on the time series patterns of banknotes in circulation and of other autonomous factors. A central bank model for forecasting banknotes in circulation can be found for instance in Cabrero et al. (2002). In chapter 4 we will see what role this forecasting plays, in particular

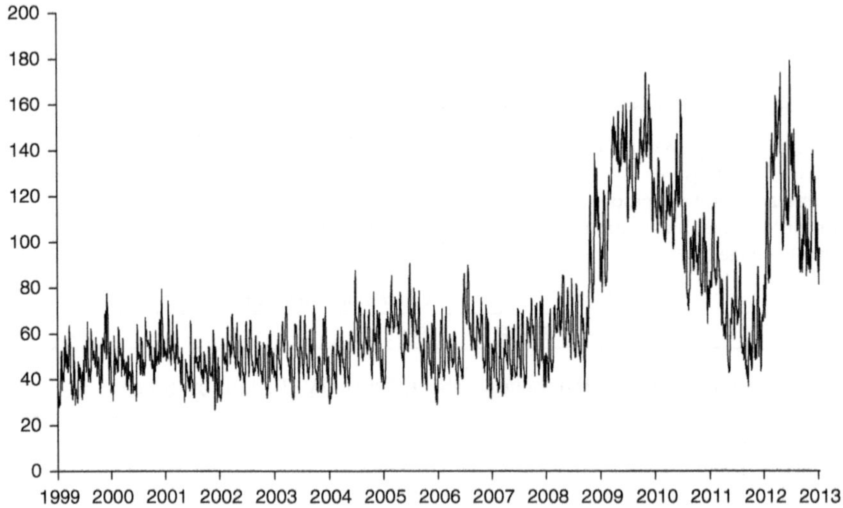

Fig. 2.12. Government deposits, Eurosystem, 1999–2013, in billion euro

in approaches to interest rate control, which do not rely on a one-directional recourse to standing facilities.

As a second example of an autonomous factor time series, figure 2.12 shows Government deposits with the Eurosystem in the same time period. This time series seems to have no clear trend, and also the seasonality is less obvious to detect. Still, central banks can typically forecast around two-thirds of the fluctuation of this position through in-depth institutional knowledge of sovereign payment flows. As also suggested by figure 2.12, Government deposits tended to increase and became even more volatile during the financial crisis, reflecting the reluctance of sovereign treasurers at some times to place their funds in markets.[2]

2.6 LIQUIDITY DEFICIT OF THE BANKING SYSTEM VIS-À-VIS THE CENTRAL BANK

Interestingly, the majority of banking systems of the world are currently in a situation in which they hold more deposits with the central bank than are

[2] It may be noted that other central banks have set up, together with the national treasury, frameworks that ensure that government deposits with the central bank are normally stable—see for example Bank of Canada (2010, 3). Also within the Eurosystem, most national central banks (NCBs) have established such frameworks, and the volatility of the government deposit account stems only from a few NCBs.

needed to fulfil reserve requirements despite the fact that they do not take recourse to central bank credit open market operations. To capture this phenomenon, the concept of the liquidity deficit of the banking system vis-à-vis the central bank is useful. The liquidity deficit may be defined in two ways:

- First, as *original liquidity deficit*: the need to provide funding in the form of monetary policy operations, including both credit operations and outright securities purchases (i.e. both types of central bank open market operations);
- Second, as *liquidity deficit post monetary policy outright operations*: the remaining need, after outright purchases, for the central bank to provide funding to banks in the form of *credit* operations.

Consider the example (figure 2.13) of a central bank balance sheet in which banks hold not only the required amount of deposits with the central bank (i.e. required reserves, RR), but also some excess reserves, XSR.

The *original liquidity deficit* is equal to B + RR. Note that excess reserves are not counted as a component of the liquidity deficit. The *liquidity deficit post monetary policy outright operations* is equal to B + RR-S_{CB}.

Recall the case of the Eurosystem in February 2012, as shown in figure 2.10. Applying the definitions of the two concepts, it is easy to calculate that the original liquidity deficit of the banking system was EUR 404 billion and that in view of the outright operations for monetary policy purposes of EUR 283 billion, the liquidity deficit post monetary policy outright operations was EUR 121 billion.

The typical emerging market economy's banking system is in a liquidity surplus (according to both concepts) vis-à-vis the central bank because of *large foreign exchange reserves of the central banks*. For example, at end 2010, in the cases of China and Korea, the sum of commercial bank deposits and central bank bonds issued (the latter to absorb excess reserves of banks) amounted to 72% and 58% of the total liabilities of these central banks, respectively. In comparison, banknotes in circulation amounted only to 16% and 8% of total liabilities. The large volumes of non-banknote liabilities are explained by the injection of reserves due to large central bank foreign reserves, which amount to 73% and 71% of the total balance sheet length, respectively (see Filardo and Yetman, 2012, 63).

Central bank			
Monetary Policy Operations		**Autonomous factor**	**B**
Credit monetary policy operations	$B + RR + XSR - S_{CB}$		
Outright monetary policy portfolio	S_{CB}	**Deposits of banks**	RR + XSR

Fig. 2.13. A central bank balance sheet to define the liquidity deficit

The US and UK banking systems currently (i.e. between end 2009 and at least end 2013) have an original liquidity deficit towards their respective central banks, but are in a surplus post monetary policy outright operations.

Table 2.1 provides a number of examples of the two concepts of a liquidity deficit of banking systems vis-à-vis the central bank for some concrete central bank balance sheets that can also be found in stylized format in this book. In some cases the precise figures may be a matter of interpretation as they may depend on the netting and classification of balance sheet items. The liquidity deficits are shown both in absolute amounts of local currency, and as a ratio to the total balance sheet lengths. Moreover, the table provides for each of these central bank balance sheets a 'leanness' indicator which is simply defined as the ratio of total balance sheet length to banknotes in circulation.[3] A perfectly lean central bank balance sheet would be one which would have a total length equal to banknotes, so having a value of our leanness indicator of one. A lean balance sheet is in principle positive as it suggests (1) a central bank focused on the core of its mandate; (2) well-functioning financial markets because the central bank is neither used as intermediary by the banking system, nor does the central bank see a need to engage in special crisis measures such as outright purchase programmes.

2.7 CREDIT MONEY CREATED BY BANKS

The financial account systems used in this book are obviously strong simplifications, and a number of further sophistications could be considered. First, in the flows-of-funds statistics maintained by the ECB, the following six sectors are distinguished: households, the banks, other financial institutions (e.g. insurance companies and pension funds), non-financial corporates, the Government, and the rest of the world. Second, all sectors have deposits with banks, and most have equity holdings with other sectors. Third, households are also leveraged, i.e. also take loans to increase their total balance sheet size beyond their equity. Finally, banks create additional bank money by providing credit to the other sectors. For example a bank provides a credit to a household, which does not immediately draw on it but maintains a correspondingly increased deposit position with the bank. We will only represent the last two points in a financial accounts example.

[3] Filardo and Yetman (2012, 63) provide this leanness indicator for Asian central banks (value in parentheses) in 2011: China (6.2), Indonesia (3.5), Korea (12.2), Malaysia (8.4), Singapore (12.6), and Thailand (5.8). These high values are all driven by the large foreign exchange reserves of these countries. Japan showed a value of only 1.6, also reflecting that the Government holds most of the foreign reserves.

Table 2.1. The liquidity deficit of the banking system: post monetary policy outright holdings; original; and leanness indicator of the central bank balance sheet

Central bank	Date; currency	Source, see:	LD original (I)	LD post outright (II)	Total BS length (III)	(IV) = (I)/(III)	(V) = (II)/(III)	Banknotes (VI)	Leanness (VII) = (III)/(VI)
German Reichsbank	31.12.1900 Million RM	Figure 4.2	1319	1234	2049	64%	60%	1410	1.5
Eurosystem	29.06.2007 Billion EUR	Figure 4.9	463	463	912	51%	51%	633	1.4
Fed	27.06.2007 Billion USD	Figure 7.1	780	–10	845	92%	–1%	775	1.1
BoE	27.06.2007 Billion GBP	Figure 4.8	80	47	80	100%	59%	40	2.0
Eurosystem	24.02.2012 Billion EUR	Figure 2.10	404	121	2178	19%	6%	867	2.5
Fed	02.01.2013 Billion USD	Figure 4.3	1108	–1562	2723	41%	–57%	1127	2.4
BoE	02.01.2013 Billion GBP	Figure 13A.4	156	–248	410	38%	–60%	60	6.8

To represent credit money creation in our system of financial accounts, we start from the simplest case of a financial account system with two banks and with all financing to the real economy being done through the banking system. Beforehand, recall Tobin's famous critical presentation of banks' credit money creation as a climax of any introductory course on monetary economics (Tobin, 1963, 408):

> Perhaps the greatest moment of triumph for the elementary economics teacher is his exposition of the multiple creation of bank credit and bank deposits. Before the admiring eyes of freshmen he puts to rout the practical banker... The banker is shown to have a worm's-eye view, and his error stands as an introductory object lesson in the fallacy of composition. From the Olympian vantage of the teacher and the textbook it appears that the banker's dictum must be reversed: depositors entrust to bankers whatever amounts the bankers lend. To be sure, this is not true for a single bank: one bank loan may wind up as another bank's deposit. But it is, as the arithmetic of successive rounds of deposit creation makes clear, true of the banking system as a whole. Whatever their other errors, a long line of financial heretics have been right in speaking of 'fountain pen money'—money created by the stroke of the bank president's pen when he approves a loan and credits the proceeds to the borrower's checking account.

Tobin criticizes this textbook 'old view' of the money supply for a number of reasons, and indeed, as argued in section 3.3, the associated money multiplier and money supply approach to monetary economics is hardly convincing.

It is helpful to represent credit money supply in the framework of a financial account system, as this easily allows precise statements to be made on the constraints to money creation by banks. Denote by C_1 (C_2) the credit money creation by bank 1 (bank 2) to the households. We assume that households keep the money in the form of deposits with banks, but not necessarily with the same bank. Concretely we assume that the household splits up its additional credit money holdings equally across the two banks, regardless of which bank provided the credit. Figure 2.14 shows the resulting financial accounts.

What could be the possible limits to credit money creation by banks?

- Assuming that credit claims to households are not central bank eligible collateral, then the collateral constraint is a natural break to *over-proportional* credit money creation by a *single* bank. If credit claims to households can be securitized and pledged in this form as central bank credit, then the haircuts imposed by the central bank would still constitute a limitation for the single bank.
- If $C_1 = C_2$ (i.e. parallel credit money creation by both banks), there would be no limit in the system above for credit money creation by the two banks, unless the central bank imposes reserve requirements (see also chapter 8).

Households / Investors			
Real Assets	$E-D-B$	Household Equity	E
Deposits Bank 1	$D/2+(C_1+C_2)/2$	Credit from bank 1	C_1
Deposits Bank 2	$D/2+(C_1+C_2)/2$	Credit from bank 2	C_2
Banknotes	B		

Corporate / Government			
Real assets	$D+B$	Credits from banks	$D+B$

Bank 1			
Lending to corporates	$D/2+B/2$	Household deposits / debt	$D/2+(C_1+C_2)/2$
Lending to households	C_1	Credit from central bank	$B/2+(C_1-C_2)/2$

Bank 2			
Lending to corporates	$D/2+B/2$	Household deposits / debt	$D/2+(C_1+C_2)/2$
Lending to households	C_2	Credit from central bank	$B/2+(C_2-C_1)/2$

Central Bank			
Credit operations	B	Banknotes	B

Fig. 2.14. Financial accounts with two banks and bank credit money creation

- In reality, however, limits to credit money creation arise out of the preferences of the household. Bank credit money creation will not be costless in the sense that the banks will require a higher remuneration rate for the claims towards the households than what they offer in terms of remuneration rate of deposits (banks have to cover their operations costs and compensate credit risk). Therefore households will have a demand for credit money only to the extent that they see a particular utility attached to it, justifying the costs of credit.

It is important to note that the credit money expansion by the bank has no impact on the central bank balance sheet in the financial accounts system above as long as the difference in the pace of additional credit provision by the two banks is not too large, i.e. as long as $|C_2 - C_1| < B$. Once this condition is violated, the length of the central bank balance sheet would expand because the bank with the more limited credit expansion would hold excess reserves.

In any case, the size of credit money expansion affects the scale of possible deposit shifts, and hence the scale of possible recourses to the central bank to compensate for resulting funding gaps. To that extent, the length of the banks' balance sheets, and their ballooning through credit money creation, are relevant in financial crisis situations, as analysed further in part II of the book.

2.8 THE 'REAL' EURO AREA FINANCIAL ACCOUNTS

We now consider the real statistical financial accounts of an economy, using the example of the euro area. This will give us a further sense of the simplifications made in the stylized financial accounts system, and on the order of magnitude of actual financial linkages. Consider the 'Integrated economic and financial accounts' of the euro area, as presented in section 3 of the ECB Monthly Bulletin (section 3.1, in particular page S28 in the December 2011 Monthly Bulletin). The methodology underlying these accounts has been explained in depth in a methodological document ('ECB Monthly Bulletin—Euro Area Statistics methodological notes, Chapter 3: Euro area accounts', 28 October 2010). This is a comprehensive and consistent system of euro area financial accounts distinguishing the key institutional sectors, similarly to our stylized system of financial accounts, although with more sectors and more types of financial inter-linkages (see table 2.2). It may be noted that the euro area integrated economic and financial accounts do not contain a position for real assets, contrary to our financial accounts. Therefore, to translate into our approach, one needs to interpret the item 'Net financial worth', as being equivalent in our system to 'Equity minus Real Assets' (i.e. reflecting a netting on the liability side).

A number of observations may be of interest. *Households* have indeed a large net worth, but, contrary to the assumption taken in our stylized financial accounts, also have financed through loans around one-third of their total financial assets. These loans are mostly mortgage loans, but also consumer loans. Their largest single asset item are deposits (and currency), while their debt securities holdings are more limited, and actually less than one-half of shares and equity. Shares and other forms of equity are the biggest source of funding of *non-financial corporations*, followed by loans, and to a much lesser extent debt securities. In our financial accounts representation we ignore equity as the vulnerability regarding liquidity shocks comes from the large share of funding through bank loans. Only companies financed fully through equity would be resilient against liquidity crises. For the *Government*, the main financing source is debt issuance. *MFIs* ('Monetary financial institutions', i.e. banks) fund mainly through deposit collection (as assumed in our financial accounts), but also through debt issuance. Banks' largest asset type is loans, but also debt securities holdings and deposits (mainly with other banks) are

Table 2.2. Euro area integrated economic and financial accounts, end Q2 2011

	House-hold	Non-financial corporations	Monetary financial institutions (banks)	Other financial institutions	Government	Rest of the world
Financial assets	**19**	**17**	**32**	**22**	**4**	**17**
Currency and deposits	7	2	9	3	1	4
Debt securities	1	0	7	5	1	5
Loans	0	3	13	4	1	2
Shares, Equity	4	8	2	9	1	6
Other financial assets	6	4	1	1	1	1
Liabilities	**19**	**17**	**32**	**22**	**4**	**17**
Currency and deposits			22		0	3
Debt securities		1	5	6	7	6
Loans	6	9		2	1	6
Shares, Equity		13	3	9		
Other liabilities	1	4	1	5	1	3
Net financial worth	*12*	*−10*	*1*	*1*	*−5*	*0*

Source: ECB monthly bulletin, pages S28–S29, in trillions of euro, rounded to the full trillion.

relevant. Finally, the *rest of the world* provides funding in the form of shares, debt securities and loans (in this order), and vice versa. All sectors, including households, are structurally dependent on funding if engaging in maturity transformation and hence are vulnerable to funding crises.

It should be noted that the financial structure and the debt markets of an economy will have various implications on the details of monetary policy implementation, even in normal times. Filardo et al. (2012) is an example of a paper analysing the relation between central bank operations and sovereign debt management.

3

Operational Target of Monetary Policy

3.1 CONCEPT OF AN OPERATIONAL TARGET OF MONETARY POLICY

The operational target of monetary policy is an economic variable, which the central bank wants to control, and indeed can control, to a very large extent on a day-by-day basis through the use of its monetary policy instruments. It is the variable for which (i) the policy decision-making committee decides the level in each of its meetings, which (ii) gives guidance to the implementation officers in the central bank on what really to do on a day-by-day basis in the inter-meeting period, and (iii) serves to communicate the stance of monetary policy to the public. Today, there seems to be consensus among central banks that the short-term interbank interest rate is the appropriate operational target *in normal times*. During crises, the concept is more ambiguous, as will be discussed in part II.

One may categorize the pre-2007 approaches taken by central banks towards the operational target of monetary policy as follows.

Explicit versus implicit operational target. The Fed defined its federal funds rate target at least since around 1990 explicitly, while e.g. the Bank of England and the ECB chose an implicit target in the sense that it is revealed through the rate at which they operate in the market, being—before 2007—an implicit commitment to achieve similar market rates. The Bank of Japan defined for a number of years (2001–2006) an explicit quantitative target, namely the amount of total reserves of banks with the Bank of Japan (see e.g. the press release of 19 March 2001 announcing the policy). The Bank of Japan's target implied huge excess reserves, and close to zero short-term market interest rates.

Specified versus non-specified operational target. An operational target is specified in terms of value if an exact figure is assigned to it after each meeting of its decision-making body—at least for internal purposes. The Fed's quantitative operational targets set in the 1950s and 1960s were normally not precisely quantified.

Public immediate release, or not. Most central banks now publish immediately after the meeting of their monetary policy committee the value specification of the operational target variable. However, this was not always done: for instance the Fed before 1994 did not immediately announce its target specification, and thus the markets tried to extract it from the (variable rate tender) operations of the New York Fed.

A unique versus a variety of operational targets. The Fed, for example, specified between 1994 and 2007 one unique operational target, the federal funds rate, and thus seemed to consider the fed funds rate as a sufficient measure for its monetary policy stance. The opposite approach is described e.g. by Anderson (1969, 69), according to whom there were in the 1960s eight measures of money market conditions considered by the Fed, namely 'the Treasury bill rate, free reserve of all member banks, the basic reserve deficiency at eight New York money market banks, the basic reserve deficiency at 38 money market banks outside New York, member banks' borrowing from the Federal Reserve, United States government security dealer borrowings, the Federal funds rate, and the Federal Reserve discount rate'. Also in today's special (post-)crisis environment, central banks seem again to have more than one operational target. For instance, the Fed seems to care not only about the Fed funds rate, but also about long-term treasury rates and RMBS rates, in the sense that it conducts operations to directly affect these rates (even if no precise target is provided, and control of these rates is not supposed to be perfect). Also the ECB was concerned during the financial crisis about various euro bond yields, and has conducted operations to directly affect those for monetary policy reasons. One could argue that often, the overnight rate is considered as primary operational target, but that if the overnight rate is no longer considered 'sufficient' in terms of capturing the monetary policy stance, additional variables are identified as 'secondary' operational targets: in Japan from 2001 to 2006 the level of banks' reserves with the Bank of Japan, and in the US after 2010 the ten-year yields of treasuries, agency bonds, and RMBS. In both cases the primary operational target is an overnight interest rate at (or close to) zero, but this target is no longer considered sufficient.

Type of operational target. There are essentially three main types of operational targets: (i) a short-term interest rate (pre-1914, and post-1990 the dominating type of operational target, and in between also playing at least implicitly an important role); (ii) a quantitative, reserve-related concept—officially in the US the operational target in the period 1920–1983 (in numerous variants as explained in section 3.3); (iii) a foreign exchange rate, for central banks which peg their own currency strictly to a foreign one. In the present text, the focus will be on large monetary areas for which this approach is not an alternative.

Section 3.2 will provide more insight into the short-term interest rate as operational target of monetary policy. In section 3.3, the history of the operational targets of monetary policy in the twentieth century will be further analysed. This is not only a disturbing piece of history of economic thinking, but also helps to interpret correctly large parts of academic writing on monetary policy implementation during the twentieth century. During this period (to be precise: between 1920 and 1983), central banks, and first and foremost the Fed, tended to deny that the central bank bears responsibility for short-term rates, and in different variants suggested instead the following quantitative operational targets (the list tries to order the different quantitative concepts from broad to narrow, which is however not obvious in all cases):

(i) The monetary base, which is the sum of reserves of banks with the central bank and currency. This tended to be the preferred operational target concept of monetarists, who did not want to go into the details of day-to-day monetary policy implementation and the implied need to split up the monetary base further into sub-elements.
(ii) Reserves of banks. As mentioned, this operational target was applied between 2001 and 2006 by the Bank of Japan and was also occasionally advocated by academics.
(iii) The total volume of open market operations (Friedman, 1982).
(iv) 'Non-borrowed' reserves, applied by the Fed 1979–1982.
(v) Excess reserves, i.e. reserves in excess of required reserves (critical review by Dow, 2001).
(vi) Free reserves, i.e. excess reserves minus the reserves the banks have borrowed at a borrowing facility (in the US case: at the discount window). This concept was applied, at least in theory, by the Fed during the period 1954–1970 (see e.g. Meigs, 1962).
(vii) 'Borrowed reserves', applied by the Fed from 1982 to 1990 (see e.g. Meulendyke, 1998).

From today's perspective, these concepts appear doubtful, as already argued convincingly and in detail by Moore (1988). In section 3.3, the history of thought of these various variants of 'reserve position doctrine' (a term coined by Meigs, 1962) is summarized.

3.2 SHORT-TERM RATE AS OPERATIONAL TARGET OF MONETARY POLICY

Already Thornton (1802, 254), who is usually praised as the most advanced monetary policy theorist before the twentieth century, views central bank policy as 'Bank rate' (discount facility rate) policy, and analyses how Bank rate policy should be conducted. The idea that Bank rate needs to follow the real rate of return of capital, in order to allow control of the expansion of money and hence inflation, was probably first spelled out by him:

In order to ascertain how far the desire of obtaining loans at the bank (the Bank of England) may be expected at any time to be carried, we must inquire into the subject of the quantum of profit likely to be derived from borrowing there under the existing circumstances... We may, therefore, consider this question as turning principally on a comparison of the rate of interest taken at the bank with the current rate of mercantile profit. The bank is prohibited, by the state of (usury) law, from demanding, even in time of war, an interest of more than five per cent, which is the same rate at which it discounts in a period of profound peace. It might, undoubtedly, at all seasons, sufficiently limit its paper by means of the price at which it lends, if the legislature did not interpose an obstacle to the constant adoption of this principle of restriction.

A key point of Thornton is that the bank rate is always an adequate and sufficient tool of central bank policy to prevent over-issuance of money and hence inflation (except if the central bank is constrained in the use of this tool, e.g. by usury law). Thornton's concept of a 'rate of mercantile profit' indeed looks much like the 'natural rate' of interest described in 1898 by Wicksell (1898/1936, 102) as follows:

There is a certain rate of interest on loans which is neutral in respect to commodity prices, and tends neither to raise nor to lower them. This is necessarily the same as the rate of interest which would be determined by supply and demand if no use were made of money and all lending were effected in the form of real capital goods. It comes to much the same thing to describe it as the current value of the natural rate of interest on capital.

The arbitrage diagram in figure 3.1 (see also Richter, 1990), with two goods (wheat and money) at two points in time (today and tomorrow) and with the relevant relative prices, shows that, under stable prices, the rate of interest on money, i, has to correspond to the real rate of interest, r, which can be thought as independent from the 'monetary sphere' of the economy. P_1 is the price of wheat prevailing today, and P_2 is the expected spot price of wheat prevailing tomorrow.

Arbitrage logic allows some basic relationships between prices to be established by moving within the diagram from one good to another via different

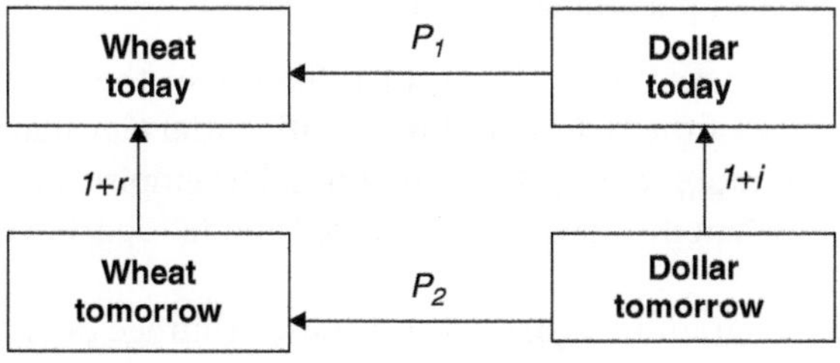

Fig. 3.1. Arbitrage diagram between real and nominal interest, and inflation rate

paths. Indeed, by moving from 'Wheat today' to 'Wheat tomorrow' through different ways, one can show that in equilibrium:

$$1 + r = P_1 \ (1 + i)/P_2 \tag{3.1}$$

Defining $(1 + \pi)$ as P_2/P_1, we also obtain the Fisher equation:

$$(1 + r) = (1 + i)/(1 + \pi) \tag{3.2}$$

Equation (3.2) is approximately equivalent to $i = r + \pi$, i.e. in equilibrium the nominal interest rate should be the sum of the real rate and the (expected) inflation rate. If the central bank manages to keep the money (nominal) interest rate, i, always equal to the real interest rate, r, no inflation occurs, i.e. $\pi = 0$. Where does the real rate of interest come from? The real rate of interest is simply a relative price between 'wheat tomorrow' and 'wheat today', which, like all relative prices for goods that can be transformed into each other, depends on the production function (inter-temporal in this case) and on relative preferences (consumption today versus consumption tomorrow, from today's perspective of course). As we may die before being able to consume tomorrow, we normally prefer consumption today to consumption tomorrow (or we may simply be impatient), while the inter-temporal production function is normally producing positive returns. Hence, real interest rates are normally positive.

The most blatant case of central bank denial of this arbitrage logic in modern history was probably the application of a 5% discount rate policy by the Reichsbank from 1914 to 1922—despite the fact that the inflation rate reached 40% already in 1915, and remained at least in the two-digit area every year until it totally exploded in the years after World War I. Stolper (1940/1969) notes about credit provision during this period that (p. 83):

> Persons who were resourceful and had the necessary banking connections to procure a maximum of commercial credit had nothing to do but invest the money without delay in 'physical values' in order to amass a gigantic fortune in no time at all. The most typical example of such practice and, in general, of the trend towards capital accumulation, was Hugo Stinnes... He began to buy up at random and in large numbers the most varied businesses, including banks, hotels, paper mills, newspapers and other publishing concerns.

Hugo Stinnes, who was named 'King of Inflation' in the Weimar Republic, died in 1924 as one of the richest and most influential German industrialists, with ownership in more than 4,500 companies. His empire, however, ran into liquidity troubles when the mark was stabilized and fell apart in 1925 (Schacht, 1927).

Of course the diagram in figure 3.1 is a static arbitrage device and, in reality, we may be most of the time in complex dynamic states of disequilibrium. Taylor's rules of different kinds can be thought of as being derived from a dynamic version of the arbitrage diagram. In a dynamic disequilibrium situation, setting the right interest rate becomes more complicated, and this is why central banks have large economics departments. Also, complicated issues arise in practice in identifying in practice and measuring the real rate of interest. Laubach and Williams (2001) recall that economic theory allows the derivation, within an optimal growth steady state model, of a simple relationship between the real rate of interest, the intertemporal elasticity of consumption, the rate of labour augmenting technological change, the rate of population growth, and the rate of time preference.[1] If population growth and technological change are negative, real interest rates could also be negative, with interesting implications for monetary policy in the context of the danger of a deflationary trap (as nominal rates cannot normally be negative). In principle, the solution to this problem would be a higher inflation-rate target, such that a negative real rate is obtained while the nominal rate remains positive. In the context of this book, it is enough to have provided the rationale for the basic logical relationship between interest rates and inflation, which is the foundation of the reliance on interest rates as operational target of monetary policy. Modern macroeconomics as represented by e.g. Woodford (2003) starts from this perspective.

Once it is clear that an interest rate should be the operational target, the question remains: which interest rate? Three dimensions may be distinguished: (i) Should one select an interbank rate or the rate at which funds are provided to banks through central bank monetary policy operations? (ii) If an interbank rate is chosen, should this be a secured (repo) or an unsecured interbank rate?[2] (iii) What should be the maturity of the targeted interest rate (overnight, one week, one month)? The first two dimensions are normally, i.e. under well-functioning markets, not so crucial, since the rates in question (unsecured versus secured interbank rates, policy operations rates) should be very close one to the other, and indeed far closer than the smallest interest rate step central banks normally take (which is 25 basis points).

With regard to the third dimension, most central banks aim explicitly or implicitly at the shortest maturity, namely the overnight one. In fact it can be shown easily that anticipated changes of longer-term rates implemented from one day to the next would cause extreme movements of the short end of the yield curve. Assume that the central bank would steer the three-day rate and that it will decide tomorrow, i.e. in $t + 1$, to lower the three-day rate from 4% to 3%. Also assume that the market anticipates fully the change, as the central

[1] The real rate of interest would equal the quotient of labour augmenting technological change to the inter-temporal elasticity of consumption, plus the rate of population growth, plus the time preference rate.

[2] While the majority of central banks target unsecured overnight rates, the Bank of Canada recently chose the collateralized overnight rate as operational target; see Bank of Canada, 2010, 2).

bank has a rule-based and transparent monetary policy strategy. What does that mean for the path of overnight interest rates? Call $i_{\tau,t}$ the τ-day interest rate at point in time t, and $E(i_{1,t+k} \mid I_t)$ the expectation, at point in time t and hence on the basis of information set I_t, of $i_{1,t+k}$, i.e. of the overnight rate on day t + k. Assume moreover that the expectations hypothesis of the term structure of interest rate holds in its simplest possible form, i.e.:

$$(1+i_{3,t})^{\frac{3}{360}} = (1+i_{1,t})^{\frac{1}{360}}(1+E(i_{1,t+1} \mid I_t))^{\frac{1}{360}}(1+E(i_{1,t+2} \mid I_t))^{\frac{1}{360}} \tag{3.3}$$

For our purposes, this can be approximated by:

$$i_{3,t} = \frac{(i_{1,t} + E(i_{1,t+1} \mid I_t) + E(i_{1,t+2} \mid I_t))}{3} \tag{3.4}$$

We know that $i_{3,t} = 4\%$ and $i_{3,t+1} = 3\%$. The latter implies, if we in addition assume that there will be no further policy rate changes for the next three days, according to our simple term structure model, that $E(i_{1,t+1} \mid I_t) = E(i_{1,t+2} \mid I_t) = 3\%$ (and also that $E(i_{1,t+3} \mid I_t) = 3\%$). This however implies, through equation (3.4), that:

$$4\% = \frac{\left(i_{1,t} + 3\% + 3\%\right)}{3} \Rightarrow i_{1,t} = 6\% \tag{3.5}$$

In other words, we will see a temporary spike of the overnight interest rate because there is an anticipated one-off decrease of the three-day rate. This movement is obviously much more extreme in case the central bank steers e.g. the three-month (90-day) rate instead of the three-day. In the example above, the peak of the overnight rate would be close to 100%.

Hence, targeting longer-term rates requires the central bank to either (a) accept anomalies at the short end of the yield curve; or (b) surprise the market when implementing changes of the operational target level; or (c) implement changes in a gradual way.[3]

[3] Another way to express this problem is to note that overnight is the only maturity which never spans over the dates of rate decisions. The 'straddling' implied by targeting longer-term rates would mean that the actual value of the operational target would be affected by the future and not only by the prevailing monetary policy stance. Accordingly, in order to steer the operational target, the central bank would need to commit to a certain path of future decisions. However, in this case, the future rate decisions would either be redundant—because they were already committed—or, worse, they would be inconsistent with previous commitments. Again, the only solution would be to implement changes in a gradual manner whilst not being explicit about what is actually, at each specific point in time, the level of the operational target.

3.3 QUANTITY-ORIENTED OPERATIONAL TARGETS OF MONETARY POLICY IN THE TWENTIETH CENTURY—A BRIEF HISTORY

The Operational Target of Monetary Policy in the Pre-1914 World

Thornton (1802) and Wicksell (1898/1936) stand for the pre-1914 assumption that short-term interest rates should be the operational target of monetary policy. Many other nineteenth-century findings on central banking are associated with Bagehot (1873). One crucial point highlighted by Bagehot (1873, 58), which is of particular relevance in the context of the operational target of monetary policy, is the inherent instability of the money market when left alone by the central bank. It results from the combination of the volatility of the (price-inelastic) supply of central bank reserves with the extremely low short-term interest rate elasticity of the demand for reserves in the money market. It is a sufficient argument for choosing rates, and not quantities, as operational target. According to Bagehot:

> But though the value of money is not settled in an exceptional way, there is nevertheless a peculiarity about it, as there is about many articles. It is a commodity subject to great fluctuations of value and those fluctuations are easily produced by a slight excess or a slight deficiency of quantity. Up to a certain point money is a necessity. If a merchant has acceptances to meet tomorrow, money he must and will find today at some price or other. And it is this urgent need of the whole body of merchants which runs up the value of money so wildly and to such a height in a great panic. On the other hand, money easily becomes a 'drug', as the phrase is, and there is soon too much of it.

What is important to note is that all of these short-term demand and supply shocks in the market for reserves have nothing or very little to do with macroeconomic developments, and it is thus wrong to view the 'rates versus quantity' decision on the operational target, like Poole (1970), as one depending on macroeconomic relationships, such as the interest rate elasticity of money demand, or the relative importance of real and monetary shocks in the macroeconomy. Bagehot's insight into the inherent instability of the money market implies that any serious setting of a quantitative operational target would mean extreme noise in interest rates. Such noise is not compatible with stable financial and economic conditions.

In line with this understanding, and in the context of the classical gold standard, central bank monetary policy implementation basically consisted in setting the rate of discount at which the central bank discounted trade bills. King (1936) describes the various nineteenth-century debates in the Bank of England and the London financial market around this principle. Using the term of Moore (1988), central bank monetary policy implementation before 1914 was as 'horizontalist' as it can be. 'Verticalism' would be invented in the US around 1920.

The Rise of Reserve Position Doctrine in the US: 1914–1960

It is well documented (e.g. Warburg, 1930, Friedman and Schwartz, 1963, Meltzer, 2003) that the organizational set-up of the Federal Reserve System in 1914 suffered from a series of shortcomings. The first ten years of the Fed were overshadowed in addition by a lack of experience, a too high influence of commercial banks, and the confrontation of a major challenge, namely the Government's wish to finance World War I at low interest rates. As again Warburg (1930, II, 296) puts it: 'In the life and death struggle of war, sound economic precepts have to give way to the dictates of self-preservation.' All issues together caused a failure of the Fed to raise interest rates as it would have been required to maintain price stability. The economic impact of the too loose monetary policy of the Fed in its first years was substantial: while the wholesale price index increased from 1914 to 1920 by 150%, it declined in the following phase of restrictive policy (beginning in November 1919) again within two years by around 35%, the latter development being associated with a decline in real GDP of more than 20% (see e.g. Meltzer, 2003).

What makes the episode extraordinary in the case of the Fed and distinguishes it from other national monetary histories of World War I and the early 1920s, was the ex-post rationalization given to it, namely that the reasons for the inflation in the first six years of the Fed had not been the (deliberate) failure of the monetary authorities to hike the discount rate, but excessive borrowing by the banks through the discount window. In other words not rates were the problem, but quantities, and not the Fed had failed, but the banks. This switch of paradigm seems to take place rather precisely around 1920, with discussion after this date highlighting consistently the quantity dimension. Two main events seem to explain the switch exactly in 1920, namely (i) the above-mentioned start of the tightening of monetary policy in November 1919 and its substantial impact on economic activity, and (ii) an academic event, namely the invention of the money multiplier by the American C. A. Philipps (1920). Even Friedman and Schwartz (1963, 250), who otherwise strongly oppose interest rates as operational targets of monetary policy, are astonished by the fact that e.g. in the 1921 annual report of the Board of Governors, explicit discussion of the Fed's aggressive hiking of interest rates after November 1919 and the implied deflation and recession is avoided:

> It is hard to escape the conclusion that . . . this . . . is designed to turn aside criticism without either meeting them or making explicit misstatements . . . For example, in

> the whole nine-page section, neither the words 'discount rate' nor any synonyms occurs...As implied by the absence of the words discount rate, nothing at all is said in the discussion of fundamental principles about the criteria for discount rates or about the effect of the level of discount rates on the total level of Federal reserve credit...It is natural human tendency to take credit for good outcomes and seek to avoid the blame for bad.

After this denial of previously undisputed monetary policy logic, the Fed for some reason did not manage to return to normality with regard to its official operational target doctrine for seventy years. In the early 1920s, we find Fed officials more and more rationalizing why interest rates are secondary, and quantities are more relevant as operational target (e.g. Warburg, 1930, II, 851).

Open market operations thus had become the key official monetary policy instrument. Open market operations, by injecting free bank reserves, were supposed to trigger credit and monetary expansion via the money multiplier. An inherent element of this doctrine was right from the beginning the view that recourse to discount borrowing was potentially evil, as the inflation until 1919 had been attributed to excessive recourse to the discount window. To rationalize the failure to hike rates during World War I, it was necessary to argue that raising the level of the discount rate would not have been sufficient to limit monetary expansion, and that therefore, non-price disincentives—mainly moral suasion—were necessary to discourage use of the discount facility. This new approach went so far that discount rates were from then onwards kept below market rates, such as to make clear that moral suasion and burdensome administrative procedures indeed are necessary to prevent banks from making use of the facility. It was of course too obvious that this technique was quite different from the one that the Bank of England had established on the basis of its rich nineteenth-century experience, and Fed officials thus saw a need to defend the change of paradigm in half-official publications. For instance Goldenweiser (1925, 46) argues that (rather unspecific) financial and institutional differences would have required a different approach.

From the early 1930s until the early 1950s, monetary policy had, in the US and many other countries, a break in the sense that short-term interest rates were anyway at or close to zero, and that the main danger was deflation, not inflation. Reserve position doctrine emerged in the 1950s as dominant in the US, and it is plausible that one reason for this was the enthusiastic support for it by Keynes, starting in the second volume of his *Treatise on Money* of 1930. Keynes also advocated the use of changes of reserve requirements as a monetary tool to absorb or inject reserves. As one example of the countless changes of reserve requirements in the US during that period, and how directly they were apparently motivated by money multiplier logic, consider the following Fed policy action of August 1960 (from Annual Report, Digest of Principal Federal Reserve Policy Actions; similar changes were implemented again in November of the same year): 'Authorized member banks to count about $500 million of their vault cash as required reserves, effective for country banks August 25 and for central reserve and reserve city banks September 1. Reduced reserve requirements against net demand deposits at central reserve city banks from 18 to 17½ per cent, effective September 1, thereby releasing about $125 million of reserves.'

Reserve Position Doctrine According to Monetarism

Generally, monetarists, who liked quantities, but tended to dislike the idea of central bank control of (short-term) interest rates, broadly supported reserve position doctrine, although they were often not so keen on being bothered with a need to split up their most cherished concept for monetary policy implementation, the monetary base, into petty-minded technical concepts like excess reserves, free reserves, borrowed reserves, etc. It seems likely that popular monetarists, such as especially Milton Friedman, played an important role in preventing reserve position doctrine from being silently buried already in the late 1960s. Maybe the most detailed discussion of monetarist theory applied to monetary policy implementation is Friedman (1960). Friedman (1960, 50–1) argues that open market operations alone are a sufficient tool for monetary policy implementation, and that standing facilities (e.g. the US discount facility) and changing of reserve requirements could thus be abolished.

What may be most striking in Friedman's (1960) analysis is his silence on the role of short-term interest rates and in particular about the fact that his proposals would imply a very high volatility at least of short- and medium-term rates. Similarly, Friedman and Schwartz (1963), in their critique of the Fed policy in the 1930s, show little curiosity for interest rates, but argue again and again in a strict multiplier framework. They follow the historical development of the monetary base and monetary aggregates to argue within the multiplier model that open market operations could have increased the monetary base and hence the money stock, preventing or at least attenuating the crisis of the 1930s (p. 393): 'If the deposit ratios had behaved as in fact they did, the change from a decline in high powered money of 2½ per cent to a rise of 6½ per cent... would have changed the monetary situation drastically, so drastically that such an operation was almost surely decidedly larger than was required to convert the decline in the stock of money into an appreciable rise.'

Probably the most extreme statements of monetarist views on monetary policy implementation can be found in Friedman (1982). Friedman (1982, 101) makes a rather concrete proposal regarding open market operations:

> Set a target path for several years ahead for a single aggregate—for example M2 or the base... Estimate the change over an extended period, say three or six months, in the Fed's holdings of securities that would be necessary to approximate the target path over that period. Divide that estimate by 13 or 26. Let the Fed purchase

precisely that amount every week in addition to the amount needed to replace maturing securities. Eliminate all repurchase agreements and similar short-term transactions.

This proposal is in fact neither a reserves nor a monetary base target, but an 'open market operations quantity' target, and thus an additional variant of an operational target of monetary policy inspired by reserve position doctrine. It is again too difficult to imagine how this proposal would work in practice, and why it should make sense.

Reserve Position Doctrine in the Practice of the Fed

One may distinguish six episodes in the practice of US Fed reserve position doctrine.

1920–1930: This period appears to be characterized by a relatively undogmatic application of reserve position doctrine. After the refusal to discuss the level of the discount rate in the early 1920s' annual reports, this ban seems to get partially lifted and open market operations and discount rate setting are presented in the annual reports jointly as main policy measures. Still, no explicit responsibility for short-term rates is taken, and changes of discount rates are often presented as *following* changes in market rates.

1931–1952: During this period, the Fed tended to leave the market with substantial excess reserves, such that money market rates were mostly close to zero (while still reflecting to a significant degree credit risk). According to Friedman and Schwartz (1963), the Fed was too restrictive in its excess reserves policy during the 1930s, which contributed to shrinking monetary aggregates; i.e. they criticize that the Fed should not have acted by reliance on a supposedly stable money multiplier.

1952–1970: The official approach of the Fed during this period was 'free reserves targeting', i.e. targeting of excess reserves minus borrowed reserves. The practical approach was eclectic both with regard to the measurement of the monetary conditions (as suggested by Anderson, 1969), and with regard to the use of instruments. Annual reports provide evidence that changes of reserve requirements, open market operations, and changes of the discount rate were all actively used, whereby the latter was again normally presented as following market rates, instead of guiding them. Taking into account in addition the frequent changes with regard to 'direct measures of monetary control', like margin requirements or deposit rate ceilings, one gets the impression that monetary policy was overly complex, and that the effects of all the policy measures and their interaction cannot really have been well controlled.

1970–1974: Towards the end of the 1960s, the federal funds rate was becoming more important as an indicator of monetary policy. However, in 1972, another quantitative operational target was defined, namely reserves on private deposits (a subset of total required reserves). According to Meulendyke (1998), the FOMC set two months growth rates for this quantity, consistent with the desired M1 growth and instructed the New York Fed trading desk to alter reserve provision in a way to achieve the targets. However, fearing that this would raise the fed funds' volatility, the FOMC also constrained the fed funds rate. In fact, the relatively narrow fed funds rate limits eventually dominated, and the reserves targets were often missed. In 1973, reserves on private deposits were redefined from an operational to an intermediate target, taking its place with M1. It was dropped as an indicator in 1976.

1974–1979: In this period, the Fed implicitly targeted a federal funds rate level, intervening in the market whenever the fed funds rate moved out of a very narrow band (see e.g. Cook and Hahn, 1989).

1979–1982: In October 1979, Paul Volcker became chairman of the Board of Governors and felt that inflation, which had two-digit levels during most of the 1970s, needed eventually to be stopped. The Fed concluded that the time was ripe for taking a monetarist approach that was also serious about day-to-day monetary policy implementation, by substituting interest rate targeting again by a reserve target, which this time was defined as non-borrowed reserves, i.e. reserves held by banks minus borrowed reserves, the recourse to the discount window. Although Axilrod and Lindsey (1981) provided an official scientific motivation for the 1979–1982 approach, it seems difficult today to reconstruct what was exactly done. According to Strongin (1995, 475): 'Non-borrowed reserves targeting was the most complicated of the reserves operating procedures that the Federal Reserve has ever used and it lasted the shortest length of time... Considerable debate within the Federal Reserve system about how these procedures actually worked is still going on.' The domestic policy directive formulated by the FOMC and effective on 1 January 1980 for instance specified:

> the FOMC seeks to foster monetary and financial conditions that will resist inflationary pressures while encouraging moderate economic expansion... The Committee agreed that these objectives would be furthered by growth of M-1, M-2, and M-3 within ranges of 1½ to 4½ %, 5–8%, and 6–9%, respectively... In the short run, the Committee seeks to restrain expansion of reserve aggregates to a pace consistent with decelerating in growth of M-1, M-2 and M-3 to rates that would hold growth of these monetary aggregates... within the Committee's longer run ranges, provided that in the period before the next regular meeting the weekly average federal funds rate remains within a range of 11½ to 15½%.

Some, as for instance Goodhart (2001) and Mishkin (2004), argue that the whole approach was just about the Fed avoiding taking responsibility for the necessary brutal increase in interest rates to bring down inflation, and the associated economic effects such as a strong rise in unemployment. In the words of Goodhart (2001), the episode, 'if properly analysed, reveals that the Fed continued to use interest rates as its fundamental modus operandi, even if it dressed up its activities under the mask of monetary base control…there was a degree of play-acting, even deception…' The 'smokescreen' created by Volcker would thus have been simply a necessary condition for bringing inflation to an end under conditions of imperfect central bank independence.

The Decline of Reserve Position Doctrine

Already in the 1970s, reverse open market operations (repos) become the predominant tool of central banks to steer reserve market conditions, questioning the strict distinction in the US reserve position doctrine literature between 'borrowed' and 'non-borrowed' reserves, as well as the praising of open market operations and the condemnation of discount window borrowing. Indeed, considering the leeway in specifying reverse open market operations, the distinction between the two instruments is far less clear than reserve position doctrine suggests (e.g. a reverse open market operation at a fixed tender rate and pre-announced full allotment is quasi-equivalent to a borrowing facility).

After the 1979–1983 episode of 'non-borrowed' reserve targeting, the 1983–1990 period of borrowed reserves targeting (see Meulendyke, 1998) is most likely an attempt to retreat from reserve position doctrine without needing to admit it too openly. Attempts made by the Fed to justify borrowed reserves targeting within a coherent framework indeed seem to be missing. In 1994, the gradual move to federal funds rate targeting is completed by announcing, after each FOMC meeting, the decision with regard to the fed funds target rate.

In 1998, for the first time, the 'Domestic Policy Directive', which is part of the minutes of the FOMC, contains again a reference to the fed funds target rate, instead of a reference to the vague concept of 'reserve pressure'. For instance, the domestic policy directive in effect on 1 January 1997 still contains the formula 'in the implementation of policy for the immediate future, the Committee seeks to maintain the existing degree of pressure on reserve position', while the one in effect on 1 January 1998 reads for the first time in the fed history 'in the implementation of policy for the immediate future, the Committee seeks conditions in reserve markets consistent with maintaining the federal funds rate at an average of around 5½%'. Moreover, still in 1998, contemporaneous reserve accounting is substituted again by lagged reserves accounting, which facilitates life of both banks and the Fed (as both now again know the level of required reserves before the start of the reserve maintenance period; contemporaneous reserve accounting had been advocated by Friedman as a supposed key element of quantity-oriented monetary policy implementation since 1960). Finally, in 2003, the Fed implemented a reform to its discount window, setting the discount rate systematically 100 basis points above the federal funds target rate and thus ending, after more than eighty years, the setting of the discount rate below market rates. The 100 basis points spread between the targeted market rate and the discount rate corresponds in principle to the pre-1914 approach of the Bank of England.

On the academic side, Basil Moore (1988) and Charles Goodhart (e.g. Goodhart, 1999) were the first during the 1980s to explicitly refute reserve position doctrine and to argue for a return to explicit interest rate control by central banks. With work such as Taylor (1993) or Woodford (2003), the view that central bank monetary policy is at least in normal times interest rate policy became again the predominating academic view.

What Remains of Reserve Position Doctrine?

The idea that there is a meaningful and important monetary policy transmission channel via the monetary base and the money multiplier is not dead. For example, Kuttner and Mosser (2002) and Gray et al. (2013) provide a figure as a summary of their perception of the monetary policy transmission mechanism in which there are two equally important channels of monetary policy, one via interest rates and one via the monetary base.

Likewise, the Bank of Japan's 'quantitative and qualitative easing programme' (QQE) explicitly includes a transmission channel via the monetary base (see press release of the Bank of Japan of 5 April 2013; see also section 13.3).

4

Three Basic Techniques to Control Short-term Interest Rates

On the basis of the balance sheet logic explained in chapter 2, and the choice of the interbank overnight rate as operational target of monetary policy as motivated in chapter 3, we now illustrate basic techniques of short-term interest rate control through monetary policy operations. Sections 4.1 to 4.3 all look at an aggregate model of the banking system, assuming that interbank markets work perfectly. Moreover, it is assumed throughout the chapter that there is no specific demand for excess reserves beyond required reserves, reflecting again an assumption of full market efficiency.[1]

4.1 ONE-DIRECTIONAL STANDING FACILITY-BASED MONETARY POLICY IMPLEMENTATION

Under this approach, the banking system takes systematic recourse to one central bank standing facility and the interest rate of this systematically used facility determines interbank interest rates as a result of arbitrage. This is actually the simplest way to steer short-term interest rates. Two variants are possible, depending on whether the banks are kept systematically dependent on the borrowing facility or the deposit facility provided by the central bank. To implement this technique in its first variant, the central bank needs to do the following:

- Taking into account the level of autonomous factors, ensure through low or zero liquidity provision via outright open market operations, or if needed through liquidity-*absorbing* outright operations (e.g. issuance of

[1] Bindseil et al (2006) provide an economic model of the banks' demand for excess reserves and explain that the demand for excess reserves needs to be treated in monetary policy implementation like an autonomous factor.

Household			
Real assets	E − D − B	Equity	E
Banknotes	B + d		
Deposits bank	D − d		

Corporate			
Real assets	D + B	Loans from banks	D + B

Bank			
Loans to corporate	D + B	Deposits of HH	D − d
Reserves of banks (incl RR)	RR	CB borrowing facility	RR + B + d

Central bank			
Borrowing facility	RR + B + d	Banknotes	B + d
		Reserves of banks (incl RR)	RR

Fig. 4.1. Financial account system of one-directional standing facility based monetary policy implementation

central bank debt certificates) that the banking system has a systematic liquidity deficit vis-à-vis the central bank after outright operations;

- Conduct no credit open market operations;
- Set the rate of the borrowing facility i_B to the level of the intended policy target rate i^*, i.e. $i_B = i^*$; in case of changes of the target, simply change i_B accordingly.

The set of financial accounts in (figure 4.1) represents this technique, which ensures that the interbank overnight rate will systematically correspond to the rate of the borrowing facility chosen by the central bank: overnight interest rates cannot exceed the borrowing facility rate because it would always be cheaper for a bank to go to the borrowing facility than to the interbank market (assuming sufficient collateral availability). Also, overnight rates cannot fall below the borrowing facility rate since at the margin the banking system needs to borrow at the latter rate, and hence no bank should be willing to lend at a lower rate. This approach was largely used by central banks in the nineteenth century, when banks had to take structural recourse to the discount facility and the discount rate determined market rates. Figure 4.2 provides as example the balance sheet of the German Reichsbank in 1900.

The monetary policy operations of the Reichsbank were dominated by the discounting of bills. Moreover, banks took recourse to the Lombard facility, which was priced 100 basis points above the discount facility. The choice between the two facilities was determined by the availability of discountable

Reichsbank, end 1900 (in million Reichsmark)			
Autonomous factors		**Autonomous factors**	
Gold and coins	730	Banknotes	1410
		Government deposits	110
Monetary policy operations		Other autonomous factors	142
Securities held outright	85		
Bills discounted	1088	**Current accounts of banks**	**387**
Lombard lending	146		
Sum	**2049**	**Sum**	**2049**

Fig. 4.2. German Reichsbank balance sheet as example of a one-directional standing facility-based monetary policy implementation
Source: Deutsche Bundesbank, 1976, p. 36–7.

bills, and because of its higher price, the Lombard facility was typically more a tool for short-term liquidity needs. In any case, monetary policy was implemented by setting rates of standing facilities. Current accounts of banks with the central bank were not driven by reserve requirements, but by working balances (reflecting the technically less advanced payment system environment).

The second variant of this approach (in which banks systematically use the deposit facility) was used by the Federal Reserve or by the Bank of England after 2009. To implement this technique, the central bank needs to do the following:

- Taking into account the level of autonomous factors, ensure through sufficiently high liquidity-injecting outright monetary policy operations that the banking system has a systematic liquidity surplus vis-à-vis the central bank after outright operations;
- Conduct no credit open market operations;
- Set the rate of the deposit facility, i_D (or the remuneration of excess reserves), to the level of the intended policy target rate i^*, i.e. $i_D = i^*$; in case of changes of the target, simply change i_D accordingly.

Figure 4.3 illustrates this technique for the case of the US Fed in January 2013. It may be noted that the ability of the Fed to pay 'interest on reserves', i.e. to remunerate excess reserves of banks held with the Fed, and the implied existence of a new monetary policy instrument for the Fed, got significant attention in some recent US academic literature. Kashyap and Stein (2012) argue that central banks should use the rate of remuneration of excess reserves (or, equivalently, of the deposit facility), and the level of excess reserves, as two independent policy tools, with the mix depending on conditions in the real economy and in financial markets. From a practical perspective, it seems true that the central bank can choose between a symmetric corridor approach and a one-directional reliance on one standing facility, and that the choice may depend on financial

Federal Reserve System, 2 January 2013 (in billion USD)			
Autonomous factors		**Autonomous factors**	
Net Foreign assets	42	Banknotes	1127
Other autonomous factors	110	Government deposits	84
Monetary policy operations		**Monetary policy operations**	
Outright holdings	2670	Reverse repo operations	103
Short term credit operations	0		
Borrowing facility (discount window)	1	**Deposits of banks**	**1509**
Sum	**2823**	**Sum**	**2823**

Fig. 4.3. The Fed in January 2013 as example of a one-directional standing facility based monetary policy implementation

Source: Board of Governors of the Federal Reserve System.

conditions. But a more subtle independent use of the two instruments as envisaged by Kashyap and Stein (2012) appears not to be practical.

The Fed's outright purchase programmes increased central bank assets such that the banking system was systematically in a state of excess reserves (reserve requirements were less than 10% of actual deposits of banks with the Fed). The Fed remunerated excess reserves at 25 basis points, which is equivalent to a deposit facility with this remuneration and automated transfer of excess funds to such a facility.

4.2 SYMMETRIC CORRIDOR APPROACH WITH OPEN MARKET OPERATIONS VOLUME SET BY THE CENTRAL BANK

Under this approach, the central bank offers both a borrowing and a deposit facility, sets the rate of these two facilities symmetrically around the target interest rate, and steers the scarcity of reserves such that there is an equal probability that at day end (or end of reserve maintenance period), the banking system will need one or the other facility. Then, the equilibrium interbank interest rate is the mid-point of the corridor set by standing facilities. Changes of the level of the target interest rate (monetary policy changes) are carried out by moving the corridor set by the standing facilities and the target rate (in its middle) in parallel up or down, while not changing the scarcity of reserves. To capture the technique more precisely, assume the following daily timeline of events, as also summarized in figure 4.4, and as reflected in the financial accounts of figure 4.5:

(1) In the morning, the central bank adjusts its securities position S by means of open market operations, such that S = B + RR. B is the level

of autonomous factors in the morning, while d is a stochastic unpredictable autonomous factor element that occurs in the afternoon with E(d) = 0 and with a symmetric density function. RR are the required reserves. As S = B + RR, in the morning, the total bank reserves will be equal to RR.

(2) At midday, a trading session takes place, in which in a competitive market (assume a high number of banks trading, with some of them short of reserves and others long), the interbank rate is set as the weighted average of the two standing facility rates, the weights being the perceived probabilities of the banking system being short or long at day end.

(3) In the afternoon, the true level for autonomous factors (B + d) is revealed, i.e. the stochastic variable d gets realized.

(4) Accordingly, the banks need to take recourse to one or the other facility.

This technique can also be implemented with reliance on central bank credit open market operations, as shown in figure 4.6.

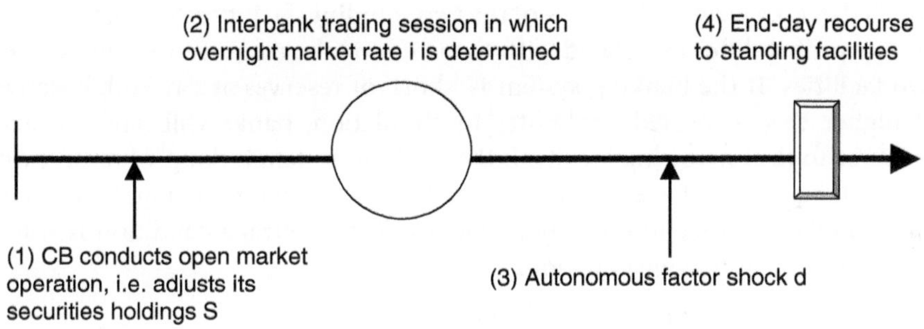

Fig. 4.4. A stylized daily timeline of central bank operations and interbank trading

Bank			
Loans to corporate	D – RR	Deposits of HH	D – d
Reserves of banks (incl RR)	RR	CB borrowing facility	max (0, d)
CB deposit facility	max (0, – d)		

Central bank			
OMO - Corporate bond holdings	RR + B	Autonomous factors	B + d
CB borrowing facility	max (0, d)	Reserves of banks (incl. RR)	RR
		CB deposit facility	max (0, – d)

Fig. 4.5. Financial account representations of symmetric corridor approach with outright open market operations volume determined by the central bank

Bank			
Loans to corporate	D + B	Deposits of HH	D – d
Reserves of banks (incl RR)	RR	Credit from CB (OMO)	RR + B
CB deposit facility	max(0, – d)	CB borrowing facility	max(0, d)

Central bank			
OMO – credit operations	RR + B	Autonomous factors	B + d
CB borrowing facility	max(0, d)	Reserves of banks (incl. RR)	RR
		CB deposit facility	max(0, – d)

Fig. 4.6. Financial account representations of symmetric corridor approach with credit open market operations volume determined by the central bank

The equality between assets and liabilities for both the central bank and the banks follows from the fact that max(–d, 0) = –d + max(d, 0) and max(d, 0) = d + max(–d, 0).

How exactly will the interbank interest rate i be determined? The basic idea is that for risk-neutral banks, arbitrage requires that the overnight interbank market rate is equal to the expected end-of-day marginal value of reserves, which itself is a weighted average of the two standing-facility rates. The weights are the probabilities associated with the need to take recourse to either of the two facilities. If the banking system is 'short' of reserves at day end, because of higher than expected banknotes in circulation, banks will have to take recourse to the borrowing facility. If the banking system is 'long' of reserves at day end, because of lower than expected banknotes in circulation, banks will have to take recourse to the deposit facility. This arbitrage condition is summarized in the following equation.

$$\begin{aligned} i &= P(\text{"}short\text{"})i_B + P(\text{"}long\text{"})i_D \\ &= P(S \le RR + B + d)i_B + P(S > RR + B + d)i_D \\ &= i_D + P(S \le RR + B + d)(i_B - i_D) \end{aligned} \tag{4.1}$$

Substituting $S = B + RR$ allows us to write:

$$i = i_D + P(0 \le d)(i_B - i_D) \tag{4.2}$$

If d is symmetrically distributed around zero, then:

$$i = i_D + 0.5(i_B - i_D) = (i_B + i_D)/2 \tag{4.3}$$

The recourse to the standing facilities will simply be equal to d, with the recourse to the borrowing facility being max(d, 0) and the recourse to the deposit facility being max(–d, 0). If one assumes that $d \approx N(0, \sigma_d)$, then one may also express equation (4.1) above as ($\Phi()$ being the cumulative standard normal distribution):

$$i = i_D + \Phi\left(-\frac{S - RR - B}{\sigma_d}\right)(i_B - i_D) \tag{4.4}$$

Based on this, one can calculate the effect on interest rates of S deviating from *RR* + *B*. If the central bank would like to implement an asymmetric corridor approach, it could base its liquidity supply *S* on this logic. Figure 4.7 illustrates the relationship between i and S in case of $RR = 0$; $B = 3$; $i_D = 1$; $i_B = 2$; $\sigma_d = 1$.

If the central bank aims at a steering of the overnight rate in the middle of the corridor, i.e. $i^* = 1.5\%$, it needs to set $S = 3$. If it set $S = 4$ it would obtain $i^* = 1.16\%$ and if it set $S = 2$, it would obtain $i^* = 1.84\%$.

Some authors have imagined that changes of the interest rate target would be implemented through changing liquidity conditions, i.e. through changing *S* (for example Hamilton, 1996, seems to be motivated by the question of how a central bank can influence the interest rate level through liquidity management). For example, in the case of figure 4.7, one could imagine that the central bank would like to implement a change of the interest rate target i^* from

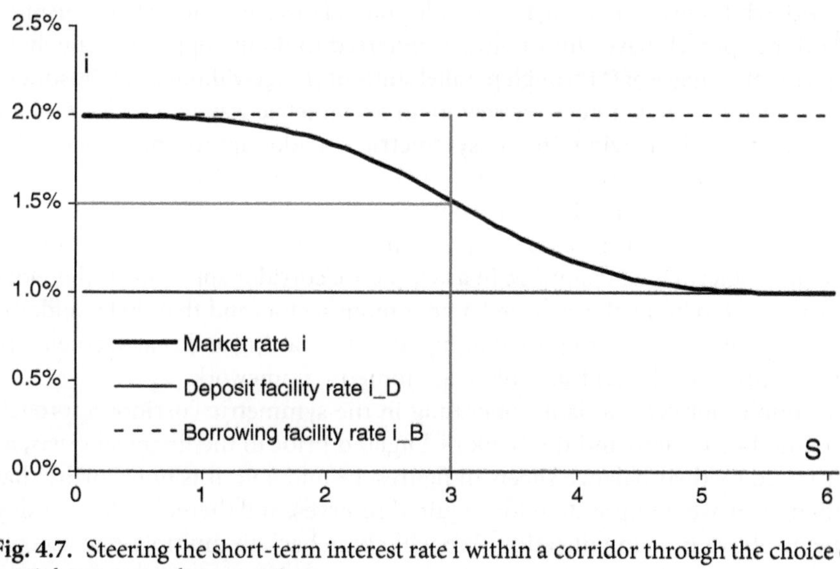

Fig. 4.7. Steering the short-term interest rate i within a corridor through the choice of outright open market operations

Bank of England, 27 June 2007 (in billion pounds Sterling)			
Autonomous factors		**Autonomous factors**	
		Banknotes	40
		Net other autonomous factors	20
Monetary policy operations			
Domestic assets held outright	33		
Short term credit operations	32		
Longer term credit operations	15		
Borrowing facility	0	Deposit facility	0
		Current accounts of banks	**20**
Sum	**80**	**Sum**	**80**

Fig. 4.8. Bank of England balance sheet in June 2007, as example of a symmetric corridor approach

Source: Bank of England.

1.5 to 1.25. What level of S does it have to choose for that? Transforming (4.4) provides the solution, namely:

$$S^* = RR + B - (\sigma_d)\Phi^{-1}\left(\frac{i^* - i_D}{i_B - i_D}\right) \tag{4.5}$$

In the concrete example, we obtain thus $S^* = 3 - \Phi^{-1}(0.25) = 3.675$. In theory, one could even imagine that the corridor $[i_D, i_B]$ would be so wide, say [0%, 10%], that changes of the target rate would always be implemented by varying S as needed, while never changing the corridor rates. However, central banks using a corridor approach have almost always preferred to do the opposite, namely to implement changes of i^* through parallel shifts of $[i_D, i_B]$ without any adjustment of S. Steering interest rates precisely in an asymmetric way in a wide corridor is in fact very challenging. In an asymmetric corridor approach, higher-order moments of the density function of d become relevant. For example, as (4.5) reveals, S^* would need to be adjusted whenever σ_d changes. Equation (4.5) also shows why this is not the case when i^* is in the middle of the corridor: in this case the last term is zero anyway. In a symmetric corridor approach, it therefore only matters to know the expected autonomous factors and that their randomness is symmetric. This implies that liquidity forecasting and management are much simpler for the central bank in a symmetric framework.

Examples for central banks operating in the symmetric corridor approach were the Eurosystem and the Bank of England prior to the financial crisis, as illustrated by their balance sheets in figures 4.8 and 4.9). It is noteworthy that both had an averaging system for required reserves, and therefore the one-day scheme above is a simplification. We will come back to multiple-day reserve requirements in chapter 5.

Eurosystem, 29 June 2007 (in billion euro)			
Autonomous factors		**Autonomous factors**	
Net Foreign assets	317	Banknotes	633
Domestic investment assets	131	Government deposits	70
		Net other autonomous factors	27
Monetary policy operations			
Short term credit operations	313		
Longer term credit operations	150		
Borrowing facility	0	Deposit facility	0
		Current accounts of banks	**182**
Sum	**912**	**Sum**	**912**

Fig. 4.9. The Eurosystem balance sheet in June 2007 as an example of a symmetric corridor approach

Source: ECB.

The majority of monetary policy assets held by the Bank of England was in the form of credit operations. Current accounts had the observed level mainly to fulfil the (voluntary) reserve requirement system. Recourse to the two standing facilities was negligible, reflecting the symmetry of the approach.

The Eurosystem had no outright monetary policy portfolio at that point in time. Current accounts of banks are again explained by the reserve requirement system. The level of standing facilities was practically zero, illustrating the application of a symmetric corridor approach.

4.3 FULL ALLOTMENT OPEN MARKET OPERATIONS WITHIN A CORRIDOR SET BY STANDING FACILITIES

In this case, the sequence of events is in principle similar to the previous case, but the open market operation consists in open market operation with *full allotment*, i.e. banks get whatever quantity they have asked for, conducted at some fixed rate i_{OMO}. This rate needs to be somewhere within the corridor $[i_D, i_B]$, but not necessarily in its middle. In this approach, banks will bid in the operations such that the expected interbank rate prevailing after the conduct of the open market operation will be equal to the rate at which the full allotment OMO is offered, i.e. *Bid* is such that $E(i|Bid) = i_{OMO}$. Hence, the bid needs to be such that $(i_{OMO} - i_D)/(i_B - i_D)$ = P("short") and therefore, assuming that d is $N(0, \sigma_d^2)$ distributed:

$$\frac{i_{OMO} - i_D}{i_B - i_D} = \Phi\left(-\frac{Bid - RR - B}{\sigma_d}\right) \tag{4.6}$$

Bank			
Loans to corporate	$D + B$	Deposits of HH	$D - d$
Reserves of banks (incl RR)	RR	CB credit (OMO)	$RR + B - \sigma_d\Phi^{-1}\left(\frac{i_{OMO} - i_D}{i_B - i_D}\right)$
CB deposit fac.	$\max\left(0, -d - \sigma_d\Phi^{-1}\left(\frac{i_{OMO} - i_D}{i_B - i_D}\right)\right)$	CB facility	$\max\left(0, d + \sigma_d\Phi^{-1}\left(\frac{i_{OMO} - i_D}{i_B - i_D}\right)\right)$

Central bank			
OMO	$RR + B - \sigma_d\Phi^{-1}\left(\frac{i_{OMO} - i_D}{i_B - i_D}\right)$	Banknotes	$B + d$
		Reserves of banks (incl. RR)	RR
CB facility	$\max\left(0, d + \sigma_d\Phi^{-1}\left(\frac{i_{OMO} - i_D}{i_B - i_D}\right)\right)$	CB deposit fac.	$\max\left(0, -d - \sigma_d\Phi^{-1}\left(\frac{i_{OMO} - i_D}{i_B - i_D}\right)\right)$

Fig. 4.10. Financial account representations of full allotment open market operations within a corridor set by standing facilities

$$\Leftrightarrow Bid = RR + B - \sigma_d\Phi^{-1}\left(\frac{i_{OMO} - i_D}{i_B - i_D}\right) \tag{4.7}$$

The bid leads in principle to an equivalent result as in the previous approach (corridor with open market operations volumes determined by the central bank). The key difference is that the amount of liquidity injected in the system is chosen by banks while bidding (variable bid) instead of being decided by the central bank in selecting the size of its operations (credit operations or securities holdings). Figure 4.10 illustrates this in the financial accounts.

In practice, information asymmetries (e.g. the central bank having a better aggregate banknote forecast than the banks[2]) and bid aggregation issues will make a difference, relative to the approach of section 4.2. The latter will imply that the sum of bids is likely to contain an extra random term relative to the actual neutral bid as determined in the equation (4.7), and this additional

[2] Indeed, central banks operating a symmetric corridor approach invest considerable resources in forecasting autonomous factors. On a daily basis, a fresh forecast of autonomous factors is produced relying on econometric models and data collected from specific sources (Government to forecast the level of the Government deposit account with the central bank; payment system operators in the event that frictions in the payment system lead to non-settled balances; foreign exchange function within the central bank if the central bank is active in foreign exchange markets, etc.). Aggregate bids of banks in a fixed-rate full allotment system will contain noise relative to a well-done central bank forecast of autonomous factors since (i) banks have no access to many of the relevant information sources; (ii) deposit shift shocks dominate at the level of the individual bank the aggregate autonomous factor shocks, and it is the main interest of the bank to forecast its own liquidity needs. See also section 2.5.

random term will impact upon overnight interest rates as soon as the total bid volume becomes public. In the financial accounts, this issue can be presented by adding an extra random variable in the volume of the open market operation.

An approach with fixed-rate full allotment open market operations within a corridor set by standing facilities has been applied by Danmarks Nationalbank and Suomen Pankki (the Finnish central bank) for some years (see Välimäki, 1999, 2003, for a description of the Finnish experience). The European Central Bank moved to such a framework in October 2008. Interestingly, during the crisis, euro area banks often bid in excess of what would have been implied by equation (4.7). Therefore, the post-allotment short-term interbank overnight interest rate was driven well below the rate of the fixed-rate tender. This signals that some aspects, which became important during the crisis, are not present in this simple model with only one representative bank.

5

Several Liquidity Shocks, Averaging, and the Martingale Property of Overnight Rates

In the previous chapter, a one-day, one autonomous factor shock, one trading session model of the interbank overnight rate was introduced. Now, the time dimension is generalized in two directions. First, section 5.1 presents a one-day model of the overnight rate with three distinct interbank trading sessions and three distinct autonomous factor shocks. Then, section 5.2 presents a three-day reserve maintenance period with one interbank session and one autonomous factor shock each day. Both generalizations capture relevant aspects of reality, notably the pattern of overnight rates to become more volatile at day-ends and at end of reserve maintenance periods (for empirical studies see e.g. Angelini, 2000, Bartolini et al., 2001, and Brousseau and Manzanares, 2005).

5.1 THREE SHOCKS AND THREE TRADING SESSIONS ON ONE DAY

As illustrated in figure 5.1, it is assumed that every day contains one open market operation, three interbank trading sessions, and three autonomous factor shocks.

For the sake of simplicity of notation, it is assumed now that $i_B = 1; i_D = 0$ while required reserves are assumed to be zero. The random aggregate autonomous factor shock d is now split up into three independently distributed components which occur after each of the three trading sessions and which are denoted as d_1, d_2, d_3, with realizations of these variables written as d_1, d_2, d_3, with $\mathrm{d} = \mathrm{d}_1 + \mathrm{d}_2 + \mathrm{d}_3$. The random variables d_1, d_2, d_3 are assumed to be independently and identically $\mathrm{N}(0, \sigma_d)$ distributed (alternative assumptions are possible of course—below, the assumption of constant volatility across the day

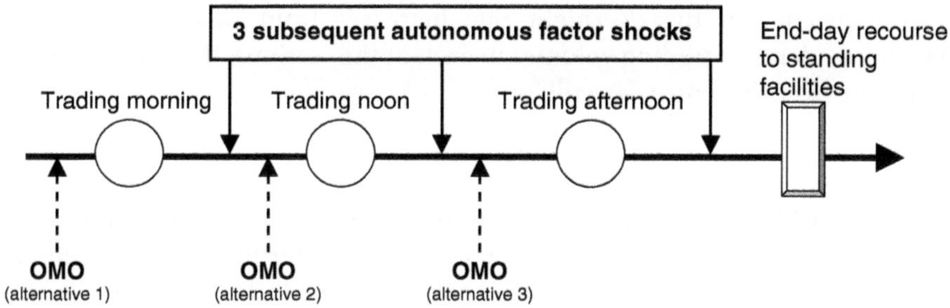

Fig. 5.1. Stylized timeline of the day with three trading sessions (with three alternatives for the timing of the OMO)

will be varied). Autonomous factors at day end are thus *ex ante* $B + d_1 + d_2 + d_3$. Assume that the central bank conducts a symmetric liquidity policy, i.e. aims at steering short-term rates to the middle of the corridor set by standing facilities. The first decision of the central bank is *when* to conduct the open market operation. One option is to conduct it before the first autonomous factor shock materializes. It would thus choose the volume of open market operations S as S = B, which implies, using the balance sheet identity, that the expected level of deposits with the central bank $S - B - E(d_1 + d_2 + d_3)$ is equal to zero, i.e. neutral in the absence of reserve requirements. Then the market interest rate in the first market session will be (noting that $d_1 + d_2 + d_3$ is $N(0, 3\sigma_d^2)$):

$$\begin{aligned} i_1 &= P(\text{'long'})^*0 + P(\text{'short'})^*1 = P(\text{'short'}) \\ &= P(S - B - (d_1 + d_2 + d_3) < 0) \\ &= P(-(d_1 + d_2 + d_3) < 0) = \Phi(0/(3\sigma_d^2)^{0.5}) = 0.5 \end{aligned} \quad (5.1)$$

The market rate in session 1 will be in the middle of the corridor as liquidity conditions will be balanced. This changes in session 2, as market players are assumed to observe the realization of the first autonomous factor shock. The market interest rate in session 2 will be (noting that $d_1 + d_2 + d_3$ is a random variable with probability distribution $N(d_1, 2\sigma_d^2)$).

$$i_2 = P\left(-\left(d_1 + d_2 + d_3\right) < 0\right) = \Phi\left(-d_1 / \left(2\sigma_d^2\right)^{0.5}\right) \quad (5.2)$$

In the last trading session, two autonomous factor shocks, but not the third, will have materialized, such that the interest rate will be, again assuming that the realized values of the first two shocks are common knowledge:

$$i_3 = P\left(-\left(d_1 + d_2 + d_3\right) < 0\right) = \Phi\left(-\left(d_1 + d_2\right) / \left(\sigma_d^2\right)^{0.5}\right) \quad (5.3)$$

The variance of the overnight rate increases from session to session. Assuming identical trading volumes in each of the sessions, the effective overnight rate over the entire day will be:

$$i = (i_1 + i_2 + i_3)/3 \tag{5.4}$$

Now consider the approach, instead, in which the central bank conducts its open market operation later in the day, namely after the first autonomous factor shock.[1] It is assumed that the central bank neutralizes this first shock, together with the structural level of autonomous factors, i.e. S = B + d_1. The interest rates in the three trading sessions will be:

$$i_1 = P\left(-(d_2 + d_3) < 0\right) = \Phi\left(0/\left(2\sigma_d^2\right)^{0.5}\right) = 0.5 \tag{5.5}$$

$$i_2 = P\left(-(d_2 + d_3) < 0\right) = \Phi\left(0/\left(2\sigma_d^2\right)^{0.5}\right) = 0.5 \tag{5.6}$$

$$i_3 = P\left(-(d_2 + d_3) < 0\right) = \Phi\left(-d_2/\left(\sigma_d^2\right)^{0.5}\right) \tag{5.7}$$

The overnight rate will deviate from the target only in the last session of the trading day. Obviously, $i = (i_1 + i_2 + i_3)/3$ will be less volatile. Finally, the central bank could also conduct its open market operation at the very end of the day, in which case it would fully stabilize the rate. Table 5.1 shows simulated volatilities of interest rates as a function of volatility of autonomous factor shocks. Cases are also considered in which the volatility of autonomous factor shocks decreases or increases over the course of the day (i.e. now we assume that each of the three autonomous factor shocks d_1, d_2, d_3 have their own variance, $\sigma_{d1}^2, \sigma_{d2}^2, \sigma_{d3}^2$ respectively).

First, it appears that the absolute level of the standard deviation of autonomous factor shocks does not matter for interest rate volatility in this model. Intuitively, this is because a higher end-of-day uncertainty (which drags interest rates towards the middle of the corridor) exactly compensates for the higher average size of early-day shocks (which push interest rates towards the outer bounds of the corridor). Second, unsurprisingly, conducting the open market operation at midday leads to lower interest-rate volatility than conducting the open market operation early in the morning. Third, if the volatility of aggregate autonomous factor shocks increases over the day, the overnight rate will be relatively stable (again because post-trading uncertainty on autonomous

[1] For example Bank of Canada (2010, 2) explains that its daily open market operation is 'at midday to encourage market participants to trade with each other during the morning, when a large portion of daily funding activity occurs'.

Table 5.1. Standard deviation of interest rates for different values of autonomous factor shock volatilities

Standard deviation of autonomous factor shocks			Standard deviation of interest rates							
			Open market operation in the morning				*Open market operation in midday*			
Morning	**Midday**	**Afternoon**	**Morning**	**Midday**	**Afternoon**	**All day**	**Morning**	**Midday**	**Afternoon**	**All day**
1	1	1	0	0.24	0.34	0.18	0	0	0.29	0.10
2	2	2	0	0.24	0.34	0.18	0	0	0.29	0.10
1	2	4	0	0.16	0.20	0.10	0	0	0.18	0.06
2	1	0.5	0	0.28	0.45	0.23	0	0	0.39	0.13

factors stabilizes interbank overnight rates around the middle of the corridor). Symmetrically, if the volatility of aggregate autonomous factor shocks decreases over the day, the overnight rate will be relatively volatile.

Figure 5.2 draws histograms of simulated overnight interest rates at the two relevant trading sessions (in the first session, rates are always in the middle of the corridor) for the case of an early-morning open market operation. The three sub-charts reflect constant, increasing, and decreasing volatility of autonomous factor shocks during the day. For the *constant* volatility of autonomous factor shocks (figure 5.2a), the shape of the distribution changes between the midday and the afternoon session: from a sort of bell curve to a distribution with the highest frequencies at the boundaries set by standing facilities. The intuition here is that as the shocks are revealed in the course of the day, the uncertainty about whether the day will end with a lack or an excess of liquidity subsides. When the volatility of autonomous factor shocks gradually *increases* in the course of the day (figure 5.2b), then in both market sessions a bell-shaped curve is obtained as the residual uncertainty dominates the shocks that have already materialized. Finally, if the volatility of autonomous factor shocks *declines* sufficiently in the course of the day (figure 5.2c), the opposite applies, and the probability clusters at close to the corridor boundaries in both the midday and the day-end market session.

It can be easily verified in these examples that, also thanks to unlimited intra-day over-drafting (i.e. intra-day, banks can run negative positions on the sight deposits with the central bank), the *martingale property of short-term interest rates* holds, i.e.

$$i_1 = E(i_2 | I_1) = E(i_3 | I_1); \quad i_2 = E(i_3 | I_2) \tag{5.8}$$

In equation (5.8) I_t is the information set of banks at time t. In words, the martingale property means in this context that in the first and second trading sessions, the expected value of the interbank interest rate to prevail in the subsequent trading session(s) of the day is equal to the interbank interest rate prevailing in the current trading session. Assume that $i_1 > E(i_2 | I_1)$ would apply, contradicting the martingale property. This would mean that any risk-neutral bank would make money by lending in session 1 and by borrowing in the interbank market in session 2. But since all banks would try to lend in the interbank market at the high rate of session 1 and try to borrow at the low rate in session 2, $i_1 > E(i_2 | I_1)$ cannot be an equilibrium. The same holds for $i_1 < E(i_2 | I_1)$.

5.2 THREE-DAY RESERVE MAINTENANCE PERIOD WITH AVERAGING

The model in section 5.1 can be re-interpreted relatively easily as one of a three-day reserve maintenance period with an open market operation in the

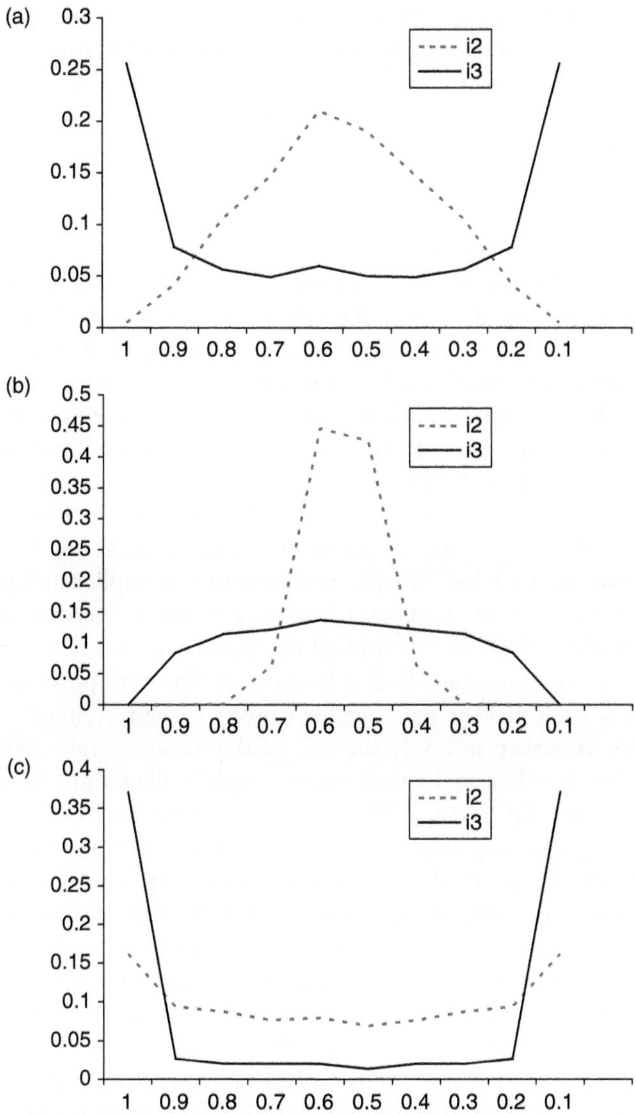

Fig. 5.2. Frequency diagram of interest rates, three trading sessions (midday session i2, afternoon session i3). Assuming that the open market operation is conducted in the morning, for three combinations of volatilities of the autonomous factor shocks. (a) Constant volatility of autonomous factor shocks, $\sigma_{d1} = 1, \sigma_{d2} = 1, \sigma_{d3} = 1$. (b) Increasing volatility of autonomous factor shocks $\sigma_{d1} = 1, \sigma_{d2} = 2, \sigma_{d3} = 4$. (c) Decreasing volatility of autonomous factor shocks $\sigma_{d1} = 2, \sigma_{d2} = 1, \sigma_{d3} = 0.5$. X-axis: market interest rate; Y-axis: probability)

morning of the first day with three days' maturity and one trading session and one autonomous factor shock on each day of the reserve maintenance period. In a reserve maintenance period with averaging over three days, reserve fulfilment is controlled (i) at the end of each day, in the sense of a prohibition of negative balances on the current accounts, and (ii) at the end of the reserve maintenance period, in the sense of an average fulfilment of reserve requirements.

To understand the mechanics of such a reserve maintenance period, assume first that only the second control would be carried out and thus there would be no overdraft constraint at the end of every day. One can show that in this case, the model presented in section 5.1 continues to apply, i.e. it makes no difference if reserve requirement fulfilment is controlled only on the last day or as average over the three days.[2] Banks continue to optimize their reserve holdings across the days of the reserve maintenance period with a view to achieving cost-minimizing reserve fulfilment, and undertake inter-temporal arbitrage accordingly. In this case, interbank rates will always reflect the forward-looking analysis of banks, encompassing autonomous factor forecasts for the entire reserve maintenance period. The martingale property applies in the same way as in the previous section: if on day 1, banks expected an increase of the interbank rate for day 2 then they would all try to borrow as much as possible to fulfil their reserve requirements at a lower cost. This will push up interbank rates on day 1, such that the martingale property is again fulfilled.

In practice, however, not only the end-of-day no-overdraft constraint, but also a number of other real-world factors explain deviations of time series properties of overnight rates within reserve maintenance periods from the martingale property, and some other specific time series properties. A relatively old literature has studied these phenomena. Ho and Saunders (1985) focus on the role of risk aversion of banks for the time series properties of overnight rates. Campbell (1987) assumes that liquidity benefits of reserves vary across the days of the reserve maintenance period, for instance due to differing payment system activity. Transaction costs are introduced by e.g. Kopecky and Tucker (1993), Hamilton (1996), Clouse and Dow (1999) and Bartolini et al. (2001). Limits to interbank trading have been analysed by Spindt and Hoffmeister (1988) and Hamilton (1996). Effects of payment systems are analysed by Furfine (2000). So-called window dressing by banks is studied by Allen and Saunders (1992) for the US, and by Bindseil et al. (2003) for the euro area. Bartolini et al. (2002) focus on volatility effects of operating procedures, confirming the increased end-of-day volatility also suggested in the simple model above. Further empirical models of short-term interest rates in the euro

[2] In order to obtain the full equivalence, the autonomous factor shocks must however be effective until at least the end of the reserve maintenance period (i.e. they must be persistent)—otherwise the calculus is slightly different.

area are Hartmann et al. (2001), Angelini (2002), and Würtz (2003). Schmidt and Nautz (2009) treat the case of the US Fed funds rate, while Nautz and Scheithauer (2011) provide a comparison across four central banks.

Perez Quiros and Rodriguez (2006) derive from the no-overdraft constraint the existence of an inherent asymmetry, according to which overnight rates tend to creep upwards over the reserve maintenance period with a measurable peak at its end. While they demonstrate this effect with a numerical example of a model, they also prove empirically the existence of a small effect for overnight rates in pre-EMU Germany, and show that the effect has practically vanished under monetary union (probably because of the higher total amount of reserve requirements). The intuition is that banks prefer to backload their reserve fulfilment within the reserve maintenance period (i.e. prefer to under-fulfil at the beginning and catch up at the end of the reserve maintenance period) since this reduces the probability of a too-early fulfilment of reserve requirements, which would imply a limited ability to offset shocks in the rest of the maintenance period. The calculus of Perez Quiros and Rodriguez (2006) to solve their model numerically is complex. Abolishing the no-overdraft constraint would be one option to simplify the reserve requirement system. However, central banks would probably feel uncomfortable, from a risk and incentive perspective, to let banks remain in overdraft for such a long period as the current standard length of reserve maintenance periods (e.g. two weeks in the US and around one month in the euro area).

Finally, it should be noted that limited collateral buffers may, even if the end-of-day no-overdraft constraint were abolished, create an asymmetry of somewhat similar nature. Indeed, banks can over-fulfil reserve requirements on a given day without limits but cannot under-fulfil them to the same extent because overdrafts need to be collateralized.

6

Standing Facilities and the Interest Rate Corridor

6.1 TYPES OF STANDING FACILITIES AND HISTORY

Borrowing facilities have two aims.[1] First, they serve as a monetary policy instrument as they contribute to steering short-term interest rates. Second, they contribute to the stability of payment flows and to financial stability in so far as they ensure that banks can always overcome temporary liquidity problems (as long as they have central bank eligible collateral). Historically, recourse to a liquidity-providing standing facility was sometimes not very clearly distinguished from emergency liquidity assistance (ELA—see chapter 14). Indeed, the US discount window had a reputation for revealing grave liquidity problems of the banks taking recourse to it, and the Fed for a long time did not really try to overcome this perception. Today, there is consensus among central bankers that recourse to standing facilities and ELA should be fully separated, to make sure that the one is as far as possible at the discretion of commercial banks and bears no stigma, while the other is as far as possible at the discretion of the central bank. Consider now the different types of borrowing facilities in turn.

Discount facility in the original sense: In a classical rediscounting operation, the holder of an eligible bill (typically a commercial bill with residual maturity of less than three months) sells the bill to the central bank outright (that is, for good), whereby the price charged in the transaction is determined by 'discounting' the nominal value of the bill through the 'discount' rate. In the first two decades of the twentieth century, monetary policy was still more or less equivalent to 'discount policy', that is, to defining the discount rate and the eligibility criteria for bills, since both Lombard lending (see below) and, even

[1] In this book, liquidity-injecting credit facilities are called 'borrowing facilities', reflecting the perspective of the one who takes recourse to the facility. Elsewhere such facilities are often called 'lending facilities'.

more, open market operations, were of limited relevance. Today, no major central bank offers any longer a discount facility in the original sense, although the US Fed still uses this term for its Lombard facility.

Until the first decades of the twentieth century, classical rediscounting was preferred by central banks to Lombard loans due to some kind of real bills doctrine, which in its original sense states that banknotes which are lent in exchange for 'real bills', that is, titles to real value or value in process of creation, cannot be issued in excess (see, for example, Reichsbank, 1910; McCallum, 1986; Green, 1987; Meltzer, 2003). The origin of the real bills doctrine lies in eighteenth-century England and possibly relates to the fact that usury laws prevented the Bank of England's discount rate from being set above 5%. Therefore, when the appropriate Bank rate would have been higher, the Bank of England tried to limit the gold drain by restricting the set of eligible paper, for example to 'real bills', claiming that this type of paper had specific properties since it represented real commerce. H. Thornton (1802, 252–3) had already convincingly refuted the real bills doctrine:

> If it should be said that the bank [Bank of England] loans ought to be afforded only to traders, and on the security of real bills, that is to say, of bills drawn on the occasion of an actual sale of goods, let it be remembered that real bills . . . may be multiplied to an extremely great extent; and moreover, that it is only necessary sufficiently to extend the customary length of credit, in order to effect the greatest imaginable multiplication of them.

One may add that real bills also can be multiplied by inflating the number of layers in trade. Despite Thornton's arguments, the real bills doctrine turned out to be astonishingly persistent and seems to have played an important role in the first decade of the Fed (see Meltzer, 2003). Echoes of the real bills doctrine even seem to have survived until the 1990s (e.g. Deutsche Bundesbank, 1995, 100).

Lombard facility (or 'advance' facility): Recourse to a Lombard facility means obtaining a credit from the central bank with given maturity as specified by the central bank, and pledging (or repoing) some eligible paper for the duration of the credit. This has—in the view of today's central banks—two particular advantages over discounting, namely, standardization of the maturity of operations, and allowing for a wider set of eligible paper in terms of maturity and risk characteristics. It was mainly in the 1950s that more and more central banks developed a preference for advances over discounting (Tamagna, 1963, 79–80), which was also due to a large extent to the growth of long-term government debt during World War II, which could easily be pledged. Today, all major central banks offer a Lombard facility at a penalty rate relative to the target interbank overnight rate (the US only since 2002). In the nineteenth century, central banks offered Lombard loans typically at 100 basis points above the discount rate.

Deposit facility: Central banks have only recently discovered the advantages of liquidity-absorbing facilities for monetary policy implementation. In fact the ECB and the central banks of Canada, New Zealand, and Australia were the pioneers of the symmetric corridor system around the year 2000, whereby the latter three applied this system without a reserve averaging system, while the ECB combined it with a one-month reserve maintenance period (see e.g. Whitesell, 2006). A deposit facility may appear somewhat less important since it is not needed to support financial stability. Still, it was shown in chapter 4 that interest rate control by the central bank is much simpler in a symmetric corridor relative to an asymmetric one. But this was not recognized by central banks for a long time, possibly also due to the general passion for open market operations and monetary quantities. In 2012, the US, UK, and Japan all stabilize their overnight interest rate with such an instrument, however in a context of huge excess reserves, such that in fact the remuneration rate of the deposit facility becomes the key monetary policy operations rate determining the market rate. In the case of the US, the deposit facility takes the form of a remuneration of excess reserves, which is equivalent to a deposit facility with automatic transfer of excess reserves to it.

The different approaches to monetary policy implementation explained in chapter 4 all relied in one way or the other on standing facilities, i.e. it appears that there is no standing-facility-free approach to monetary policy implementation that allows for a simple and effective steering of short-term interest rates. However, this conclusion was not standard in the twentieth century. The negative view on standing facilities in the US goes back to the 1920s, and was reinforced by monetarists like, for example, Friedman (1960), who strongly criticized at least the specification of standing facilities prevailing in the US. The strange history of the specification in practice and academic discussion of standing facilities in the twentieth-century US in fact can only be understood in the context of the related predominance of 'reserve position doctrine', as explained in section 3.3. Reserve position doctrine denies that central banks should control short-term rates, but argues that the central bank should control some quantity on a day-by-day basis. It follows from this that standing facilities, which by definition put a ceiling or floor on prices, but leave quantities to the discretion of banks, must be problematic.

That the absence of standing facilities can lead to extreme interest rate volatility is illustrated by the experience of the US before 1914. Burgess (1927, 278–9) quotes a report by the Senate Banking and Currency Committee of November 1913 which gave evidence of the volatility of interest rates before the setting up of the Fed: 'during the year 1907 the range of interest for money was from 2 to 45% in January, from 3 to 25% in March, from 5 to 125% in October, from 3 to 75% in November, and from 2 to 25% in December.' As Friedman (1960, 35) himself summarized, the Federal Reserve system was created by men whose views on the goals of central banking were shaped by the money panics during the national banking era. The solution to the problem of panics reflected in the Federal Reserve Act was the discount window, whose purpose was 'to provide an elastic currency'. Of course, a modern central bank—and this was Friedman's counter-argumentation (1960)—may also attenuate extreme fluctuations through very regular open market operations. However, as mentioned, such open market operations would in effect not be so different from standing facilities.

As central bank policy in the nineteenth century was largely discount window policy, including policies on rates and on access constraints (through limits or eligible paper constraints), one can say without exaggeration that the history of central banking in the nineteenth century is largely the history of its liquidity-providing standing facility. The best documented such history is certainly that of the Bank of England, as summarized in Bagehot (1873) and in more detail and more systematically in King (1936). Bindseil (2005a) reviews the history of this instrument for the Bank of England, the German Reichsbank, and the US Fed. The Fed, after having heavily stigmatized the discount window for the eighty years following 1920, eventually normalized its relationship to this instrument again only in the twenty-first century. Hakkio and Sellon (2000) were the first Fed economists to discuss openly fundamental reforms of the discount window towards the end of the twentieth century. They suggest that a Lombard-type facility with a rate above market rates would probably be preferable, but mention a series of technical issues which would need to be addressed. It was only in May 2002 that eventually the Fed embarked on fundamental reform of its discount window, labelling the new borrowing facility 'primary credit', and specifying it in a very similar way to the facilities in place e.g. in the UK and the euro area.

6.2 OPTIMAL WIDTH OF THE CORRIDOR SET BY STANDING FACILITIES IN THE SYMMETRIC CORRIDOR APPROACH

Reflections of central banks on the optimal width of the corridor start in the last years of the twentieth century. Bank of Canada (1995) puts the trade-off between stabilizing short-term interest rates and maintaining market turnover in the interbank market in the centre of the choice of the width of the corridor:

> The existence of a 50 basis point spread between the rate charged on overdrafts and that paid on surpluses would provide a fairly strong cost incentive for participants to deal in the market rather than to rely on the central bank, and the cost of overnight loans in the market would thus fluctuate between the rate on positive settlement balances and the Bank Rate. Since the typical spread between bids and

offers on overnight funds in the market is not more than 1/8 per cent, in principle it should always be possible for lenders and borrowers to negotiate a rate that is mutually more favorable than the rates available at the Bank of Canada. Thus, the rate spread at the central bank would encourage the participants to hold a zero balance every day, and the Bank would expect only minimal use to be made of its end-of-day facilities.

Another central bank to adopt early a corridor approach was the Sveriges Riksbank. While discussing the costs and benefits of the system in place (corridor of 150 bp), Mitlid and Vesterlund (2001) move beyond the interest rate control–interbank turnover trade-off and stress the implications of the chosen corridor width for central bank risk-taking:

> A very narrow corridor would probably be very effective in steering the overnight interest rate, but at the same time the Riksbank would take over much of the risk distribution that is currently done on the overnight market. It is uncertain how broad the corridor needs to be in order for the banks' first choice to be to even out imbalances on the overnight market, but it probably does not need to be as broad as it is now.

The issue of undue central bank exposure (and hence risk taking) and the need of an efficient interbank market (providing market discipline and allowing policy-makers to extract signals) is raised also in connection to the Bank of England's framework. Allen (2002) notes:

> Deciding on the width of the interest rate corridor was difficult. A wide corridor or band would not bind on many days and might not have much effect. A narrower band would have more effect and would have been likely to generate more business with the Bank of England, but it would erode incentives for borrowers and lenders to meet in the commercial market. We did not want our operations to overshadow normal market trading: a key feature of our current money market arrangements is that banks must test their name in commercial credit markets regularly. Related to that, any corridor would need to allow for credit tiering, since widening credit spreads are an important signal of potential financial stress.

The *academic* literature on the optimal width of the standing facilities corridor set by central banks is rather recent (see e.g. Bindseil and Jablecki, 2011a, 2011b for a review). Woodford (2003), Bindseil (2005a), and Whitesell (2006) discuss the general functioning of standing facilities corridors set by central banks. Berentsen and Monnet (2008) are the first to propose a dynamic general equilibrium model of a 'channel' system (i.e. a standing facilities corridor) with a welfare-maximizing central bank, a money market, and commercial banks subject to idiosyncratic liquidity shocks. Berentsen et al. (2010) use a dynamic general equilibrium set-up with idiosyncratic liquidity shocks and explicitly ask why not, if controlling the market interest rate is the monetary policy objective, set the corridor width to zero, which would allow perfect control of the money market rate? Hoerova and Monnet (2010) also tackle the question of why central banks allow money markets to exist. Following the logic of Allen (2002), Hoerova and Monnet explore the idea that money-market-induced discipline is an *ex ante* provision of incentives to banks to conduct business in a sound manner. The bilateral interaction between a lender and borrower in the over-the-counter money market would ensure that the borrower does not take any more risk than is socially desirable. The model, which assumes idiosyncratic liquidity shocks, allows simultaneous derivation of an optimal width of the corridor and an optimal collateral haircut, thereby bringing together different literatures. Bindseil and Jablecki (2011a) propose a structural model of a financial system (represented by a closed set of financial accounts as used frequently in the present book), which focuses on long-term two-sided recourse to central bank liquidity facilities, as observed notably in the euro area during the financial turmoil from autumn 2008 to 2010. This model will be taken up in part II of this text as it relates to a crisis situation with highly impaired money markets.

The following simple model is based on Bindseil and Jablecki (2011b). It follows the simple financial accounts logic introduced in chapter 3 and does not pretend to integrate household preference or a production stage. It nevertheless makes it possible to analyse the impact of the width of the standing facilities corridor on (i) overnight rate volatility, (ii) interbank trading volume, and (iii) central bank balance sheet length/average recourse to the facilities. The following is a specification of the simple financial accounts model with two banks introduced in chapter 2. The banks are hit by partially symmetric, partially asymmetric daily liquidity shocks. Bindseil and Jablecki (2011b) assume a symmetric corridor approach to monetary policy implementation, but with two banks. The aggregate liquidity shocks occur partially before, and partially after the interbank market session. The timeline every day is as follows:

(i) **Central bank open market operation.** In the morning, the central bank adjusts its securities position S by means of an open market operation, such that $S = B$, i.e. the expected value of autonomous factors. The actual banknote circulation at day end is defined as $B + 2d_1 + 2d_2$ (we will also sometimes write $d = 2d_1 + 2d_2$). B is the deterministic component and level of banknotes in the morning, while d_1, d_2 are stochastic shocks hitting each bank in the course of the day, with $E(d_1) = E(d_2) = 0$ and with a symmetric density function. Since $S = B$ in the morning, the total bank reserves R will equal zero in the morning.

(ii) **First liquidity shock.** After the central bank operation, a first stochastic component of autonomous factors realizes itself and becomes publicly known: $2d_1$. At the same time, a deposit shift shock occurs, k, which is neutral in terms of aggregate liquidity, but reflects that deposits of households move from one bank to another.

(iii) **Interbank trading session.** At midday, a trading session takes place, in which the interbank rate is set as the weighted average of the two standing facility rates, the weights being the perceived probabilities of the banking system being short or long at day end. It is assumed here for the time being that the banks neutralize through interbank trading the entire deposit shift shock, reflecting zero transaction costs in the interbank market. This assumption is the basis for the financial accounts representation in figure 6.2.

(iv) **Second liquidity shock.** In the afternoon, the true level of autonomous factors is revealed, as the last stochastic variable $2d_2$ gets realized.

(v) **Day end and recourse to standing facilities.** This enables banks to precisely fulfil their (zero) reserve requirements.

The daily timeline is summarized in figure 6.1. The end of day financial accounts representation under the assumption of perfectly efficient interbank markets is shown in figure 6.2. The perfect efficiency of interbank markets ensures that banks fully trade away the deposit shift shock k, such that banks are equal in terms of probability of being short or long at day end (this assumption will be relaxed later on).

How will the spread between the borrowing and the deposit facility affect the interbank market and average central bank balance sheet length? The model of Bindseil and Jablecki (2011b) allows explicit derivation of the trade-off between overnight interest-rate stability and interbank-market volume y, depending on the width of the interest rate corridor. If there are no interbank transaction costs, as assumed in figure 6.2, then banks would always trade in the interbank market until the interbank shock k could be fully offset, i.e. y = k. In contrast, if there is a *cost* C_{MM} associated with transacting in the market, the average volume of interbank trading E(y) will depend both on C_{MM} and on the width of the standing facilities corridor, i.e. on the penalty

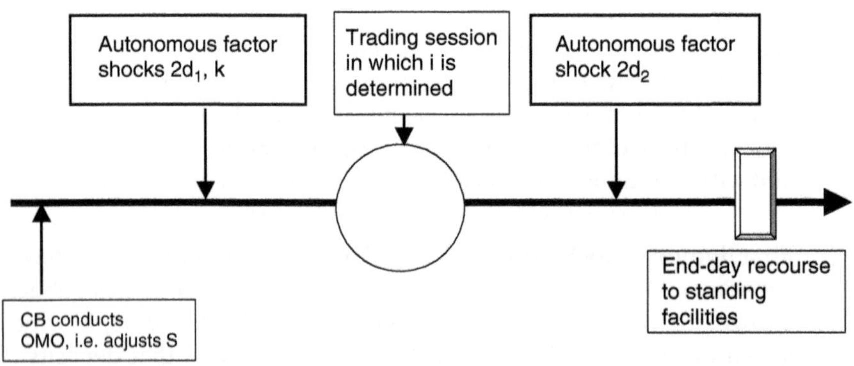

Fig. 6.1. Daily stylized timeline of central bank operations and interbank trading

Households / Investors			
Real Assets	E – D – B	Household Equity	E
Deposits Bank 1	D/2 – d/2 + k		
Deposits Bank 2	D/2 – d /2 – k		
Banknotes	B + d		

Bank 1			
Lending to corporates	D/2	Household deposits / debt	D/2 + k – d/2
Interbank lending	max(k,0)	Interbank borrowing	max(– k,0)
Deposits with CB	max(0, – d/2)	Credit from central bank	max(0, d/2)

Bank 2			
Lending to corporates	D/2	Household deposits / debt	D/2 – k – d/2
Interbank lending	max(– k,0)	Interbank borrowing	max(k,0)
Deposits with CB	max(0, – d/2)	Credit from central bank	max(0, d/2)

Central Bank			
Securities	B	Banknotes	B + d
Lending to banks	max(d,0)	Deposits of banks	max(– d,0)

Fig. 6.2. Financial accounts at end of the day ($d = 2d_1 + 2d_2$)—with zero interbank transaction costs such that interbank lending y = k

associated with dealing with the central bank. If $C_{MM} > 0$ and the corridor is zero, then—as we show below—there will never be any trading. In general, what the banking system needs to minimize when establishing the interbank trading volume is the sum of interbank transaction costs plus the expected costs of a *two-sided* recourse to standing facilities. If banks totally reverse the deposit shift shock, then the second type of costs is certainly zero (as the two banks will end the day either both in the borrowing facility, or both in the deposit facility). But if transaction costs are material, this is sub-optimal as at the end, the incremental savings relating to the second type of cost will be lower than the interbank transaction cost. Bindseil and Jablecki (2011b) solve this problem through simulation, relying on the following approach. For simplicity, they assume that $d_1 \sim N(0,\sigma_1^2)$, $d_2 \sim N(0,\sigma_2^2)$ and the interest rate on the deposit facility is zero, i.e. $i_D = 0$ (such that the width of the standing facility corridor is simply captured by i_B). First it is noted that if there were no interbank markets, the marginal value of funds at the time of the ineffective market session for the two banks, respectively, i_1, i_2, would be given by the following:

$$\text{Marginal value funds Bank 1 pre-trade}: MV_1 = \Phi\left(\frac{d_1 - k}{\sigma_2}\right) i_B \tag{6.1}$$

$$\text{Marginal value funds Bank 2 pre-trade}: MV_2 = \Phi\left(\frac{d_1 + k}{\sigma_2}\right) i_B \quad (6.2)$$

Assuming now that there is an interbank market and that interbank transaction costs are C_{MM}, then banks should transact overnight funds in the market as long as the net rent from trading is positive, i.e. as long as $|MV_1 - MV_2| > C_{MM}$. Assuming equal bargaining power, the rate at which the interbank transaction will be settled should be $i = (MV_1 + MV_2)/2$. With each currency unit transacted, the difference in the marginal valuation of funds will decline, and eventually reach the level of transaction cost C_{MM}, at which point trading will stop, as banks will consider it efficient to accept that the still different liquidity position of the banks creates a positive probability that they will have to turn to different standing facilities at day end. Thus, for every value of d_1 and k (and for given parameter values C_{MM}, i_B, and σ_2), one can calculate the interbank transaction size y. Simulating d_1 and k thus allows us to calculate an expected level of interbank turnover, E(y), as well as interest-rate volatility conditional on the corridor width and transaction cost.

Consider the illustration in figure 6.3. The figure shows the situation at the interbank trading session, i.e. after the morning shocks d_1 and k, but before the day end shock d_2. It is assumed that $d_1 > 0$ and hence the banking system on aggregate is short of reserves; moreover, a realization of the shock $k > 0$ has driven MV_1 and MV_2 apart. An interbank transaction of size y will now

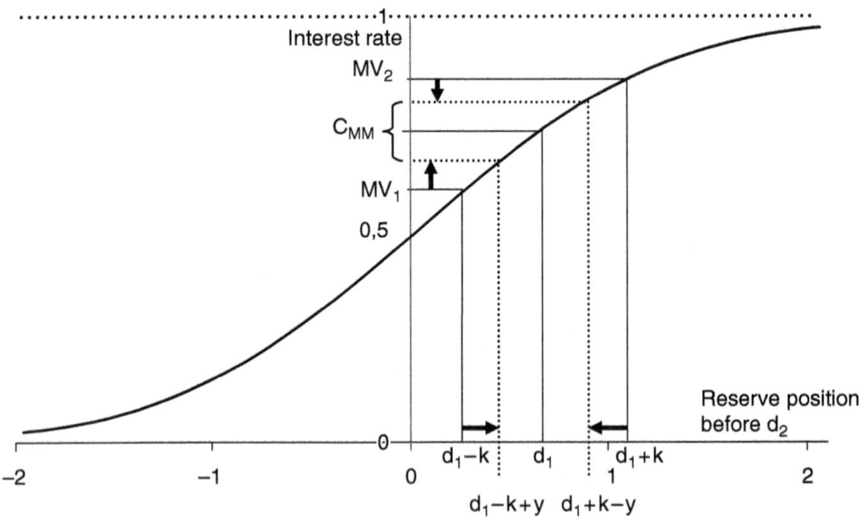

Fig. 6.3. Illustration of the calculus of banks when deciding on the interbank transaction volume y

drive back the two marginal valuations of reserves closer to each other, namely exactly to the point in which they differ only by C_{MM}, as shown on the vertical axis. This determines the size of the interbank transaction as it can be read from the horizontal axis.

Figure 6.3 illustrates that for a given k, the larger the shock d_2, the lower the trading volume will be because the slope of the cumulative standard normal distribution flattens for values more distant to 0.

Simulation results are presented in figure 6.4 (taken from Bindseil and Jablecki, 2011b, 20). It is assumed that the morning and afternoon aggregate

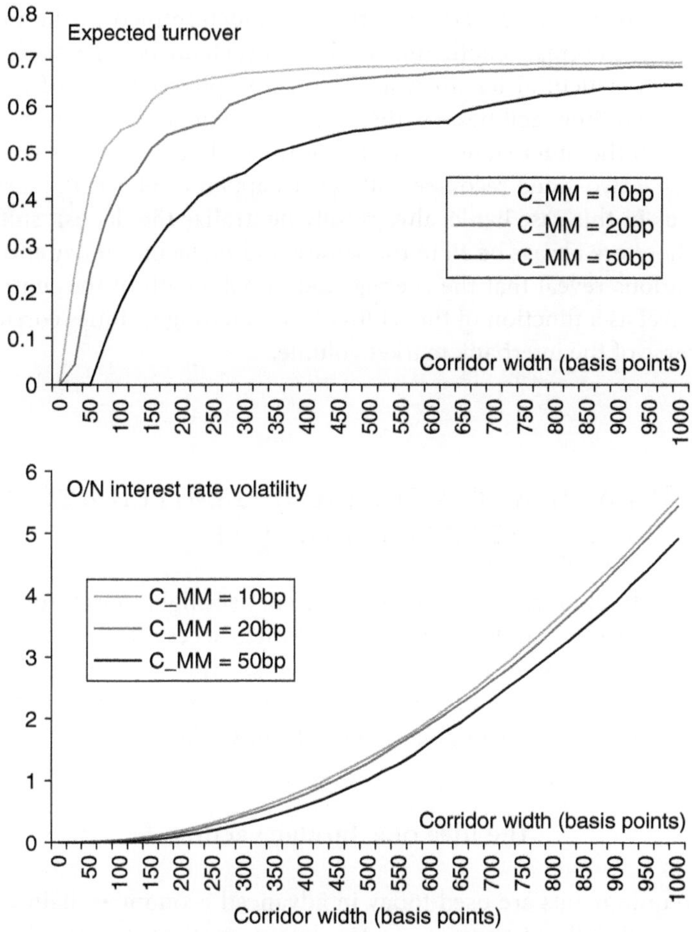

Fig. 6.4. Expected volumes of interbank trading (first panel) and interest rate volatility (second panel) for different widths of the standing facilities corridor and transaction costs C_{MM} equal to 10 basis points (bp), 20 bp, and 50 bp ($\sigma_1 = \sigma_2 = \sigma_k = 1$)—from Bindseil and Jablecki (2011b)

shocks as well as the interbank shocks have a standard deviation of one billion and that transaction costs increase from 10 basis points (bp), to 20 bp and 50 bp (and that $\sigma_1 = \sigma_2 = \sigma_k = 1$). The simulations illustrate how wider standing facilities corridors are associated with greater interbank trading volumes and greater volatility of the overnight interest rate. In view of the concavity of the turnover function, and the convexity of the variance function, it seems plausible that a central bank with normally shaped preferences in both a stable overnight rate and a healthy market turnover will prefer an interior value for the width of the corridor, i.e. neither a very narrow nor an extremely wide corridor.

The level of interbank turnover is also reflected in the *length of the central bank balance sheet*. In fact, the two are codetermined in the proposed model since the average lengthening of the central bank balance sheet beyond its minimum structural length results from the phenomenon of two-sided recourse to standing facilities, i.e. the first bank being in one, and the second bank being in the other standing facility at the end of the day. As was shown above, such a two-sided recourse will never happen if interbank markets are cost-free, as in this case banks always fully neutralize the deposit shift shock and will therefore always be all in the same standing facility at day end. In fact the simulations reveal that the average additional length of the central bank balance sheet as a function of the width of the standing facilities corridor will be an inverse of the interbank market volume.

6.3 IDEA OF A 'TARGET RATE—LIMITED ACCESS' (TARALAC) FACILITY

This section develops an idea of stabilization of overnight rates through a new buffering tool, called Taralac ('target rate—limited access') facility, substituting the averaging function of reserve requirements, while conventional standing facilities with unlimited access at penalty-level interest rates would remain. Holthausen et al. (2008) also discuss this type of facility.

The Idea of a Taralac Facility

Reserve requirements are used today in advanced economies mainly to provide buffers for daily autonomous factor shocks, so that the central bank does not need to intervene every day through open market operations. In this section, a framework of daily buffers to aggregate reserve shocks is introduced that does not rely on reserve requirements and avoids the need of daily open market operations. It can be integrated rather easily into a standard symmetric corridor framework, namely through one or two target-rate limited-access ('Taralac') standing facilities. The 'target rate' is the interbank interest rate the central bank aims at, i.e. the chosen level for the operational target of monetary policy.

In the one-directional variant, there would be only one facility, at the target rate, say a borrowing facility, through which the central bank stands ready to lend liquidity to banks at any time at the target rate. In order to ensure that the limited access facility anchors the overnight rate, the daily liquidity deficit should require *ex ante* an aggregate half-use of the standing facilities' limit. This means that the system is symmetric, in the sense that the probability that, due to large aggregate liquidity-absorbing shocks, the full use of the facility cannot avoid a lack of reserves, is equal to the probability that, without any use of the facility, the banks would be in a surplus.

In the two-directional variant, both a limited-access lending and a deposit facility at the target rate are offered. In this case, the open market operations need to be calibrated so that the *ex ante* probability of aggregate use of these two Taralac facilities is equal, which implies, for symmetric autonomous factor distributions, that the *ex ante* probabilities of aggregate use of either of the two penalty-level (unlimited access) facilities are the same.

Assume the financial accounts model and timeline introduced in the previous section (see in particular figures 6.1 and 6.2). Thus assume again that the central bank operates in a symmetric approach, i.e. the target interest rate i^* is in the middle of a corridor set by the borrowing and deposit facilities. Moreover assume that $i^* = 0.5, i_D = 0, i_B = 1$ and that there is only one Taralac facility, namely a borrowing facility offered at an interest rate $i_\psi = 0.5$. The Taralac facility has a limit (a capacity) of ψ. For risk-neutral banks, the interbank rate should simply be the weighted average of the three possible end-of-day marginal costs of funds, the weights being the respective perceived probabilities of day-end recourse. Assume that the aggregate liquidity shock is again d.

$$i = P\left(\text{'short'}\right)i_B + P\left(\text{'Taralac'}\right)i^* + P\left(\text{'long'}\right)i_D \tag{6.3}$$

$$\Leftrightarrow i = P(S-(B+d) < -\psi)i_B + P(-\psi < S-(B+d) < 0)i^* + P(S-(B+d) > 0)i_D \tag{6.4}$$

In this case, one obtains P('short') = P('long') only if $P(S - (B+d) < -\psi) = P(S - (B+d) > 0)$. This holds only for $S = B-\psi/2$. Substituting this indeed yields:

$$P(-\psi/2 - d < -\psi) = P(-\psi/2 - d > 0) \Leftrightarrow P(-d < -\psi/2) = P(-d > \psi/2)$$

$$\Leftrightarrow P\left(d > \psi/2\right) = P\left(d < -\psi/2\right) \tag{6.5}$$

This holds for any symmetric density function of the shock d. In words: the central bank provides through open market operations the amount of reserves such that the expected use of the Taralac facility at day end is one-half of the limit of this facility. The probability of having recourse to either of the two standing facilities at penalty rates is the same (while both depend, inversely, on the size of the Taralac facility). Given that the rates of the two penalty facilities are symmetric around the target rate and that the probability of having recourse to one or the other facility is the same, the market interest rate will be equal to the target rate, itself in the middle between the two penalty rates.

Interest Rate Volatility and Interbank Trading Volume with a Taralac Facility

The framework presented in section 6.2 to model the impact of the width of the standing facilities corridor on interest rate volatility, market turnover, and central bank balance sheet length can also be applied easily to the case of a Taralac facility in the middle of a symmetric corridor. Obviously, the larger the capacity of the Taralac facility (ψ), the larger the probability that it will be sufficient to absorb the shocks and therefore the lower the probability that banks will need to have recourse to either of the penalty facilities, and the more stable the overnight rate will be. If rate stability were the only criterion, then the higher the size of the Taralac facility, the better. Unfortunately, activity in the interbank overnight trading also depends on the capacity of the Taralac facility, i.e. the higher the capacity, the lower will be the incentive of banks to trade in the market. In fact, the whole idea of limiting the access to a facility at the target rate reflects that such a limit supports the interbank market. What is, in the model proposed, the trade-off between overnight interest rate stability and interbank market volumes, depending on the size of the Taralac buffer? The trading volume y between the two banks should be chosen again such as to minimize the sum of market transactions costs and the expected costs of simultaneous two-sided recourse to penalty standing facilities, with the solution to this problem being some function of $\psi, \sigma_2, d_1, k, C_{MM}$ (assuming that the width of the corridor is kept constant at 1—otherwise it would need to be added as a further argument). Table 6.1 summarizes a numerical simulation of this model, using the same method as in section 6.2. The morning and afternoon aggregate shocks have a standard deviation of one. Transaction costs C_{MM} have been set to 0.001%. The table provides expected trading volumes for buffer sizes between 0 and 4, and for three alternative sizes of standard deviations of interbank shocks (standard deviations of 1, 2, and 4). Moreover, the table contains aggregate overnight rate volatilities depending on the buffer size ψ (last row), and trading volumes under the assumption that there would

Table 6.1 Average interbank trading volumes for different Taralac buffer sizes (ψ) and different values of interbank shock volatility σ_k (relative to aggregate shocks $\sigma_d = 1$)

	$C_{MM} = 0.001\%$					$C_{MM} = 0$ (regardless of ψ)
	$\Psi = 0$	$\Psi = 1$	$\Psi = 2$	$\Psi = 3$	$\Psi = 4$	
$\sigma_k = 1$	0.27	0.20	0.06	0.01	0.00	0.80
$\sigma_k = 2$	0.94	0.84	0.52	0.23	0.08	1.60
$\sigma_k = 4$	2.08	1.97	1.55	1.02	0.60	2.77
ONR volatility	*0.29*	*0.22*	*0.11*	*0.04*	*0.01*	-

be no transaction costs, i.e. that all interbank shocks are always fully offset by interbank trading.

The central bank has to choose an optimal point on a trade-off between interest rate volatility and the amount of interbank trading, by means of choosing the size of the Taralac facility. Confirming intuition, it appears that, with a Taralac facility, the trade-off between preserving interbank market activity and stabilizing overnight rates is more favourable the higher are the interbank-shocks relative to aggregate shocks.

7

Open Market Operations in Normal Times

7.1 ORIGINS AND HISTORY

Open market operations (OMOs) are financial transactions with monetary policy purposes conducted by the central bank at its own initiative and discretion. Originally, the expression meant that the central bank operates in the interbank market (the 'open market') as a normal, possibly anonymous participant, for instance by buying Treasury paper in the secondary market. Also, the original expression was limited to outright (as opposed to credit) operations. Open market operations appeared chronologically as a monetary policy instrument after standing facilities. Different views can be found in the literature on what was the first open market operation in history. Wood (1939, 80–9) discusses security operations of the Bank of England before 1844, and calls them 'open market operations'. Clapham (1944, 290–7) judges that the first open market operations of the Bank of England took place in the 1830s, and sees 'very large scale' liquidity-absorbing operations to make bank rate effective in the 1860s. Bloomfield (1959, 45) sees only 'two clear-cut cases... of open market operations by a central bank between 1880 and 1914 as a deliberate instrument of monetary policy':

> The main device used by the Bank of England during this period to make its (discount) rate effective, when such was necessary, was that of 'borrowing in the market' from the commercial banks... Closely related to this, although apparently of much less importance, were occasional open market sales of consols. On a number of occasions, the Reichsbank similarly sold ('rediscounted') Treasury bills in the market in order to withdraw funds and to force market rates up.

Jobst (2009) notes that the Austrian central bank also conducted before World War I foreign exchange-based open market operations to influence domestic liquidity conditions.

For Mishkin (2004, 420), it is the US Fed which invented the instrument:

> In the early 1920s, a particularly important event occurred: The Fed accidentally discovered open market operations... After the 1920–21 recession, the volume

> of discount loans shrank dramatically, and the Fed was pressed for income. It solved this problem by purchasing income earning securities. In doing so, the Fed noticed that reserves in the banking system grew and there was a multiple expansion of bank loans and deposits... A new monetary policy tool was born, and by the end of the 1920s, it was the most important weapon in the Fed's arsenal.

It is true that it was in the US in the twenties that the term 'open market operations' came up and that the instrument started to be considered, in the context of reserve position doctrine, as a new, revolutionary, effective tool of monetary policy implementation.

As also summarized in section 3.3, various discussions can be found in the literature of the 1920s and early 1930s on the independent and superior effectiveness of OMOs relative to discount rate policy (e.g. Warburg, 1930, II, 851, or Keynes, 1930/1971, 226–30). M. Friedman (1960) and monetarists in general were strong supporters of the supremacy of outright open market operations, and suggested that they alone are a sufficient and efficient tool for monetary policy. Generations of monetary economists followed Keynes and Friedman, often not even raising again the question of why exactly open market operations should make a fundamental difference relative to liquidity provision through standing facilities. The textbook literature also adopted reserve position doctrine and the associated key role of outright open market operations until the early twenty-first century (for example, Mishkin, 2004). The Fed itself argued similarly at least from the 1950s up to the 1980s. For instance, the Board of Governors (1954, 38–9) explains the working of open market operations (as it would do in the subsequent three decades):

> If the Federal Reserve decides to buy, say, 25 million dollars of Government securities, it places an order with a dealer in such securities... The result is that the Reserve Bank has added 25 million dollars to its holdings of United States Government securities, and the same amount has been added to the reserve accounts of some member banks... These member banks are now in a position to expand their loans and investments and deposits. In so doing the banks will lose funds to other banks which in turn may expand... The reserves, the loans and investments, and the deposits of the banking system as a whole will be increased—the loans and investments and the deposits by several times the amount of the added reserves.

In the pre-2007 age of explicit short-term interest rate targeting, most of the historical justifications of open market operations were no longer relevant. Instead, it was recognized that, before anything else, open market operations will affect money-market interest rates and the recourse to standing facilities—as in the models presented in chapter 4. In 2009, a number of historical justifications of open market operations could be reactivated in the context of the asset purchase programmes launched by a number of central banks. Even reserve position doctrine, according to which open market operations directly affect the expansion of credit and money in the banking system, was used again by a few central banks as a basis for conducting outright purchases (see section 13.3 in part II of this book).

7.2 OPEN MARKET OPERATIONS AS DETERMINANTS OF THE MONETARY POLICY IMPLEMENTATION APPROACH

Assume a central bank with autonomous factors of B and no reserve requirements. The level of open market operations, 'OMO', can first of all be considered to determine the approach to monetary policy implementation in the following sense (see also sections 4.1 and 4.2):

(i) If $OMO < B$: systematic recourse of banks to borrowing facility, central bank to set $i_B = i^*$

(ii) If $OMO > B$: systematic recourse of banks to deposit facility, central bank to set $i_D = i^*$

(iii) If $OMO = B$: symmetric corridor approach, central bank to set i_D, i_B such that $(i_D + i_B)/2 = i^*$

In particular three degrees of freedom of the central bank can be identified beyond the choice between these three approaches through the setting of the OMO level.

First degree of freedom: difference between OMO and B in asymmetric standing facility-based approaches. Under the first two approaches, it is only clear that there should be a sufficient difference between OMO and B such that short-term fluctuations of B cannot reverse the sign of OMO-B. Beyond this, it is not clearly prescribed how big the difference should be. Under (i), OMO could be zero, or 20% of B, or 80%. Under (ii), OMO could be 120% of B, or 300%. If one takes the position that a central bank balance sheet should be lean, then obviously the difference between OMO and B should be kept small. If instead the outright operations fulfil a certain purpose, then, to reach the purpose, the central bank can use its freedom and set OMO at the desired level. For instance, the Fed in its outright purchase programmes during the crisis chose OMO levels far beyond B, implying huge excess reserves of the banks. The exact level of OMOs depended on the specific objectives of the outright purchase programmes (e.g. keeping long-term yields low).

Second degree of freedom: choice between outright and credit OMOs. At least under (i) and (iii), the central bank *can choose freely between outright OMOs and credit OMOs*. Examples for different choices in this respect are the Eurosystem and the Fed pre-crisis. The Eurosystem operated only with credit OMOs, while the Fed chose to have outright OMOs cover more than 95% of the OMO volume, while credit operations covered the remaining 5%.

US Fed, 27 June 2007 (in billion USD)			
Autonomous factors		Banknotes	775
Net other autonomous factors	11		
Monetary policy operations			
Domestic assets held outright	790	Reverse Repo	30
Credit operations	20	Deposit facility	16
Borrowing facility	0		
		Current accounts of banks	**20**

Fig. 7.1. US Fed balance sheet in June 2007, as example of a system with predominance of outright open market operations for the structural provision of liquidity
Source: Board of Governors of the Federal Reserve System.

A stylized 2007 Eurosystem balance sheet was shown in Figure 4.9. Figure 7.1 shows the US Fed balance sheet in June 2007. It may be noted that the Fed also conducted liquidity-absorbing repo operations, and that in fact in net terms credit open market operations were slightly liquidity-absorbing.

Outright operations may be preferred to credit operations for the following reasons. *First,* outright operations may be preferred for long-term structural liquidity adjustments as they do not bind both parties into the transaction, thanks to the existence of secondary markets. For liquidity-absorbing operations, issuing central bank paper makes it possible to provide a liquid instrument to market participants. *Second,* outright operations allow reserves to be injected at the discretion of the central bank even when the lower interest rate bound is reached, while credit operations require the willingness of counterparties to take credit. *Third,* if the central bank wants to hold to the maximum extent only risk-free assets and wants to minimize interaction with the banking system, then holding outright Government paper appears to be logical.

Credit operations may be considered to have the following advantages. *First,* they may be considered more neutral with regard to the relative prices of securities, as the collateralization does not change ownership and therefore affects the relative scarcity of securities less than outright purchases focused on a few specific asset classes. *Second,* one could argue that if the operational target of the central bank is a short-term interest rate, then it is natural to conduct a large share of its OMOs as credit operations at the target rate. *Third,* credit operations have similar properties as standing facilities in so far as they allow banks access to the central bank as lender of last resort (see part II of this book). Only the collateral constraint puts a limit to banks closing (temporarily) their funding gaps through a recourse to the central bank. This will stabilize market access of banks. However, it could also be argued that this may create scope for moral hazard.[1]

[1] See e.g. Bindseil and Nyborg (2008) for a discussion of the frequency and maturity of credit open market operations.

Third degree of freedom: What assets to hold in the outright portfolio? For its outright operations part, the central bank can choose quite freely what assets it wants to purchase. One approach could start from the argument that the consolidated state balance sheet should be lean as the role of the state in the economy should be minimized as long as no good reasons require state activities. In the case of the central bank, this could imply that it should hold most of its assets in the form of Government paper, such as to allow for the relevant shortening of the state balance sheet when consolidating the central bank and the Government. This argument has likely been relevant in the US Fed's decision to hold a large Treasury paper portfolio pre-crisis.[2]

An opposite approach could be to argue that the *central bank should view itself as independent from the Government* (as central bank independence has been argued to be positive for central bank performance). Accordingly, it could be concluded that the central bank should avoid any direct exposure to the Government, or that at least it should be neutral, i.e. hold Government and private securities according to market capitalization. Indeed, in history, excessive central bank crediting of the Government has led to hyperinflation or currency reforms (notably in Germany in 1924 and 1948). The 'monetary financing prohibition' in article 123 of the EU Treaty is motivated by this belief. More generally, it could be argued that the central bank should seek orientation from market capitalization to guide its outright portfolios to be generally as neutral as possible with regard to asset prices and yields, and hence with regard to the allocation of credit to the real economy. In crisis times, central banks have sometimes over-weighted certain assets in their outright portfolio to e.g. support the prices of these assets, i.e. to be non-neutral, assuming that the market fails to function efficiently, such that an unbalanced central bank asset structure ameliorates social welfare. In crisis times, a high number of special policy objectives of focused outright holdings arise, which will be discussed in more detail in section 13.3 of this book.

Also, *in normal times, central banks have sometimes tried to influence the yield curve of Government bonds* for perceived policy reasons. According to Sayers (1953), controlling the yield curve and in particular longer-term rates through open market operations had already been a topic in monetary policy implementation (that is, not only in fiscal policy) in the early 1930s. After

[2] Indeed, in the US, reverse operations were used only for the day-to-day control of reserve conditions, while outright holdings of securities provide the greater share of the total supply of reserves through open market operations. The Fed has been systematically very transparent with regard to its outright portfolio. According to e.g. Federal Reserve Bank of New York (2002), the domestic 'System Open Market Account' (SOMA), which includes all the domestic securities held on an outright basis, stood at $575 billion at the end of 2001. Normally, changes in the level of the SOMA were used to accommodate structural changes in autonomous factors. The SOMA consisted almost entirely of Treasury securities. The distribution of securities across maturity and individual issues aimed at achieving a liquid portfolio without distorting the yield curve or impairing the liquidity of the market for individual Treasury securities.

World War II, the Bank of England eventually seems to have adopted such an approach (Sayers 1953, 394): 'After the war came the Dalton episode, with the official attempt to get the long-term rate down to a 2½ per cent basis. Whether the bank itself, as well as Government Departments, joined in the heavy buying of medium and long-term bonds, in this ultra-cheap money drive, has never been satisfactorily established.' The US Fed in 1937 bought for the first time long-term paper with the exclusive aim of keeping capital market rates low. For instance, the 1940 annual report of the Board of Governors states the purpose of open market operations as follows (p. 3): 'The system's open market policy in 1940, as in 1939, involved the use of a flexible portfolio for the purpose of maintaining orderly conditions in the Government securities market.' Orderly conditions consisted in the pegging of the rate at which it would transact in Treasury bills at three-eighths of 1%. Similar policies were continued until 1951. After 1953, the Fed pursued what became known as a 'bills only' policy—that is, it confined outright open market operations to short-term paper. But in 1961 the bills-only doctrine was abandoned, and some experience in controlling the yield curve was again sought through open market operations (Meulendyke, 1998, 35): 'The extent to which these actions changed the yield curve or modified investment decisions is a source of dispute, although the predominant view is that the impact on yields was minimal.' In 1974, the Deutsche Bundesbank started to purchase systematically longer-term government paper in order to keep capital market rates low. In July 1975 the programme was intensified on the recommendation of the government, after which the portfolio of government paper reached a maximum of DM 7.5 billion (from only DM 6 million as at end 1973). In October 1975, the policy was abandoned as ineffective.

7.3 TENDER PROCEDURE FOR CREDIT OPEN MARKET OPERATIONS

First, it should be noted that open market operations do not necessarily have to be conducted via tender procedures. In 'bilateral operations', the central bank enters the market like a normal market participant to provide credit or undertake securities transactions bilaterally with a commercial bank. Bilateral operations have the advantage that they do not require specific procedures to be set up since the central bank follows normal market convention. Also, bilateral procedures are advisable in the event that the central bank would prefer to keep the operation secret. The potential disadvantage of bilateral operations lies in the discretionary selection of a single counterparty by the central bank and hence potential preferential treatment. Of course, the central bank can try to rotate its counterparties in these operations or to spread volumes through several bilateral operations conducted in parallel or sequentially. Still, this is unlikely to lead to a totally equal treatment of all market participants. Therefore, tender procedures have increasingly become the standard tool for open market operations since the late 1970s.

In *fixed-rate tenders*, the central bank pre-announces the interest rate (or price) applicable to the transaction, and the counterparties submit the amounts they wish to obtain at that rate/price. Two sub-variants have been used. Under the discretionary allotment variant, if the total amount bid is above the amount the central bank wishes to provide, it allots pro rata, that is, each bid is satisfied at a certain percentage. This method was applied extensively by, for example, the Bundesbank during the 1980s and 1990s, and also by the Eurosystem from January 1999 to June 2000. Also, the Bank of England systematically applied fixed-rate tenders throughout the twentieth century. The Fed, in contrast, never applied fixed-rate tenders in that century. Under the full allotment variant, the central bank pre-commits to allot the full amount of bids. This method was applied e.g. by the Deutsche Bundesbank in the 1950s and by the Bank of Finland in the years preceding 1999. It was massively used during the financial crisis starting in 2008, and the ECB, for example, has exclusively conducted fixed-rate full allotment operations since autumn 2008. The disadvantage of full allotment relative to pro rata allotment is that the central bank gives away its power to adjust the total allotment to make it correspond to its forecast needs. This disadvantage becomes relevant in the symmetric corridor approach, but less so in asymmetric approaches with systematic recourse to one standing facility (see section 4.3).

Under *variable-rate tenders*, bidders submit rate/quantity pairs such that the central bank, after aggregating all bids, is confronted with a downward-sloping demand curve. The central bank's allotment decision then consists of choosing one point on this curve. Above the selected rate, called the marginal rate, all bids are fully allotted. Bids below the marginal rate are disregarded. Bids exactly at the marginal rate are allotted pro rata, the central bank choosing the allotment ratio. Several sub-variants of variable rate tenders may be distinguished. The pure variable-rate tender with discretionary allotment amount was the usual tender procedure in the US. Under the variable-rate tender with pre-announced allotment amount, the allotment decision by the central bank is automatic, since the intersection of the demand curve with the vertical pre-announced supply curve determines the marginal rate. Its advantage is that it avoids a situation in which the market assigns any signalling content to the allotment decision and the resulting marginal rate. The ECB applied such a procedure to its monthly longer-term refinancing operations between 1999 and 2008. Under the variable-rate tender with a one-sided restriction to bid rates, like for example a minimum bid rate, the central bank announces beforehand that it will disregard bids below a certain minimum level. The ECB applied such an approach in its main refinancing operations between 2001 and 2008.

Finally, all variable-rate tenders can generally be specified either as a 'multiple price auction' (English auction), in which each successful bidder pays the price he bid for, or as a 'uniform price auction' (Dutch auction), in which each successful bidder pays the marginal rate. Today, multiple price auctions are generally preferred in monetary policy operations since they are said to provide more incentives to bid realistically. According to the Deutsche Bundesbank (1982), which for a long time used the Dutch tender procedure, this latter procedure has the advantage that it helps smaller bidders who may be unable to bid in a competitive way in a multiple price auction.

Central bankers normally cite *four main advantages of fixed-rate tenders*:

(1) They can send a strong signal on the central bank's monetary policy stance. Indeed, they constitute an implicit pre-commitment by the central bank to steer the corresponding short-term market rates to levels around the tender rate.

(2) Under the variable-rate tender, the public could attribute signalling content to the marginal rates. However, the policy content of marginal rates in variable-rate tenders should depend on the central bank's allotment policy. For instance, the Bundesbank aimed to send signals through the marginal rates in its variable-rate tenders. Also, the Fed until 1994 signalled to the market its monetary policy decisions through the market rates at which it would intervene. Today, the idea of signalling policy through marginal rates in variable-rate tenders is generally rejected as too noisy and complex. Since 1995, the Fed has announced the Fed funds target directly after each FOMC meeting, and banks have since then attributed no policy content to marginal tender rates (Federal Reserve Bank of New York 2000, 46). Another technique for preventing policy content being attributed to marginal rates in variable-rate tenders is to pre-announce the allotment volume, such as the ECB did until 2008 in its three-month variable-rate tenders.

(3) Fixed-rate tenders are consistent with interest-rate steering. Today, central banks again explicitly steer short-term interest rates. It therefore appears natural to offer reserves at the target rate. In contrast, it may appear counterintuitive to let the rates of central bank operations fluctuate, although they are in a clear arbitrage relationship with the market rates which the central bank wants to control.

(4) Fixed-rate tenders may not put less sophisticated bidders (for example, smaller banks) at a disadvantage. Indeed, bidding in fixed-rate tenders appears simpler than in variable-rate tenders, since in the latter case the bank also has to make up its mind on the rates at which to bid.

Variable-rate tenders are supposed to have two main advantages relative to fixed-rate tenders. *First,* they allow banks to express their relative preferences for central bank funds through the bid price or, more generally, they contain all the efficiency advantages of genuine auctions as an allocation mechanism. *Second,* they make it possible to avoid the phenomena of overbidding and underbidding, which potentially impair the efficiency of fixed-rate tenders. Moreover, under normal conditions, longer-term credit operations (i.e. credit operations going beyond the next meeting of the central bank policy-making body, i.e. beyond the next possible change of the policy interest rate) should be conducted as automated variable-rate tenders, otherwise the central bank would fix interest rates at a horizon beyond the maturity of the operational target of monetary policy.

The *analytical and empirical literature with regard to central bank tender procedures* is very recent. No literature on the US experience exists, possibly due to the non-availability of data. The research on the ECB's fixed-rate tenders was triggered initially by the 'overbidding' phenomenon. Nautz and Oechsler (2003) model specifically this phenomenon as experienced in the ECB's fixed-rate tenders. Ayuso and Repullo (2003) also focus on the overbidding phenomenon and argue that the ECB had an asymmetric preference function under which it systematically tended to provide too little liquidity, causing the overbidding. Välimäki (2003) and Bindseil (2005b) present equilibrium models of the determination in the interbank market for overnight liquidity when the central bank uses fixed-rate tenders. Linzert et al. (2006) study Bundesbank repo auctions, focusing on banks' decision to participate and the quantity they demand. Craig and Fecht (2007) study ECB auctions with more detailed bidder data for German banks. Linzert et al. (2007) provide evidence of the smooth working of pure variable-rate tenders in the ECB's longer-term refinancing operations. Bindseil et al. (2009) also study ECB tender operations and find that the tenders are informationally efficient, but that auction allocations affect banks' subsequent behaviour in a way that would be consistent with a high degree of allocational and operational inefficiency. Further recent studies of bidding behaviour of banks in Eurosystem tender operations include Ewerhart et al. (2010), Fecht et al. (2011), and Drehmann and Nikolaou (2013).

Finally, it should be noted that the allotments in both variable- and fixed-rate tenders can be automated or discretionary. Automation implies being rule-based, which also supports transparency. Being rule-based also presupposes having reached a high level of understanding of the economic relationships at stake and of the role the central bank plays. Discretion may sometimes be unavoidable, but often it may reflect the inability to understand precisely the interaction between the central bank and the market. Overall, monetary policy implementation does not appear so complex that it could not, at least to a very large extent, be rule-based, i.e. be automated. If tender

	Discretionary allotment	*Automated allotment*
Variable rate tender	No pre-announced volume	Pre-announced volume
Fixed rate tender	Discretionary *ex post* decision on allotment ratio	Full allotment (pre-announced 100% allotment ratio)

Fig. 7.2. Automated versus discretionary tender procedures

procedures for open market operations are based on automated allotments, then the banks, when submitting bids, know exactly what determines allotment amounts. There are two types of automated tender procedures: first, variable-rate tenders with pre-announced volume (in which the allotment is given automatically by the intersection of the demand curve with the vertical, pre-announced supply curve) and, second, fixed-rate tenders with pre-announced 100% allotment (i.e. quasi-standing facilities). In practice, central banks have often not pre-announced the allotment volume in variable-rate tenders, making it difficult for banks to decide on their bidding, and difficult for the central bank to decide *ex post* on how to map the information content in the bidding behaviour into an allotment decision. Also, central banks (e.g. the Bundesbank prior to 1999, and the ECB in 1999 and 2000) have relied on fixed-rate tenders with an *ex ante* unknown allotment ratio, also leading to unnecessary uncertainty and overbidding. Figure 7.2 presents a matrix summarizing the cases.

7.4 LIQUIDITY-ABSORBING OPEN MARKET OPERATIONS

Many central banks of emerging market economies have operated for years, and independently from the financial crisis, in a context of a banking system which is in a liquidity surplus vis-à-vis the central bank before the conduct of monetary policy operations. Mostly, the reason for this has been large foreign exchange reserves that the central banks accumulated with the purpose of countering pressure on the currency to appreciate in a context of large current account surpluses and capital inflows. A second category of central banks that operate in a context of a banking system in excess liquidity includes the US Fed and the Bank of England, which have, for monetary policy purposes, purchased large outright securities positions. The source of the excess reserves of the banking system makes not much of a difference with regard to how to maintain the short-term interbank rate at the target level. In some sense the excess reserves need to be 'sterilized' or 'absorbed',

Central Bank			
Autonomous factors	B	Liquidity-absorbing OMOs	0
Liquidity-providing facility	0	Deposit facility	B – RR
		Current account of banks	RR

Fig. 7.3. A central bank facing a banking system with excess reserves

although in fact the central bank may also simply remunerate them at the target interest rate level (or set the deposit facility rate at this level, which is effectively identical).

Consider the stylized central bank balance sheet in figure 7.3 and assume that the deposit facility rate is above the rate of remuneration of the current accounts of banks with the central bank, such that the current accounts will correspond exactly to the reserve requirements (RR). The autonomous factors B are in net terms on the asset side, as if e.g. net foreign assets exceed the sum of banknotes and government deposits.

The deposit facility rate will in this case determine the market interest rate. This is basically the asymmetric standing facility-based monetary policy implementation introduced in section 4.1. There are no particular reasons to think that this approach does not work, as it allows effective steering of the short-term interest rate. Of course, if the aggregate excess liquidity is very large, then the interbank market will not be very active since all banks will tend to have excess reserves. If this is considered a problem, the central bank may consider one of the following three approaches to address it:

(i) Reduce the day-to-day liquidity surplus, while not changing its sign, by absorbing a large part of the excess reserves through an increase of reserve requirements (RR) or through the conduct of liquidity-absorbing open market operations (e.g. issue twelve-month central bank debt paper).

(ii) Reverse the day-to-day surplus, again through either an increase of reserve requirements or long-term liquidity-absorbing operations. Then the banking system becomes again dependent on a day-to-day basis on liquidity provision by the central bank, either through the liquidity-providing standing facility, or through short-term credit open market operations. In the latter case, the central bank can again choose to operate in the symmetric corridor approach.

(iii) Achieve directly a symmetric corridor approach through liquidity-absorbing open market operations (e.g. combining monthly longer-term absorptions and daily absorbing operations such as in the models of chapter 4).

The following four instruments are generally available to absorb excess reserves, whereby only the first two rely on open market operations:

- Conduct reverse credit operations (collection of term deposits), unsecured or with the central bank providing securities ('repo'). For example, Bernanke (2010) explains the Fed's consideration with regard to the two, in case there were a desire to absorb the excess liquidity created by the large-scale asset purchase programmes.
- Issue special central bank debt certificates or Treasury paper. These two options have been analysed for instance by Nyawata (2012).
- Impose or increase reserve requirements (see also chapter 8). This also allows the central bank to rely on the useful features of reserve requirements, such as averaging, or creates the possibility of taxing the banking system and creating an income source for the central bank (namely by not remunerating required reserves).
- Remunerate excess reserves at the target level or offer a deposit facility at the target level and thereby put a floor also to interbank interest rates. Of course this measure does not really absorb excess reserves, but only prevents their existence from leading to a drop in short-term rates to zero.

The four approaches differ in terms of liquidity of the relevant bank assets. The liquidity of bank assets is reduced most by a collection of long-term (say, one-year) deposits, and least if the central bank issues highly liquid short-term paper, or remunerates excess reserves. More liquid bank assets mean, everything else being unchanged, somewhat looser monetary conditions.

8

Reserve Requirements

8.1 INTRODUCTION

Required reserves are deposits that banks have to hold with the central bank at certain points in time, and sometimes only on average over a number of measurement points. The size of reserve requirements is typically determined as a percentage of certain bank liability items (e.g. 'Reserve requirements of bank A in December 2012 = 10% of non-bank deposits with bank A at end of October 2012'). The functions that reserve requirements theoretically can perform depend on the specification of the reserve requirement system. In the course of the twentieth century, a high number of different functions was attributed to reserve requirements. The multiplicity of perceived functions is also reflected in a multiplicity of specifications. Before World War II, reserve requirements imposed by the central bank were a US phenomenon. After 1945, the idea became popular in most countries. Germany introduced reserve requirements in 1948, Japan in 1959, and even the Bank of England made the customary 8% deposit ratio of discount houses compulsory for some time in April 1960 (Tamagna 1963, 98). We have encountered reserve requirements already in the financial accounts model of monetary policy implementation as presented in chapters 2 and 4. As again shown in figure 8.1, reserve requirements (RR) increase banks' funding needs vis-à-vis the central bank.

If reserve requirements are determined as RR = rD, with r being a positive percentage (say 10%), then total central bank credit becomes (B + rD) and the balance sheet lengths of the banking system and of the central bank are D(1 + r) + B and Dr + B, respectively. Also, collateral constraints of individual banks are reached earlier, since typically required reserves holdings with the central bank are not counted as eligible collateral. If the haircut applied to claims to corporates is h, then the collateral constraint with reserve requirements reads $(1-h)(D + B) \geq B + rD$. Also, obviously, required reserves will be a cost factor of banks if they are not remunerated. In the US, euro area and UK, they are today remunerated, but this was different in the past, and still today many emerging economies do not remunerate reserve requirements. Call the interest rate to be paid on household deposits i_{HH}, the interest rate on central bank

Bank			
Lending to corporates	D + B	Household deposits / debt	D
Deposits with CB	RR	Credit from central bank	B + RR

Central Bank			
Credit operations with banks	B + RR	Banknotes	B
		Deposits of banks	RR

Fig. 8.1. Reserve requirements in the system of financial accounts

credit operations i, and the lending rate of the bank to corporates i_{Corp}. If banks are perfectly efficient and have no operating costs, then in competitive equilibrium: $i_{corp}(D + B) = i_{HH}D + i(B + Dr) \Rightarrow i_{corp} = i_{HH}D/(D + B) + i(B + Dr)/(D + B)$. Non-remunerated reserve requirements increase the cost of bank credit to the real economy by $riD/(D + B)$.

We have also encountered reserve requirements with averaging in the three-day model of chapter 5, where we also briefly discussed the martingale property of overnight interest rates in the reserve averaging ('maintenance') period. Reserve requirements with averaging provide a buffer against day-to-day autonomous factor shocks and allow the central bank to conduct open market operations even under a symmetric corridor approach with a *less than daily* frequency.

8.2 BASIC SPECIFICATIONS OF RESERVE REQUIREMENTS

In this section we will review in more detail the main dimensions of the specification of a reserve requirement system.

Definition of the Reserve Base Categories and Size of Reserve Ratio(s)

Normally, reserve requirement systems have in the past distinguished at least between sight, time, and savings deposits of non-banks with banks to define different reserve ratios on those categories of liabilities. The reserve ratios tended to be higher, the more 'money-like' the type of deposit with banks was considered. Distinguishing between different reserve base categories and imposing different reserve ratios was linked to the perception of reserve requirements having monetary control functions or was intended to influence competition between different banks.

Lag between Calculation Period and Maintenance Period

This issue was taken very seriously whenever the monetary control function of required reserves was deemed to be relevant (see, for example, Laufenberg, 1976; Friedman, 1982, 110–13). It was felt that, if monetary control was important, the lag should be as short as possible and the reserve calculation period and reserve maintenance period should even overlap as much as possible. This, of course, makes liquidity management much more difficult for banks, since it implies that they need to start fulfilling reserve requirements before knowing their exact level. Before 1968, reserve requirements in the US were overlapping in this sense ('contemporaneous'). In that year, a lag was introduced to facilitate the life of banks. After strong lobbying for years by monetarists and continued resistance by the Fed (see Friedman 1982), contemporaneous reserve accounting was reintroduced in February 1984, ironically just after the short-term monetary control experience of Volcker had come to an end. The Fed switched back again to lagged reserve accounting only in 1998, explaining, in a press release of 26 March that year, that 'the switch will make it easier for depositories to calculate their required reserve balances for the current maintenance period and will increase the accuracy of information on aggregate required reserve balances, which is needed by the Open Market Trading Desk to carry out its operations'.

Calculation Days for the Reserve Base

The importance of this issue depends on remuneration and hence on circumvention issues. With full remuneration of required reserves and hence no incentives for banks to circumvent them, the number of calculation days does not matter, since banks will not try to manipulate their balance sheet on the calculation days to reduce their reserve base. Hence, for instance, the Eurosystem, which fully remunerates required reserves, defines only one monthly snapshot for the calculation of the reserve base. The Bundesbank, which did not remunerate reserve requirements before 1999, prescribed the calculation of its non-remunerated reserve requirement on the basis of an average over four days' snapshot of the reserve base spread over the month.

Overall Size of Reserve Requirements

Depending on the reserve base and the reserve ratio(s), an overall size of reserve requirements is obtained. Assessing whether a certain overall size is adequate depends on the relevant environment and the functions attributed to the reserve requirement.

Remuneration

Required reserves may be remunerated or not. Whether remuneration is deemed preferable depends on the perceived relevance of the taxation function and circumvention possibilities, but also on the perception of a specific monetary control function of reserve requirements. Today, reserve requirements are typically remunerated in industrialized countries, but often not in emerging market economies (or at least not fully).

Averaging within a Reserve Maintenance Period of More than One Day

This feature determines whether reserve requirements serve the function of buffering out the effect of transitory autonomous factor shocks on short-term interest rates.

Use of Vault Cash

In some countries, banks can or could fulfil reserve requirements at least partially through vault cash. Friedman (1960, 49) argues that vault cash should be counted towards the fulfilment of reserve requirements in order to allow for the most stable relationship between the monetary base and broad money, which would improve the monetary control function. Indeed, the Fed still allows each bank to satisfy its reserve requirements with vault cash. Each bank's level of 'applied vault cash' in a reserve maintenance period is calculated as the average value of the vault cash it held during an earlier computation period, up to the level of its reserve requirements, such that the level of applied vault cash is lagged and known prior to the start of each maintenance period. Other central banks like the Bundesbank and the Eurosystem did not and do not accept vault cash since it is felt not to perform any relevant functions of required reserves while being administratively burdensome.

8.3 KEY FUNCTIONS OF RESERVE REQUIREMENTS (INCLUDING HISTORICAL)

Reserve Requirements to Secure the Banks' Liquidity and Financial Stability

Goodfriend and Hargarves (1983, 35–7) and Feinman (1993, 573) describe in detail this function, which was perceived to play a role in the US from the 1860s to 1931. Reserve requirements on deposits with banks were first imposed in the US on a national level with the National Bank Act of 1863. This act provided a national charter under which banks could be constituted as an alternative to state charters. Banks with the national charter were required to keep a reserve of 25% against both note and deposit liabilities. Goodfriend and Hargraves (1983, 36) interpret this reserve requirement as 'apparently rationalized as being necessary to ensure bank liquidity, that is, the ability of banks to convert deposits into currency'. A series of bank runs and financial panics in the late nineteenth and early twentieth centuries, however, made it clear that reserve requirements were not sufficient to guarantee liquidity of the banking system. What was missing was a mechanism for accommodating temporary variations in the demand for currency, such as an averaging facility or a borrowing facility (Feinman 1993, 573). The Federal Reserve Act of 1913 was hence in large part designed to solve the two main problems of the National Banking Act period: recurrent liquidity crises and seasonal contractions due to a lack of currency. The establishment of the discount window addressed more directly and effectively the issue of individual banks' liquidity. Still, reserve requirements continued to be imposed after 1914 without any new argument in favour of that instrument being advanced.

Monetary Control I: Changes of Reserve Requirements as Policy Tool

A predecessor of this argument is found in the older literature justifying reserve requirements, which argued that only reserve requirements would ensure that the creation of deposit money by private banks did not lead to an infinite monetary expansion and thus an undetermined price level (see, for example, Richter, 1990, 324–30, for an overview of this older literature). The critical assumption for deriving this result is that currency and deposit money are perfect substitutes. This can be easily illustrated in the framework of the money multiplier: if the ratio of currency to transaction deposits is not well-defined and thus possibly zero (because of the perfect substitutability of both categories of M1), then the M1 money multiplier will be undefined or even infinite (if the voluntary reserve holdings of the banking sector are zero). In this case, a positive minimum reserve requirement ratio r limits the expansion of M1 by setting the money multiplier at 1/r and thus is a necessary condition for the existence of a finite price level. In the real world, deposits and currency are not perfect substitutes. If money holders have well-defined preferences for the different components of M1, banks will not be able to create an arbitrary quantity of deposit money, as their customers will transform a part of the bank money into currency. Although this supposed function of reserve requirements therefore appears to stand on relatively weak ground, the argument still seemed to be maintained more or less explicitly until relatively recently, for instance by the Deutsche Bundesbank (1995, 128). Section 2.7 provides a simple representation of the credit money creation problem in a financial accounts system.

The more sophisticated variant of this argument says that changing the reserve ratio(s) makes it possible, via the money multiplier, to expand or contract credit and monetary aggregates. This argument was first detailed by Keynes (1930/1971, 65–8). He introduced the case with an example from the UK, in which no reserve requirements were imposed at that time (as is practically the case today):

> The Midland Bank had... maintained for some years past a reserve proportion a good deal higher than those of its competitors. It is not obvious that this had really been worth-while from its own point of view. Accordingly, beginning in the latter part of 1926, a gradual downward movement became apparent in the Midland Bank's proportion from about 14.5% in 1926 to about 11.5% in 1929... this... in fact enabled the banks as a whole to increase their deposits (and their advances) by about GBP 100 million without any new increase in their aggregate reserves... Now, as it happened, this relaxation of credit was in the particular circumstances greatly in the public interest... Nevertheless, such an expansion of the resources of the member banks should not, in any sound modern system, depend on the action of an individual member bank... For we ought to be able to assume that the central bank will be at least as intelligent as a member bank and more to be relied on to act in the general interest. I conclude therefore, that the American system of regulating by law the amount of the member bank reserves is preferable to the English system of depending on an ill-defined and somewhat precarious convention.

Keynes (1930, 68) then proposed a concrete specification of a reserve requirement system, to conclude enthusiastically on its power: 'These regulations would greatly strengthen the power of control in the hands of the Bank of England—placing, indeed, in its hands an almost complete control over the total volume of bank money—without in any way hampering the legitimate operations of the joint stock banks.' This argumentation was taken up by central banks, and, for instance, the Board of Governors (1954, 1974) lists the three main instruments of monetary policy implementation as follows: 'Discount operations, Open market operations, *Changes in reserve requirements*' (emphasis added), that is, reserve requirements were a relevant tool especially in so far as they could be changed across time. Only in Board of Governors (1994), the argumentation changes again and reserve requirements no longer play such a role. How seriously central banks took this function of reserve requirements at different points in time can in principle be measured by observing how frequently required reserve ratios were changed. Indeed, all other arguments in favour of imposing reserve requirements should not per se require variations of the reserve ratio.

The high tide of implementing monetary policy through changes in reserve ratios was in the 1960s and 1970s. Tamagna (1963, 104) explains that the

Bundesbank was indeed during this time using changes of reserve requirements for liquidity management purposes, substituting to some extent open market operations. According to Tamagna (1963, 115), this reflected the underdevelopment of financial markets in Germany, which implied that no appropriate paper for open market operations would have been available. In any case, this explanation cannot hold for the Fed, which also in the 1950s, 1960s, and 1970s frequently changed reserve ratios for monetary control. The years with very many changes in Germany, such as 1961 and 1967, saw gradual changes in one direction, somewhat similar to gradual changes in official interest rates. Indeed, in both years, both reserve requirements and the discount and Lombard rates were gradually lowered, revealing a kind of mixture of quantitative and interest-rate instruments.

Monetary Control II: Reserve Requirements as Built-in Stabilizer

To perform this function, reserve requirements do not need to be changed as they need to be for the previous one; that is, reserve requirements act as a built-in stabilizer which modifies the properties of the monetary system such that exogenous shocks become less harmful. This argument won more support from academics than from central banks, which apparently had problems presenting it as an official position. In 1998 the ECB presented its own variant of the built-in stabilizer function, according to which non-remunerated reserve requirements would increase the interest-rate elasticity of money demand and would therefore facilitate monetary targeting.

Consider first the academic literature on the topic. Richter (1968) was the first author to analyse the role of minimum reserves as a general macroeconomic built-in stabilizer. He concludes that the stabilization effect of reserve requirements on economic activity ultimately depends on the coefficients of the model, but that the case in which minimum reserve requirements act as a 'built-in destabilizer' is 'by far the more plausible' (Richter 1968, 288). Siegel (1981) and Baltensperger (1982) argue that the variability of the monetary aggregate is minimized by a 100% reserve ratio. But the reserve ratio minimizing the variability of the price level depends on the coefficients of the model and the correlation structure of the shocks. It can take any value between zero and one. Baltensperger (1982, 214) remains agnostic in his conclusions: 'The fractional reserve system has a flexibility and elasticity that may be a disadvantage in some situations, but that may equally be an advantage in other situations. I conclude that it is difficult and probably not advisable to choose between a low and a high reserve requirement on the basis of this kind of stability considerations.' Siegel (1981) is more courageous and estimates his model for the US with quarterly data from 1952–73. He concludes that the optimal average reserve requirement would have been 7% instead of the actual 11.5% at that time. On the other hand, the difference in the standard deviation of the quarterly price level would have been only minor. Horrigan (1988) shows in the framework of a macroeconomic model with rational expectations that the size and remuneration of required reserves are irrelevant from the point of view of stabilization of the price level and economic activity, as the impact of reserve requirements can also be effected by an adequate adjustment of the interest-rate elasticity of the supply of central bank money. Horrigan is therefore the first author to explicitly merge the minimum reserve literature such as Baltensperger (1982) with the general stabilization literature based on Poole (1970). All in all, it seems right to conclude agnostically. Although especially high reserve requirements are likely to matter for macroeconomic stability, one knows little or nothing about how and in which direction this really would work.

In the second half of the twentieth century, the differentiation of reserve requirements across deposit types was often perceived as a reflection of sophisticated monetary control considerations. The Bundesbank in 1952 differentiated along the following five dimensions: type of deposit (sight; time; savings); up to six size categories (implying different marginal ratios); whether or not banks were located at major bank places; liabilities towards residents or non-residents; and stocks versus increments of deposits (Deutsche Bundesbank, 1976, 1995). The simplification of reserve base categories started only in the late 1970s. A broadly similar evolution seems to hold for the US, where twelve different reserve ratios still applied in 1978, but only two remained in 1988. As Hardy (1996, 14) argues, in practice, differentiated reserve requirements are more likely to complicate monetary control, especially since the different implicit taxes on different types of deposits will create circumvention and hence instability in the structure of deposits.

Monetary Control III: Stabilizing, Creating, or Enlarging the Demand for Central Bank Credit of the Banking System

This argument has two variants. The first depends on the uncertainty that the demand for working balances creates for day-to-day control of the overnight rate. The second is independent from this uncertainty. Consider the two in turn.

(1) Stabilizing the demand for reserves by making the demand for working balances irrelevant to short-term market rates. We ignored in most of this text the demand of banks for excess reserves or 'working balances'. This either assumed that this demand was negligible due to extremely efficient payment systems, or that reserve requirements anyway exceed this demand. If these assumptions are given up, the central bank would need to forecast the daily demand by banks for excess reserves. However, since the demand for excess reserves depends on various factors that are unstable and difficult to predict, the control of short-term interest rates is difficult under such circumstances. By making reserve requirements the binding constraint on banks' demand for reserves—that is, by keeping required reserves above the shifting and unpredictable level needed for clearing purposes—the central bank can more accurately determine the banking system's demand for reserves, and eventually exercise better control over short-term interest rates. The Board of Governors (1994, 56) argues exactly in this way (see also Clouse and Elmendorf, 1997). To that extent, reserve requirements allow for better control of short-term interest rates, independently of the averaging function.

(2) Increasing the refinancing needs of the banking system vis-à-vis the central bank. While the first variant refers to an increase in the reserve holdings, the second refers to an increase in refinancing needs, the two being differentiated in terms of the level of autonomous liquidity factors. Schmid and Asche (1997, 76), for instance, explain this second variant of the function as follows: 'In order to ensure efficiency of monetary policy, i.e. the central bank leadership in the money market, the banking system must be kept sufficiently dependent on central bank refinancing.' Hence, reserve requirements, which increase the level of refinancing needs, would improve the efficiency of monetary policy implementation. The ECB in a press release of 8 July 1998 also refers to this argument as the second amongst the three it cites: 'such a system will contribute to enlarging the demand for central bank money and thus creating or enlarging a structural liquidity shortage in the market; this is considered helpful in order to improve the ability of the ESCB to operate efficiently as a supplier of liquidity and, in the longer term, to react to new payment technologies such as the development of electronic money'.

It is at least understandable that central banks probably prefer to operate in an environment in which the liquidity position of the banking system does not change its sign easily. Indeed, the switch of open market operations from the asset side to the liability side of the central bank balance sheet requires a review of procedures both for the central bank and for the market, which may be deemed costly. Also, open market operations that are too small, whether on the asset or the liability side of the central bank balance sheet, could be problematic because they probably lead to relatively unstable aggregate bidding behaviour. Finally, it should be noted that the enlargement function is also regularly considered key by central banks of smaller monetary areas and emerging economies. These central banks often have large foreign exchange reserves such that they would have to absorb liquidity through open market operations if they did not impose reserve requirements. These central banks have sometimes argued that absorbing liquidity in day-to-day open market operations makes less effective monetary policy operations, compared to making banks depend on a day-to-day basis on the central bank credit provision.

Averaging Out Transitory Liquidity Shocks and Allowing the Central Bank to Conduct Open Market Operations with a Lower Frequency

Reserve requirements can provide a temporary source of individual banks' and the banking system's aggregate liquidity if they are not enforced on a day-by-day basis, as suggested in chapter 5 (where we also reviewed the literature on imperfections of averaging and the martingale hypothesis). Section 2.4 provided a simple financial accounts representation of the degree of freedom of banks in fulfilling reserve requirements when averaging is allowed. In the practice of monetary policy implementation, averaging implies that any divergence of reserve holdings from reserve requirements in the course of the reserve maintenance period should not affect overnight interbank rates as long as money market players expect that it will be reversed before the end of the reserve maintenance period. Therefore, one late open market operation in the reserve maintenance period (for example, on the last day of the reserve maintenance period) in which the central bank is expected to compensate any accumulated excess or deficit of reserves relative to reserve requirements should be enough to fully stabilize overnight interest rates up to the moment of the open market operation. Besides the level of reserve requirements, the length of the reserve maintenance period, that is, of the averaging period, is crucial for this function. Averaging periods in central banking in the twentieth century ranged from half a week to one month. Carry-over provisions are also relevant to assessing the liquidity buffers provided by the reserve requirement system. Carry-over provisions serve as bridging reserve maintenance periods by allowing banks to shift limited reserve surpluses or deficits into the next reserve maintenance period. This has the advantage of reducing the volatility of overnight interest rates at the end of the reserve maintenance period, which normally cannot be avoided in an averaging system without carry-over. For example, the Fed currently allows for carry-over of 4% of required reserves as a deficit or a surplus into the following reserve maintenance period. It needs to be recognized that averaging can also be achieved without reserve requirements if banks are allowed to overdraft their end-of-day reserve account position ('averaging around zero'). Indeed, such a system has been successfully applied by the Bank of Canada (see, for example, Clinton, 1997) and was studied by the Bank of England (Davies, 1998).

Although elements of averaging in the fulfilment of reserve requirements can be traced back in the US to as early as 1863 (Stevens, 1991, 12), astonishingly, the implications of averaging and the possibility of deriving from it an explicit rationale for reserve requirements were systematically ignored for a long time, and the first publications which are outspoken on the averaging function appear only in the early 1990s (for example, Stevens, 1991, 12). In Board of Governors (1994) or Deutsche Bundesbank (1995) this function is already made explicit. Deutsche Bundesbank (1995, 125–6), for example, puts it as follows:

> Minimum reserve requirements, through which central bank balances have to be maintained only on average over a month, rather than daily, act in the money market as a liquidity cushion which absorbs unforeseen fluctuations in liquidity needs, generally with no intervention by the Bundesbank. This contributes to stabilizing interest rates and enables the central bank to adopt a 'non-interventionist' stance in the money market.

One may wonder why central banks have never adopted averaging periods of longer than one month. The issue is probably that by definition averaging excludes anticipated changes of overnight interest rate targets within the reserve maintenance period. Indeed, expectations of the central bank interest rates and the liquidity conditions at the end of the maintenance period are relevant to the interbank rates at any moment in time. Suppose as an extreme case a reserve maintenance of one year. Then, market participants would mainly speculate about what the central bank rates will be at the end of this reserve maintenance period, and the central bank would have difficulty influencing rates independently of this channel. In particular, it could not engineer anticipated changes of interbank rates within the course of the year. With fixed-rate tenders, expected rate changes within the maintenance period also cause overbidding and underbidding problems. If expected rate hikes within the reserve maintenance period exceed half the width of the corridor set by standing facilities, the banking system could also be tempted to fulfil its reserve requirements for the entire year through one huge recourse to the borrowing facility.

While in the first years of the euro, interest rate target changes occurred within the reserve maintenance period and destabilized reserve averaging and bidding behaviour, the ECB solved the problem in spring 2004 by aligning reserve maintenance periods with meetings of the ECB's Governing Council in which discussions of the monetary policy stance are pre-scheduled (see European Central Bank, 2005a, for an assessment of the effects of the changes made). Interest rate decisions since then have always been implemented as of the start of the next reserve maintenance period.

Reserve Requirements as a Tax

Unremunerated or only partially remunerated reserve requirements are a tax on the deposits of non-banks with banks, and are hence a source of income for the central bank, and eventually for the government. For a given level of deposits of customers with the central bank subject to reserve requirements, D, a reserve ratio r, and an interest rate level i, the total yearly tax income of reserve requirement will simply be irD. Already Keynes (1930, 62) gives prominence to this argument: 'The custom of requiring banks to hold larger reserves than they strictly require for till money and for clearing purposes is a means of making them contribute to the expenses which the central bank incurs for the maintenance of the currency.'

In general, taxes imply some form of allocative distortion. However, as long as free public goods need to be provided, such distortions may be unavoidable and the issue is to find the optimal way to distribute the tax burden on different goods or activities. Freeman (1987) elaborates on the role of reserve requirements for the total seigniorage and the relevance of inflation to that. A number of papers analyse in a rather abstract form the allocative effects of the taxation component of reserve requirements in the context of models of overlapping generations. For instance, Romer (1985) points out that reserve requirements are not exactly equivalent to a tax on deposits. He derives an optimal combination of public income from monetary expansion, minimum reserve requirements, and debt expansion. Mourmouras and Russel (1992) analyse the conditions under which an unremunerated minimum reserve and a tax on deposits are broadly equivalent. Ultimately, one has to ask whether the tax effect of non-remunerated reserve requirements represents an optimal tax according to the theory of optimal taxation, which postulates the optimality condition that the marginal welfare costs of different tax incomes should be equal. In the case of open capital markets, the international mobility of at least a part of deposits is high, such that small differences in the tax on deposits (implicit in the reserve requirement) can imply large outflows of the relevant types of deposits. In addition, technical innovations have made it possible to circumvent deposits subject to required reserves even without international dislocation.

In emerging economies, the taxation of bank intermediation through non-remuneration can have two specific merits, in addition to the considerations above. First, this tax may be viewed as a way to slow down an excessively rapid growth of bank intermediation, as the growth may be considered as unsound and fuelling a financial bubble. Second, central banks in emerging economies may have an income generation problem if they hold large foreign reserves, and need to conduct liquidity-absorbing monetary policy operations at rates above the remuneration rate of foreign reserves, while at the same time facing appreciation pressures of their own currency. To preserve central bank independence, it may be wise in these circumstances to increase the structural profitability of the central bank by absorbing a part of the excess liquidity through non-remunerated reserve requirements.

9

Collateral

9.1 IMPORTANCE OF THE COLLATERAL FRAMEWORK FOR MONETARY POLICY IMPLEMENTATION

Collateral availability is the ultimate constraint to accessing central bank credit. In this sense, it is difficult to overstate the importance of the collateral framework for monetary policy and financial stability. Unencumbered central bank-eligible collateral is potential central bank money, as banks can, dependent on the rest of the operational framework, swap it more or less easily into actual deposits with the central bank. If the central bank operates largely through outright operations and its credit operations are stigmatized and expensive, the collateral framework may be limitedly relevant. If the central bank, however, conducts large-scale credit operations at the operational target rate and without stigma, then collateral becomes almost equivalent to central bank money. Bindseil and Papadia (2006) and Chailloux et al. (2008) touch upon the economics of the central bank collateral framework. Gonzalez and Molitor (2009) present a methodology for deriving a central bank risk-control framework for credit operations. Chapman et al. (2010), Ashcraft et al. (2011), Bindseil and Jablecki (2013) and Bindseil (2013) model the role of the collateral and risk-control framework of the central bank for financial stability and monetary policy transmission. Overviews of collateral frameworks are provided by Chailloux et al. (2008), Tabakis and Weller (2009), Cheun et al. (2009), European Central Bank (2013b), and Markets Committee (2013).

The Collateral Constraint in Accessing Central Bank Credit

Consider a bank with differentiated bank assets, such as is shown in Figure 9.1.

For instance, asset type 1 could be 'AAA-rated sovereign bonds with residual maturity between 0 and 1 year' and asset type n could be 'impaired loans to corporates located in a certain region with a residual maturity of more than

Bank			
Asset type 1	a_1	Deposits / market funding	D
Asset type 2	a_2	Credit from central bank	$\Sigma a_i - D + RR$
Asset type...	...		
Asset type n	a_n		
Deposits with CB	RR		

Fig. 9.1. A financial accounts representation to illustrate the role of the collateral framework

3 years', etc. On each of these assets, *the central bank decides on eligibility of assets as collateral*, and for the eligible assets, it decides on a haircut. Let the vector of central bank haircuts be $H = \{h_1, h_2, \ldots, h_n\}$, with for each i, $0 \leq h_i \leq 1$. The differentiation of haircuts serves to achieve some sort of post haircut 'risk equivalence' across collateral types (see section 9.3). Haircuts of 1 are equivalent to non-eligibility of the respective assets. The total central bank borrowing potential of the representative bank is the collateral value post-haircut, 'CVPH', therefore $CVPH = \Sigma a_i(1 - h_i)$. Central bank borrowing cannot exceed CVPH, i.e. $\Sigma a_i - D + RR \leq CVPH$ or $D - RR > \Sigma a_i h_i$. The difference $CVPH - (\Sigma a_i - D + RR) = D - RR - \Sigma a_i h_i$ is the further potential recourse to central bank credit.

The Example of the Euro Area

It is interesting to consider as example the case of the Eurosystem. According to the ECB website, at end 2012, Eurosystem-eligible securities consisted in total of an amount of EUR 14 trillion (see also table 9.2 at the end of the chapter). The total length of the euro area banks' balance sheet was around EUR 32 trillion, with around EUR 5 trillion of eligible assets post-haircut (CVPH). The liquidity deficit of the euro area banking system towards the central bank post-outright operations (i.e. the one to be covered through collateralized credit operations) is around EUR 0.5 trillion. Therefore, at the *aggregate* level, eligible collateral was more than sufficient to cover the liquidity deficit of the banking system towards the central bank. However, one can also conclude that for the average *individual* bank, only a relatively small part of its balance sheet can be financed through Eurosystem credit operations (on average 5/32), i.e. a loss of capital market access and depositors outflows will over time lead to a funding gap that can no longer be financed through Eurosystem credit due to collateral scarcity. In this sense, central bank collateral scarcity will always be a key consideration in the liquidity management strategies of banks.

A Continuous Haircut Function

Typically haircuts applied to the most liquid assets of banks (e.g. to sovereign bills) are close to zero, while the less liquid assets are not eligible at all (in some sense equivalent to a haircut of 1). Assume now that total assets of the bank would be equal to 1, and that there would be a continuum of assets and that they are ranked from those with the lowest uncertainty on liquidation value (highest quality collateral) to the ones with the highest uncertainty on liquidation value (lowest quality collateral). One could then think of haircuts to be captured by a continuous function x→h(x), from the asset space x in [0,1] into the haircut level h in [0,1]. Specifically, the form of a power function could be assumed to apply:

$$h(x) = x^{\delta} \text{ with } \delta > 0 \tag{9.1}$$

If δ is close to 0, then the haircuts increase and converge quickly towards 1. If in contrast δ is large (say 10) then haircuts stay at close to zero for a long time and only start to increase in a convex manner when approaching the least liquid assets. The total haircut (and the average haircut) is $1/(\delta + 1)$, and hence CVPH is $\delta/(\delta + 1)$. This is obtained from the integration rule $\int x^{\delta}\, dx = x^{\delta + 1}/(\delta + 1)$. Figure 9.2 illustrates the haircut function h(x) for various values of δ.

For values of the parameter δ of 0.05, 0.2, 1, 5, and 10, the average haircut applied by the central bank is 0.95, 0.84, 0.51, 0.17, and 0.05, respectively. For example, in the case of the Eurosystem, EUR 32 trillion of aggregated bank assets yield around EUR 5 trillion of eligible collateral after haircuts, which

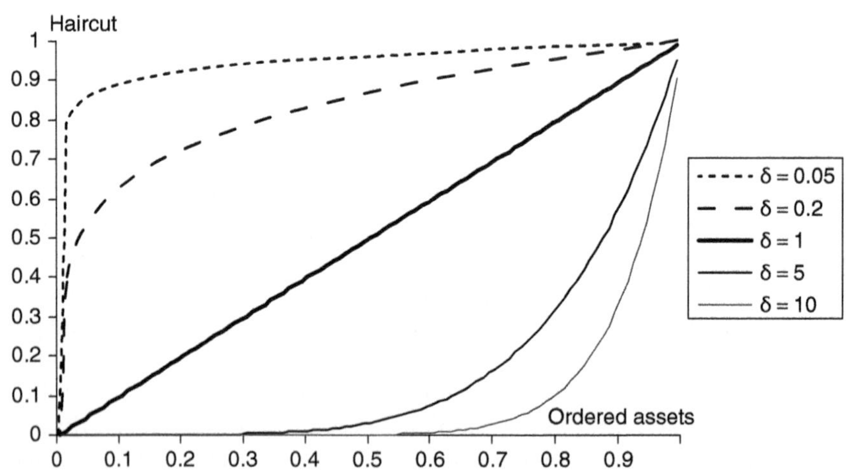

Fig. 9.2. A haircut function as a simple power function for different parameters. Haircut function h(x) = x δ, x in [0,1], for various values of the parameter δ

implies that the average haircut applied by the Eurosystem to (the entirety of) bank assets is around 84%, and central bank refinancing power is 16% of bank assets, which approximately implies a parameter value $\delta = 0.2$. We will use the power haircut function again in part II of this book.

In practice, the collateral framework is much more complex and can hardly be captured in a parameter value δ and a simple functional form $h(x) = x^{\delta}$. One can say that central banking in essence relies on two legs: (i) monetary base issuance and (ii) related asset purchasing or collateralized credit provision. The monetary base issuance leg is homogeneous, while the asset/collateral leg is normally heterogeneous, complex and risky to manage. Indeed, it is noteworthy that e.g. two-thirds of the European Central Bank's 'General Documentation' on monetary policy implementation (European Central Bank, 2011b) consists in the description of eligible collateral and associated risk-control measures. Similarly, the place devoted to collateral issues in historical accounts of central banking, such as Reichsbank (1900/1910), or Bagehot (1873), is remarkable. In all models of monetary policy implementation introduced so far in this text, it was implicitly assumed that collateral availability was not constraining the borrowing of banks from the central bank. Once this assumption has to be abandoned, the basic models used so far need refinement (this will also be illustrated further in particular in section 12.1).

A World Without Central Bank Collateral Scarcity

It is useful to think about two hypothetical scenarios in which collateral scarcity would not be an issue, as implicitly assumed so far.

First, consider the case in which the central bank has a perfect collateral analysis and management technology, such that it could accept all assets of banks as collateral without haircut. This would ensure that indeed the collateral constraint could never become binding, since each bank could in theory finance all its assets through central bank credit. Theoretically, one could imagine that central banks could constantly and perfectly measure the fair value of assets and, as they are not subject to liquidity risk, would not need to worry about delays in liquidation due to less than perfect market liquidity. However, the central bank would still have a positive expected loss because of the following three issues applying jointly: first, perfect asset valuation does not mean that true asset values will not fluctuate randomly after the point in time of valuation; second, asset liquidation after counterparty default takes time also relating to legal procedures; third, there is a fundamental profit and loss asymmetry when collateral needs to be liquidated due to counterparty default: in case the liquidation value exceeds the claim against the counterparty, the resulting excess must be handed over to the administrator of the defaulted bank; in case of a shortfall, the central bank suffers losses. Therefore, perfect asset valuation is not sufficient to have an expected zero loss after default. Instead, a haircut on the value of the collateral remains necessary to achieve close to zero expected losses.

A *second*, theoretically feasible, and more radical approach leading to an absence of collateral scarcity would obviously be to offer to banks *uncollateralized* central bank credit. There are, however, various reasons for the principle that central banks should not provide lending without collateral. First, their function, and area of expertise, is the implementation of monetary policy aimed at price stability, not the management of credit risk (and offering uncollateralized credit is subject to high credit risk). Second, while access to central bank credit should be based on the principles of transparency and equal treatment, unsecured lending is a risky art, requiring discretion, which is neither compatible with these principles nor with central bank accountability. Third, central banks need to act quickly in monetary policy operations and, exceptionally, also in operations aiming at maintaining financial stability. Unsecured lending would require careful and time-consuming analysis and limit setting. Fourth, central banks need to deal with a high number of banks, which can include banks with a rather low credit rating. Fifth, to reflect the different degrees of counterparty risk in unsecured lending, banks charge different interest rates. By contrast, central banks have to apply uniform policy rates and thus cannot compensate the different degree of credit risk.

As a consequence of rejecting both hypothetical scenarios leading to a non-scarcity of collateral, it needs to be accepted that collateral will tend to be scarce, and that the collateral framework will have to achieve an optimal balance between a number of considerations, namely central bank risk protection, possible moral hazard on the side of banks, sufficient availability of collateral to allow for a smooth implementation of monetary policy, and financial stability. Part II of the book will develop further the role of collateral for central bank risk taking, moral hazard, and financial stability in the context of stressed markets.

9.2 LOGIC OF ESTABLISHING A COLLATERAL FRAMEWORK

Desirable Properties of Collateral

Consider which desirable properties the assets accepted as central bank collateral should have.

Legal certainty. There should be no doubt about the ability and legal right of the central bank to appropriate and liquidate the collateral after a counterparty default. If it turns out (e.g. through the decision of a court), that this is not the case, then the entire claim vis-à-vis the defaulted counterparty may be lost. No risk-control measure can address such kinds of uncertainty.

Credit quality. Central banks usually set a minimum credit quality for collateral. The argument that credit quality is reflected in prices, and that therefore a sound valuation sufficiently reflects different degrees of credit quality is wrong for the following two reasons: (i) Lower-rated collateral has a higher probability of default, and even a higher probability of downwards credit-quality migration. While credit migration can be addressed through haircuts (as done for instance by the European Central Bank when assigning an extra 5% haircut to BBB-rated collateral), it is not clear how to address default risk through haircuts. (ii) Lower-rated securities tend to be more information-intensive and hence less liquid and more difficult to value; therefore, the central bank may take longer to sell the assets (implying more market risk) and it is also more likely to be the victim of adverse selection phenomena (i.e. banks submitting assets with hidden problems).

Simplicity. Some securities are relatively simple (e.g. bullet bonds issued by large issuers), while others are more complex (e.g. multi-layer CDOs). Complexity per se does not need to be a problem, but in any case requires that resources are devoted by the central bank for due diligence to ensure that the complexities are understood and do not potentially lead to losses in the case of collateral liquidation. If the central bank is unwilling to spend these resources, it should not accept complex collateral.

Market transparency/price availability. Some securities are traded on markets with well-established rules that also ensure post-trading transparency and/or binding price quotations. Others are traded only over-the-counter (OTC) and no rules and regulations support the transparency of prices. Non-availability of true market prices means that assets need to be valued theoretically, which requires resources, and even with sufficient resources, valuation is likely to remain less precise than pricing on the basis of observed market transactions.

Market liquidity of collateral. While some types of assets are constantly traded (Government debt), others are only rarely (e.g. many Asset Backed Securities, ABS) and still others are never (e.g. credit claims, such as accepted by the Eurosystem). Obviously, liquidity of collateral is desirable because, first, it ensures price availability and, second, it means that the collateral can likely be sold easily (fast, without depressing prices) in case of a counterparty default.

Cost of handling and settlement. Settlement costs (for both the bank and the central bank) differ across collateral types. For instance, some settlement and securities depository systems may charge lower fees than others and some may be more automated for the users than others. In particular cross-border settlement may be more costly and work-intensive.

Currency denomination of collateral. In normal practice, central banks tend to limit collateral eligibility to assets located and denominated in their own currency/jurisdiction. In a crisis situation, the readiness of central banks to relax such constraints may increase, whereby (i) additional settlement costs may arise and (ii) a currency mismatch typically needs to be addressed through some extra haircut on collateral.

Five-Step Logic of Establishing a Collateral Framework

The setting-up of a central bank's collateral set and associated risk-control framework has to take into account the uneven suitability of financial assets for use as central bank collateral and their *ex ante* heterogeneous risk properties. The following five-step approach does so.

First, a list of all asset types that could be eligible as collateral in central bank credit operations has to be established. All need to fulfil minimum requirements such as legal certainty.

Second, the specific aim of risk mitigation measures is to bring the risks that are associated with the different types of assets to the same level, namely the level that the central bank is ready to accept. The idea to equalize residual (i.e. post haircut) risks across collateral types is called the *risk equivalence principle* of the collateral framework. The fact that risk mitigation measures can reduce residual risks for a given asset to the desired level, is not sufficient to conclude that such an asset should be made eligible. This also requires the risk mitigation measures and the general handling of such a type of collateral to be cost effective, as addressed in the next two steps.

Third, the potential collateral types should be ranked in increasing order of cost (handling, due diligence, application of risk-control measures, analysis) per unit of potential central bank credit..

Fourth, the central bank has to choose a cut-off line in the ranked assets on the basis of a comprehensive cost–benefit analysis, matching the marginal social benefits of central bank collateral with its increasing marginal cost. The social benefits of enlarging the collateral set are very high at the beginning, because a too-small collateral set interferes with a smooth monetary policy implementation and the implied lack of liquidity buffers in the form of central bank borrowing potential is detrimental to financial stability. The larger the collateral set, the less likely it is that liquidity-absorbing shocks to individual banks or to the banking system as a whole exhaust the collateral buffers and hence the marginal value of further increases of collateral buffers becomes lower and lower, when the eligible collateral set grows. On the other side, as the collateral types are ranked in this exercise from the most convenient, and hence cheapest to use, to the least convenient ones (which are expensive to provide, difficult to risk-manage and to handle; which need to be made subject to high haircuts, etc.), the marginal cost curve of widening the collateral set increases. In view of the decreasing marginal social benefits, and the increasing social cost of widening the central bank collateral set, a unique optimum can be identified, at least in theory.

Finally, the central bank has to monitor how the counterparties use the opportunities provided by the framework, in particular which collateral they use and how much concentration risk results from their choices. The actual collateral use by counterparties, while being very difficult to anticipate, determines the residual credit risks borne by the central bank. If actual risks deviate much from expectations due to unexpected collateral use practices, there may be a need to revise the framework accordingly. The monitoring of the use of the collateral framework also relates to the issue of limits (section 9.3) and of segregation of collateral pools (section 9.5).

Collateral frameworks are in practice very diverse (e.g. Chailloux et al., 2008; Cheun et al., 2009; Tabakis and Weller, 2019) and one may wonder why such different frameworks may arise if indeed the logic under which the frameworks were derived would have been similar. Cheun et al. (2009) review a number of external factors, as well as some variations in the principles underlying the frameworks. They consider inter alia legal constraints and different financial market structures. Cheun et al. (2009, 10) note that legal constraints have a direct impact on the operational and collateral frameworks in the case of the Eurosystem and the Fed. The Eurosystem is obliged not to treat public sector issuers more favourably than private sector issuers, except where this is justified by objective considerations, such as levels of credit or liquidity risk. These statutory requirements enable the Eurosystem to accept a wide range of assets, not only in its capacity as lender of last resort, but also in the implementation of monetary policy. In the case of the Federal Reserve, lending to depository institutions in the capacity of lender of last resort and conducting open market operations to implement monetary policy are viewed as very distinct activities, which are even governed by different bodies: the Board of Governors and the Federal Open Market Committee (FOMC), respectively. The Federal Reserve Act (FRA) restricts discount-window lending to banks, except under 'unusual and exigent conditions', but allows for a wide range of collateral to be eligible for this safety-valve purpose. By contrast, collateral eligible for open market operations is very restricted under the FRA: only Treasury, agency, and agency mortgage-backed securities (MBSs) are accepted. Of course, such legal constraints should not be considered as genuinely exogenous to an optimal design of the collateral framework, as the legislative could be convinced of the merits of changing the relevant laws and regulations.

9.3 RISK MANAGEMENT TECHNIQUES

As any other economic actor with a balance sheet, the central bank cannot (and should not) protect itself at 100% from risks. Instead, the central bank must choose some risk tolerance level and define on that basis adequate risk mitigation measures. Since the risk associated with collateralized operations depends, before the application of credit risk mitigation measures, on the type of collateral used, the risk mitigation measures will need to be differentiated according to the collateral type to ensure consistent compliance with the defined risk tolerance of the central bank. The following risk mitigation measures are typically used in collateralized lending operations.[1]

Limits can directly avoid undue concentration risk. Limits can typically take one of the following forms: (i) limits to credit the exposure to individual counterparties; (ii) limits to the use of specific collateral by single counterparties, e.g. percentage or absolute limits per issuer or per asset type. Examples of collateral limits would be: 'ABS must not exceed a share of 20% in a collateral pool submitted by a bank'; 'Securities issued by any single issuer must not exceed 5% of the collateral pool submitted by a bank'; 'Securities issued by any single issuer (except sovereigns) must not exceed a value of EUR 100 million in the collateral pool submitted by a bank'; etc.

Valuation and margin calls. Collateral needs to be valued accurately to ensure that the amount of central bank credit provided to the counterparty does not exceed the collateral value. As asset prices fluctuate over time, collateral needs to be re-valued regularly, and new collateral needs to be called in whenever a certain trigger level is reached. In a world without monitoring and handling costs, collateral valuation could be done on a real-time basis, and the trigger level for margin calls would at the limit be zero. In practice, costs create a trade-off. For instance, the Eurosystem, in line with market practice, values collateral daily and has a symmetric trigger level of 0.5%, i.e. when the collateral value, after haircuts, falls below 99.5% of the cash leg, a margin call is triggered, while if it exceeds 100.5%, some collateral is returned to the counterparty.

Haircuts. In case of counterparty default, the collateral submitted by that counterparty needs to be sold. This takes some time and, in the case of less liquid markets, a sale in the shortest possible time would have a negative impact on prices. To reduce the probability of losses at liquidation, a certain percentage h of the collateral is deducted when accepting the collateral, to establish what amount of credit can be provided in exchange of the collateral. The haircut should depend on the price volatility of the relevant asset and on the prospective liquidation time. The Eurosystem, for example, according to European Central Bank (2004), sets haircuts to cover 99% of price changes within the assumed orderly liquidation time of the respective asset class. An

[1] In many central banks, including the ECB, risk management was recently established as a function independent from market operations, so as to ensure that decision-making bodies receive an independent and unbiased picture of the risks associated with central bank assets. This also reflects the perception that risk-taking of central banks has increased considerably in the financial crisis (see chapter 15 in part II of this book).

additional haircut may address uncertainty regarding the initial value of the asset.

To illustrate the calibration of haircuts to achieve risk equivalence, consider two assets, asset 1 and asset 2. Assume asset 1 is traded regularly on a market with transparent prices, such that every day a true market price can be established, which can be considered a price without valuation uncertainty. Assume, moreover, that in case of a counterparty default, the asset could be liquidated in markets without an undue negative influence on prices within a one-week period, and that the asset has negligible credit risk (i.e. it is close to a credit risk-free asset). Asset 2 is assumed not to be traded regularly on markets and hence a theoretical value needs to be calculated every day on the basis of some theoretical valuation approach (such as discounting the future cash flows of the assets using an appropriate yield curve). Moreover, for asset 2, an orderly liquidation time of four weeks is assumed. Finally, for asset 2, specific risk factors, namely spread and credit risk, can influence negatively prices over the liquidation horizon. Such risk factors were deemed to be of negligible relevance for asset 1.

The uncertainty of the liquidation value of asset 1 is thus driven by only one factor, namely the general market price risk within a one-week liquidation period driven by the volatility, at that horizon, of the risk-free yield curve. Assume that this risk is normally distributed, and that the related one-week price change is $N(0,\sigma_{M,1}^2)$, whereby the 'M' in the index stands for 'Market risk' and the '1' for asset 1. The uncertainty of the liquidation value of asset 2 is driven by three factors, which we all assume to be normally distributed and independent from each other. We assume that asset 2 has a four-week orderly liquidation period, and that the four-week price change due to market risk is $N(0,\sigma_{M,2}^2)$; the uncertainty on the true asset value at the moment of valuation is $N(0,\sigma_{V,2}^2)$, the V in the index standing for 'valuation'; the value uncertainty stemming from spread and migration risks during the liquidation period is $N(0,\sigma_{S,2}^2)$, the S in the index standing for 'spread and migration'. Total uncertainty on liquidation values of asset 1 will be $N(0,\sigma_{M,1}^2)$ and of asset 2 will be $N(0,\sigma_{M,2}^2 + \sigma_{V,2}^2 + \sigma_{S,2}^2)$, assuming that the risk factors are uncorrelated. Call $\sigma_{T,i}^2$ the variance of total liquidation value uncertainty for asset i. If the risk tolerance of the central bank has been defined as 'preventing with 99% probability that the asset value at liquidation falls short of the last valuation post-haircut', then haircuts need to be set for each asset at $\sigma_{T,i}\Phi^{-1}(0.01)$, where $\Phi()$ is the cumulative standard normal distribution. If, for example, $\sigma_{M,1}^2 = 1\%$; $\sigma_{M,2}^2 = 4\%$; $\sigma_{V,2}^2 = 2\%$; and $\sigma_{S,2}^2 = 2\%$, then the haircut array that establishes *risk equivalence* is $H = \{h_1;h_2\} = \{2.33\%; 6.60\%\}$. Some assumptions underlying the approach taken in this example deserve refinement in practice: (i) the assumption that the uncertainties affecting the eventual liquidation value follow a normal distribution; (ii) the assumption that the different factors are independently distributed; (iii); the assumption that past time series' properties provide an accurate picture of the likely behaviour of these risk factors after a counterparty default.

Table 9.1 presents an excerpt of the ECB haircut scheme, showing only two out of the five maturity buckets. The ECB haircut scheme is a mapping of three features of each security onto a haircut, namely (see ECB Press Release of 18 July 2013; European Central Bank, 2009, Chapter 6):

- *Rating:* BBB-rated assets have higher haircuts than A–AAA-rated ones;
- *Residual maturity:* The longer the residual maturity of bonds, the higher the price volatility and hence the higher the haircut.
- *Institutional liquidity category of asset:* The ECB has established six such categories, which are supposed to group assets in homogeneous institutional groups in terms of liquidity. Of course any such grouping will be a simplification. For instance, Government bonds of a relatively small euro area country with relatively little debt outstanding (e.g. Slovakia, classified in category I) will tend to be less liquid than the bonds of a large Government-linked issuer in category II, such as the German development bank KfW. The approach taken reflects the need to establish a sufficiently simple, transparent, and manageable framework.

The Bank of England and the Fed are also highly transparent on their haircuts (see Bank of England: 'Sterling Monetary Framework—Summary of

Table 9.1. ECB's haircuts for different securities classified in liquidity categories according to issuer types, for the maturity bucket 0–1 and 7–10 years' residual maturity, as published by ECB on 18 July 2013 (annex to Press release of that date)

	Category I	Category II	Category III	Category IV	Category V	Category. VI*
Issuer types → Assets ↓	Central Government debt	Local Gvt debt; Jumbo covered bonds	Covered bonds; corp. bonds	Unsecured bank debt instruments	ABS	Credit claims to corporates
0-1Y (A–AAA)	0.5	1.0	1.0	6.5	10.0	12.0
3-5Y (A–AAA)	1.5	2.5	3.0	11.0	10.0	21.0
0-1Y (BBB)	6.0	7.0	8.0	13.0	22.0	19.0
3-5Y (BBB)	9.0	15.5	22.5	32.5	22.0	46.0

* For credit claims: referring to nominal value, as applicable to most credit claims accepted by Eurosystem.

haircuts for securities eligible for the Bank's lending operations, 02 October 2012'; US Fed: 'Federal Reserve Discount Window & Payment System Risk Collateral Margins Table1—Effective Date: October 19, 2009, updated January 3, 2011'—both found on the central banks' websites).

There is one key feature of the central bank as collateral-taker that must not be overlooked when designing and assessing the collateral framework and haircuts set by a central bank. *Haircuts are a powerful risk mitigation tool if credit risk is asymmetric and the collateral provider* (repo borrower) is more credit-risky than the cash investor (repo lender). The power of haircuts is limited if cash-taker and cash-lender are equally credit-risky. Although haircuts protect the cash-provider, they expose the cash-taker to unsecured credit risk which increases with the haircut level (Ewerhart and Tapking, 2008). Anecdotal evidence suggests that haircuts applied in repos between banks of similar credit quality tend to be rather low, while haircuts applied to other, non-regulated, market participants, as for example hedge funds, tend to be higher. For similar reasons, banks would never question haircuts imposed by the central bank (repo lender), because the central bank cannot default. From this perspective it is economically sensible that the central bank accepts less liquid collateral, but at relatively high haircuts, even if such collateral is not used in interbank markets.

9.4 MARKET IMPACT OF THE COLLATERAL FRAMEWORK AND COLLATERAL AS MONETARY POLICY INSTRUMENT

Assume three asset types {A, B, C} with A being eligible as central bank collateral, while B and C are not. Everything else being equal, A will trade with an eligibility premium, reflecting that the holder of these assets also benefits from the fact that they can be submitted at any time to the central bank to obtain cash. Now assume that B is made eligible. First, this will reduce the eligibility premium in general, since the overall scarcity, and hence the marginal benefit of central bank collateral, will decrease. Hence, the impact on the price of A of this central bank decision will be negative, while the price of B will increase.

Sometimes, the effects of collateral eligibility decisions on asset prices have been considered to be 'distortions'. For instance, the compression of spreads between different asset types (e.g. Government bonds versus ABS), implied by the fact that they are both eligible in the euro area, has been considered problematic because relative prices would no longer adequately reflect the different liquidity risks inherent in these assets.

The price impact of central bank eligibility should however not a priori be considered as a distortion, assuming that indeed the central bank (i) follows correctly the five-step approach to establish a collateral framework as described in section 9.2, (ii) in particular applies risk-control measures that make the assets risk-equivalent from the central bank perspective, and (iii) charges to counterparties the costs of assessing, handling, and risk-controlling assets. For instance, if complex ABS are accepted, higher haircuts should be applied to them and a fee should be imposed on banks submitting these complex ABS, for the necessary analysis and risk control. Then, still, it could well be that complex ABS are used for central bank operations and not for interbank operations, because of certain central bank specificities (absence of liquidity risk, hence no hurry in asset liquidation even in a crisis; haircuts as effective risk mitigation tool in collateralized operations between agents with unequal credit risk). If haircuts on complex ABS are relatively high and counterparties are charged for handling and assessment costs, then obviously the eligibility premium for complex ABS will be lower than that for Government bonds. The remaining impact on securities prices is not a distortion, but the result of the participation of a large player with specific characteristics (i.e. the central bank) in a market. If the central bank in contrast deviates from these principles, the price impact of eligibility may indeed contain an element of 'distortion'. Just accepting only Government bonds as eligible central bank collateral is in any case not a solution to avoid distortions. This would likely mean a collateral set which is narrower than the socially optimal one and the implied very high eligibility premium on Government paper compared to any other paper would mean a deviation from relative asset prices prevailing under the optimal (wider) collateral set. Such an approach could even be considered a case of financial repression (i.e. a trick to force financial institutions to hold sovereign bonds, in order to ensure that the sovereign can place its debt in the market).

The issue of distortion of asset prices due to an inadequate differentiation of haircuts by a central bank was for instance raised by Buiter and Sibert (2005), who argued that the Eurosystem was undermining incentives for fiscal discipline as it did not reflect the differences in credit risk of euro area governments in collateral haircuts. Bindseil and Papadia (2006) questioned these conclusions.

If Haircuts are Effective Leverage Constraints

Ashcraft et al. (2011) model within an overlapping generations model the impact of binding collateral constraints in the sense of leveraging constraints, and how these affect the effective funding costs of the underlying economic activities and the overall economic equilibrium. They find that 'a reduction in the haircut of an asset unambiguously lowers its required return and can ease the funding constraints on all assets. Empirically, we estimate that lowering haircuts through lending facilities significantly decreased the required return during the recent crisis, and we provide unique survey evidence suggesting a strong demand sensitivity to haircuts.' Here, we only consider a very simple arbitrage condition between assets to which different haircuts are applied, starting from the idea that total assets are equal to one and are ordered from the most to the least asset in [0,1] (such as in figure 9.2). If haircuts are binding in the sense that they set effective leveraging constraints, the effective funding cost of an asset x in [0,1], i(x), essentially depends on the shadow cost of equity, i_e, the rate at which central bank credit is available, i*, and the allowed leveraging as determined by the central bank haircut h(x). Indeed, it can be argued that any asset can be financed partially through equity, and partially through central bank credit, whereby the weight of the former is h(x) and of the latter is (1 – h(x)):

$$i(x) = h(x)i_e + (1 - h(x))i^* \tag{9.2}$$

If haircuts have the form of a power function for x in [0, 1], $h(x) = x^\delta$, then $i(x) = x^\delta\, i_e + (1 - x^\delta)\, i^*$. The average funding costs of the economy i# would be:

$$i\# = \int i(x)dx = i_e\ [1/(\delta + 1)] + i^*\ [\delta/(\delta + 1)] \tag{9.3}$$

In this sense, as postulated by Ashcraft et al. (2011) in the title of their paper, effective monetary conditions would depend as much on the central bank policy rate i* as on the haircut setting of the central bank, as captured above in the parameter δ. Figure 9.3 plots the effective average funding costs as a function of the monetary policy interest rates, for different values of the haircut setting parameter δ. The figure (and the underlying formula) suggest for instance that one can achieve monetary conditions in the sense of average funding costs of 3% with the following combinations of parameters: (i*, δ) = (1.6%; 5) or (2.3%, 10) or (2.93%, 100). Of course, these three alternatives should not be equivalent from a microeconomic perspective, in the sense that the first option is relatively more favourable to liquid assets, while the last is relatively favourable for illiquid assets. This is illustrated by figure 9.4. As far as this model holds, it seems that the effects of central bank haircut decisions would not only be strong in terms of setting actual monetary conditions (in the sense of actual funding costs of the real economy), but also in terms of allocative effects. Moreover, changes in the haircut schedule would imply the need to re-allocate resources across projects.

Both from a theoretical and an empirical perspective, it seems that this simple model is not directly applicable in reality. First, not all assets are refinanced with the central bank. The central bank could choose its outright holdings such that the actual reliance of the banking system on central bank credit is small, zero, or even negative. Even if the entire amount of banknotes in circulation were matched by central bank credit, only a small part of the banks' assets

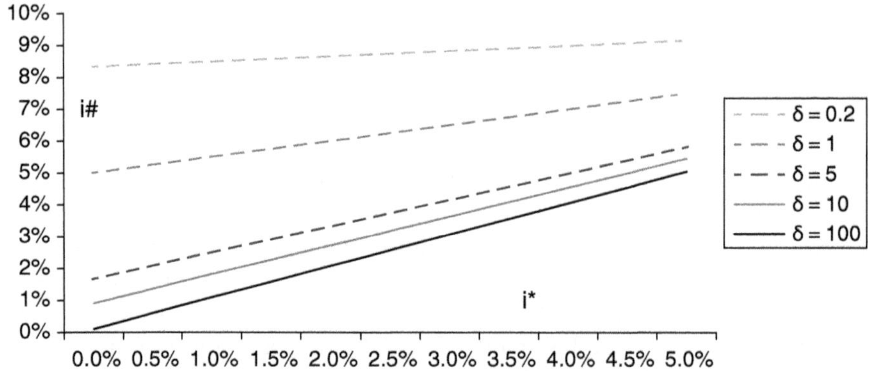

Fig. 9.3. Effective funding costs of the economy depending on central bank credit rate i* and on haircut-setting parameter δ. The alternative curves refer to alternative values of δ, namely δ = 0.02, δ = 1, etc.

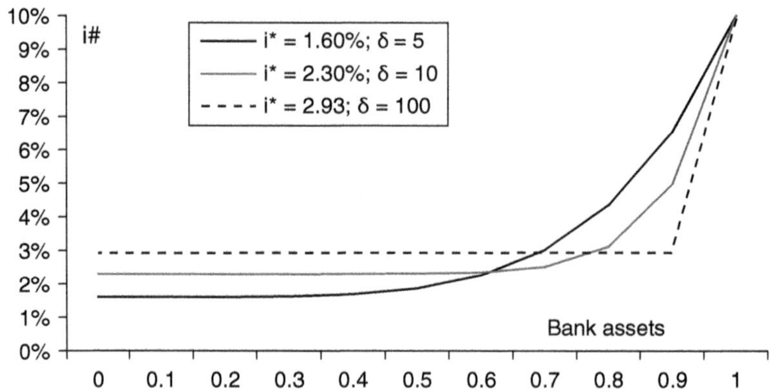

Fig. 9.4. Funding costs across assets for three policy parameter combinations which are equivalent in terms of achieving aggregate average funding costs of the economy of 3%: (i*, δ) = (1.6%; 5) or (2.3%, 10) or (2.93%, 100)

would be refinanced by the central bank (in case of the euro area, bank total assets are around EUR 32 trillion, while banknotes in circulation are around 1 trillion). Then it becomes less clear why the arbitrage condition postulated in the model should be binding. Second, empirically, it should be remembered that the haircut function parameter δ in the case of the Eurosystem is around 0.2, and that for other central banks it is even lower. This would imply, however, in the simple model above, that practically all assets have yields close to the shadow cost of equity, which is also not plausible.

It is useful to establish financial accounts of an economy that would come close to supporting the logic of the model above. This should be the case for figure 9.5. In particular the following assumptions have been

Households / Investors			
Real Assets	$E - 1$	Household Equity	E
Bank equity	$\delta/(1 + \delta)$		
Banknotes	$1/(1 + \delta)$		

Banking system			
Real assets	1	Equity	$\delta/(1 + \delta)$
		Credit from central bank	$1/(1 + \delta)$

Central Bank			
Credit operations with banks	$1/(1 + \delta)$	Banknotes	$1/(1 + \delta)$

Fig. 9.5. A simple system of financial accounts in which central bank haircuts are effective leverage constraints and thereby determine yields

made: (i) households want to diversify exactly one unit of their equity from real assets into financial assets, whereby only banknotes and bank equity exist as financial assets; (ii) equity is remunerated at $i_e > 0$ and households are willing to accept any allocation of financial assets at these remuneration rates; therefore, the central bank haircut parameter δ can determine the split between the two types of financial assets; (iii) banks directly hold real assets (or corporates are simple pass through structures). Obviously, all of these assumptions are excessively strong simplifications of reality.

In this model, real assets outside the household sphere are financed totally through equity and central bank credit. In competitive equilibrium, banks, who can be heterogeneous in terms of their asset composition and in terms of haircuts, and therefore also in terms of their liability structure, will trade assets such as to establish prices and hence yields according to equation (9.2).

To address some of the shortcomings of the model above, the model below does not assume that bank assets are systematically refinanced through the central bank in such a way as to reach the maximum leverage ratio determined by central bank haircuts.

A Simple Model Taking into Account the Actual Recourse to Central Bank Credit

The following model should yield more realistic results as it reflects the fact that most bank assets are not refinanced through central bank credit (e.g. in the case of the euro area only around 2% are). Consider the simple model in figure 9.6 of the price impact of collateral eligibility, assuming the identical banks being subject to a deposit shift shock k.

Assume that the haircut array set by the central bank is $H = (h_A, h_B, h_C)$ with each haircut in [0,1], such that total eligible collateral value post haircut is

$$CVPH = (3 - h_A - h_B - h_C) \tag{9.4}$$

Assume that asset A is a risk free asset, and that the two other assets trade at a yield premium relative to asset A. Assume that the yield spreads prevailing under $H^0 = (0,0,0)$ are s_B and s_C. A general zero haircut would mean that banks are not really subject to any funding risk as they can always take the necessary recourse to the central bank. How will changes in the haircut array H relative to H^0 influence the yield spreads s_B and s_C? To establish this, we need (i) a probability distribution of k, say f(k), and (ii) a marginal cost function of running out of collateral. Define the 'collateral gap' (CG) as the potential shortfall of CVPH relative to central bank funding needs (for bank 1: 1.5 + k). Hence, for bank 1:

$$CG = \max\,(0, 1.5 + k - (3 - h_A - h_B - h_C)) \tag{9.5}$$

Call the marginal cost function of running out of collateral q(CG), whereby $q(0) = 0$ and for $CG > 0$: $q(CG) > 0$ and $dq/d(CG) \geq 0$. The actual costs underlying q could be manifold: they can consist in convincing the other bank to provide an interbank credit, or in finding at short notice some capital market funding. They can also consist in the cost of requesting ELA (emergency liquidity assistance) from the central bank, or in asset fire sales costs. At some stage, when q is quite large, the bank will become insolvent.

The expected cost of running out of collateral, Q, will thus be:

$$\begin{aligned} Q &= \int_{CVPH-1.5}^{+\infty} f(k)q(1.5 + k - CVPH)dk \\ &= \int_{1.5-hA-hB-hC}^{+\infty} f(k)q(-1.5 + h_A + h_B + h_C + k)dk \end{aligned} \tag{9.6}$$

The spread between asset yields induced by different collateral eligibility/central bank haircuts can now be approximated as follows. Assume that bank 1 would reduce its holding of asset B by 1 and increase its holding of asset A by 1, whereby we assume that $h_A < h_B$ (it is assumed here that assets are not divisible, i.e. banks can hold one unit or zero). Then the expected cost of running out of collateral decreases by:

$$\begin{aligned} &\int_{1.5-hA-hB-hC}^{+\infty} f(k)q(-1.5 + h_A + h_B + h_C + k)dk \\ &- \int_{1.5-2hA-hC}^{+\infty} f(k)q(-1.5 + 2h_A + h_C + k)dk \end{aligned} \tag{9.7}$$

Bank 1			
Asset type A	1	Household deposits / debt	1.5 - k
Asset type B	1	Credit from central bank	1.5 + k
Asset type C	1		

Bank 2			
Asset type A	1	Household deposits / debt	1.5 + k
Asset type B	1	Credit from central bank	1.5 - k
Asset type C	1		

Fig. 9.6. Two banks' balance sheets to illustrate the impact of collateral eligibility on asset prices

This decrease of expected cost of running out of collateral is the upper bound to an additional spread component of the yield difference between asset A and asset B resulting from a haircut array different from H^0. The actual increase in the spread as a consequence of moving from H^0 to a haircut vector in which $h_A < h_B$ will be lower in case other (non-leveraged) investors are interest-rate elastic in their asset demand. If the only way to trade asset B against asset A is to trade with the other (identical) bank, then indeed the spread impact of moving away from H^0 to a different H is given by (9.7). It can be shown easily within this model that this additional spread component will be higher for higher values of (i) $h_B - h_A$ (ii) h_C; (iii) the variance of k; (iv) the structural reliance of the banks on central bank funding.

Example: suppose that the shock k is normally distributed with expected value 0 and standard deviation 1. Also suppose that the marginal cost of running out of collateral is constant and equal to 1, that the balance sheet above applies, and that H = (0,0.2,0.5). Then, the decrease of expected costs to run out of collateral from changing the asset allocation from (1,1,1) to (2,0,1) for the assets A, B, and C is:

$$\int_{0.8}^{+\infty} \varphi(k)(k-0.8)dk - \int_{1}^{+\infty} \varphi(k)(k-1)dk = (0.12-0.083) = 0.037 \qquad (9.8)$$

Therefore, provided that no other investor is available to trade asset A against asset B (but the other bank), an extra spread component of 0.037 should prevail that reflects the difference of central bank collateral haircuts between assets A and B.

Further Recent Literature on the Role of Central Bank Collateral for Monetary Policy

A number of further recent papers discuss the role of the central bank collateral framework as monetary policy instrument. Koulischer and Struyven (2013) define credit quality of collateral as the ability of the collateral receiver to value the collateral, implying that lower-quality collateral will be subject to higher haircuts. In their model, collateral provision to lenders has favourable incentive effects on borrowers, but at the same time collateral provision is costly because of imperfect collateral quality and implied low valuation (equivalent in this model to high haircuts), also leading to an asset encumbrance issue. The model of Koulischer and Struyven (2013) shows that exogenous shocks to the quantity or the quality of collateral available to banks can increase interest rates in the economy even with an unchanged central bank policy rate. A loosening of the central bank collateral policy can therefore make more accommodating monetary conditions and thereby contribute to alleviating a credit crunch and increasing output (in particular at the zero lower bound to nominal interest rates).

Bindseil (2013) obtains similar results, but with a bank run model. The paper analyses the potential roles of bank asset fire sales and recourse to central bank credit to ensure banks' funding liquidity and solvency. Funding stability is captured as a strategic bank run game in pure strategies between depositors. Asset liquidity, the central bank collateral framework, and regulation determine jointly the ability of the banking system to deliver maturity transformation and financial stability. The model also explains why banks tend to use the least liquid eligible assets as central bank collateral and why a sudden non-anticipated reduction of asset liquidity, or a tightening of the collateral framework, can destabilize short-term liabilities of banks. As in the model of Koulischer and Struyven (2013) (also Ashcraft et al., 2011 and Chapman et al., 2010), central bank collateral policies are shown to be relevant for effective monetary conditions.

Majnoni d'Intignano (2013) also proposes a model in which collateral constraints impact on effective monetary conditions, and uses a financial accounts framework similar to the one used in the present book. He models a credit multiplier linking the availability of secured bank funding to the credit provision to the real economy, and finds (p. 1) that this multiplier's 'sensitivity to interest rates significantly changes across states of nature and leads to state-contingent equilibria allowing for multiple equilibria and calling for state-dependent money and credit stabilization policies. According to this framework, often labeled "unconventional" monetary policies can be reinterpreted as "conventional" policies for exceptional situations.'

Finally, Singh (2013, 4) also 'tries to highlight the important role of collateral in monetary policy issues' and in particular integrates collateral into a text book IS-LM framework.

9.5 SEGREGATION OF COLLATERAL SETS, ADVERSE SELECTION IN COLLATERAL USE, AND PRICING

In principle, central banks have reasons to accept wide collateral sets with limited a priori constraints and relying essentially only on the *ex post* risk equalization through haircuts. As already mentioned, this requires at least a careful monitoring of the collateral use, to detect whether the use of collateral becomes overly concentrated on some types of assets, and if so, it needs to be analysed why this is the case, and whether it creates undue central bank risks or market distortion. The central bank is in principle always subject to a double adverse selection threat (a double Gresham's law): weaker banks tend to rely over-proportionally on the central bank, and they will tend to use weaker collateral as the best (i.e. most liquid) collateral can also be used in interbank markets or be sold without fire sale discounts. If the central bank is indeed unhappy with the degree of concentration it experiences in collateral use, it could in principle consider the following four measures.

First, the central bank may increase the haircuts on the assets for which it observes an over-proportional use. This addresses risk-taking concerns, and lowers incentives to use this asset type as central bank collateral. However, this method may be considered to have the disadvantage that it uses a parameter (haircuts) which should be used for achieving risk-equivalence for anti-concentration and anti-arbitrage purposes.

Second, the central bank may set asset-specific limits. For instance, the central bank could impose a requirement that only 25% of a collateral pool may be composed of a certain less liquid asset type (e.g. non-standard ABS). The Bank of England imposes a *single issuer limit* in any collateral pool that 'shall be the greater of £250 million or 25% of the total market value of the securities it delivers to the Bank as collateral' (Bank of England 2010). Limits are highly effective for addressing concentration. However, they also have the drawback of limiting flexibility of counterparties in a rough way.

Third, the central bank may conduct in-depth individual analysis of less liquid and overused assets, and charge the posting banks the costs of this work. This could mitigate risk-taking and adverse selection concerns and would at the same time provide additional financial incentives against overusing such assets.

Fourth, the central bank may segregate asset pools across operations and limit the amount of credit operations against the pool of less liquid assets through different mechanisms (see also Chailloux et al., 2008, for a more detailed discussion of this issue, as well as Cheun et al., 2009, 17–18). A number of central banks have chosen such segregation approaches.

The Fed, even after its reform of the discount window in 2001, has continued with a full segregation of its eligible asset set for credit open market operations from the one for discount-window lending. While the collateral set for the latter is very wide (and includes e.g. credit claims, even with lower ratings), the former is very narrow and well defined and consisted pre-crisis only in US treasury paper, US AAA agency bonds, and RMBS. According to Chailloux et al. (2008), in 2007 around 55% of collateral used in the Fed repo operations was US treasury paper, the rest being equally split up into agency bonds and RMBS. In contrast, the paper pledged in the Primary Credit Facility (the discount window) consisted to the amount of 73% in credit claims (i.e. loans to corporates), the rest being ABS (15%), Corporate bonds (7%), and other (5%). The Term Auction Facility (TAF) operations introduced in March 2008 merged these two types of collateral pools temporarily to reduce stigma and collateral scarcity.

The Bank of England segregates collateral for credit open market operations in two pools and even talks about 'liquidity insurance' (and not of monetary policy) with regard to its open market operations against the wide collateral set (Bank of England, 2012a). Also, access to a special borrowing facility (the discount window) is against an even wider collateral set, and in fact is foreseen to be normally conducted in the form of an asset swap to be liquidity-neutral (that is, illiquid assets of banks are repoed against gilts, i.e. British government securities). Bank of England (2012a) explains that in fact it differentiates its collateral pools potentially across five types of operations, whereby in 2011 in practice the first three types of operations (intra-day, normal borrowing facility, and short-term open market operations) had the same collateral set, namely consisting only in high-quality sovereign debt. The fourth type of operations, 'indexed long-term open market operations', allow in addition for Level B collateral, i.e. 'wider collateral' containing 'liquid and high quality mortgage and corporate bonds'. Finally, the fifth type of operation, the discount window facility, allows in addition Level C and Level D collateral, i.e. 'illiquid transferable securitized loans and mortgages' and 'own name securitizations and covered bonds and loans'. The Bank of England also provides in its quarterly bulletin detailed information on the relative size of its different operations against the relevant collateral sets and on price differentials across collateral sets.

In view of full pooling of collateral of different liquidity by the Eurosystem, it is of interest to check to what extent this approach lead to concentration of collateral use towards the least liquid assets. Table 9.2 provides evidence of this as of the end of 2010 (although limited to marketable debt instruments, i.e. securities, excluding credit claims).

When interpreting this table, it is important to note that 'posted' eligible collateral does not necessarily mean that actual Eurosystem credit is requested and obtained by the counterparty against this collateral. For instance, some

Table 9.2. Eurosystem-eligible marketable debt instruments, end 2010

	Eligible assets		Posted assets		'usage ratio'
	(i) Nominal value (in bn euro)	% over total	(ii) Market value after haircut (in bn euro)	% over total	= (ii)/(i)
Government bonds	6492	47%	404	25%	6%
Covered bank bonds	1413	10%	249	16%	18%
Corporate bonds	1516	11%	110	7%	7%
Unsecured bank bonds	2646	19%	329	21%	12%
ABS	1272	9%	480	30%	38%
Other marketable assets	626	4%	31	2%	5%
Total	**13965**		**1603**		**11%**

Source: ECB data.

banks may take zero recourse to Eurosystem credit, but may have posted in advance collateral on the relevant central bank accounts as this advance posting is considered convenient.

Usage ratios vary between 6% for Government bonds and 38% for ABS, and overall it appears indeed that there is an inverse relationship between usage ratios and liquidity. Whether this is problematic is another question. As mentioned, the central bank may be more suitable than others to accept less liquid collateral against a relatively high haircut, and it may therefore be natural that the used collateral pool for central bank credit operations has a lower average liquidity than the eligible one.

10

Optimal Monetary Policy Operations Frameworks in Normal Times

10.1 HUNDRED WAYS TO SKIN A CAT

This chapter discusses briefly the idea of an 'optimal' monetary policy implementation technique under functioning financial markets, such as prevailing largely in the decades before 2007. There are many different ways to implement monetary policy in the sense of controlling short-term rates, as noted by Borio (2001, 1):[1] 'Just as there are a hundred ways to skin a cat, so there are a hundred ways to implement monetary policy... Such differences reflect a mixture of purely historical factors and different views regarding the fine balance between the pros and cons of the various choices. At the end of the day, however, the proof of the pudding is in the eating.'

Borio suggests that from a monetary policy perspective, it is doubtful that the implementation details are very important as long as the signalling and the short-term rate objectives are achieved. But these are relatively straightforward to meet. Signalling can take the form of publicly announcing the target level of short-term interest rates. Controlling short-term rates can be done for instance by pegging the market rate to a standing facility rate. However, monetary policy implementation arguably has ramifications and implications beyond the pure monetary policy perspective, for example on cost effectiveness of banks' liquidity management, on bank business and funding models, on financial markets, and financial stability.

10.2 POTENTIAL OBJECTIVES OF THE DESIGN AND USE OF THE MONETARY POLICY IMPLEMENTATION FRAMEWORK

Beyond the effective control of the overnight rate, the following objectives of the design and use of a monetary policy implementation framework may be regarded as relevant.

[1] For overviews of operational frameworks, see Borio (1997), Markets Committee (2009), Sellin and Sommar (2013).

(1) Leanness and efficiency. If a certain result (effectively steering the overnight interest rate) can be achieved with few instruments and only standardized and simple operations, then one should not try to achieve the same result through a more complex framework (a synonym for 'lean' in this sense is 'parsimonious'). A complex and opaque operational framework will be inefficient as it may not only lead to a failure to control interest rates but it is also resource-demanding for both the central banks and banks. If monetary policy operations are complex and regularly generate surprises because they are not transparent, banks must be prepared for the surprises and have incentives to spend resources on trying to forecast the action of the central bank. Compared with the 1920–1990 period, monetary policy implementation approaches in the years preceding 2007 were well-focused and transparent. In particular: (i) they aimed at achieving well-defined operational targets (typically the overnight interest rate), (ii) monetary policy operations were not supposed to contain signals on the monetary policy stance, (iii) reserve requirements were kept stable, i.e. were no longer used as an active instrument of reserve absorption or injection. Still, particularly central banks from the large monetary areas had preserved in 2006 the luxury of a number of complexities. First, the use of reserve requirements with averaging to absorb liquidity shocks created a non-trivial inter-temporal structure of liquidity demand. Second, operational frameworks were often specified in such a way that significant discretion was exerted in conducting open market operations (see the next point).

(2) Reliance on rules. Being rule-based also presupposes having reached a high level of understanding of the economic relationships at stake. Discretion may sometimes be unavoidable, but often it reflects the inability on the side of the central bank to understand precisely the interaction between the central bank and the market, or, at least, to come up with a model that captures a large part of this interaction. Overall, monetary policy implementation does not appear so complex that it could not, at least to a very large extent, be rule-based. As one example, central banks before 2007 often used auction procedures in which the allotment decision contained discretionary elements. When bidding in such auctions, banks had to speculate about what quantity the central bank would allot (and what would be the lowest successful interest rate). It seems preferable that central banks rely on automated allotment procedures, such as fixed-rate full allotment, or variable-rate tender with pre-fixed allotment volume.

(3) Ensuring, for a given achievement of the policy mandate, an adequate financial return on the enormous financial resources with which the central bank is normally endowed (relating to banknote issuance, reserve requirements, and capital). If two frameworks allow for the same degree of achievement of policy objectives, but the first leads to higher financial returns than the second, then the second cannot be efficient.

(4) Minimizing the extent to which the operational framework imposes costs on the cash management of commercial banks. For instance, asking banks to fulfil precisely a reserve requirement every day imposes a cost on banks in terms of managing their end-of-day account in order to avoid costly recourse to standing facilities.

(5) The operational framework should facilitate financial stability, including, for instance, support incentives to banks to run a sound and secure business model, and more generally an adequate functioning of various segments of the financial market. This has received particular attention during the crisis, which has highlighted the question of how far the central bank should, in the short and the long run, act as an intermediary to remedy the malfunctioning of parts of the financial market. For this criterion, there are three dimensions of the refinancing operations of the central bank which are particularly important: (i) the variety of assets which are eligible as collateral and the haircuts applied; (ii) the number of counterparties which have access to refinancing; and (iii) the size and/or frequency with which the central bank offers refinancing opportunities to banks.

(6) Relating closely to the previous point, the framework should not undermine incentives for active interbank and capital markets. This is ensured in particular if the central bank minimizes the length of its balance sheet, and only transacts with the market to provide the counterpart of the monetary base. If the central bank buys, for instance, large amounts of assets outright such that all banks are in excess liquidity (such as is the case for many of the major central banks in 2012), then all banks will tend to use at the margin for day-to-day liquidity management the central bank's deposit facility, and there will be very little interbank market activity. Also, going one step back, if the central bank liquidity provision is extremely elastic for any single bank (also because of a very wide collateral set), then the banks are tempted to steer their liquidity to a large extent by increasing or reducing their recourse to central bank credit, instead of adjusting permanently through interbank and capital markets. It should be taken into account that a solid interbank and capital market access cannot be gained at short notice, as the readiness of investors and other banks to have exposure to a certain name has to be built up over time. Supporting efficient interbank and capital markets is particularly important in normal times. In stressed times, strong pressure to rely on markets (say through limitations in central bank access and penalty rates) may backfire as it may stigmatize and contribute to triggering a run on parts of the banking system (see part II of this book).

(7) Market neutrality. Choices with regard to the monetary policy implementation technique should avoid having distorting effects on the relative prices of financial assets. Due to the scale of central bank assets, outright purchase or sale operations can potentially influence relative asset prices. There are two potential approaches to define 'neutrality', also dependent on how independently one views the central bank from the government. Under one approach, the central bank should treat the government as a normal issuer and not overweight its role in outright portfolios or in the collateral framework. Under the other approach, the central bank aims at a lean state balance sheet under the assumption that the central bank and the government should be consolidated, implying a preference of the central bank for exposures to the government.

(8) Universality, which means allowing an efficient control of the operational target across different financial and macroeconomic environments. Universality is desirable because it avoids the need for changes to the operational framework across time, which are normally costly because of the necessary investments on the side of both the central bank and the banks to learn and understand the working of any new framework. Often, central banks have defended changes in their frameworks or differences relative to frameworks in other countries by saying that one approach cannot fit all, and that they have to adapt to the environment in which they operate. This was not always fully convincing.

10.3 STATEMENTS OF CENTRAL BANKS ON THEIR OBJECTIVES AND PRINCIPLES

On some occasions central banks have been explicit on the principles that they applied to derive their operational framework. We consider three examples. The *Federal Reserve System* (2002, 1-1), which reflects the outcome of an extensive Fed study group established to work out alternative monetary policy implementation approaches under the assumption that the outstanding US sovereign debt would continue to shrink to the extent of questioning the Fed approach so far, states four basic principles for monetary policy implementation (called there 'set of principles for managing the composition and operations of the System Open Markets Account'):

> The starting point for developing a set of principles is the Federal Reserve Act, which gives the central bank its goals of achieving price stability and fostering sustainable economic growth. To accomplish its long-run objectives, the Federal Reserve should adhere to the following principles: (1) Exercise effective control over the stock of high-powered money and the size of the System's balance sheet…(2) Structure its portfolio and undertake its activities so as to minimize their effect on relative asset values and credit allocation within the private sector. (3) Manage its portfolio to be adequately compensated for risks and to maintain sufficient liquidity in its portfolio to conduct potentially large actions on short notice. (4) Place a high priority on transparency and accountability in its monetary policy operations.

The first point refers to the effectiveness of the control of the monetary policy operational target, whereby the reference to the 'stock of high-powered money' and the absence of a reference to interest rates may appear surprising in view of the fact that since 1994 the Fed has been announcing the Fed funds target rate as operational target of monetary policy.

Also the *Bank of England* (2008, 4, 6) has established two key and two further principles on the basis of which it would like to derive its operational framework:

> The Bank's market operations have two Objectives, stemming from its monetary policy and financial stability responsibilities as the United Kingdom's central bank. They are: (i) To implement monetary policy by maintaining overnight market interest rates in line with Bank Rate, so that there is a flat risk-free money market yield curve to the next MPC decision date, and there is very little day-to-day or intraday volatility in market interest rates at maturities out to that horizon. (ii) To reduce the cost of disruptions to the liquidity and payments services supplied by commercial banks. The Bank does this by balancing the provision of liquidity insurance against the costs of creating incentives for banks to take greater risks, and subject to the need to avoid taking risk onto its balance sheet... In designing the longer-run framework for its market operations, the Bank also takes into account two other considerations. The first is the wish that market operations have broadly neutral effects on relative asset prices, in normal circumstances... The second consideration is that the Bank wishes to foster competitive and fair sterling money markets. Individual banks obtain the reserves they need not only directly via the Bank's operations but also indirectly via the money markets. It is therefore important that markets are efficient, since the effective distribution of reserves will affect the stability of overnight rates and the ability of banks to manage their day-to-day liquidity position.

The first objective is again an effective control of the operational target—although this time formulated in a more modern way.

The *ECB* explains the objectives and general principles of its framework in European Central Bank (2011a, 94–5). Accordingly, the operational framework of the ECB complies with the following principles:

(i) The overriding principle is operational efficiency. This can be defined as the capacity of the operational framework to enable monetary policy decisions to feed through as precisely and as quickly as possible to short-term money market rates.

(ii) The operational framework has to be consistent with the principles of a market-oriented economy in which competition is key to ensuring the efficient allocation of resources.

(iii) Other important principles are equal treatment of financial institutions and the harmonization of rules and procedures throughout the euro area. Given the area-wide focus, credit institutions must be treated equally across the euro area, irrespective of their size or location.

(iv) The operational framework also needs to be consistent with the principles of simplicity, transparency, continuity, safety and cost efficiency. Simplicity and transparency ensure that financial market participants understand the intentions behind monetary policy operations. The principle of continuity requires the avoidance of frequent and major adjustments in instruments and procedures, so that central banks and their counterparties can rely on past experience when participating in monetary policy operations. The principle of safety requires the Eurosystem's financial and operational risks to be kept to a minimum, while cost efficiency should ensure low operational costs for both the Eurosystem and its counterparties arising from the operational framework.

10.4 FOUR EXAMPLES OF FRAMEWORKS

Sellin and Sommar (2013) survey systematically the control of short-term interest rates by various major central banks in normal and crisis times. The following only refers to four central banks, and mainly to normal times. Collateral aspects are not analysed.

The Reserve Bank of Australia has a symmetric corridor framework at ±25 basis points around the overnight rate target, conducts daily credit open market operations, and has no reserve requirement system. Similar frameworks are in place in e.g. Canada and New Zealand. Control of the overnight rate appears almost perfect (see figure 10.1). This is achieved essentially by conducting a daily open market operation at the target rate after the money market has taken place, such that at the time of the market session, all banks can rely on the perfect supply elasticity of central bank overnight credit. The model of the Reserve Bank of Australia scores high in terms of simplicity and effectiveness. There is no particular reason to expect that it impairs market activity, as long as the daily open market operation at the target rate is only in one direction, and hence only adjusts the netted overall liquidity position of the banking system after the interbank trading has exploited the relative dislocation of liquidity within the banking system.

Bank of England, 2001–2006. The Bank of England had during those years an implicit overnight rate target, no reserve averaging, and credit open market operations with a daily frequency. The volatility of the overnight rate (SONIA) within the standing facilities corridor was remarkably high, compared to e.g. the Reserve Bank of Australia (see figure 10.2). Tucker (2004, 361–2) explains the pre-2006 system and its problems as follows. Open market operations (OMOs) with a two-week maturity were conducted each day at the policy rate.

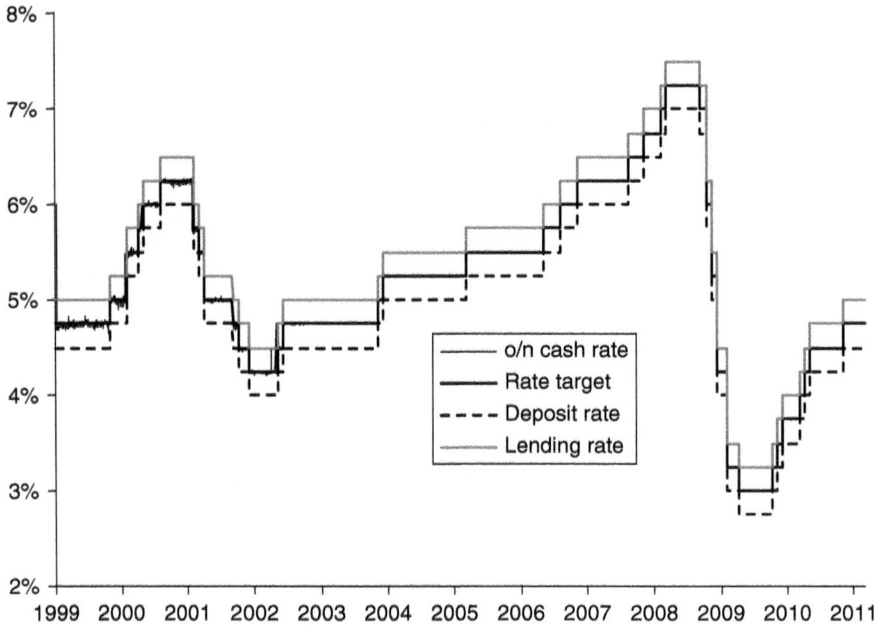

Fig. 10.1. Overnight rate control by the Reserve Bank of Australia, 1999–2011
Source: Sellin and Sommar (2013).

> There are three types of problem with the current framework. First, it is overly complex: the system provides for four rounds of operations each day and on most days there are at least two. The end-of-day arrangements are especially elaborate. Second, when the MPC is expected to change rates, the ultra-short maturity rate structure 'pivots' in a rather perverse way, because the daily two-week repos span the MPC meeting but are conducted at the existing rate... And third, the overnight rate is highly volatile by international standards—from day to day, and intraday... this volatility has troubled the Bank for some years.

Tucker (2004, 362) moreover notes that the market is non-competitive, and large money-market players can regularly exert a manipulative influence on markets.

In 2006, the Bank of England introduced an *ex ante* voluntary reserve averaging system, which considerably reduced volatility. The objective of the reforms was 'to ensure that monetary policy would be implemented reliably, i.e. there would be a close and stable relationship between overnight market rates and Bank Rate' (Clews et al., 2010, 297). The new framework comprised a corridor system in which banks set their own reserves targets every month. Reserves balances that on average over the month fell within a relatively narrow range around those targets were remunerated at the target rate. The fact that reserve requirements need to be fulfilled *within a range* provides

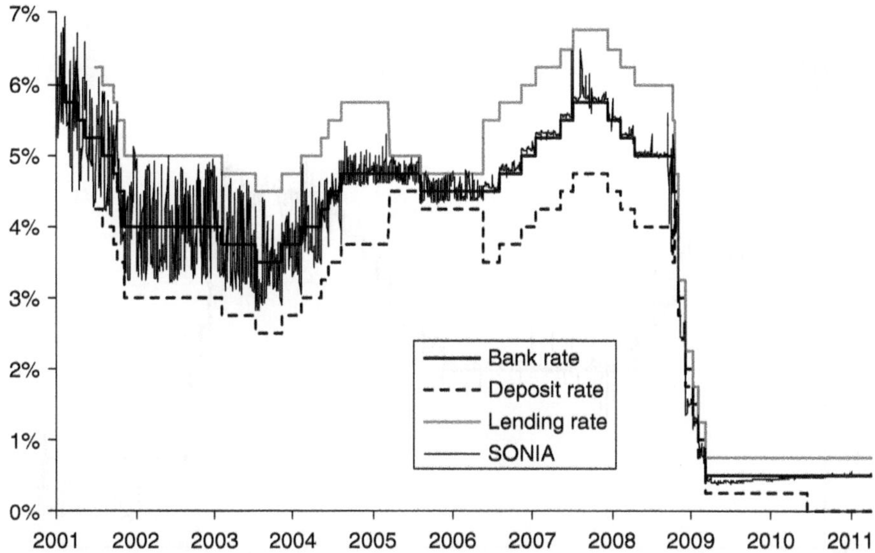

Fig. 10.2. Overnight rate control by the Bank of England, 2001–2011
Source: Sellin and Sommar (2013).

for an extra liquidity buffer and makes it possible to avoid the end of reserve maintenance period interest-rate volatility that was experienced e.g. by the Eurosystem. Moreover, a narrow ±25 basis point standing facilities corridor applied on every final day of the reserve maintenance period, and there 'will closely resemble the corridors to be found in the "channel" systems of Canada, Australia and New Zealand. But there the narrow corridors apply on every day, and because there is no reserve averaging the central banks have to manage liquidity in their systems day by day' (Clews, 2005, 219).

The 2006–2010 system of monetary policy implementation of the Bank of England was clearly innovative, well-designed, and effective. It dramatically reduced overnight rate volatility without reducing money market activity. It is, however, still somewhat more complex than the Australian approach.

Eurosystem, 1999–2006. The Eurosystem applied reserve averaging over a one-month maintenance period and weekly credit open market operations, with the overnight rate as an implicit operational target and standing facilities at ± 100 basis points around the operational target. Until 2007, control of overnight rates was precise, but for the end-of-maintenance-period volatility that can be seen in figure 10.3 as periodic spikes. In 2004, the ECB changed the exact timing of the monthly reserve maintenance periods such as to normally exclude the possibility that decisions to change the operational target become effective within the reserve maintenance period, as this destabilized bidding in open market operations and the reserve fulfilment path. Also, the

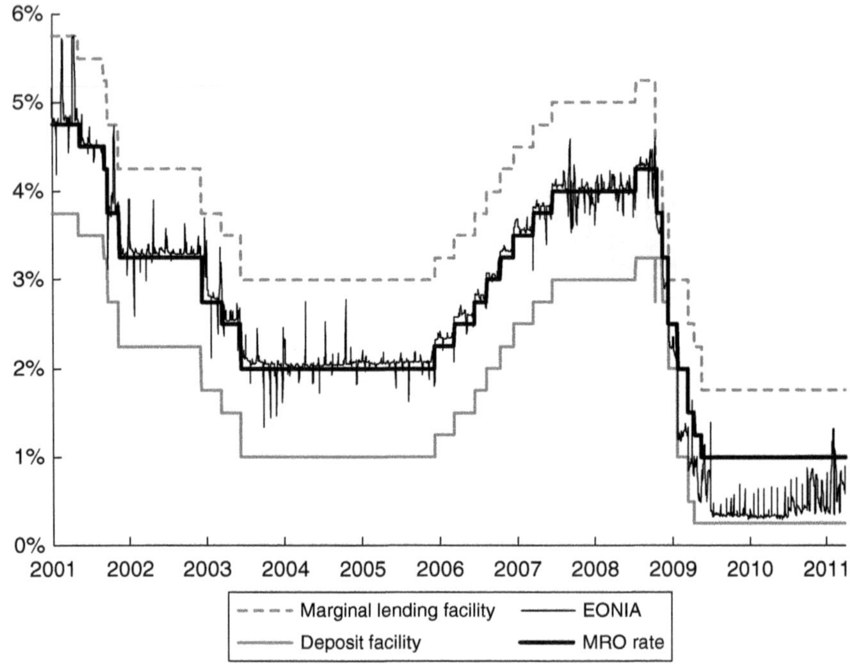

Fig. 10.3. Overnight interest rate control by the ECB, 2001–2011
Source: Sellin and Sommar (2013).

ECB reduced the maturity of its weekly main refinancing operation from two weeks to one week, such that instead of two, always one such operation is outstanding. Overall, the ECB's system was effective and sufficiently transparent and did not impair the money market (see European Central Bank, 2005a). However, the end-of-maintenance-period spikes were an anomaly that could have been overcome with the Bank of England innovations of 2006.

The US Fed's control of the overnight rate is summarized in figure 10.4. The Fed lagged other central banks with regard to the introduction of standing facilities (for the reasons explained in the section 3.3). A normal borrowing facility was introduced only in 2002, and a deposit facility (in the form of remuneration of excess reserves) only in 2009. The Fed had a reserve averaging system with rather low requirements, with several credit open market operations a week. The one-directional system of the Fed seemed to have some similarity to the 'classical' system of the Bank of England applied between 1890 and 1970, as described by Tucker (2004). Different from the case of an asymetric corridor approach, the Fed needed to adjust its reserve supply whenever it changed its overnight interest rate target, i.e. it was not sufficient in this case to adjust the central bank rates. This is because any

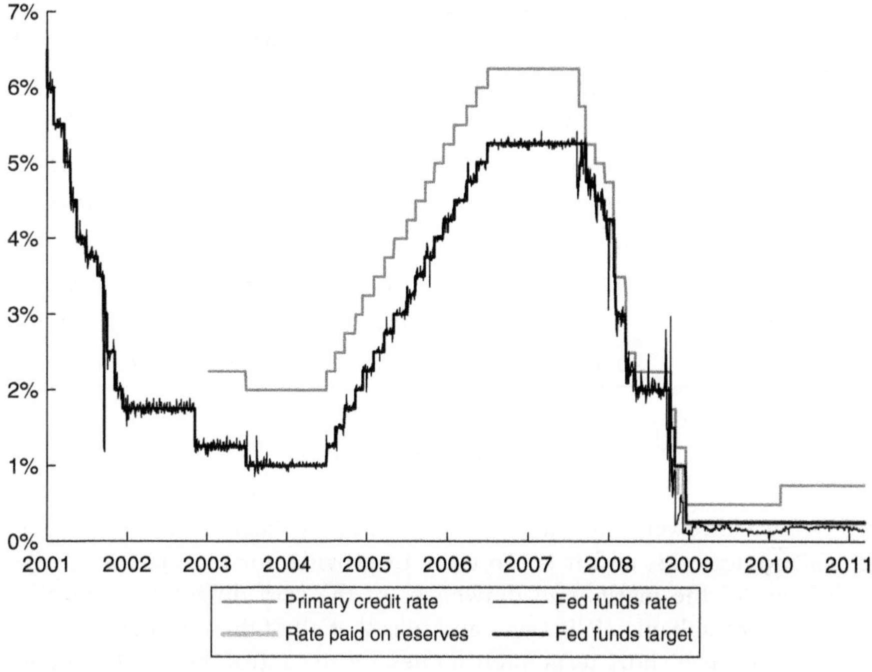

Fig. 10.4. Overnight interest rate control by the US Fed, 2001–2011
Source: Sellin and Sommar (2013).

target rate change also changes the exact asymmetry of the corridor (as the lower corridor bound always stays equal to zero). Moreover, since the corridor is asymmetric, the Fed would in principle need to care about higher-order moments of the probability distribution of autonomous factor shocks to control short-term rates precisely (this can be shown easily in the model framework of section 4.2).

Table 10.1 (extracted from Sellin and Sommar, 2013) provides summary information on the precision of the control of overnight rates by the four central banks. The following observations may be highlighted: (i) all central banks managed to achieve a mean overnight rate very close to the target rate; (ii) the Bank of England in the period 2001–2004 was an outlier in terms of high volatility of the overnight rate; (iii) the volatility of three-month rates seems largely independent of the volatility of the overnight rate, and is in the range of 7–19 basis points. The Reserve Bank of Australia and the US Fed, which had the most perfect control of the overnight rate, had a relatively high volatility of the three-month rate. In sum, there seem to be no reasons to doubt that the central banks examined were in sufficient control of short-term interest rates as starting point of the transmission of monetary policy.

Table 10.1. Spread between interbank rate and target rate in pre-crisis times (in %), with standard deviation of spread in parenthesis, according to Sellin and Sommar (2013)

Country	Overnight rate	1-week rate	1-month rate	3-month rate
Australia 2001–07	0.00 (0.02)	0.01 (0.07)	0.03 (0.10)	0.08 (0.17)
UK 2001–04	−0.05 (0.46)	−0.02 (0.20)	0.04 (0.10)	0.10 (0.16)
UK 2005–06	0.01 (0.14)	0.07 (0.05)	0.09 (0.04)	0.11 (0.07)
UK 2006–07	0.07 (0.10)	0.13 (0.06)	0.19 (0.06)	0.30 (0.08)
Euro Area 2004–07	0.07 (0.07)	0.10 (0.05)	0.14 (0.07)	0.22 (0.11)
US 2001–07	0.00 (0.10)	0.08 (0.08)	0.10 (0.11)	0.16 (0.19)

10.5 CONCLUSIONS

Overall, we have yet only partial knowledge on optimal central bank operational frameworks, and it is too early to provide, for example, a relative assessment of the merits and drawbacks of the very different approaches taken by central banks. What we can say is that all of these frameworks are easily able to steer short-term interest rates, i.e. to control the standard operational target of monetary policy. One can also be conclusive about some past frameworks' mistakes and establish a set of best practices that avoid those. On some aspects though, we are still not sure about best practice, or how to map environmental parameters (e.g. regarding the structure of a country's financial system) into optimal framework specifications. One may try to summarize as follows.

First, frameworks of central banks operating in developed and efficient financial markets should be parsimonious and well-focused on achieving a single operational target of monetary policy. This speaks against the multitude of instruments and targets applied e.g. in the 1960s by many central banks. It is unlikely that in such complex frameworks the central bank understands well what it is doing and what it aims at exactly. Banks and financial markets are also unlikely to understand, and this further complicates the interaction between the central bank and the market. In normal times, the separation principle (or 'dichotomy') should apply within the central bank between macroeconomic analysis and setting of the operational target level on one side, and the implementation of the target through monetary policy operations on the other side. For central banks in emerging economies with yet less developed financial markets, this conclusion is less straightforward, as in fact many of the considerations made in part II of this book relating to impaired markets apply.

Second, there seem to be three reasonable frameworks for controlling short-term interest rates:

- **One-directional standing-facility-based approach,** in which banks systematically have recourse to a standing facility and the rate of this facility determines essentially the short-term interbank market rate. Such systems have been applied in Denmark and Norway before the crisis, and the current (i.e. 2009–2013) Bank of England and Fed approaches also fall into this category. Such an approach is in principle very simple and effective. It does not necessarily have to lead to excessive central bank intermediation provided the structural dependence of the banking system on the central bank is not too large (and this approach is not to be confounded with a zero-width standing facilities corridor approach).
- **Symmetric narrow (e.g. ± 25 basis points) standing facilities corridor** with a daily open market operation (not too early in the day) at the target rate such as to guide the interbank market rate. Again, this approach appears rather simple and effective, as demonstrated e.g. in Australia, Canada, and New Zealand. If the daily open market operation is conducted as a fixed-rate tender with full allotment, the system becomes similar to the previous approach.
- **Reserve requirements with averaging, relatively wider symmetric corridor** (± 100 basis points), including maybe the Bank of England innovations of 2006 (reserve fulfilment corridor and narrow end-of-maintenance-period interest-rate corridor) and the ECB innovations of 2004 (normally no policy decision on rate changes within the reserve maintenance period). This system is certainly more complex than the preceding ones (as the reserve requirement system unavoidably creates a complex inter-temporal structure). But for some reason, large monetary areas with money markets with many participants have revealed a preference for this framework, relative to the more simple previous ones.

Third, the following further conclusions on best practice emerged. The width of the standing facilities corridor should be such as to avoid that the central bank becomes an intermediary in the money market and lengthens its balance sheet accordingly. Under normal circumstances, a corridor of ± 25 basis points is considered accurate for central banks without reserve requirements and averaging, and ± 100 basis points in the case of an averaging system. Reserve requirements, if any, should be remunerated at close to the target rate (i.e. at close to market rates), and fulfilment should be on average within a reserve maintenance period. This holds for industrialized countries with limited foreign reserves and hence a banking system in a liquidity deficit vis-à-vis the central bank. For emerging economies with a central bank with huge foreign reserves, other monetary control functions of (non-remunerated) reserve requirements may remain important. Tender procedures for open market operations should have no discretionary elements in allotments, i.e. they should be automated. There are two types of such tender procedure: variable-rate tender with pre-announced volume, and fixed-rate tender with full allotment. Central bank credit open market operations should be parsimonious, i.e. should be limited to e.g. two or at most three maturities, and the number of outstanding operations at any moment in time should be limited. For example, it is difficult to understand why a central bank would conduct every day a two-week operation (implying ten overlapping operations at any moment in time), as the Bank of England did prior to 2006.

Fourth, the following two issues remain rather *unclear*: There are still very different approaches with regard to the relative role of *outright versus credit operations*. While it is a consensus today that open market operations at the margin, i.e. to control short-term interest rates, should be credit operations, it is unclear what share of central bank assets should be covered through outright holdings. For example, the US Fed held pre-crisis around 95% of its monetary policy assets in the form of its SOMA outright portfolio, and less than 5% in the form of credit operations with banks, while the Eurosystem had all of its monetary policy operations in the form of credit operations. The choice makes obviously a difference for financial markets and the funding of banks, but it is not obvious what to conclude on the superiority of either of these approaches. Also, still fundamentally different approaches prevail with regard to the *central bank asset composition (for outright holdings and collateral) in terms of preferential treatment of sovereign debt versus private assets*. There are two distinct views on that, which both have their merits but which lead to opposite conclusions: (i) the consolidated state sector should have a lean balance sheet, and hence the central bank should prefer exposures to the government to exposures to the private sector; (ii) central banks should not treat the government in a privileged way relative to the private sector. The two views emanate from different philosophies: on one side, the view that the state sector should act in a coordinated way in view of the interrelation of policies, and that it should be possible to assume that the state as a whole acts in a wise way, also without 'artificial' segregations. On the other side, various countries, and in particular in continental Europe and Latin America, have experienced that states have behaved poorly when this segregation was weak, and seem to have exploited monetary policy in a short-sighted way that eventually harmed social welfare.

Part II

Monetary Policy Operations in Times of Crisis

11

The Mechanics of Liquidity Crises

11.1 INTRODUCTION

A financial crisis is normally associated with a liquidity crisis, which has typically a funding and a market dimension. In a *funding* liquidity crisis the willingness of investors to maintain exposures to indebted entities is destabilized, triggering funding stress on economic agents who depend on external refinancing. In a *market* liquidity crisis, turnover in securities markets drops, bid–ask spreads go up, and much higher discounts have to be accepted when selling assets, in particular if sales volumes are large and if sales have to be conducted rapidly because cash is urgently needed. The implied lack of liquidity may lead to the inability of debtors to fulfil their contractual obligations and hence to their default, with additional economic damage.

Most authors analysing financial crisis highlight the role of strong downward revisions of asset values as a crisis trigger (from Bagehot, 1873, to e.g. Kindleberger and Aliber, 2005 or Adrian and Shin, 2009). In the crisis that started in August 2007, the inversion of an unsustainable trend in real estate prices and related securitizations (and associated malpractices) in the US played this role. Strong declines of asset values have various negative effects on economic agents. Even for non-leveraged households, wealth effects imply a decline in consumption. For leveraged entities, asset value declines may imply insolvency (a shortfall of asset value relative to debt) or, at least, a narrowing of capital buffers, which undermines the ability to access funding sources and the willingness and the ability to undertake new risky projects. In the case of banks, an additional factor comes into play: a decline in capital puts at risk compliance with capital adequacy regulations, adding urgency to deleveraging through the shrinking of lending or through asset fire sales.

A number of historical quotes, which keep all their relevance, illustrate the mechanisms of liquidity crisis and their similarity across time. Already Thornton (1802) noticed the problem of liquidity hoarding and bank runs, and how they relate to a lack of trust.

> That a state of distrust causes a slowness in the circulation of guineas, and that at such time a great quantity of money will be wanted in order to effect only the

> same money payments, is a position that scarcely needs to be proved...When a season of extraordinary alarm arises, and the money of the country in some measure disappears, the guineas, it is commonly said, are hoarded. (p. 99)
>
> If any one bank fails, a general run upon the neighbouring ones is apt to take place which if not checked in the beginning by pouring into the circulation a large quantity of gold, leads to very extensive mischief. (p. 180)

Bagehot (1873, all of the following from chapter 6 'Why Lombard Street is often very dull, and sometimes extremely excited') argues that while liquidity crises can be triggered by various exogenous events, their consequences tend to be similar (p. 124):

> Any sudden event which creates a great demand for actual cash may cause, and will tend to cause, a panic in a country where cash is much economised, and where debts payable on demand are large... Such accidental events are of the most various nature: a bad harvest, an apprehension of foreign invasion, the sudden failure of a great firm which everybody trusted, and many other similar events, have all caused a sudden demand for cash. And some writers have endeavoured to classify panics according to the nature of the particular accidents producing them. But little, however, is, I believe, to be gained by such classifications. There is little difference in the effect of one accident and another upon our credit system. We must be prepared for all of them, and we must prepare for all of them in the same way—by keeping a large cash reserve.

Bagehot also highlighted the systemic nature of liquidity crises (p. 125):

> Most persons who begin to think of the subject are puzzled on the threshold. They hear much of 'good times' and 'bad times,' meaning by 'good' times in which nearly everyone is very well off, and by 'bad' times in which nearly everyone is comparatively ill off. And at first it is natural to ask why should everybody, or almost everybody, be well off together? Why should there be any great tides of industry, with large diffused profit by way of flow, and large diffused want of profit, or loss, by way of ebb?

This chapter provides a set of simple partial models of liquidity crises. Understanding the logic of liquidity crises is a precondition for understanding the role of the central bank in stopping the escalation of liquidity crises and in addressing their economic consequences. Sections 11.2 to 11.6 will each describe one key element of the mechanisms of liquidity crisis. Section 11.7 will elaborate on the interaction between the various effects, describe the resulting vicious loops, and provide some illustration from the recent financial crisis. Section 11.8 briefly overviews the role of the central bank in preventing the escalation of liquidity crises and address their economic consequences. References to more comprehensive (often general equilibrium) models in the academic literature are provided.

11.2 INCREASED CREDIT RISK, ADVERSE SELECTION, AND FUNDING MARKET BREAKDOWN

Increased Credit Risk

The default risk of borrowers is opaque, and it is the core competence of banking to assess and monitor credit risk. Credit risk increases in financial crisis when the value of assets owned by the borrower declines and/or becomes more volatile. Consider the leveraged corporate or financial institution balance sheet shown in figure 11.1, with ε being a random variable impacting on asset values.

While the level of debt is given, asset values are subject to a random shock depending on various uncertain events. Assuming that ε is a normally distributed random variable over the relevant horizon with expected value 0 and standard deviation σ_ε, then the probability of default (PD) of the company, in the sense of the probability that its asset values will be below the value of debt, could be estimated as (with $\Phi()$ being the cumulative standard normal distribution):

$$PD = P(E + \varepsilon < 0) = P(A + \varepsilon < D) = \Phi\left(-\frac{A - D}{\sigma_\varepsilon}\right) \tag{11.1}$$

For a number of reasons, this is a strong simplification. First, asset values are not really normally distributed. Second, variables such as σ_ε are not directly observable. Third, time is continuous and there is no unique horizon to consider. Fourth, it is not clear that default occurs exactly when $A + \varepsilon$ touches D, as in fact default is eventually triggered by illiquidity. Modelling default risk while taking into account all of these issues has been undertaken e.g. by Crosbie and Bohn (2003) applying Merton's structural credit model (Merton, 1974).

It is also important to consider what losses debtors make in case of default. If (i) the default point were exactly equal to the point when $A + \varepsilon = D$, and (ii) the default event would not be in itself disruptive, then the 'Loss-given-default' (LGD, = 1 –recovery ratio) of investors should be zero. However, in reality, rating agencies typically mention out of their empirical studies LGDs of 40–50%

Assets		Liabilities	
Assets	$A + \varepsilon$	Debt	D
		Equity	$E + \varepsilon$

Fig. 11.1. A leveraged firm balance sheet

on average (e.g. Moody's, 2008), implying that assumptions (i) and (ii) cannot both be valid. Indeed, often default occurs only when A is already clearly below D (i.e. creditors typically would not notice in time that the company has a solvency problem). At the same time, the default event itself tends to be disruptive, since default typically implies that organizational and human capital gets lost and physical assets need to be liquidated at fire sale prices (e.g. a sophisticated machine may have to be sold at its raw material value). Empirical estimates of default costs in the corporate finance literature vary between 10 and 44% (see e.g. Glover, 2011, and Davydenko et al., 2012). The fact that default is costly is one crucial aspect in assessing the merits of the central bank's acting to prevent default due to illiquidity. We will see below that in settings of asymmetric information, which are typical for the high uncertainty prevailing in financial crisis, credit markets can break down such that default can occur even when A > D. In these cases, it seems plausible that the central bank can contribute to social welfare if it assures funding liquidity.

The role of banking supervision and bank resolution may be described as follows in this context. Good banking supervision is one which has a relatively accurate view at any time of the true value of the bank assets, and of the outlook for the future performance of the bank. When necessary, this allows the bank supervisor to ask in a timely manner for (i) a recapitalization of the bank; (ii) changes in the management and the business model of the bank; or (iii) a closure of the bank. This should reduce the probability of defaults of banks and the severity of default as measured by the gap between assets and liabilities at the moment of default. A good bank resolution framework is one in which the closing of banks and the re-assignment of assets to a new entity work as efficiently as possible, and with as few surprises as possible with regard to the sharing of the asset value amongst creditors. This helps to minimize additional damage relating to wasteful default and resolution procedures, and lowers *ex ante* risk premiums.

Higher credit-riskiness due to lower capital has been identified for a while as an issue for monetary policy transmission in the literature on the 'credit channel'. Lower capital of corporates means higher agency costs in the lending between banks and corporates. Lower capital of banks means higher agency costs between holders of bank liabilities and banks. Higher agency costs result from the fact that the alignment of incentives between debt and equity owners is likely to suffer for lower levels of capital (e.g. Jensen and Meckling, 1976; Bernanke and Gertler, 1989; Holmström and Tirole, 1997; and Jimenez et al., 2012). Moreover, indebted corporates and banks will aim at overcoming the implied frictions in accessing credit by aiming at deleveraging, also causing economic contraction.

Adverse Selection and Market Breakdown

The potential of information asymmetries to impact negatively on financial markets and thereby to potentially harm the funding of the real economy has been identified as a key issue in the economic literature for a while: see for example Stiglitz and Weiss (1981), Glosten and Milgrom (1985), Bernanke and Gertler (1989), Mishkin (1991), Bernanke et al. (1996), Stein (1998), Morris and Shin (2004), Bolton and Freixas (2006), Acharya and Yorulmazer (2008). The following simple model is a variant of the model of Flannery (1996). It assumes a one-period economy with many potential borrowers, of whom some are 'Good' and others are 'Bad'. An adverse selection problem in the spirit of Akerlof (1970) arises. The model assumes that projects require an investment of one monetary unit, which needs to be obtained by the entrepreneur from a bank through a loan. At the end of the project period, Good loan applicants' projects will be worth $V_G > 1$, which is sufficient to repay loans provided that the contracted interest rate is not higher than $V_G - 1$. Bad applicants will not pay back one cent (if they had obtained a loan). The number of borrowers and their quality are exogenous: the proportion of Good borrowers is δ, while the proportion of Bad borrowers is (1 – δ). Banks have a costless but imperfect technology for assessing the creditworthiness of a loan applicant. Assume that this technology consists in a signal, which can be either S_G or S_B. If the borrower is Good, then with probability p > δ, a Good signal (S_G) is captured, and the bank may lend. With probability (1 – p), the signal Bad (S_B) is captured, and no lending will take place. If the borrower is Bad, instead, then, the signal Bad will be received by the bank with probability p, and the signal Good with probability (1 – p). This allows application of Bayes Law in the sense that:

$$P(S_G|G) = \frac{P(S_G \cap G)}{P(G)} \Rightarrow P(S_G \cap G) = p\delta \tag{11.2}$$

$$P(S_B|B) = \frac{P(S_B \cap B)}{P(B)} \Rightarrow P(S_B \cap B) = p(1-\delta) \tag{11.3}$$

$$P(S_G|B) = \frac{P(S_G \cap B)}{P(B)} \Rightarrow P(S_G \cap B) = (1-p)(1-\delta) \tag{11.4}$$

$$P(S_B|G) = \frac{P(S_B \cap G)}{P(G)} \Rightarrow P(S_B \cap G) = (1-p)\delta \tag{11.5}$$

A perfect technology is one in which p = 1. Figure 11.2 summarizes the probabilities of the four possible cases.

The bank needs to fulfil, in competitive equilibrium, the no-loss constraint or, equivalently, an equilibrium rate of return. The profit it achieves if it lends to a Good borrower must on average compensate the credit losses it experiences with Bad borrowers. Define the minimum interest rate that a bank needs to set in order not to make losses as i*. As a loan is only provided in case a Good signal was obtained, non-zero pay-offs to the bank occur only in

	Good signal	Bad signal
Good borrower	δp	$\delta(1-p)$
Bad borrower	$(1-\delta)(1-p)$	$(1-\delta)p$

Fig. 11.2. Matrix of probabilities in lemons market model

the two subcases (Good signal column in figure 11.3), and therefore the no loss-constraint can be written (assuming that banks are funded at a zero interest rate level):

$$i\,\delta p + (-1)(1-\delta)(1-p) \geq 0 \Rightarrow i^* = (1-\delta)(1-p)/\delta p \qquad (11.6)$$

For instance, for $\delta = 0.5$, if $p = 0.5$ (no useful signal), then the interest rate i^* needs to be 100%, if $p = 0.8$. the interest rate needs to be 25%, if $p = 0.95$, it needs to be 5.3%, and if $p = 1$, then it needs to be zero (assuming indeed that the bank is otherwise perfectly efficient). Lending will take place as long as $V_G - 1 \geq i^*$ (since otherwise, the Good borrowers would no longer be profitable).

The model makes it possible to identify three intuitive triggers that can cause a breakdown of lending: (i) a decline of δ, the share of Good loan applicants in the population, (ii) a decrease of $V_{G,}$ the return-generating power of Good loan applicants, (iii) a decrease of p, the power of the screening technology. All three effects are likely to occur in the case of a major negative economic shock, such as an asset bubble burst, and may hence cause a lending freeze. Therefore, the adverse selection model explains why negative economic shocks trigger liquidity crises, and why these effects can be large and abrupt.

Before a deterioration of economic conditions such as that captured in (i) and (iii) leads to a complete funding market breakdown, it is already felt in the form of an increasing equilibrium lending rate i^* for a given level of funding costs of banks (which were assumed to be zero). This will affect the transmission mechanism of monetary policy in the sense that for unchanged central bank policy rates (for an unchanged operational target of monetary policy), suddenly higher funding costs to the real economy materialize. To that extent, the effective monetary conditions have tightened due to a change of the transmission mechanism of monetary policy.

Inferior Non-Lending Equilibrium in Interbank Markets

Above it was argued that the market may break down because of asymmetric information and adverse selection. Once a liquidity crisis has broken out, and everybody starts hoarding liquidity, this 'dreadful state' (Bagehot, 1873) may constitute an inferior equilibrium which is difficult to overcome. It may be useful

		Bank 2	
		Lend	*Do not lend*
Bank 1	*Lend*	*1* *1*	*0.8* *0.6*
	Do not lend	*0.6* *0.8*	*0* *0*

Fig. 11.3. Strategic game matrix—stable interbank market

to illustrate the switch from an elastic interbank market to a 'hoarding' equilibrium without interbank lending as a simple strategic game between two banks, whereby three different cases may be distinguished. It is always *socially* optimal that both banks are ready to lend to each other (i.e. they establish positive and significant limits to each other). In this case, banks do not have to fear funding liquidity constraints in case of non-anticipated liquidity outflows and capital market constraints, and hence can engage in more profitable (and welfare-enhancing) business opportunities. Consider now the three strategic game constellations that could describe the state of the money market at any point in time.

- **Stable unique lending equilibrium,** in which banks are ready to lend to other banks when needed (i.e. positive and significant limits for interbank exposure). Banks would have no incentive to deviate from this, in the sense that being ready to lend is better than not being ready to do so, regardless of what the other bank does. This could reflect a sufficient confidence on the existence of other funding sources (capital market access, non-encumbered collateral allowing for central bank access, etc.). The strategic game is reflected in figure 11.3.
- **Two equilibria: one superior (both banks are ready to lend to other banks) and one inferior (both banks hoard, i.e. do not lend to each other).** If bank 1 lends, and bank 2 does not, then bank 1 may be in a particularly bad situation as it may have given away its liquidity buffer to bank 2, but in case of an adverse liquidity shock may have to default because it does not find itself a lender in the interbank market. In normal times the latter case may not be so dramatic as there may be alternative (moderately costly) solutions to avoid default. But in bad market circumstances, illiquidity risks become significant. Therefore, in a generally illiquid environment, not lending to each other may become a stable equilibrium as well. This idea is reflected in figure 11.4.
- **Prisoners dilemma with a unique inferior equilibrium:** It could be imagined that in a severe crisis, regardless of what the other banks are doing, not lending to other banks is best to support the survival of one's own bank. In that case a strategic game as illustrated in figure 11.5 would apply.

		Bank 2	
		Lend	*Do not lend*
Bank 1	*Lend*	*1* *1*	*0.5* *− 0.5*
	Do not lend	*− 0.5* *0.5*	*0* *0*

Fig. 11.4. Strategic game matrix—breakdown of interbank market as a multiple equilibrium problem

		Bank 2	
		Lend	*Do not lend*
Bank 1	*Lend*	*1* *1*	*2* *− 2*
	Do not lend	*− 2* *2*	*0* *0*

Fig. 11.5. Strategic game matrix—breakdown of interbank market as a prisoner's dilemma problem

We will use simple strategic game representations with more economic underpinnings in the next section and on several occasions in the rest of the book to illustrate the multiple equilibrium problem in bank funding and the role of the central bank in supporting the case of a unique superior equilibrium. Only the simplest possible equilibrium concept will be used, although there is no doubt that additional insights can be obtained from more sophisticated equilibrium concepts (including mixed strategies). Obviously there is a large, more sophisticated literature on multiple equilibria in funding markets, including in the specific case of money markets (see, also for further references, e.g. Morris and Shin, 2001; Caballero and Krishnamurthy, 2008; Heider et al., 2009; or Acharya et al., 2012).

Furfine (2002) analyses the reaction of US money markets to the 1998 crisis, and notes that the market was sufficiently resilient to not break down at that time. This was different in the crisis starting in 2007.

For further illustration, Table 11.1 illustrates the development of interbank secured and unsecured money market lending quantities by a sample of around 100 banks active in the euro area money market (for the details of the data collection methodology, see European Central Bank, 2012).

Table 11.1 illustrates the shrinking of the unsecured markets, and the higher resilience of the secured markets during the crisis. Post-crisis, a clear dominance of secured over unsecured markets emerges for all maturities but overnight.

Table 11.1. Secured and unsecured lending in euro area money markets, volumes in billions of euro. Assumed average maturity: mid of range, or: 3–12 months: 6 months; more than 1 year: 15 months

	Turnover		Outstanding		
	Q2 2007	Q2 2012	Q2 2007	Q2 2012	Change
Unsecured deposits					
Overnight	55.0	26.7	55.0	26.7	–51%
Tom/Next to 1 Month	24.3	5.1	364.2	75.9	–79%
1 Month to 3 Months	1.5	0.3	88.4	16.5	–81%
3 Months to 1 Year	0.9	0.2	163.4	38.0	–77%
More than 1 Year	0.1	0.1	30.3	54.7	80%
Total	**81.8**	**32.4**	**701.4**	**211.8**	**–70%**
Secured deposits (reverse repo)					
Overnight	33.2	26.6	33.2	26.6	–20%
Tom/Next to 1 Month	151.3	145.0	2270.2	2174.0	–4%
1 Month to 3 Months	6.6	4.0	397.2	244.0	–39%
3 Months to 1 Year	2.9	2.5	528.4	445.6	–16%
More than 1 Year	0.2	0.2	113.2	105.3	–7%
Total	**194.4**	**178.4**	**3342.2**	**2995.5**	**–10%**

Source: European Central Bank (2012), ECB data.

11.3 BANK RUNS AND INVESTOR STRIKES

Retail Depositor Bank Runs

According to Laeven and Valencia (2008, 19), bank runs are a common feature of banking crises, with 62% of crises experiencing momentary sharp reductions in total deposits. That even industrialized countries are still not secure from bank runs was illustrated by the retail depositor bank run on Northern Rock, experienced in 2007 in the United Kingdom. House of Commons (2008, 3) notes that the run on Northern Rock was 'the first run on the retail deposits of a United Kingdom bank since Victorian times' and provides a very detailed description of the causes, sequence of events, and lessons of that bank run (see also Shin, 2009). One may also identify a limited *aggregate* run in the fact that the growth rate of the demand for banknotes had in many industrialized countries a peak at the end of 2008, i.e. after Lehman. For example, euro banknotes experienced a 13% increase from October 2007 to October 2008, above the preceding trend increase of 8%. Finally, during 2011 and 2012, there was a 'cold' bank run on Greek banks, in particular in 2012 in the context of fears of an exit of the country from the euro area: corporate and household deposits with (the top 16) Greek banks stood at EUR 203 billion at end 2010, at EUR 161 billion at end of 2011, and EUR 151 billion at end 2012. In mid July 2013 they had recovered again somewhat to reach EUR 166 billion. This bank run materialized through electronic transfers of deposits to accounts with non-Greek euro area banks, i.e. at no time were there queues in front of the banks to withdraw cash. In the early 1930s there had been a multitude of bank runs, which led to the decision to establish deposit insurance schemes (for the US bank runs in the early 1930s see e.g. Wicker, 1996; for the German bank run of July 1931 see e.g. Priester, 1932).

Bank runs have been modelled e.g. by Diamond and Dybvig (1983), Cooper and Ross (1998), Chen (1999), Rochet and Vives (2004), and Ennis and Keister (2006), Chen and Hasan (2006). More generally, multiple equilibria in financial markets have been modelled in particular in the global games literature as represented by e.g. Morris and Shin (1998; 2001), Angeletos et al. (2006), Heinemann et al. (2004), Heinemann and Illing (2002). In the following, only the simplest possible model of the bank run problem and multiple equilibria in funding markets will be provided. Still, this model will make it possible to illustrate the basic link between asset liquidity, funding structure, central bank collateral, lender of last resort policies, and financial stability.

The particularity of bank runs is their self-fulfilling property: once a run on a bank starts, it can lead to the default of the bank, confirming the individual wisdom of those who were first in the queue to withdraw their money. The deposit run problem can be modelled in a simple way in the form of a strategic game. Assume the bank balance sheet shown in figure 11.6, with two depositors who each deposit one currency unit in the bank. The bank moreover has equity E. It holds fully liquid assets at a proportion of Λ and totally illiquid ones at proportion $(1 - \Lambda)$, with $1 \geq \Lambda \geq 0$.[1]

Assume that there are no central bank credit facilities (an assumption that will be changed in chapter 12), that deposits are overnight deposits, and that a depositor can either leave his deposits completely stable or withdraw them as much as possible (i.e. totally if the liquidity of the bank allows so). Also assume that a disorderly default event implies costs of $C > 0$. The strategic 'bank run' game now depends on the relative sizes of the various parameters. The extreme case is that $\Lambda = 1$, i.e. all bank assets are liquid. In this case, there is no liquidity risk. Still, there can be a bank run in case the bank has possible solvency problems, since then the last depositor will have to bear losses. We assume that the solvency of the bank is revealed at the end of the game, so that a possible

[1] The separation of assets into totally liquid and totally illiquid ones is obviously a strong simplification of reality. Alternatively, one may describe asset liquidity of the bank's asset as a continuous function (see Bindseil, 2013).

negative equity is allocated pro rata to the depositors that are still with the bank. The exact time line of this bank run model is as follows:

- Initially, the bank has the balance sheet composition shown in figure 11.6.
- Short-term depositors play a strategic game with two alternative actions: to run or not to run. 'Running' means to withdraw the deposits and to transfer them to another account. If successful, this means that the value of deposits is afterwards equal to the initial value minus a small cost capturing the transaction cost of withdrawing the deposits, which we call ε.
- It is not to be taken for granted that depositors can withdraw all their funds, as the pay-out is limited to the ability of the bank to sell liquid assets. If it is impossible to pay out the depositors that want to withdraw their deposits, illiquidity-induced default will occur, implying extra damage.
- If the bank was not closed due to illiquidity in the previous stage, still its solvency is analysed and if capital is negative, the bank is resolved, and negative equity leads to pro rata losses for creditors.

The model timeline is summarized in figure 11.7.

Assume that the cost of disorderly default C is larger than E (and of course $C > 0$), i.e. any positive equity gets wiped out in case of a disorderly default.

The decision set of depositor i (i = 1,2) from which he will choose his decision D_i consists in $\{K_i, R_i\}$, whereby 'K' stands for 'keeping' deposits and 'R' stands for 'run'. Call the pay-off function of depositor i $U_i = U_i(D_1,D_2)$. Note that the strategic game is symmetric, i.e. $U_1(K_1,K_2) = U_2(K_1,K_2)$;

Assets		Liabilities	
Liquid assets	$\Lambda(2 + E)$	Depositor 1	1
Non-liquid assets	$(1 - \Lambda)(2 + E)$	Depositor 2	1
		Equity	E

Fig. 11.6. A bank threatened by illiquidity due to a possible depositor run

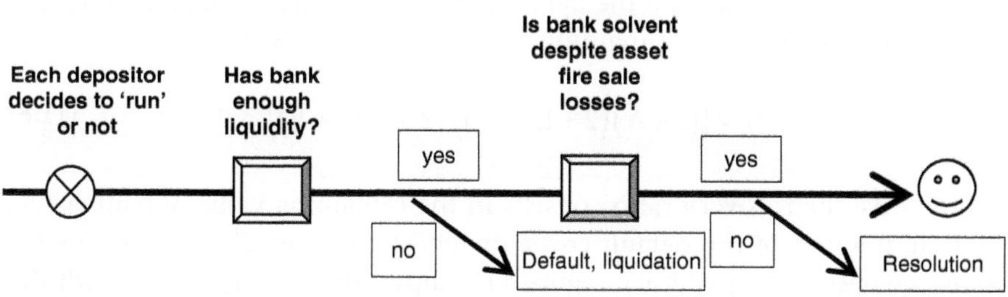

Fig. 11.7. Time-line of bank run model

$U_1(K_1,R_2) = U_2(R_1,K_2)$; $U_1(R_1,K_2) = U_2(K_1,R_2)$; $U_1(R_1,R_2) = U_2(R_1,R_2)$. This allows expressing conditions only with reference to one of the two players. A *Strict Nash equilibrium* is defined as the solution to a strategic game in which each player has a unique best response to the other players' strategies (see Fudenberg and Tirole, 1991, 11). A *Strict Nash No-Run (SNNR) equilibrium* in our bank run game is therefore one in which the no-run choice dominates the 'run' choice regardless of what the other depositor decides, i.e. an SNNR equilibrium is defined by:

$$U_1(K_1,K_2) > U_1(R_1,K_2) \cap U_1(K_1,R_2) > U_1(R_1,R_2) \qquad (11.7)$$

Consider now three cases of parameter constellations leading to different strategic games. We ignore the case $\Lambda(2 + E) \geq 2$ as trivial (both depositors could withdraw their deposits at any time as that there are sufficient fully liquid assets to pay them out—there would therefore be no scenario of default triggered by a deposit run).

Case (A): First, assume that $2 > \Lambda(2 + E) \geq 1$ and $E > 0$. In this case, default occurs when both depositors 'run', but not when only one of them runs. Figure 11.8 illustrates this case. In this and the following figures, the default outcomes are shaded in grey—these outcomes are the socially inferior ones, in the sense that social costs C arise due to an illiquidity-induced disorderly default, that could have been avoided if one had had enough liquidity to maintain orderly operations (regardless of whether equity is positive or not).

In this case, not-running is the unique equilibrium strategy for the two players, and hence the social optimum is achieved. Formally, this can be verified by checking the formal condition $U_1(K_1,K_2) > U_1(R_1,K_2) \cap U_1(K_1,R_2) > U_1(R_1,R_2)$

Case (B): Consider now instead the case in which $\Lambda(2 + E) < 1$ and $E > 0$, so that already the withdrawal of one depositor will lead the bank to default and hence the related damage $C > E$ will materialize and the remaining depositors will face losses pro rata. To understand the pay-off, note that if one depositor runs, this depositor will have withdrawn $\Lambda(2 + E)$, and will have still in the bank $1 - \Lambda(2 + E)$ deposits at the moment of default. Total remaining bank assets will be $(1 - \Lambda)(2 + E)$, i.e. the non-liquid assets remain at default. If both depositors run in parallel, both will have withdrawn deposits of $\Lambda(2 + E)/2$, and will still have claims on the banks of $1 - \Lambda(2 + E)/2$ at default. Note that the recovery ratio (rr) for remaining deposits at default will be

$$rr = \big((1-\Lambda)(2+E)-C\big)/\big(2-\Lambda(2+E)\big) < 1 \qquad (11.8)$$

In words: the recovery ratio consists in the remaining value of bank assets after subtraction of the default costs, divided by the remaining deposits (as equity owners are wiped out). Figure 11.9 shows the strategic game with the various pay-offs.

		Depositor 2	
		Keep deposits	*Run*
Depositor 1	*Keep deposits*	1 / 1	1 / 1 − ε
	Run	1 − ε / 1	1 − (C − E)/2 / 1 − (C − E)/2

Fig. 11.8. The bank run game with sufficient liquidity for exit of one depositor and positive equity

		Depositor 2	
		Keep deposit	*Run*
Depositor 1	*Keep deposits*	1 / 1	rr / Λ(2 + E) + rr(1 − Λ(2 + E))
	Run	Λ(2 + E) + rr(1 − Λ(2 + E)) / rr	Λ(2 + E)/2 + rr(1 − Λ(2 + E)/2) / Λ(2 + E)/2 + rr(1 − Λ(2 + E)/2)

Fig. 11.9. The bank run game with insufficient liquidity to allow exit of one depositor and positive equity

In this case, two equilibria are observed—the superior, in which no depositor runs, and the inferior one, in which both run. Formally, not running is no longer a single equilibrium because $U_1(K_1,R_2) < U_1(R_1,R_2)$.

Case (C): Now consider the case of a bank with negative equity but with sufficient liquidity buffers to sustain a run by one of the two depositors, i.e. $2 \geq \Lambda(2 + E) \geq 1$ and $E < 0$. It is assumed that in any case, the negative equity is discovered after the run game is played, and that the bank is then liquidated (in an orderly manner) because it has negative equity. It is assumed that the cost C of default materializes not only in case of an illiquidity-induced default, but also in case of a closing of the bank by the supervisor due to negative equity. The strategic game is shown in figure 11.10.

Not running does not seem to be a stable equilibrium any longer as running makes it possible to avoid having to share eventually the burden of negative equity. There is instead a unique inferior equilibrium in the game (run-run). Running is the superior strategy whatever the other depositor does, i.e. $U_1(R_1,K_2) > U_1(K_1,K_2) \cap U_1(R_1,R_2) > U_1(K_1,R_2)$. The strategic game has taken the form of a prisoner's dilemma.

Overall, one can conclude that only if the bank has positive equity and sufficient liquidity to sustain at least one depositor running (i.e. $E \geq 0$ and $\Lambda(2 + E) \geq 1$) will the social optimum be achieved. In principle, it could be assumed that banks have themselves an interest in respecting this constraint, in order

		Depositor 2	
		Keep deposits	*Run*
Depositor 1	*Keep deposits*	1 - (C - E)/2 1- (C - E)/2	1 - ε 1- (C - E)
	Run	1- (C - E) 1 - ε	1 - (C - E)/2 1 - (C - E)/2

Fig. 11.10. The bank run game with sufficient liquidity for exit of one depositor and negative equity

to ensure the stability of their deposits. However, competition is likely to force banks to go to the limit in terms of asset–liability structure, i.e. banks will choose liquid assets to be equal to exactly 1, and not hold more liquid assets and more equity than necessary to sustain a single no-run equilibrium. This is because equity is more expensive than deposits as a funding source, and liquid assets generate less interest income than illiquid ones. If banks implement the profit-maximizing asset–liability structure for a given asset liquidity, the problem arises that if asset liquidity deteriorates, in the sense that a part of the assets that were formerly liquid are no longer liquid (for the reasons described e.g. in section 11.5), then what was formerly a stable no-run equilibrium will suddenly turn into a vulnerable situation with two equilibria, and a significant probability of a bank run. A loss of asset value and the implied reduction of equity E can have the same effects (to push $\Lambda(2 + E)$ to less than 1, even if E is still itself positive).

In sum, the bank run problem provides for another important channel of contagion and escalation of liquidity crisis. It also provides for a potential justification of liquidity and/or capital adequacy regulation: regulation can impose some Λ', E', such that small deteriorations of asset liquidity (implying a fall of Λ), or small deteriorations of asset values (implying an erosion of equity E) no longer lead to a direct switch from a situation with a single no-run equilibrium to a situation with multiple equilibria (or a single inferior equilibrium). Of course it could be argued that forward-looking banks have themselves incentives to ensure that they do not easily run into problems of destabilization of short-term deposits. However, banks may be myopic, or may have suboptimal incentives because of the negative externalities of bank liquidity problems and bank defaults. This will be taken up in chapter 13.

It is straightforward to show in the model above that depositor runs can be made more likely through additional public information, implying that sometimes, less public information may lead to higher social welfare than more public information, being the opposite of what one would expect in normal adverse selection models. For example, if the alternative to holding deposits with one bank is to hold them with another bank, then the rationale of withdrawing deposits from one bank relies on knowledge that this bank is worse with respect to liquidity or equity than the other bank. Chen and Hasan (2006) and Allenspach (2009) provide models in which more information can increase the probability of bank runs and hence reduces social welfare. The global games literature also demonstrates similar effects (e.g. Morris and Shin, 2001). Regulators would therefore sometimes face a trade-off: while enhancing transparency may be useful to strengthen market discipline, it could also increase the probability of a destabilization of liabilities. Others have argued that more information can reduce the probability of bank runs, e.g. Schotter and Yorulmazer (2009), who also validate this finding in a laboratory experiment (see also Heinemann et al., 2004). The intuition is that as weak banks would fail anyway, expected welfare would be higher with disclosure as it is likely to prevent runs on strong banks.

Roll-over of Debt Securities Issued and 'Investor Strikes'

In principle, the logic of bank runs also applies to the *roll-over of debt securities issued*, even if the potential dynamics are different, and may be more limited if the maturity dates of debt are well distributed and average duration of liabilities is high. Indeed the best protection against such runs, called sometimes 'investor strikes', is to issue longer-term paper. The pre-2007 practice of setting up special purpose vehicles ('SPVs') holding long-term assets and issuing short-term (say three months) Asset Backed Commercial Papers ('ABCPs') was going in the opposite direction, and was one of the triggers of the 2007/2008 liquidity crisis. The simple model of a depositor bank run proposed above and the way it links asset liquidity and funding instability in fact also explains well the spillovers between asset and funding liquidity observed in the break-out of the current crisis in 2007, as described for example by Acharya and Viswanathan (2011, 103), and as serving as motivation to their more sophisticated model:

> Starting August 9, 2007, the subprime crisis took hold of the financial sector... In fact, since the beginning of 2007, information about the deteriorating quality of mortgage assets hit markets on a repeated basis... An important element that contributed to the sharp reaction of financial markets was the highly short-term nature of debt with which these assets, and more broadly balance sheets, had been financed... It became increasingly clear in the following months that funding conditions had tightened and the roll-over of short-term debt would be limited... The cost of issuing Asset Backed Commercial Paper over the Federal funds

rate rose from benign levels of 10–15 basis points to over 100 basis points in the months following 9 August 2007…

Further, there was a substantial increase in liquidation risk over this period. In particular, if assets had to be liquidated, prices would be far cry from 'fair' or 'normal time' valuations because natural buyers of such assets were themselves hit by the shock to asset quality.

Central banks around the world had to act as lenders of last resort starting in 2007 to help out to banks who had funded themselves too short-term or who had provided liquidity lines to vehicles with a considerable maturity mismatch (like ABCPs or other special investment vehicles). While Northern Rock (see Shin, 2009) was the only example of a bank in the industrialized world during the current crisis which faced a physical retail depositor bank run, there was a multitude of banks that were under acute liquidity stress and needed central bank rescue through Emergency Liquidity Assistance (ELA—see section 14.4). Wholesale funding market liquidity and roll-over risks and their systemic consequences have been modelled for example by Cifuentes et al. (2005), Acharya et al. (2011), Acharya and Viswanathan (2011), and Huang and Ratnovski (2011).

Sovereigns as Victims of Investor Strikes?

Whether sovereigns can also be subject to self-fulfilling investor strikes is a more controversial issue. One of the often cited arguments as to why the financial markets and banking crisis of 2007–2009 turned in 2011, *in the euro area*, into a sovereign debt crisis is that the euro area lacks a lender of last resort for Governments due to the prohibition of monetary financing in Article 123 of the EU Treaty. To simplify, in Germany the ECB has been attacked for supposedly not fully respecting this treaty article, while criticism in the rest of the world mostly went in the opposite direction. Looking briefly at the facts, it is in any case noteworthy how much sovereign debt the central banks of e.g. the US, UK, and Japan bought relative to the Eurosystem (see also section 12.4). While the purchases were never motivated with the lender of last resort function, but more generally as a monetary policy measure, they nevertheless drove sovereign debt yields down, and thereby at least indirectly lowered the funding costs of the Government, facilitated market access, and improved the sovereigns' solvency.

A number of differences between Governments and banks or other private indebted entities can be identified: (i) Compared with banks, Governments have even less liquid assets that they could repo or sell to obtain funding in markets; (ii) however, Governments can increase taxes such as to ensure their liquidity, although democracy may impose constraints on this; (iii) dangers of loss of central bank independence are more serious in case the central bank acts as lender of last resort for Governments.[2]

The issue could also be approached as follows: Banks and Governments can both be thought to have, for given assets, maximum sustainable leverage ratios. Such maximum leverage ratios will depend on whether or not a lender of last resort is available. Without a lender of last resort, the optimal leverage ratio is lower, to take into account the vulnerability relating to sudden stops of investors' willingness to provide funds. In principle, these lower leverage ratios may be inferior, as leverage may have economic merits.

In any case, the current very high sovereign debt levels of many industrialized countries appear excessive, and can hardly be justified as optimal in view of aging societies and mediocre growth perspectives. In this sense, the availability of an unconstrained central bank as lender of last resort may be seen to be a pre-condition for managing the current high debt situation without major disruptions. Taking a different perspective, it could however also be argued that such a central bank role facilitates the delay of necessary adjustments, with even higher adjustment costs later on.

Reinhart and Rogoff (2009) confirm the difference in debt sustainability depending on whether the Government debt is in the country's *own* currency or in a genuine *foreign* currency, and more generally note that the two types of debt are subject to very different economic laws. Their statistical evidence suggests that more than half of *external* defaults of emerging economies occur at a ratio of external debt to GDP of less than 60%. This contrasts with the much higher domestic-currency debt levels that seem to be supportable when the central bank is unconstrained in its lender of last resort function for banks and sovereigns, as illustrated by the current debt-to-GDP ratios of e.g. the US, the UK, and Japan.

The issue of the need of a lender of last resort (LOLR) for sovereigns is analysed further in De Grauwe (2011) and Buiter and Rahbari (2012a). Both come to the conclusion, discussing the case of the euro area, that indeed even Governments would need a lender of last resort. Previously, Calvo (1988) and Cole and Kehoe (2000) had modelled the role of expectations and multiple equilibria in sovereign funding. In section 17.1, we will briefly model the run on a country under a fixed exchange rate regime.

11.4 INCREASE OF MARGIN

Collateralizing financial claims is a widespread financial market technique. It is used in particular in the following three types of operations.

[2] See also Buchheit et al. (2013) for a more general review of the particularities of sovereign default.

- Interbank repo operations (i.e. collateralized interbank lending—see e.g. European Central Bank, 2012).
- Lending of banks to non-banks, e.g. mortgage loans to household and commercial real estate developers; loans of banks to corporates collateralized by equipment or receivables; loans of banks to hedge funds collateralized with the funds' financial investments, etc.
- Collateralization of the value of derivatives transactions, be they 'over-the-counter' (OTC) or via central clearing counterparties (CCPs). An overview of the use of collateral in OTC derivative markets can be found in the annual ISDA margin surveys. According to the International Swaps and Derivatives Association (2013, 2), collateral 'in circulation in the non-cleared OTC derivative markets' stood at US$3.7 trillion at end 2012. The number of active collateral agreements between counterparties supporting non-cleared OTC derivatives transactions was 118,853 at end 2012, of which 87% are ISDA agreements. Around 80% of collateral is actually cash, followed by sovereign debt (use of cash as collateral obviously would not make sense for the funding operations mentioned in the previous two bullet points).

Geanakoplos (2009, 6–7) explains the importance of margining for the generation of a liquidity crisis and for the depreciation of asset values via fire sales, as margin requirements are a limitation to leverage, both for home-owners and for

> esoteric assets traded on Wall Street, ... where the margins (i.e. leverage) can vary much more radically. Declining margins, or equivalently increasing leverage, are a consequence of the happy coincidence of universal good news and the absence of danger on the horizon. Good, safe news events by themselves tend to make asset prices rise. But they also encourage declining margins which in turn cause the massive borrowing that inflates asset prices still more. Similarly, when the news is bad, asset prices tend to fall on the news alone. But the prices often fall further if the margins are tightened... Buyers who were allowed to massively leverage their purchases with borrowed money are forced to sell.

Kiyotaki and Moore (1997), Adrian and Shin (2009), Acharya et al. (2011), and Ashcraft et al. (2011) model the role of margin requirements in the leverage cycle. Ashcraft et al. (2011) and Chapman et al. (2010) also make an explicit link to central bank collateral policies, and hence to the role of this central bank tool in financial crisis.

The IMF Global Financial Stability Report of November 2008 (p. 42) reports large increases of margins (and the implied need to reduce leverage) during the crisis, even before Lehman (see Table 11.2). It is noteworthy that the increase is not proportional through securities types, but reflects the respective perceived value uncertainties during this phase of the crisis. In particular

Table 11.2. Typical collateral haircut in per cent—April 2007 versus August 2008. In case of ranges: rounded mid-points.

	Haircut—April 2007	Haircut—August 2008
US treasuries	0.25	3
Investment grade bonds	2	10
High-yield bonds	13	33
Equities	15	20
CDOs—AAA-rated	3	95
CDOs—AA-rated	6	95
CDOs—A-rated	12	95
CLO—AAA-rated	4	15
Prime RMBS—AAA	3	15

Source: International Monetary Fund (2008, 42).

CDOs (often multi-layer securitizations) were practically no longer accepted at all as collateral.

It is easy to explain why in a financial crisis haircuts can increase so dramatically. Assume that the cash investor (or the party having an exposure out of an OTC derivative transaction) wants to maintain the probability of a loss conditional on counterparty default at a certain confidence level, i.e. say a loss should have a probability not higher than β (e.g. $\beta = 1\%$). Then, the investor should set the haircut at the level of the Value-at-Risk (VaR) from a unit exposure to the collateral. VaR is calculated on the basis of the following factors (for a definition of VaR and its role in financial risk management see any standard risk management text, such as Hull, 2012):

- The holding period T of the asset in case of counterparty default, i.e. how much time is needed to liquidate an asset without the liquidation leading to a negative market price effect?
- The volatility σ of the asset price at some standard time horizon, say one day. If daily price innovations are independently and identically normally distributed, then price changes over the horizon T will have a volatility of $\sigma\sqrt{T}$.
- The confidence level for the VaR limit (in our case of the no-loss requirement), i.e. with what probability the VaR should not be exceeded. For normally distributed price changes, the confidence level β can be translated into a multiplier of volatility using the inverted cumulative standard normal distribution, i.e. $\Phi^{-1}(\beta)$. For instance, $\Phi^{-1}(0.1\%) = -3.10$; $\Phi^{-1}(1\%) = -2.33$; and $\Phi^{-1}(5\%) = -1.64$.

The VaR reflecting a conditional daily price volatility σ, a liquidation horizon of T days, and a confidence level β is then simply equal to:

$$VaR = \Phi^{-1}(\beta)\sigma\sqrt{T} \tag{11.9}$$

Example: assume that for a certain collateral asset, a three-year corporate bond issued by Volkswagen, the daily price volatility (conditional on counterparty default) is estimated at 1% and the orderly liquidation period is estimated at four business days. Moreover, the investor wants to protect itself against a loss conditional on counterparty default at a 5% confidence level. Therefore, the investor needs to set the haircut on this bond when accepted as collateral to: $h = VaR = \Phi^{-1}(5\%)1\%\sqrt{4} = -1.64 * 2\% = -3.28\%$. In a financial crisis, unfortunately, all of these input factors to the calculation of haircuts are likely to change towards requiring higher haircuts. First, investors may want to increase their confidence level as they need to economize on their capital. Second, asset price volatility increases (also reflecting more uncertainty on credit and liquidity risk factors). Third, the orderly liquidation horizon increases as asset liquidity deteriorates. For example, if the confidence level is tightened from 5% to 1%, asset price volatility doubles from 1% to 2%, and the orderly liquidation horizon increases from four to sixteen days, then the haircut ensuring no losses at the new confidence level has to be $h' = VaR' = \Phi^{-1}(1\%)2\%\sqrt{16} = -2.33 * 8\% = -18.64\%$. Therefore, relative to the pre-crisis situation, haircuts have increased by a factor of almost five. This is dramatic in terms of leveraging capability of the collateral provider. If pre-crisis the collateral provider could, with equity of 1, run in theory a balance sheet of 1/3.28% = 30, post-crisis he can maintain only a balance sheet of a length of 1/18.64% = 5.4. In other words, he will have to shrink his balance sheet dramatically, having to fire sale the larger part of his assets.

It is noteworthy that increases of margin may also be the trigger of default of a bank, so bringing the liquidity stress of a bank to its ultimate consequence. This was reported in the case of Lehman (*Financial Times*, 6 October 2009, 'The two faces of Lehman's Fall'; see also Ashcraft et al., 2011):

> On Sept. 11, J. P. Morgan Chase & Co. effectively ended Lehman's campaign to appear strong. In its capacity as a middleman between Lehman and its clients, J. P. Morgan knew more about Lehman's predicament than most outsiders, and it didn't like what it saw. J. P. Morgan demanded from Lehman \$5 billion in additional collateral—easy-to-sell securities to cover lending positions that J. P. Morgan's clients had with Lehman—repeating an unmet request from a week earlier, people familiar with the situation say. It was a knockout blow. That \$5 billion collateral call, coupled with a huge outflow of money from Lehman's hedge-fund clients, so weakened the 158-year-old Wall Street firm that it sought Chapter 11 bankruptcy protection four days later.

11.5 ASSET LIQUIDITY IN A MARKET MAKER MODEL

A Simple Model with Insiders

In a dealer market, where dealers quote binding bid–ask prices (for certain specified amounts), the bid–ask spread is the most obvious measure of asset liquidity. Bid–ask spreads can dramatically increase during financial crises, meaning that asset sales become more costly or even prohibitive. There is an extensive microstructure literature explaining why this is so. Bid–ask spreads in a dealer market with information asymmetries have been modelled in particular by e.g. Kyle (1985) or Glosten and Milgrom (1985). Consider below a basic version of a model explaining why asset liquidity as measured through the bid–ask spread in a dealer market will deteriorate in a financial crisis. The model relies on the following set of assumptions.

- The **true value of assets,** v_t, innovates every day according to $v_t = v_{t-1} + \varepsilon_t$ with ε_t having a probability distribution $f_\varepsilon()$.
- The bid–ask spread *z* is set every day symmetrically by the **market maker** around the estimated true value v_t of the asset. However, the market maker only knows the true value of the asset on the previous day, and therefore on day t, the spread is $[v_{t-1} - z/2, v_{t-1} + z/2]$. Market makers are competitive and deliver their services without operating cost. The market makers commit to trade at the bid–ask quotation for a total value of q.
- **Noise traders** (i.e. uninformed traders) trade every day for an amount $W = W(z) \geq 0$ with $W(0) > 0$, $dW/dz < 0$, whereby it is equally split between demand and supply.
- The **insider** knows v_t on the same day. Whenever the true value is outside the bid–ask spread, i.e. whenever $v_t < v_{t-1}\text{-}z/2$ or $v_t > v_{t-1} + z/2$, the insider exploits the dealing commitment of the trader. Assume that the market maker becomes aware of an insider transaction only once he notes the imbalance in demand and supply, and that this is the case when the insider has traded a volume of q. Then, the market maker stops trading for that day, and re-opens next day again with a symmetrical bid–ask spread around the new asset value.

It is easy to show how, under these assumptions, bid–ask spreads and trading volumes reflect the existence of insider information, as captured by σ_ε^2 (price volatility is equivalent here to insider information, as the insiders are always ahead one period in time with regard to knowing the fair value of the asset). The competitive dealers will set z such as to have expected profits of zero. Expected profits have two components. First, the profit of dealers generated by the noise traders ('EPN') is:

$$EPN = zW(z) \tag{11.10}$$

Second, the expected losses inflicted on the market maker by the insiders ('ELI') are:

$$ELI = \left[\int_{-\infty}^{-z/2} (x + z/2) f_{\varepsilon}(x)dx + \int_{z/2}^{\infty} (x - z/2) f_{\varepsilon}(x)dx \right] q \tag{11.11}$$

In competitive equilibrium, z has to be set such as to bring expected profits to zero, with the first element in the expression compensating the second, i.e. EPN – ELI = 0. Taking as an example that $W(z) = 1/(1 + z)$, $q = 3$ and ε_t being N(0,1), then the competitive bid–ask spread will be 0.5, while for ε_t being N(0,5), it will be 3.6. This dealer market model with insiders explains simply the well-known inverse relation between information intensity of assets and asset liquidity, measured by the bid–ask spread. The model also explains why in a financial turmoil, where uncertainties and hence the potential for insider information dramatically increase, bid–ask spreads increase, possibly in an extremely rapid and strong way, leading to an associated collapse of market liquidity.

A Simple Model with Risk-taking Constraints of the Market Maker

One can also explain the widening of bid–ask spreads due to higher asset price volatility in a market maker model without insiders by simply assuming that the market makers are constrained in their risk-taking capability. Assume there is only one market maker and that this market maker has a risk-bearing capacity expressed as a Value-at-Risk (VaR) at the one-day horizon and at the 99% confidence level of Ω. Assume the following slightly modified setting:

- As previously, the **true value of assets** innovates every day $v_t = v_{t-1} + \varepsilon_t$ with ε_t being $N(0, \sigma_\varepsilon^2)$.
- Early in the day, the market maker can without costs set to zero its inventory at the price v_{t-1}. This assumption makes it possible to set up the model as a single-day model.
- As previously, the bid–ask spread z is set every day symmetrically by the **market maker** around the estimated true value v_t of the asset. Now assume, however, that the market maker transacts whatever the noise trader asks him for, but protects himself against too-high volumes (that may exceed his risk capacity) with the help of the bid–ask spread.

- **Noise traders** (i.e. uninformed traders) trade every day for an amount $W = W(z) \geq 0$ with $W(0) > 0$, $dW/dz < 0$, whereby now on one day W is all demand, and on the other day it is all supply, reflecting a random draw every day.
- **At the end of the day, the true value** v_t is revealed and the market maker has to book a profit or loss ('P&L').

The risk-taking by the market maker will be a function of W, which is a function of z and is therefore controlled by the market maker, and σ_ε^2. The VaR of the market maker will be $W(z) * \Phi^{-1}(0.01)\sigma_\varepsilon^2$, and it must not exceed the risk budget Ω. One can therefore derive the bid–ask spread that the market maker needs to set in order to fulfil its VaR constraint as follows:

$$W(z)\Phi^{-1}(0.01)\sigma_\varepsilon = \Omega \Rightarrow z = W^{-1}\left(\Omega / \left(\Phi^{-1}(0.01)\sigma_\varepsilon\right)\right) \quad (11.12)$$

The bid–ask spread is a monotonously falling function in the VaR risk budget Ω and monotonously increasing in asset price volatility. In a financial crisis, market makers are likely to be more capital constrained, and asset price volatility increases. Therefore, asset liquidity should deteriorate in a crisis even in the absence of insiders.

Figure 11.11 provides a time series of the bid–ask spread of German and Spanish Government bonds between 2006 and 2012, which illustrate the widening of spreads under financial stress. Before the outbreak of the sovereign debt crisis, bid–ask spreads for the sovereign debt of the two countries were essentially similar, and as low as one basis point. In contrast, as of early 2011, the bid–ask spread for Spanish bonds decoupled and become much higher and more volatile than its German counterpart.

11.6 ASSET FIRE SALES

As we have seen above, in a financial crisis, asset liquidity deteriorates (section 11.5), and leveraged entities have to shrink their balance sheet regardless of whether they were funded in collateralized (section 11.4) or unsecured (sections 11.2 and 11.3) interbank and capital markets. This creates potentially a vicious circle: asset fire sales to obtain liquidity further depress asset prices, such that, in the worst case, the asset fire sales depress market prices of assets remaining on the balance sheet by so much, that, after the fire sales, solvency and liquidity problems are even worse and require even more fire sales, and so on. Moreover, the asset fire sales of one institution impact negatively on the mark-to-market value of other institutions' assets (and hence imply losses), leading to negative externalities. Cifuentes et al. (2005) develop and simulate a model of the asset fire sale channel of systemic contagion and related negative

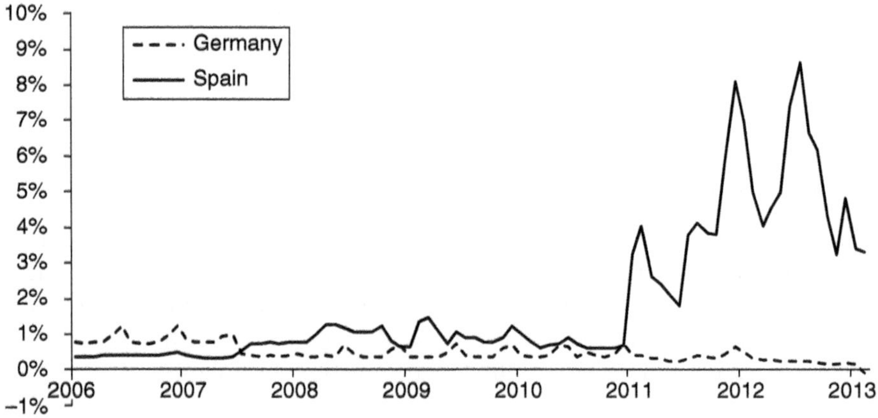

Fig. 11.11. Bid–ask spread of Spanish and German government bonds, 2006–2012, in bps

Source: Bloomberg.

externalities. They also analyse stability effects of capital and liquidity requirements in a system of interconnected banks for given portfolio choices, when mark-to-market rules are in place. A study estimating the systemic effects of asset fire sales on the basis of actual data is Duarte and Eisenbach (2013), who quantify fire-sale spillovers using regulatory US bank balance sheet data and repo market data and find that fire-sale externalities can be substantial.

Figure 11.12 illustrates the effects of the asset fire sales spiral in the case of three US ABS types. The asset swap spreads (yield spreads against interest rate swaps) increase starting in September 2007 and explode after Lehman in September 2008. Swap spread levels of up to 25% were reached after Lehman, indicating that values of securities with a duration above two years would have fallen to around 50%. Prices recovered almost as quickly as they had declined, mainly in the three last quarters of 2009, and swap spreads reached almost pre-crisis levels in 2010 and after. These price developments have to be seen against the fact that these ABS never showed noteworthy impairment rates, i.e. in retrospect, the low prices were never justified by an actual deterioration of credit quality.

11.7 INTERACTION BETWEEN CRISIS CHANNELS

The various liquidity and solvency issues that suddenly appear in a financial crisis reinforce each other and can lead to a downward spiral of ever worsening conditions. Also, once lending to the real economy becomes scarce and expensive, an economic downturn will likely occur and will lead to additional losses via asset price declines and impairment of loan portfolios (as the default

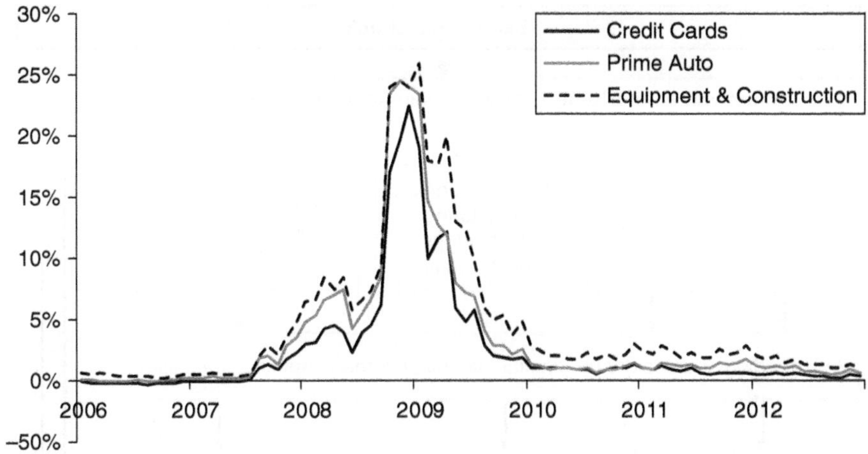

Fig. 11.12. US ABS asset swap spreads: credit cards, auto, equipment/construction
Source: JP Morgan.

frequency of debtors increases). A poor equity position of banks (and other indebted entities) resulting from these losses increases further their credit riskiness and fuels again the vicious circles inherent in liquidity crisis. The resulting economic and financial dynamic may be fatal and calls for external circuit-breakers such as in particular Government authorities, regulators, and the central bank. Central banks, which can in theory provide unlimited liquidity to banks by lending freely, have the power to suppress the liquidity part of any vicious crisis circle, making the central bank (unwillingly) the key player deciding on the fate of banks and other leveraged entities. The essential trade-off of the central bank in such circumstances, namely between on one side supporting the funding liquidity of banks to stop a vicious circle and on the other side limiting financial risk-taking and moral hazard is further discussed in chapter 16. A related fundamental trade-off that the central bank faces is the one between complementing the impaired intermediation ability of the financial market and taking away incentives from private sector intermediation. Moreover, outright purchases of financial assets (discussed in more detail in section 13.3) may cut the part of the vicious circle in which asset fire sales trigger further asset value declines (and hence also further losses and risks for the solvency of banks).

Figure 11.13 aims at capturing the various effects and contagion channels of liquidity crises as described in chapter 11, including the main loops that may lead to an endogenous intensification of a crisis and self-fulfilling expectations of disaster scenarios. These crisis dynamics also explain why the system can switch so easily from a state of comfort and liquidity into one of generalized hoarding, funding fears, asset fire sales, and default, with serious real economic consequences.

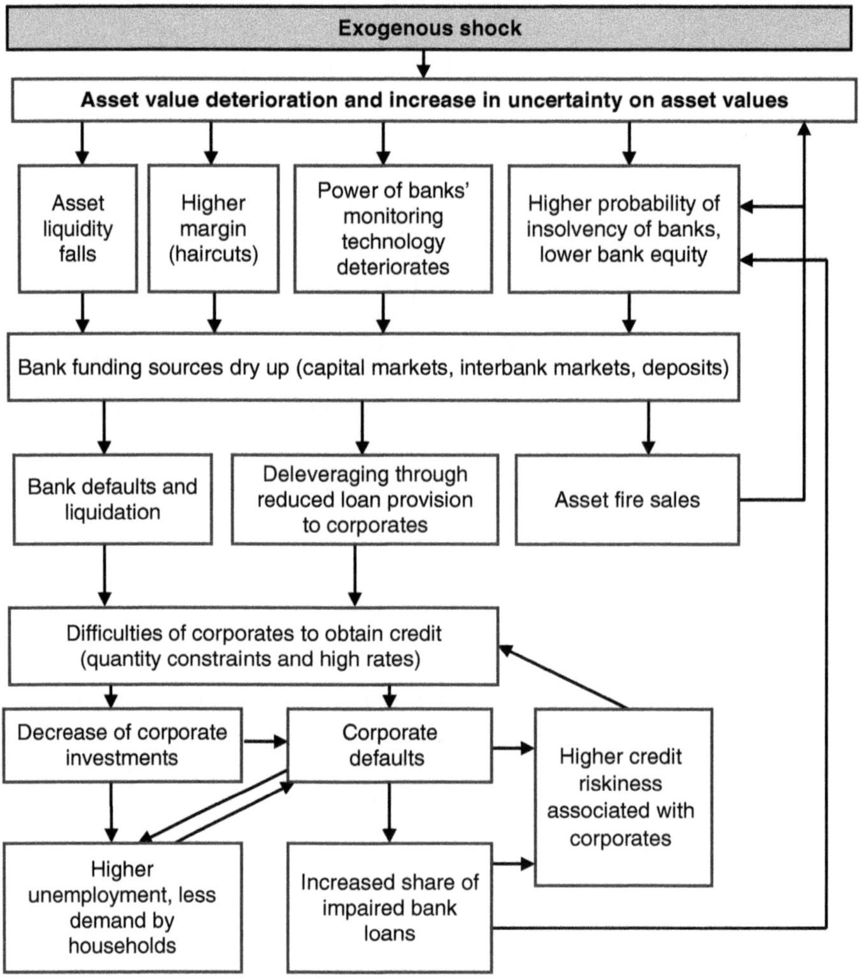

Fig. 11.13. Feedback loops and contagion channels inherent to liquidity crisis

11.8 THE ROLE OF THE CENTRAL BANK: MONETARY POLICY AND LOLR

Monetary Policy in Financial Crisis

Central banks are mandated to reach certain economic objectives through monetary policy. For example, the US Federal Reserve Act specifies that the Board of Governors and the Federal Open Market Committee should seek 'to promote effectively the goals of maximum employment, stable prices, and moderate long-term interest rates'. In the case of the Eurosystem, maintaining price stability is the primary objective of monetary policy, as stated in the Treaty on the Functioning of the European Union, Article 127 (1): 'Without prejudice to the objective of price stability', the Eurosystem shall also 'support the general economic policies in the Union with a view to contributing to the achievement of the objectives of the Union'. These include inter alia 'full employment' and 'balanced economic growth'. Normally, as explained in part I of this book, central banks control one specific operational target variable (mostly the short-term interbank interest rate) such that, in view of the central bank's knowledge of the transmission mechanism and its forecasts of the relevant exogenous variables, the ultimate policy objective(s) can be reached. What should ultimately matter, however, for inflation and real economic activity is not the control of the operational target, but what happens at the end of the transmission mechanism, such as in particular the actual price and availability of credit to the real economy, i.e. households, the state, and the corporate sector.

Funding interest rates of the real economy can be estimated by compiling a weighted average of funding rates, the weights reflecting the share of that type of funding in the total funding of the real economy. For example, for the euro area, Table 4.5 of the statistical annex of each ECB Monthly Bulletin contains a detailed split of lending rates for new and outstanding loans to various obligor classes (household consumer credit, household mortgage loans, loans to non-financial corporates, etc.), with volumes also known from the Monetary Financial Institutions (MFI) statistics. Corporate and sovereign bond yields can also be collected easily from information systems such as Reuters and Bloomberg.

The weighted-average real lending rate of the economy can be thought to reflect three main factors:

(i) The operational target of monetary policy: the short-term, and therefore quasi-risk-free interbank interest rate. This can be controlled by the central bank through conventional central bank operations such as described in chapter 4.

(ii) The slope of the risk-free benchmark yield curve. This can partially be controlled by the central bank through the use of a clear and transparent strategy, self-commitment, and forward guidance, i.e. by influencing the expected path of future central bank rates. Indeed, apart from a general term premium, the slope of the yield curve reflects to a large extent expectations on short-term interest rates (see e.g. Rudebusch, 1995). For example, the Fed used the instrument of forward guidance intensively in the current crisis, whereby the precise wording evolved over time: exceptionally low levels of the federal funds rate were announced to hold 'for some time' (16 December 2008), 'for an extended period' (18 March 2009), 'at least through mid-2013'

(9 August 2011), 'for a considerable time after the economic recovery strengthens' (13 September 2012), 'at least as long as the unemployment rate remains above 6½ percent, inflation between one and two years ahead is projected to be no more than a half percentage point above the Committee's 2 percent longer-run goal' (12 December 2012).

(iii) The various instrument-specific liquidity and credit-risk premia. These vary over time reflecting primarily the efficiency and stability of the financial system. The central bank may partially influence those though unconventional monetary policy tools and lender of last resort policies.

Recall the idea of Wicksell (1898) that the money rate needs to follow the real rate of interest plus the expected (and accepted) inflation rate across time to ensure price stability (see chapter 3). Admitting now that liquidity and credit-risk premia are substantial and time-varying, the challenge for the central bank is no longer limited to the estimation of the real rate of interest. In addition, it becomes necessary to adjust across time for the varying spread between the weighted average funding costs of the real economy and risk-free rates of the same maturity. If the real rate of interest is low (as is likely the case in a crisis), and in addition the spread between the operational target variable and effective funding costs that cannot be attributed to the term premium is high (again, as is likely in the case of a crisis), then it is likely that the central bank will quickly reach the zero lower bound of its operational target without being able to make monetary conditions expansionary.

To express this simple relationship formally, we set the following notation:

- i = the short-term interest controlled by the central bank
- j = the term premium summarizing the slope of the risk-free yield curve, i.e. the difference between the risk-free rate at the average duration of real economic projects (say five years) and the short end of the risk-free yield curve (which is close or equal to i)
- k = the spread between the weighted funding costs of the real economy and the risk-free yield with the same duration, i.e. capturing credit and liquidity premia
- r = the real interest rate, i.e. the real rate of return of real capital, which tends to decline in a recessionary economic environment
- $E(\pi)$ = the expected inflation rate.

In chapter 3 (figure 3.1), j and k were ignored and the neutral (non-accelerating) short-term central bank interest rate i^* was equal to the real rate plus inflation expectations, i.e. $i^* = r + E(\pi)$. Now, adding j and k, the neutral rate becomes:

$$i^* = r + E(\pi) - j - k \qquad (11.13)$$

In principle, the challenge of the central bank is now to track r – k, instead of only r (as presented in chapter 3). This implies the need to look at more data obviously to get its estimate of r – k right, and it adds to the danger of ending in a deflationary trap if r moves down and k moves up. For example, assuming j = 0, if E(π) = 2%, r = 2%, and k = 1%, then i* = 3%. If now a real economic shock depresses r to 0 and the related financial crisis increases k to 4, then suddenly the operational target rate should move to i* = –2%, which is a problem, as it cannot really be implemented as long as banknotes are offered unlimitedly as central bank liability with zero remuneration rate.[3] For example, Clouse et al. (1999) and Hamilton and Wu (2012) have explored the zero lower bound problem for central bank interest rate policies.

One *ex ante* remedy against this case is to set a positive inflation target π which provides a buffer against reaching the zero lower bound. Most central banks have chosen inflation targets of around 2%, while Blanchard et al. (2010) proposes 4%. *Ex post*, i.e. if the central bank has fallen into the deflationary trap, it may become essential that the central bank works directly on j (by pre-committing to keep i* at close to zero for a long time and by buying longer-term risk-free debt instruments) and k (by purchasing debt instruments which are credit-risky and imperfectly liquid; by lending to banks against such assets, etc.). Both will be essential when a major shock simultaneously moves r down and k up. This is what central banks have done over recent years.

It is important to keep in mind that the actual availability of funds to the real economy cannot necessarily be measured by contemplating interest rates alone. Indeed, as e.g. the model in section 11.2 suggested, funding markets can break down completely due to an increase of uncertainty and information asymmetries between lenders and borrowers. The role of quantitative funding constraints has been recognized as a relevant element of monetary conditions by central banks, and therefore central banks have started to collect systematically survey data in order to be able to monitor this element of the transmission mechanism. For example, the ECB collects on a quarterly basis qualitative and quantitative bank lending data (see the 'Euro Area Bank lending Survey', European Central Bank, 2013d) and data on the access of SMEs to funding ('Survey on the access to finance of small and medium-sized enterprises in the euro area', European Central Bank, 2013c).

[3] The first central bank ever (and so far the only one) that has tried to put its operational target interest rate to negative levels was Danmarks Nationalbank, as described for instance by Jørgensen and Risbjerg (2012). Monetary-policy counterparties of Danmarks Nationalbank had to pay as of July 2012 20 basis points for placing liquidity in certificates of deposit with it. As Jørgensen and Risbjerg (2012) note, the negative rates were passed through in the money market and achieved the objective of stopping the appreciation of the Krona relative to the euro. Interbank turnover fell, but no particular market disruptions were noted. One issue was that the banks did not really pass on the negative rates to retail depositors, creating a profitability issue in the long term (already in January 2013, Danmarks Nationalbank was again able to increase short-term rates).

The measurement of actual funding conditions of the real economy and of comprehensive indicators of monetary and financial conditions affecting the real economy is actually a well-developed field in academic and applied research (see for example Hatzius et al., 2010; Hollo et al., 2012; Citi, 2013). Some of these indicators (which may be called monetary conditions indicators) measure essentially i + j + k, while others (which may be called financial stress indicators) measure proxies of k. Still other indicators aim at forecasting the impact of monetary conditions on real economic developments and thereby could be interpreted as measures of the spread between the actual monetary conditions and the non-accelerating nominal interest rate. The integration of credit spreads in macroeconomic models has found renewed interest since the outbreak of the current financial crisis: see e.g. Woodford (2010), Curdia and Woodford (2010), or Friedman (2013).

Table 11.3 provides as an illustrative example some key time series for the euro area which make it possible to identify the main factors impacting on the actual monetary conditions in the euro area. Column (I) shows the ECB's main refinancing operations (MRO) rate, which can be regarded as proxy to its short-term interest rate operational target (although during the crisis actual money market rates have often been somewhat below that rate). Column (II) shows the five-year AAA Government bond curve, as published by the ECB in table 4.7 of its Monthly Bulletin. This may be a proxy for the risk-free yield at the maturity equivalent to the average funding maturity of the real economy. Column (III) shows a nominal cost-of-funding composite indicator for non-financial corporates (NFCs) as calculated by the ECB (see European Central Bank, 2005b). The overall cost of financing for non-financial corporations is calculated as a weighted average of the cost of bank lending, the cost of market-based debt and the cost of equity, based on their respective amounts outstanding derived from the euro area accounts. The maturity of the capital market funding indicator fluctuates between approximately four and six years. Column (III) can be considered to represent 'gross' monetary conditions as eventually felt by the NFC sector ('gross' in the sense that there is no matching of the nominal funding costs yet with the real rate). Column (IV) is simply the difference between (III) and (II), and captures the funding cost add-on that the real economy is confronted with due to credit risks, lower liquidity, and shortage of funds due to an imperfectly functioning financial system. This captures the variable k introduced above.

While the risk and inefficiency spread (III)–(II) seems normally to be in a range of 2–2.5% (this is the range encompassing the observations at end of years 2004–2007, and again 2009), it grows to above 3.5% at end 2008 and 2010, and even to above 4% in 2011 and 2012, indicating an exceptional impairment of monetary policy transmission in those years, despite the forceful non-conventional measures taken by the ECB.

Table 11.3. End-of-year euro area interest rates from 2004 to 2012 and implied decomposition of monetary conditions, in %

Date—end of	ECB's MRO rate (i) (I)	5 Y AAA Sovereign yield (i + j) (II)	Overall cost of external funding for euro area NFCs (i + j + k = 'gross' monetary conditions) (III)	Implied risk and inefficiency add on (k) (IV) = (III) – (II)
2004	2.00	3.06	5.56	2.50
2005	2.25	2.93	5.50	2.57
2006	3.50	3.83	6.02	2.19
2007	4.00	4.11	6.52	2.41
2008	2.50	2.95	6.55	3.60
2009	1.00	2.64	5.01	2.37
2010	1.00	2.15	5.78	3.63
2011	1.00	1.56	5.82	4.26
2012	0.75	0.58	5.12	4.55

Source: ECB, Bloomberg.

Table 11.3 illustrates the challenges caused by financial crisis for monetary policy. When growth rates are low or negative, and when the transmission of monetary policy impulses (i.e. a lowering of the operational target level) does not pass through an impaired financial system, then deflationary risks can quickly emerge even if policy rates have reached the zero lower bound. Even before the zero lower bound becomes a binding constraint, it needs to be considered, in the words of Woodford (2010, 39) that

> decisions about interest-rate policy should take account of changes in financial conditions—in particular, of changes in interest-rate spreads…this interest rate can be determined at any time given two other numbers: (i) the current value of the 'natural rate of interest'—the real interest rate required for output equal to the natural rate, in the absence of financial frictions—converted into an equivalent nominal interest rate by adding the current expected inflation rate, and (ii) the current interest-rate spread…Changes in credit spreads should be an important indicator in setting the federal funds rate; the funds rate target should be lower than would otherwise be chosen given other conditions, when credit spreads are larger.

To complement Table 11.3 with the quantity side of funding, consider as illustration figure 11.14, which compares German and Spanish *growth of bank lending* to non-financial corporations and to households during the period 2006–2012, which is likely to be driven not only by different monetary conditions as measured in prices, but also by the diverging availability of credit. Figure 11.14 provides the annual growth rates of bank lending in those two countries to those two types of debtors.

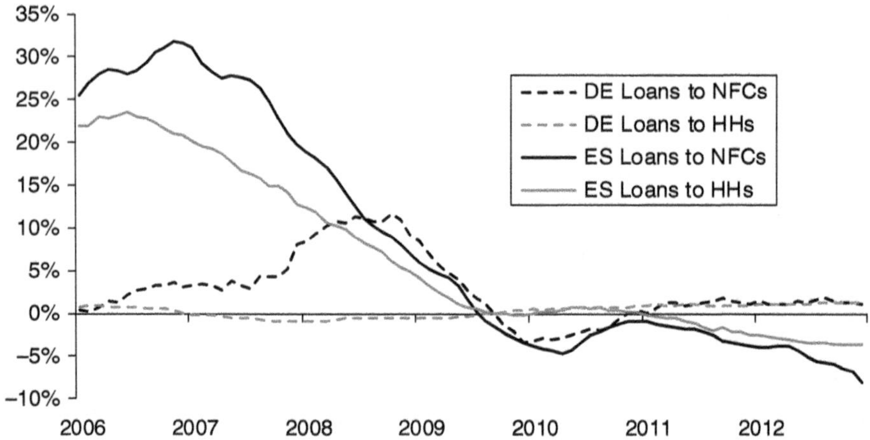

Fig. 11.14. Growth rates of lending to the real sector in Germany and Spain since 2006: annual growth rates in %.
Source: ECB.

Spanish credit growth rates were high pre-crisis and had peaked already towards end 2006. They gradually fell and in the case of loans to NFC reached negative territory towards the middle of 2009 (see also Jimenez et al., 2012, for an in-depth empirical study of the loan supply in Spain, in particular during the financial crisis). Loan provision seemed to recover until early 2011, but afterwards the euro area sovereign debt crisis led to a renewed loss of market access of banks and to a renewed fall into negative territory of lending growth rates. In contrast to that, German lending growth rates were comparatively stable, and in particular the lending growth to households was almost flat during the entire period. Lending growth to NFCs in Germany was somewhat more volatile and in particular fell from a fairly high positive level pre-Lehman (of around 10%) to around –5% post Lehman, before stabilizing again in positive territory. It seems plausible that the funding liquidity crisis hitting Spain in 2011 and 2012 is key to explaining these differences. In retrospect, the very high growth rates of loans to NFCs in Spain in 2006 also suggest that the pre-crisis economic developments in Spain may have been excessive and led to unsustainable imbalances. In this sense, part of what is observed after 2009 may be considered as a healthy correction, and it would be wrong to conclude that public policies should have necessarily prevented the negative credit growth rates to materialize. There is no doubt that in the absence of central bank funding support to the Spanish banking system (essentially in the form of allowing for a considerable temporary increase of central bank recourse to substitute the lost interbank and capital market funding), the shrinkage would have been considerably larger.

The lender of last resort function (LOLR) of the central bank will be developed in chapters 14–17. The theory of the LOLR is often presented with little reference to monetary policy, although acute funding problems are also directly relevant from a monetary policy perspective, as argued above. Without the central bank acting as a lender of last resort in a financial crisis, the crisis will risk escalating to an extent that the economy will enter deflationary and recessionary dynamics, or at least, such as in the pre-1914 US, that the economy will experience wasteful cyclicality of economic activity and price dynamics. As will be detailed in section 14.2, six main reasons can be given beyond monetary policy to justify the central bank's LOLR role.

The Logic of Monetary Policy in Times of Crisis—Summary Chart

Figure 11.15 summarizes the logic of monetary policy implementation in times of crisis. It is a modified version of figure 1.1, which summarized the logic of monetary policy implementation in normal times, i.e. when the separation principle between macroeconomic analysis and monetary policy

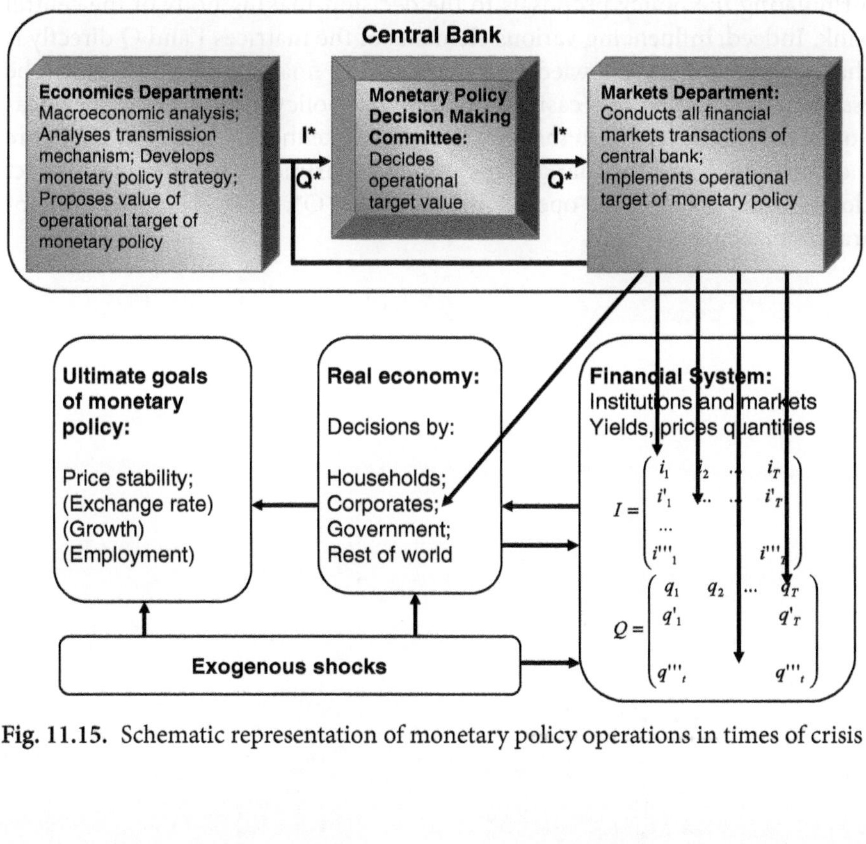

Fig. 11.15. Schematic representation of monetary policy operations in times of crisis

implementation applied. In a crisis, the separation principle has to be abandoned and the Economics department can no longer limit its setting of the operational target to a single variable (like the overnight interbank market rate), but has to set various targets reflecting the fact that one can no longer rely on a stable relationship between the previously unique operational target and the various other interest rates and financial quantities affecting the monetary conditions in which the real economy operates.

In principle, the Economics department has to take views on any element of the interest rate and financial quantity matrices I, Q, and may express operational targets for them, which may be called I*, Q* (typically this will contain targets for a subset of the comprehensive matrices I and Q). The Market Operations department will continue to aim at achieving the target level of the original single operational target variable (normally the short-term interbank interest rate). However, it will in addition aim at directly influencing markets in such a way as to achieve I*, Q*, by intervening across maturities, instrument types, and credit qualities. It can do so via outright purchases of securities or through changes of its collateral framework. Central bank market operations may even be used to support directly the funding of the real economy by providing credit to or purchasing debt instruments issued by non-financial entities. The Market Operations department will moreover be associated in formulating the policy proposals to the decision-making body of the central bank. Indeed, influencing various elements of the matrices I and Q directly is challenging, and the knowledge of markets and financial institutions will be essential in assessing the feasibility of different policy ideas and the specification of the implementation that maximizes the likelihood of success. Therefore the Economics and the Market Operations departments will have to interact closely when defining the operational targets I*, Q*, putting on hold the separation principle.

12

Collateral Availability and Monetary Policy

Central banks have undertaken various changes to their collateral framework during the crisis, with measures to *extend* available collateral predominating. For example, the Fed broadened its collateral set for credit open market operations in particular through its Term Auction Facility (TAF), in which it accepted the broad collateral set normally eligible only for discount window operations (see e.g. Armantier et al., 2008). The ECB has also widened its collateral set during the financial crisis on several occasions, although it has also tightened it in specific respects, and collateral has also been lost due to downgrades and lower mark-to-market valuation. Actually the list of collateral changes made by the ECB during the financial crisis is of substantial length (see e.g. European Central Bank, 2013a, 85–6). For a general survey of central bank collateral measures during the crisis see e.g. Markets Committee (2013). In this chapter we will analyse effects of collateral availability on the transmission of monetary policy. In chapters 14–17 collateral constraints will again play a crucial role in the context of the lender of last resort (LOLR) function of the central bank. Only simple effects within partial models will be presented. A more sophisticated model is Ritz (2012), who shows within a model of an optimizing risk-averse bank how an increase of funding uncertainty causes banks' lending volume and profitability to decline and dampens the rate of pass-through from changes in the central bank's policy rate to bank lending rates. Ritz (2012, 3) also notes that funding uncertainty has 'surprisingly strong implications for bank profitability and consumer welfare in loan and deposit markets'. These results also provide support to the relevance of maintaining or enlarging the eligible collateral basis for central bank credit operations in a financial crisis, as central bank collateral buffers are a key factor in reducing funding risks of banks.

12.1 COLLATERAL SCARCITY AND EFFECTIVE TERM FUNDING COSTS OF BANKS

This section discusses how collateral scarcity may tighten monetary conditions in a financial crisis.

If Haircuts Are Effective Leverage Constraints

According to the model of central bank collateral haircuts determining directly leverage ratios as presented in section 9.4 (equations 9.2, 9.3, figures 9.3 to 9.5; see also Ashcraft et al., 2011), central bank haircuts directly determine the average funding costs of the economy. Specifically, according to equation (9.2), the funding costs of an asset are the weighted average of the shadow cost of equity and the central bank credit operations rate, with the weights being determined by the central bank haircuts. This also makes it possible to derive a simple formula making the average funding costs of the economy a function of the shadow cost of equity, the central bank credit operations rate, and the central bank haircut function parameter δ (the exponent in the assumed haircut power function). Moreover, it makes it possible to explain why, once the zero lower bound of interest rates has been reached, the central bank may want to accept that haircuts are no longer derived exclusively from the financial risk preferences of the central bank, but also from the monetary policy objectives. Assume, for example, that the real rate of return of capital in the Wicksellian sense is r (see chapter 3 and section 11.8) and the expected (and accepted) inflation rate is E(π), such that i# in equation (9.3) should correspond to r + E(π), and hence (i_e = shadow cost of equity; i* = central bank credit operations rate):

$$r+E(\pi)=i_e\left[1/(\delta+1)\right]+i^*\left[\delta/(\delta+1)\right] \quad (12.1)$$

Also assume that the haircut parameter δ* is the value of δ obtained strictly from some risk calculus exercise, which should be respected as long as the zero lower bound has not been reached. Then the appropriate central bank credit operations rate i* is given by:

$$i^*=\left(r+E(\pi)\right)\left(\delta^*+1\right)/\delta^*-i_e/\delta^* \quad (12.2)$$

Figure 12.1 plots this function of r for three different values of δ*, assuming that E(π) = 2% and i_e = 10%.

The figure illustrates that lower haircuts (higher values of δ*) mean higher neutral central bank credit operation rates for a given real interest rate r. It also illustrates that when the real rate drops due to an exogenous shock, then

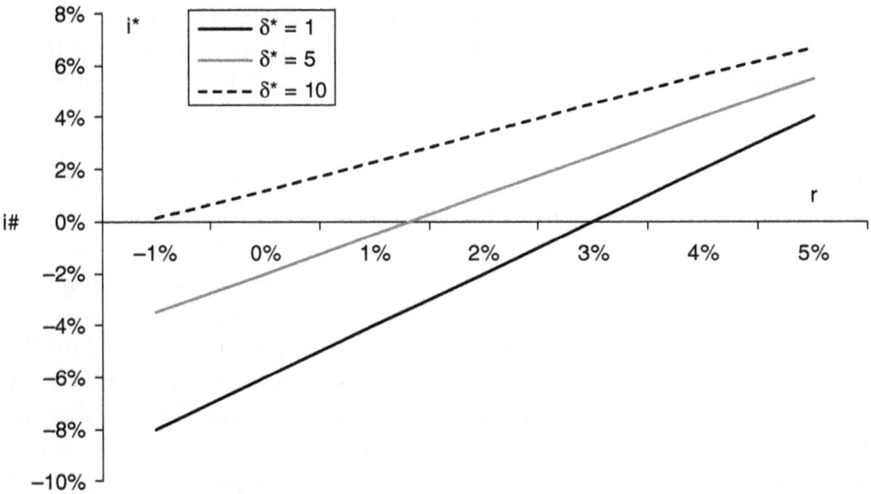

Fig. 12.1. Neutral central bank credit operation rate i* as a function of the real rate of return on capital, for three alternative values of the haircut function parameter δ*, assuming $E(\pi) = 2\%$ and $i_e = 10\%$

the zero lower bound may make it impossible to set an appropriate interest rate on central bank credit operations unless one lowers haircuts (increases δ). Assume for instance that δ* = 1 and that the real rate r had been 4%, such that the adequate central bank credit operations rate was 2%. Now, due a shock, r drops to 2%, implying a new neutral central bank rate of −2%. This is not possible, and moving the central bank rate only to 0% does not help to escape a deflationary trap with all the negative consequences for the economy. Therefore, the central bank may consider it appropriate to accept a lowering of haircuts by increasing δ to 5. This makes it possible to restore a neutral stance of monetary policy with a central bank credit operations rate of 1%.

For the reasons explained in section 9.4, this model is, though relevant, not a realistic representation of reality as bank assets are not systematically financed through central bank credit. The following model will focus instead on the expectations of hitting the collateral constraint.

Credit Risk Spread Implied by Probability of Illiquidity-induced Default

Assume a bank has assets of 1 and initial deposits of 1 > D > 0 and the rest of funding (1 − D) consisting in central bank funding. Also assume an exogenous deposit shock k, implying that deposits will be D − k and central bank funding D + k. Recall the idea introduced in chapter 9 of assuming that there is a continuum of assets and that they are ranked from the least to the most liquid and that the collateral haircut function is from [0,1] to [0,1] and has the functional form: $h(x) = x^{\delta}$ with $\delta > 0$. Recall that in this case the total (and average) haircut is $1/(\delta + 1)$, and hence CVPH (central bank borrowing potential) is $\delta/(\delta + 1)$. In the bank case above, a value of δ thus makes it possible to derive a probability of an *illiquidity-induced* default. Assuming that k is $N(0, \sigma_k)$ distributed, the probability of default due to illiquidity is $PD_L = \Phi(-(\delta/(\delta + 1) - (1 - D))/\sigma_k)$. If one assumes that the asset value destruction in case of default is such that the recovery ratio rr is 50% (this is what empirical default studies suggest as a good approximation), then one obtains for risk-neutral investors a liquidity risk implied credit spread of $0.5PD_L$. This increase of funding costs will hurt the profitability of the bank, and in fact if $0.5PD_L$ is sufficiently high for sufficiently long, may lead to the insolvency of the bank (above it was assumed that the bank has no equity, but the idea can simply be generalized to positive initial equity). In sum, it can be shown that an increase of the illiquidity-related default probability due to limited central bank collateral buffers (which may suddenly become relevant because of a decline in δ implying a decline of CVPH, or of an increase of σ_k) can lead, apart from actual direct default, to an eventual insolvency because of the implied higher bank funding costs. This phenomenon was relevant in the euro area debt crisis, in which banks in e.g. Spain, Portugal, or Ireland faced a fundamental upwards shift of their funding costs, also in relation to the perception of them having limited liquidity buffers.

Weighted Bank Term Funding Costs Including the Case of Hitting the Collateral Constraint

The following simple model also captures how the possible future scarcity of central bank collateral can affect the transmission of monetary policy. First, the focus is on banks' effective expected term funding costs, say at the one-year horizon. This is a minimum time horizon for the banks' decisions on loan provision to the real economy (households, corporates, SMEs). When deciding on lending rates and quantities, the banks will take a forward-looking attitude on their own funding costs and funding availability, focusing on the horizon of the loans to the real economy. This is an illustration of the possible differences between the operational target of monetary policy and monetary conditions, i.e. the effective funding costs of the real economy, as introduced in section 11.8.

Starting from the financial accounts system in figure 2.5 (section 2.2), but focusing now only on one liquidity shock (k) and assuming that money markets are non-existent (reflecting a state of financial crisis), assume the following stylized system of accounts for a household, a central bank, and two commercial banks. Assume bank 1 would be regarded as sound by depositors, while bank 2 would be regarded as vulnerable, such that we can focus the presentation on the

Households / Investors			
Real Assets	E − D − B	Household Equity	E
Deposits Bank 1	D/2 + k		
Deposits Bank 2	D/2 − k		
Banknotes	B		

Corporate			
Real assets	D + B	Credit from bank	D + B

Bank 1			
Lending to corporates	D/2 + B/2	Household deposits / debt	D/2 + k
Deposits with CB	max(0, − B/2 + k)	Credit from central bank	max(0,B/2 − k)

Bank 2			
Lending to corporates	D/2 + B/2	Household deposits / debt	D/2 − k
		Credit from central bank	B/2 + k

Central Bank			
Credit operations	B/2 + k + max(0, B/2 − k)	Banknotes	B
		Deposits bank 1	max(0, − B/2 + k)

Fig. 12.2. Financial account system showing household deposit and interbank lending shifts—with two separate banks

case k > 0, i.e. the deposit shift k increases deposits with bank 1 at the expense of the deposits with bank 2. As previously, the households have equity E and are unleveraged (to keep it simple). They hold assets in the form of cash (banknotes) of value B, and deposits D, initially split equally between the two banks, and real assets with value E − D − B. The deposit shift k changes the liquidity situation of the two banks that need to adjust their operations with the central bank accordingly (assuming the absence of interbank markets). Figure 12.2 shows how this adjustment takes place in the financial accounts.

The refinancing potential of banks with the central bank is limited by collateral availability, which is constrained by (i) restrictive eligibility criteria (e.g. excluding certain non-transparent asset classes and setting a minimum credit quality for the collateral obligor), (ii) conservative collateral valuation (to reduce the risk of assuming too-high collateral values), (iii) haircuts (to cater for possible losses in value during the liquidation period of the asset, i.e. after a counterparty default), or (iv) quantitative collateral limits (to address concentration and correlation risks). To simplify, we assume that all loans of banks to corporates are eligible collateral and are subject to a haircut of h, implying that for one unit of collateral value, the bank can obtain $(1 - h)$ units of central bank funding.[1] The actual borrowing of Bank 2 from the central bank, $B/2 + k$, must not exceed this, i.e.: $(1 - h)(D/2 + B/2) \geq B/2 + k$. If the shock k exceeds $(1 - h)D/2 - hB/2$, bank 2 is hit by the collateral constraint, and either defaults, or is saved by the central bank with some emergency liquidity assistance (ELA; see section 14.4). Recall the concept of the collateral gap $CG = \max(0, (B/2 + k) - (1 - h)(D/2 + B/2))$. The expected collateral gap, E(CG), will increase in a financial crisis, both because CVPH ('collateral value post haircut') will tend to decrease, and because central bank borrowing inevitably becomes more volatile.

First, consider the factors impacting in a financial crisis on the future evolution of CVPH, i.e. on $(1 - h)(D + B)/2$, whereby we should have in mind the horizon of credits of the bank to the real economy. Assume this now for simplicity to be a one-year horizon. For the bank, CVPH is uncertain at that horizon, and in a crisis is likely to decline for the following reasons.

(i) Collateral may lose eligibility because:
   a. the central bank may, as a proactive measure, make an asset ineligible to protect itself in view of a new, more critical assessment of the properties of the asset;
   b. the asset is downgraded to below the minimum rating threshold required by the central bank.

(ii) Collateral may be assigned a lower value by the central bank, in line with the likely evolution of market prices in a financial crisis and the central bank principle of valuing collateral according to market prices.

(iii) The haircuts applied by the central bank could increase because:
   a. the central bank wants to protect itself better against risk and proactively increases haircuts (because it has more doubts about understanding the asset class, or because it doubts its liquidity, or because it wants to protect against increasing volatility), or
   b. the assets migrate, e.g. through rating downgrades, into an asset class subject to a higher haircut category. For example, the Eurosystem applies a 5% haircut add-on to assets which have a rating below A (i.e. to assets that have a BBB rating, as BB assets are normally not eligible at all).

In a crisis situation, all factors will tend to put downward pressure on CVPH, meaning that the collateral framework of the central bank has some inherent pro-cyclicality. Central banks may want to counteract this pro-cyclicality in the crisis, either through an adequate *ex ante* design of the framework which minimizes pro-cyclicality, or through proactive measures in a crisis.

[1] In this simplified setting, *h* also implicitly covers conservative valuation of bank assets when being submitted as collateral, and the fact that not all assets are eligible as central bank collateral.

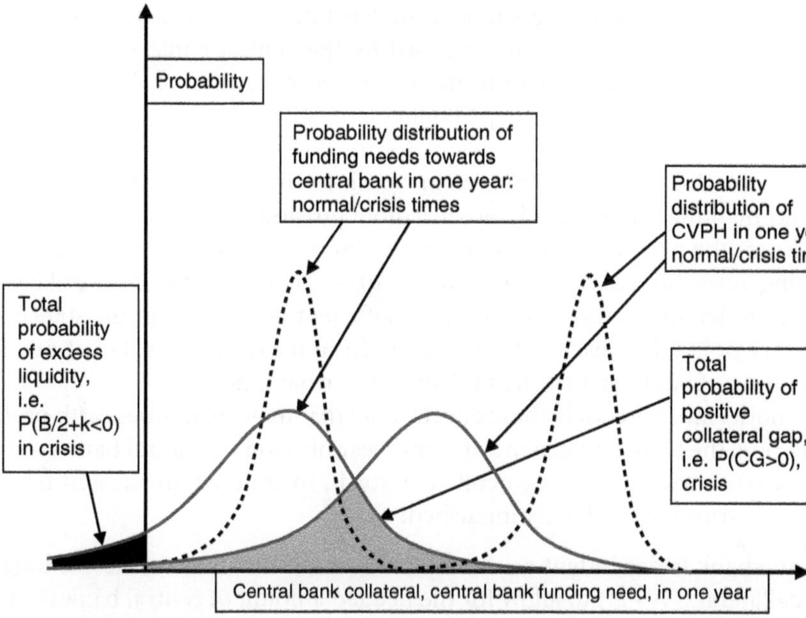

Fig. 12.3. Probability of running out of standard funding sources (including normal central bank credit) in a stressed environment

Second, central bank borrowing, B/2 + k will become more uncertain because deposits and capital markets tend to destabilize in a financial crisis. In normal times, the bank can choose D through the remuneration rate of its deposits (and does so in view of its business model and profitability considerations). Therefore, in normal times, from a liquidity management perspective, market funding and central bank borrowing are choice variables. In a financial crisis, market access and deposit outflows become uncertain and uncontrollable, and therefore the level of deposits (including capital market access) at a certain horizon becomes an exogenous random variable.

In sum, in a financial crisis (i) the collateral values post-haircut (CVPH) tends to decrease and to become less certain; (ii) central bank borrowing (B/2 + k) tends to become less certain; and (iii) the two will have a stronger negative correlation (which we ignore in the simple model reflected in figure 12.3). Therefore, the probability that the collateral gap CG = max(0,B/2 + k – CVPH) also gets positive in a crisis, i.e. P(CG > 0) will tend to increase, starting from a negligible value in normal times. This is illustrated in figure 12.3.

Taking a monetary policy perspective, one has to ask what the significant probability of the scenario CG > 0 means for the effective expected term funding costs of banks, and therefore for the pricing and quantity constraints of the banks' lending to the real economy. When CG > 0, either the bank may be saved through Emergency Liquidity Assistance (ELA), although with significant costs to its business model (higher interest rate charged by central bank on ELA; extra conditions imposed by the central bank; stigma; additional loss of market access), or it may even be restructured or default, which typically means that equity is wiped out completely and management loses its job, which is the most painful outcome for the decision-makers in the bank. If access to funding markets is uncertain, scenarios in which the bank exhausts its funding buffer are suddenly not a remote possibility any longer, but a real risk. From the perspective of the manager and equity owners, the likelihood of losing everything in this event is rather high. This implies that central bank short-term lending rates are no longer a sufficient description of the stance of monetary policy, because the transmission from the operational target rate to the lending of banks is disturbed relative to normal times.

To model more precisely these effects, note that in normal times, with probability one, the bank will depend at a one-year horizon on central bank credit, and the bank will have enough collateral for it. In contrast, in stressed times, three scenarios have to be distinguished:

- The bank is dependent on central bank credit but does not have enough collateral (CVPH) to allow for the needed amount of central bank credit. Assume that the marginal cost of funding when collateral buffers are exhausted is $i_{ELA} > i^*$ (in the best case the bank gets emergency liquidity assistance, ELA, from the central bank; in the worst case, it defaults—we mix the two cases here in one marginal cost variable). This event has probability P('lack of collateral') = $P(CG > 0)$
- The bank is in excess reserves as $B/2 - k < 0$, which has probability P('Excess reserves') = $P(B/2 - k < 0)$. In this case the marginal value of money is i_D, i.e. the rate of remuneration of excess reserves.
- The bank is dependent on central bank credit and has enough collateral (the 'normal' state): marginal funding costs are i^*, the policy rate of the central bank. This event has probability P('normal') = $1 - (PCG > 0) - P(B/2 - k < 0) = P(CG = 0) - P(B/2 - k < 0)$.

In sum, the true expected funding costs of the (risk-neutral) bank may be presented as the following expression providing a weighted average of three rates.

$$\begin{aligned} i\# &= P(\text{'lack of collateral'})i_{ELA} + P(\text{'normal'})\, i^* + P(\text{'excess reserves'})\, i_D = P(CG>0)i_{ELA} \\ &+ \left(P(CG=0) - P(B/2-k<0)\right)i^* + P(B/2-k<0)\, i_D = P((1-h)(D/2+B/2)-(B/2-k)<0)\, i_{ELA} \\ &+ [P((1-h)(D/2+B/2)-(B/2-k)\geq 0) - P(B/2-k<0)]\, i^* + P(B/2-k<0)\, i_D \end{aligned} \tag{12.3}$$

For banks with ample collateral buffers and if uncertainty on the future evolution of central bank funding needs and CVPH is low, bank term funding costs closely follow the central bank rate. This is no longer the case if collateral scarcity has positive probability and hence i# > i*. Collateral scarcity leads to an effective tightening of monetary conditions, even if materializing only in some future scenario. This raises the question how policies can counterbalance this effect. As long as the zero lower bound of nominal interest rates is not reached, it could be compensated by a *lowering of the central bank policy rate*. If the zero lower bound is reached, it may be considered useful to broaden the collateral set in a crisis, or to *give reassurance to the banks that CVPH will not shrink over time* (similar to Bagehot's dictum that the central bank should continue in crisis times to lend against collateral that is good in normal times). The central bank may have to accept the need to strike a compromise between the stance of monetary policy and risk protection, as one of the policy parameters, the nominal interest rate target, gets lost when the zero lower bound is reached.

Example

Consider now a simple example of distortion of term funding costs and hence of the transmission of monetary policy because of prospective collateral scarcity. Assume that from the perspective of the bank, the haircut at the relevant time horizon (e.g. in one year) is $h = h_0 + \theta$ with θ being $N(0,\sigma^2_h)$, and that at the one-year horizon k is $N(0,\sigma^2_k)$. Then (12.3) can be written as:

$$i\# = P(x<0)i_{ELA} + \big(P(x \geq 0) - P(y<0)\big)i^* + P(y<0)i_D, \qquad (12.4)$$

with x being $N((1 - h_0)(D/2 + B/2) - B/2, (D/2 + B/2)^2 \sigma^2_h + \sigma^2_k)$; y being $N(B/2, \sigma^2_k)$.

Table 12.1 provides some examples of how exogenous parameters and policy variables are impacting on the effective one year term funding rate, which will be the basis of banks' lending rates to the real economy. Consider briefly the eleven scenarios in Table 12.1.

- Scenario I: In this scenario, i# = i* as both the probabilities of running out of collateral and of ending with excess reserves are negligible.
- Scenario II assumes that both deposit outflows and collateral values become more uncertain (standard deviation of deposit changes increases from 1 to 4 and of haircuts from 0.01 to 0.2). The effective term funding rate increases to 5.43%, driven by the fact that the probability of ELA becomes significant while the probability of excess liquidity is still small.
- In Scenario III, the previous monetary conditions (i#) of 4% for the effective one-year funding cost is restored by changing the central bank operations rate to 2.12% for the OMO credit operations rate and to 0% for the deposit facility. In other words, *conventional* monetary policy

Table 12.1. Effects of possible collateral scarcity and excess liquidity on 1-year term funding rate. Fields in grey indicate changes of input variables relative to Scenario I

	I	II	III	IV	V	VI	VII	VIII	IX	X	XI
B	**20**	20	20	20	20	4	4	20	20	17.5	20
D	**20**	20	20	20	20	20	20	20	20	20	20
h_0	**0.30**	0.30	0.30	0.00	0.00	0.30	0.30	0.30	0.30	0.30	0.27
σ_k	**1**	4	4	4	4	1	4	6	6	6	6
σ_h	**0.01**	0.2	0.2	0.2	0	0.01	0.2	0.2	0.2	0.2	0.2
i_{ELA}	**10%**	10%	10%	10%	10%	10%	10%	10%	10%	10%	10%
i*	**4%**	4%	2.12%	4%	4%	4%	4%	4%	1.66%	2%	2%
i_D	**2%**	2%	0%	2%	2%	2%	2%	2%	0%	0%	0%
P(ELA)	***0.00***	*0.24*	*0.24*	*0.04*	*0.01*	*0.00*	*0.09*	*0.29*	*0.29*	*0.27*	*0.26*
P(i)*	***1.00***	*0.75*	*0.75*	*0.96*	*0.99*	*0.98*	*0.61*	*0.66*	*0.66*	*0.66*	*0.69*
$P(i_D)$	***0.00***	*0.01*	*0.01*	*0.01*	*0.01*	*0.02*	*0.31*	*0.05*	*0.05*	*0.07*	*0.05*
i#	***4.00%***	***5.43%***	***4.00%***	***4.22%***	***4.02%***	***3.95%***	***3.89%***	***5.64%***	***4.00%***	***4.00%***	***4.00%***

counterbalances the non-standard effects of potential collateral scarcity on monetary policy transmission and on the effective monetary conditions. Of course this approach depends on not having reached already the zero lower bound to interest rates.

- In Scenario IV, the central bank attempts instead to heal collateral scarcity through a lowering of haircuts to zero. This implies a deviation from the central bank's risk tolerance. Moreover, in our example, it does not even enable restoration of the initial monetary conditions.
- In Scenario V, the central bank not only reduces the haircuts to zero, but also 'promises' that it will not change over a one-year horizon collateral eligibility, haircuts, and valuation, such that the standard deviation of haircut changes at the one-year horizon is reduced to zero. This enables approximate restoration of the previous stance of monetary policy, but again at the expense of changing the previous risk tolerance of the central bank.
- Scenario VI returns to the initial parameters, but assumes that banknotes in circulation B are only 4, implying that deposit inflows can quickly make a bank over-liquid, while it is less likely that a bank runs out of collateral buffers (initially, the bank now has a balance sheet length of 12, but only a dependence on the central bank of 2). The effect is that the effective one-year term funding rate is driven below 4%.

- Scenario VII changes Scenario VI in the same way as Scenario II changed Scenario I—however, with opposite effects. The effect of a further increase of the probability of a recourse to the deposit facility dominates the effect of the increase of probability of ELA, and i# is even lower than under Scenario VI.
- Scenario VIII describes a more extreme increase of σ_k, namely an increase to 6. This will be maintained in all the subsequent scenarios. Each of the subsequent scenarios will combine conventional policies and one unconventional tool of monetary policy, as conventional monetary policy alone (i.e. shifting the interest corridor downwards) will be insufficient to restore the previous stance of monetary policy. The combinations will all be effective in restoring the desired stance of monetary policy.
- Scenario IX combines a conventional lowering of interest rates (parallel shift of i^* and i_D by 200 basis points) with a narrowing of the corridor from 200 basis points to 166 basis points achieved by a further lowering of i^* by 34 basis points.
- In scenario X, the central bank combines a conventional lowering of policy rates by 200 basis points with outright purchases of corporate bonds of 2.5 (see chapter 2, section 2.1, figure 2.1 with regard to the balance sheet representation of outright holdings of securities by the central bank). This lowers the initial recourse of the banks to central bank credit.
- In scenario XI, the same conventional policy change is combined with a lowering of the initial collateral haircut from 0.3 to 0.27.

12.2 COLLATERAL SCARCITY, STIGMA, AND THE CONTROL OF THE OVERNIGHT RATE

We adjust now the model of the previous section to fit the day-to-day interbank market and central bank daily control of overnight rates in a symmetric corridor system. It will be shown to what extent open market operations can be used to counterbalance the effects of possible collateral tightness and stigma on the overnight interest rate. Assume that the interbank market still exists and that the central bank wants to control short-term interest rates, i.e. its normal operational target of monetary policy. For example, after years when the ECB had operated a symmetric corridor approach by maintaining neutral liquidity conditions, tensions started to emerge in the first days of August 2007 which intensified suddenly on 9 August, leading to a sudden increase of bid–ask spreads and traded overnight rates despite the fact that on aggregate, liquidity conditions had not changed. The ECB reacted with a large liquidity

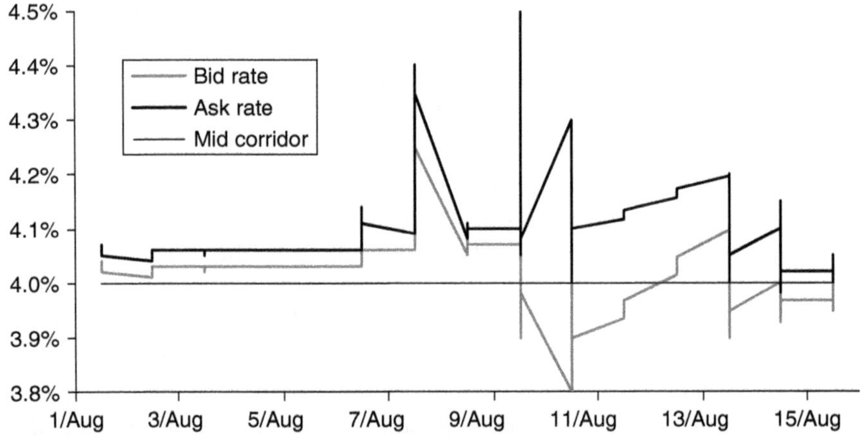

Fig. 12.4. Evolution of overnight rates (bid–ask quotations as provided by the Frankfurt money market broker Kliemm), in %, first half of August 2007
Source: Reuters.

injection through an additional repo operation. This somewhat lowered the level of rates again, but not in a really controlled manner, and the pre-August 2007 genuine symmetric liquidity approach would actually never return (at least until end 2013). Bid–ask quotations (by the Frankfurt money market broker Kliemm) are shown in figure 12.4. Note that at that time the ECB deposit facility interest rate was 3%, the ECB marginal lending facility rate was 5%, and the rate of the ECB main refinancing operations was 4% (and the ECB pursued a symmetric corridor approach as described in section 4.2).

The excerpt of a Bloomberg news report of 9 August 2007 describes the background of that day and the ECB liquidity injection. Today, 9 August 2007 is considered to be day 1 of the financial crisis:

> By Gavin Finch and Steve Rothwell Aug. 9 (Bloomberg)—The European Central Bank, in an unprecedented response to a sudden demand for cash from banks roiled by the subprime mortgage collapse in the U.S., loaned 94.8 billion euros ($130.2 billion) to assuage a credit crunch. The overnight rates banks charge each other to lend in dollars jumped to the highest in six years. The so-called dollar London interbank offered rate rose to 5.86% today from 5.35% and in euros gained to 4.31% from 4.11%…'Liquidity in the market has completely dried up as investors aren't recycling their money back because of subprime concerns,'…The ECB said today it provided the largest amount ever in a single so-called 'fine-tuning' operation, exceeding the 69.3 billion euros provided on Sept. 12, 2001, the day after the terror attacks on New York.

Why did this increase of overnight rates take place and why did the European Central Bank, as many other central banks, react through liquidity injections? The version of the symmetric corridor model presented in chapter 4 suggests that an increase in the variance of liquidity shocks should have in itself no effect on the level of interbank overnight rates, as the probability attached to a recourse to either of the standing facilities is independent of the variance of any symmetric probability distribution, if the interest rate target is in the middle of the corridor set by standing facilities. The explanation for the observed behaviour of the overnight rate and the ECB reaction is that the true, effective corridor must be different from what it appears from the official standing-facility rates.

First, an excess of funds at the end of the day does not oblige a bank to go to the deposit facility, in particular if the bank has still a considerable amount of reserve requirements to fulfil. Indeed, if the excess of funds can be used for fulfilling reserve requirements, then there is no immediate cost of holding them. On the contrary, as noted in Chapter 5, when a bank has an end-of-day overdraft, it has to take a corresponding recourse to the borrowing facility. So there is a built-in asymmetry, and therefore a deviation from the martingale property, if reserve requirements with averaging apply and if an end-of-day overdraft is not allowed. This effect, described in particular by Perez Quiros and Rodriguez (2006), intensifies in a financial crisis with higher liquidity uncertainty.

Second, if a bank faces a liquidity-absorbing shock and can neither refinance in the unsecured interbank market, nor in normal central bank operations because it has run out of eligible collateral, then it will need emergency liquidity assistance (ELA) from the central bank, or it may even default, as described above. Again, this introduces an asymmetry of the effects of liquidity shocks.

Third, even if a bank has enough collateral to borrow from the borrowing facility of the central bank, the stigma problem may arise. Will the central bank ask questions? Will other banks find out that the bank had this recourse and will these banks be even more suspicious and cut further their credit lines to the bank? For instance, Armantier et al. (2011) provide empirical evidence for the existence, magnitude, and economic impact of stigma associated with banks borrowing from the Federal Reserve's discount window facility and find that during the height of the financial crisis, banks were willing to pay an average premium of at least 37 basis points (and 150 basis points after Lehman's bankruptcy) to borrow from the less stigmatized Term Auction Facility rather than from the discount window.

Fourth, overnight interest rates such as EONIA ('Euro overnight interest average', a transaction-based euro interbank overnight interest rate) are unsecured interest rates, containing a credit-risk premium, which should increase when perceived credit risk increases.

Under normal market conditions and low variance of liquidity shocks, each of these issues has limited relevance, which explains why the symmetric corridor system is normally simple to operate. The more intense the crisis, the less symmetric the effective corridor and thus the higher will be the equilibrium rate in the overnight interbank market.

The re-interpretation of the model of section 12.1 in this context is as follows. Section 12.1 associated the 'intermediate' outcome in which the bank would neither have to take recourse to ELA, nor to the deposit facility, with the OMO credit operations rate, and hence the target rate i*. In the day-to-day symmetric liquidity management model of chapter 4, instead the daily OMO has taken place, and any lack of reserves at day end is translated into a recourse to the borrowing facility. We assume here that the central bank conducts its daily OMO in the form of a securities purchase transaction S = B + x, where x is the component of the outright OMO going beyond the neutral amount, i.e. beyond the amount ensuring that i would be in the middle of the corridor under the assumptions of chapter 4. The system of financial accounts in figure 12.5 applies.

Note that it is assumed in this model that part of the claims of the banks to the corporate are in the form of corporate bonds that the central bank can purchase from or sell to the banks on a daily basis. Assuming homogeneous banks, let $i_{B+stigma}$ be the perceived costs of the central bank borrowing facility including the stigma ($i_{B+stigma} > i_B$), and 'CVPH' be the collateral value post haircut available to each of the (identical) banks, with i_{ELA} being the full cost, expressed as an interest rate, of a recourse to emergency liquidity assistance ($i_{ELA} > i_{B+stigma}$). The daily interest rate–determining equation of chapter 4 can be adjusted accordingly:[2]

$$i\# = P(\text{'lack of collateral'})i_{ELA} + P(\text{'borrowing facility'})i_{B+\,stigma} + P(\text{'excess reserves'})i_D \quad (12.5)$$

We consider the example of Bank 2 (Bank 1 is identical, but with different signs):

$$\begin{aligned} i\# = {} & P\big((1-h)(D/2-x/2)-(k-x/2)<0\big)i_{ELA} \\ & +\Big(P\big((1-h)(D/2-x/2)-(k-x/2)\geq 0\big)-P\big(k-x/2<0\big)\Big)i_{B+\,stigma} \\ & + P\big(k-x/2<0\big)i_D \end{aligned} \quad (12.6)$$

The expression $((1-h)(D/2-x/2)-(k-x/2))$ is $N((1-h)(D/2-x/2)+x/2, \sigma_k)$, and $(k-x/2)$ is $N(-x/2, \sigma_k)$. Table 12.2 applies formula (12.6) and varies σ_k, and, as policy response x, the OMO amount beyond the neutral liquidity injection (i.e. beyond B). It is shown that indeed additional liquidity injections through outright OMOs can drive back the overnight rate to the middle of the corridor. Scenario VI shows that a lowering of haircuts can also do the job at least for small increases of deposit volatility, but at the cost of weakening the central bank's risk protection.

[2] See equations 4-.1 to 4-.3, although we now set now reserve requirements to zero, such that S – B is the expected reserve position of banks; recall also that chapter 4 presented an aggregate model with only one bank, in contrast to the model here with two banks.

Households / Investors			
Real Assets	E – D – B	Household Equity	E
Deposits Bank 1	D/2 + k		
Deposits Bank 2	D/2 – k		
Banknotes	B		

Corporate			
Real assets	D + B	Credit from banks	D – x
		Central bank outright OMO	B + x

Bank 1			
Lending to corporates	D/2 – x/2	Household deposits / debt	D/2 + k
Deposits with central bank	max(0, – (– k – x/2))	Credit from central bank	max(0, – k – x/2)

Bank 2			
Lending to corporates	D/2 – x/2	Household deposits / debt	D/2 – k
Deposit with central bank	max(0, – (k – x/2))	Credit from central bank	max(0, k – x/2)

Central Bank			
OMO outright	B + x	Banknotes	B
Borrowing fac.	max(0,k – x/2)+max(0, – k – x/2)	Deposits	max(0, – (+ k – x/2)) + max(0, – (– k – x/2))

Fig. 12.5. Another financial account system with household deposit and interbank lending shifts—with two separate banks

If collateral reserves can cover every possible daily liquidity shock, and stigma is absent, then equation (12.6) reduces back to the standard case introduced in section 4.2. If in addition x = 0, then $i = (i_B - i_D)/2$. The asymmetry in terms of interbank overnight rates relative to the mid-point of the corridor will be higher, (i) the larger the volatility of (symmetrically distributed) liquidity shocks; (ii) the less collateral is available; (iii) the larger the stigma associated with the borrowing facility. All of these factors intensify in a financial crisis such as to intensify the effective asymmetry of a corridor. Of course, the increase of short-term interbank rates relative to the central bank target negatively affects interest rate control. The central bank will wish to offset this effect.

12.3 THE ASSET ENCUMBRANCE PROBLEM

In this section we briefly review the asset encumbrance problem that may result from a large recourse of banks to central bank credit, including the

Table 12.2. Effects of collateral scarcity and stigma on overnight interest rates and possible policy responses. Fields in grey indicate changes of input variables relative to Scenario I

	I	II	III	IV	V	VI
B	20	20	20	20	20	20
D	20	20	20	20	20	20
h	0.70	0.70	0.70	0.70	0.70	0.30
σ_k	1	2	4	2	4	2
x (OMO beyond neutral)	0	0	0	0.9	3.75	0
i_{ELA}	10%	10%	10%	10%	10%	10%
$i_{B + stigma}$	4%	4%	4%	4%	4%	4%
i_D	2%	2%	2%	2%	2%	2%
P(ELA)	0.001	0.067	0.227	0.030	0.061	0.000
P('borrowing facility')	0.499	0.433	0.273	0.381	0.259	0.500
P('excess reserves')	0.500	0.500	0.500	0.590	0.680	0.500
i#	**3.01%**	**3.40%**	**4.36%**	**3.00%**	**3.00%**	**3.00%**

use as collateral of non-liquid assets to which the central bank applies high haircuts. The asset encumbrance problem is not only linked to the recourse of banks to collateralized central bank credit, but always arises when banks pledge a relevant part of their assets for collateralized credit or debt issuance (e.g. covered bonds) or in the context of margin provision for derivative trades. However, for example, the rating agency Fitch ('Banks' Use of Covered Bonds: 2013 Update, Fitch Rating, Special Report', published 6 June 2013, page 4) notes that

> Collateralised funding had increased as a result of the financial and eurozone crisis and the dislocation of the financial markets, with many banks not able to access unsecured markets. The most substantial increase in asset encumbrance resulting from the crisis in Europe has been the build-up of collateral for ECB funding; this is particularly true for banks in peripheral eurozone countries unable to access the senior unsecured funding markets.

Consider the bank balance sheet as shown in figure 12.6. Now E is bank equity, and D is the initial deposit of the household with this specific bank.

Assume that the value of assets is distributed $N(A,\sigma_\varepsilon)$—say, at the one-year horizon. Therefore, and assuming that default occurs exactly when E = 0, the probability of default is $\Phi(-E/\sigma_\varepsilon)$ with $\Phi()$ being the Gaussian cumulative distribution. Assume moreover that in the case of default, there is a share of the asset value at default of LGD ('loss given default') being destroyed. Empirical

Assets		Liabilities	
Assets	1+ ε	Deposits and debt instruments Central bank funding Equity	D 1-D-E E+ε

Fig. 12.6. A stylized bank balance sheet

default studies indicate a LGD of around 50% (see e.g. Standard & Poors, 2009). The recovery ratio rr is defined as (1 – LDG), i.e. the value of debt after default relative to nominal value.

If investors are risk-neutral, and if the risk-free rate is i, and if all creditors would be uninsured and rank *pari passu*, then the interest rate investors will ask for from the bank is:

$$i_D = i + \Phi(-E/\sigma_\varepsilon)LGD \tag{12.7}$$

Asset encumbrance will have an effect on the actual LGD of unsecured lenders and creditors. Assume that all creditors are ranked *pari passu* and no creditor had imposed collateralization. Call the actual loss given default for uncollateralized claims LGD# and the actual recovery ratio rr#. To calculate LGD# and rr#, note that the assets left after a default are rr(1 – E). However, the central bank had obtained C as collateral, with C > 1 – D – E because of the positive effective average haircut on the encumbered collateral, whereby we assume that the central bank sets its haircuts according to equation 9.1 (see Chapter 9). The value of C can then be derived from the haircut-setting formula. The share of central bank credit in total assets is 1 – D – E. The average haircut imposed on the assets that are pledged as collateral is:

$$\left(\int_0^{1-D-E} x^\delta dx\right) = \frac{(1-D-E)^{\delta+1}}{(\delta+1)} \tag{12.8}$$

We also know that C(1 – effective average haircut) = (1 – D – E), and hence:

$$C = \frac{1-D-E}{\left(1-\frac{(1-D-E)^\delta}{(\delta+1)}\right)} \tag{12.9}$$

The value of assets left to pay out to the depositor will be rr(1 –E) – C and the effective recovery ratio and loss given default for the depositors will thus be:

$$rr\# = \frac{rr(1-E)-C}{D}; LGD\# = 1-\frac{(1-LGD)(1-E)-C}{D} \tag{12.10}$$

Table 12.3. Effective LGD (LGD#) for unsecured depositors if the central bank imposes haircuts and 'consumes' them in case of default ('bp' = basis points)

	D = 0.8; E = 0.1; LGD = 50%					
δ	0.1	0.2	0.3	0.5	1	10
Collateral pledged	0.36	0.21	0.16	0.13	0.11	0.10
LGD#	66%	57%	54%	52%	50%	50%
Interest rate add-on due to asset encumbrance	32 bp	14 bp	8 bp	3 bp	1 bp	0
	D = 0.7; E = 0.1; LGD = 50%					
Collateral pledged	0.88	0.51	0.38	0.28	0.22	0.20
LGD#	99%	72%	63%	56%	52%	50%
Interest rate add-on due to asset encumbrance	98 bp	44 bp	26 bp	12 bp	3 bp	0

The interest rate that the bank will thus have to pay to compensate for solvency-induced default will be:

$$i_D = i + \Phi(-E/\sigma_A)\text{LGD\#} \tag{12.11}$$

Table 12.3 provides an overview of LGD# and implied credit spread add-on due to asset encumbrance for a specific example. The length of the balance sheet is always 1 and moreover in all cases it is assumed that LGD = 50% and that the probability of default due to insolvency is $\Phi(-E/\sigma_\varepsilon) = 2\%$. The interest rate add-on displayed is the interest rate surcharge resulting from asset encumbrance due to positive haircuts. Two cases are distinguished with regard to the share of central bank refinancing in the total assets of a bank (10% and 20%, whereby market funding is adjusted correspondingly). Moreover, various haircut parameters δ are distinct. It may be recalled that in the case of the Eurosystem, this haircut parameter is in the order of magnitude of 0.2.

With a very conservative collateral haircut, e.g. δ = 0.1, the bank needs to pledge collateral with a value of 0.36 to collateralize its central bank credit of 0.1. This leads to an effective loss given default of the unsecured depositor (LGD#) of 66%. If the bank is even more dependent on the central bank, namely 1 – D – E = 0.2, then with δ = 0.1 the depositor will lose practically everything (99%) in case of default. Obviously such a bank is not attractive for unsecured deposits or other forms of fixed income investment. The credit risk-related interest rate add-on increases proportionally with the effective LGD#. It may be noted that in the euro area debt crisis, in which national banking systems were temporarily cut off from capital markets, the ratio of central bank funding in total assets reached, at least for individual banks, levels comparable to the lower part of Table 12.3 (i.e. 20%, and in some cases even higher). Moreover, and this is not even reflected in the model above, the collateral valuation tended to be low, reflecting prevailing market prices. For instance, Portuguese ten-year Government bonds were partially valued at below 50% by the Eurosystem in 2011/2012 (which in the model above should be treated like an extra haircut). For Greek Government bonds, valuation even fell temporarily to below 20%.

It should be acknowledged that the simple calculus presented above assumed that the central bank always completely absorbs the collateral that it has received, and never gives back to the insolvency administrator any excess value it may have after collateral liquidation. In reality, in particular with very high haircuts, there should be on average excess collateral value, which improves the eventual recovery ratio of the unsecured creditors, and thereby weakens somewhat the effects of asset encumbrance on unsecured funding rates.

12.4 THE BANK RUN PROBLEM AND CENTRAL BANK COLLATERAL

We return now to the bank run problem introduced in chapter 11 to determine how it can affect the stance of monetary policy. In contrast to the models of sections 12.1 and 12.2, this makes deposit flows endogenous and does not rely on taking ad hoc assumptions on deposit volatility. We consider only a very simplified setting (again, we do not aim at presenting here more than the most rudimentary model of the bank-run and multiple-equilibrium problem—for more sophisticated models, see e.g. Morris and Shin, 2001, Freixas and Rochet, 2008, or Chapman et al., 2010). Recall the bank balance sheet as shown in figure 11.6, reproduced in figure 12.7 with two modifications:

- Now three types of assets are distinguished: those that are always liquid (share $\Lambda \geq 0$), those that are mostly liquid, but may become non-liquid in case of a crisis (share $\Pi \geq 0$) and those which are never liquid (the rest). Obviously we require $\Pi + \Lambda \leq 1$. Recall that liquid assets can be sold at zero losses, while illiquid ones cannot be sold at all.
- The central bank applies a homogeneous haircut h on all assets (in chapter 11 we had not considered the recourse to central bank credit at all). This implies that potential recourse to the central bank is $(1 - h)(2 + E)$. We assume that initially there is no recourse to central bank credit, but we insert the relevant balance sheet item already.

Assets		Liabilities	
Liquid assets	Λ(2+E)	Depositor 1	1
Mostly liquid assets	Π(2+E)	Depositor 2	1
Non-liquid assets	(1-Π-Λ)(2+E)	Central bank credit	0
		Equity	E

Fig. 12.7. A bank threatened by a bank run

Assets		Liabilities	
Non-liquid assets	(1-Π-Λ)(2+E)	Depositor 1	1-L/2
		Depositor 2	1-L/2
		Central bank credit	(1-h)(1-Π-Λ)(2+E)
		Equity	E

Fig. 12.8. The bank from figure 12.7 at default having suffered a run by two depositors (with L<2, L being the maximum liquidity that the bank can generate)

Suppose for the time being that we are in 'good' times in the sense that the mostly liquid assets are indeed fully liquid (and in fact no one has in mind that they could turn illiquid). The bank can now generate a maximum liquidity in case of a run of $L = (\Lambda + \Pi)(2 + E) + (1 - h)(1 - \Lambda - \Pi)(2 + E)$. In analogy to chapter 11, it can be shown that a single no-run deposit equilibrium exists if $(\Lambda + \Pi)(2 + E) + (1 - h)(1 - \Lambda - \Pi)(2 + E) \geq 1$ and $E \geq 0$. It may be noted that at the moment of default, when both depositors run, the bank balance sheet takes the shape shown in figure 12.8.

The decision problem for the bank is: how much equity E is needed to sustain short-term funding of 2, depending on Λ, Π, and h? And, relatedly, how high will the average funding costs be, depending on these variables? One can transform the equilibrium condition as follows:

$$
\begin{aligned}
&(\Lambda+\Pi)(2+E)+(1-h)(1-\Lambda-\Pi)(2+E)\geq 1\\
&\Leftrightarrow (\Lambda+\Pi+(1-h)(1-\Lambda-\Pi))E+(\Lambda+\Pi)2+(1-h)(1-\Lambda-\Pi)2\geq 1\\
&\Leftrightarrow E+2\geq 1/(\Lambda+\Pi+(1-h)(1-\Lambda-\Pi))\\
&\Leftrightarrow E\geq 1/(1-h+h(\Lambda+\Pi))-2 \qquad (12.12)
\end{aligned}
$$

It is clear from this formula that the critical value $E^* = 1/(1 - h + h(\Lambda + \Pi)) - 2$ increases with h and decreases with $(\Lambda + \Pi)$. Table 12.4 shows for different values of h and the share of liquid assets the necessary amount of equity E.

Consider now an example with initially: $h = 0.8$, similar to the effective average haircut that the ECB applies; $\Lambda = 20\%$; $\Pi = 20\%$. If the banks do not take into account that the mostly liquid assets may become illiquid one day, then the banks will not hold any equity and the effective funding costs of the

Table 12.4. Equity needed to sustain short-term funding of two, under different assumptions regarding the central bank haircut (h) and the share of liquid assets

E*		**Share of liquid assets** (Λ + Π in good times; Λ in bad times)					
		0.001	**0.1**	**0.2**	**0.3**	**0.4**	**0.5**
	0.99	89.0	7.2	2.8	1.3	0.5	0.0
	0.9	7.9	3.3	1.6	0.7	0.2	0.0
h (haircut)	**0.8**	3.0	1.6	0.8	0.3	0.0	0.0
	0.7	1.3	0.7	0.3	0.0	0.0	0.0
	0.6	0.5	0.2	0.0	0.0	0.0	0.0
	0.5	0.0	0.0	0.0	0.0	0.0	0.0

bank are equal to the rate of remuneration of deposits, which we assumed to be equal to the central bank policy rate. Indeed, without any equity, the liquidity L that the bank can generate is equal to $(0.4*2 + 0.6*2*0.2) = 1.04 \geq 1$ and hence sufficient to sustain a unique no-run equilibrium.

If now, however, a (non-anticipated) crisis breaks out and the mostly liquid assets stop being liquid, then L drops to $L = (0.2*2 + 0.8*2*0.2) = 0.72 < 1$, and therefore, as shown in section 11.3, there is no longer a single no-run equilibrium, but there are now two equilibria, one characterized by a run and the default of the bank. Two cases can then be distinguished: first, that immediately a run starts, and indeed the bank defaults, with associated costs for society. Here we assume the favourable case that for some time no immediate bank run destroys the bank (i.e. the favourable of the two equilibria prevails). Still, in this case, the bank will have to adjust its funding structure in order to restore the uniqueness of the no-run equilibrium. The minimum equity holdings of the bank are now $E \geq 1/(1 - h + h\Lambda) - 2 = 0.8$. This need to hold equity in the new environment of less liquid assets, however, leads to an increase of average funding costs. The bank lending rates to the real economy need in principle to increase in parallel, which means a significant tightening of the effective monetary conditions.

The central bank could neutralize this effect by reducing the average haircut to 60%, as then, once again, no equity would be needed to sustain the stable no-run equilibrium. If the central bank has not yet reached the zero lower bound, it should prefer to lower its policy rate instead of compromising on its risk tolerance. Once the zero lower bound is reached, a compromise between the two conflicting targets could be considered. Acting also on the collateral side could help to prevent a deflationary spiral. At the same time it may create moral hazard if being anticipated. Diamond and Rajan (2012) also note this effect, as well as Chapman et al. (2010, 4), who conclude that 'if the central bank can commit not to repeat [it] in the future, a temporary surprise cut in the haircut can be welfare improving'.

In chapter 16, we will turn to the question of moral hazard caused by supportive central bank collateral policies in financial crisis, and the fact that *ex ante* liquidity regulation may be necessary to address this problem.

12.5 SECURITIES LENDING PROGRAMMES BY CENTRAL BANKS

Securities lending is a widespread activity in financial markets with various purposes (see e.g. Financial Stability Board, 2012). Securities lending involves a transfer of securities (such as shares or bonds) to a third party (the borrower), who will give the lender collateral in the form of other securities or cash and pay a fee (see e.g. Association of British Insurers et al., 2010, 2).

Central banks offer securities lending services in normal times for two purposes: first, for generating an additional investment return on their investment portfolios (domestic or foreign reserves); second, for some secondary policy purposes, such as to contribute to smoothening sovereign bond markets, acting as an agent to the Government.

During the financial crisis, a number of central banks activated special securities lending programmes (SLPs) to foster the funding liquidity of financial institutions. As these SLPs are 'securities against securities' and therefore do not constitute central bank credit operations, and as they are about providing something liquid (not cash, but liquid securities) against something less liquid, we present them as a collateral measure. In a securities lending programme conducted for crisis management purposes, the central bank provides liquid securities that it has on stock and that can be used by banks in interbank repo markets. This is particularly relevant, of course, when unsecured interbank markets, and interbank markets collateralized with less liquid assets, have broken down, such that the availability of additional liquid high-quality securities makes it possible to increase correspondingly interbank market volumes (see section 11.2 on the shrinkage of unsecured interbank markets in crisis, and section 11.4 on the reduced usability of less liquid assets as collateral in interbank repo during crises).

SLPs do not inject central bank money into banks under funding stress, and therefore do not change per se the central bank balance sheet. However, indirectly, by allowing additional interbank collateralized credit, they may allow for a more effective netting of the total dependence of the banking system on the central bank, and thereby also shorten the central bank balance sheet if it was previously inflated due to *absolute* central bank intermediation.

It may be noted that the collateral constraint of bank 2 does not depend on whether the central bank decides to widen its collateral set or introduces an SLP against the extra collateral set. The two approaches, however, are still fundamentally different in terms of control of the overnight interest rate. Imagine that one group of banks experiences deposit inflows, and that these banks have still a rather good perceived credit quality such that some interbank overnight trading takes place between these banks to adjust their liquidity position at the margin. Assume that this overnight interbank trading is measured as 'the' overnight rate of the currency. Then, under the alternative without SLPs, the overnight rate will be bound to the deposit facility rate, while under the alternative with an SLP, conditions in the market for reserves with the central bank will be neutral, and both the unsecured overnight rate between the liquid subset of banks and the repo rates between liquid and stressed banks can be in the middle of the corridor set by central bank rates.

Moreover, it could be argued that the SLP approach has the advantage that it keeps some segments of the interbank market active, and therefore engages markets in the allocation of credit in some sense. This also slows down the deterioration of credit lines and interbank contacts during a crisis, contributing to a faster recovery of markets when the main causes of a crisis have been overcome.

Finally, it should be noted that an SLP can also have additional effects if access is granted to entities which do not have access to normal central bank credit operations. If these entities normally receive bank credit, but lost that ability due to a crisis, then granting them access to an SLP may allow them to prevent default as it grants to them access to secured lending markets. Of course, alternatively, the central bank could also decide to grant them direct counterparty status for central bank credit operations.

Below, two crisis-related SLPs are summarized, as explained by their respective central banks.

The Fed's Term Securities Lending Facility (TSLF)

The TSLF was addressed to financial firms who had no access to the Fed's other liquidity facilities. According to the Federal Reserve's website,[3]

> in March 2008, the Federal Reserve established the Term Securities Lending Facility (TSLF) as a means of addressing the pressures faced by primary dealers in their access to term funding and collateral. Primary dealers often obtain funding by pledging securities as collateral. When the markets for the collateral became illiquid, primary dealers had increased difficulty obtaining funding and, therefore, were less able to support broader markets. The TSLF supported the liquidity of primary dealers and fostered improved conditions in financial markets more generally. Under this program, the Federal Reserve loaned relatively liquid

[3] http://www.federalreserve.gov/newsevents/reform_tslf.htm, accessed 10 August 2013.

> Treasury securities for a fee to primary dealers for one month in exchange for eligible collateral consisting of other, less liquid securities. Loans were allocated through auctions... TSLF auctions against Schedule 1 collateral were... closed on February 1, 2010. All securities loans made under the facility were repaid in full, with interest, in accordance with the terms of the facility.

The Bank of England's Special Liquidity Scheme (SLS)

According to Cross et al. (2010, 38), the Bank of England

> introduced the SLS in April 2008 to improve the liquidity position of the banking system by allowing banks to swap high-quality, but temporarily illiquid, mortgage-backed and other securities for UK Treasury bills. As the SLS was designed to deal with existing assets on banks' balance sheets following the unexpected closure of some asset-backed securities markets in 2007, only assets already on commercial banks' balance sheets at the end of 2007 were eligible collateral. Banks are required to pay a fee for the bills they borrow against this collateral. SLS swaps may be renewed for a period of up to three years... The drawdown window was extended to 30 January 2009. The last swaps under the SLS will therefore expire at the latest in January 2012, at which point the SLS will terminate. After the closure of the drawdown period, the Bank announced in February 2009 that Treasury bills with a face value of approximately £185 billion had been lent under the Scheme. Given its scale, the Bank's operations in the SLS are indemnified by the Government.

Cross et al. (2010, 38) also explain that the *Discount Window Facility* (DWF) of the Bank of England (which exists in addition to a normal borrowing facility) is offered (since October 2008) as a permanent SLP.

> Under the DWF, banks may borrow gilts against a wide range of collateral, at fees reflecting the type of collateral and the size of drawing. The terms were designed to be consistent with avoiding creating incentives for commercial banks to take greater liquidity risk in future. And they were also designed to protect the Bank itself against risk to its balance sheet. Transactions under the DWF will normally be for 30 days... The Bank is considering further widening the collateral eligible for use in the DWF, subject to the basic principle that the Bank must be able to value the underlying assets, and manage the associated risks.

13

Open Market Operations and Standing Facilities

13.1 THE USE AND WIDTH OF THE STANDING FACILITIES CORRIDOR

A number of major central banks have engineered during the crisis as a side product *a switch from a symmetric corridor approach* (see section 4.2) *to a one-directional standing facility-based approach* (see section 4.1 and chapter 10, as well as the balance sheets of central banks in the annex to this chapter). While in the case of the Fed and the Bank of England, this switch resulted from large-scale asset purchase programmes, in the case of the ECB it was the result of a market segmentation and the readiness of the ECB to intermediate the interbank market. In all cases, the main contributors to the overnight interbank market (as measured through the Fed funds rate in the US, and EONIA and SONIA in the euro area and UK, respectively) were put into a large excess reserves position and relied systematically on the deposit facility (or the remuneration of excess reserves). While this switch was not the main reason for the underlying measures, it was probably considered useful as it allowed:

(i) Keeping short-term interbank rates stable. Indeed, it is difficult to maintain a close control of overnight rates in a symmetric corridor system with reserve requirements and averaging and significant and varying money market impairment. In other words, day-to-day liquidity management and interest rate control were kept manageable thanks to this move.

(ii) Keeping a large number of banks in a comfortable liquidity position, contributing to the resilience of the financial system. This argument applies to the case of the US and UK, as indeed almost all banks were put into excess liquidity thanks to the asset purchase programmes. In the case of the euro area, the excess liquidity of those banks who contribute to EONIA was more a consequence of the crisis and reflected the lack of funding of other ('periphery') banks. To that extent, this second argument does not really apply to the euro area.

A change, notably a narrowing, in the width of the standing facilities corridor is an unconventional measure applied by a number of central banks during the financial crisis (see Bindseil and Jablecki, 2011a, 2011b for an overview of changes and of literature on the subject). Three considerations with regard to a narrowing of the corridor set by standing facilities may be particularly relevant, of which we will develop in detail the last one.

Better Control of Short-term Interest Rates

The most obvious motivation for narrowing the interest rate corridor is to lower short-term interest rate volatility, since overnight rates normally fluctuate within this corridor. This was also one of the official reasons provided by the Federal Reserve for introducing the remuneration of excess reserves during the crisis, which is equivalent to introducing an automated deposit facility (see also the press release of the Board of Governors of 5 November 2008). A lowering of the borrowing facility rate relative to the target rate contains interbank interest rate fluctuations as long as the stigma associated with its use does not add a significant premium and as long as there is sufficient collateral available.

Stigma Associated with the Use of the Borrowing Facility

In the US, the discount window had, for a long time, the stigma of being associated with emergency liquidity assistance, and hence with serious liquidity problems of the relevant bank. The Federal Reserve had itself contributed over decades, ever since 1920, to this stigmatization. Moreover, as noted previously, standing facilities were considered highly problematic by leading US academic economists (e.g. Friedman, 1982).

As bank treasurers know, nothing is more important for a bank than appearance and reputation with regards to liquidity buffers. An often-quoted case is that of Continental Illinois, which had to borrow $3.6 billion through the Federal Reserve discount window on 11 May 1984. This recourse became known, and made everyone believe that the bank must be in deep problems. This was a self-fulfilling assessment that led to the eventual end of the bank. The recourse of Barclay's to the Bank of England's discount window at the end of August 2007 for some hundreds of millions of pounds Sterling also found considerable attention and created nervousness in financial markets. According to *The Guardian* of 31 August 2007 (article by Ashley Seager, Larry Elliott, and Julia Kollewe):

> Barclays has been forced to borrow hundreds of millions of pounds from the Bank of England's emergency lending facility for the second time in a fortnight, it was revealed last night. In a hurried and emotive statement after London's markets had closed, Barclays attempted to calm fears that it faces a cash crisis. Rumours had circulated all day that Barclays was forced to go to the Bank of England after

the central bank said it had lent £1.6bn at its penal rate of 6.75%. It is thought that Barclays borrowed the entire amount. Barclays said: 'There are no liquidity issues in the UK markets. Barclays itself is flush with liquidity. In these challenging times the dramatisation of such situations is of no help to markets, their members or their customers.'

It was mentioned in section 12.2 that Armantier et al. (2011) estimate the stigma premium on the Fed's discount window post Lehman to be up to 37 basis points. Narrowing the penalty associated with a recourse to a central bank borrowing facility may reduce in addition stigmatization as it is an invitation to use the facility also for banks that do not have particular liquidity problems.

Making Cheaper Absolute Central Bank Intermediation to Moderate a Tightening of Monetary Conditions

Bindseil and Jablecki (2011a, 2011b) analyse the role of the width of the standing facilities corridor in conjunction with interbank transactions costs, applying the financial accounts model also used throughout this text. The Bindseil and Jablecki (2011b) model has been summarized in section 6.2. This model also makes it possible to capture the effects of parameter changes that are likely to occur in a crisis (namely the decrease in interbank market efficiency as captured by an increase of interbank transaction cost C_{MM} and the increased volatility of deposit shift shocks) on the recourse to standing facilities and the volatility of overnight rates, and on the role that the width of the standing facility corridor plays in these effects.

The model of Bindseil and Jablecki (2011a), which is a structural financial accounts model, shows how an interbank market breakdown makes the width of the corridor an essential parameter also for the transmission of monetary policy. It can be considered a concrete example of how the cost of financial intermediation can be integrated into monetary analysis, as outlined by Woodford (2010, 29–32), including the modelling of the impact of a concrete monetary policy instrument on this cost. The financial accounts in figure 13.1 are the basis of the model, whereby the notation is somewhat different relative to previous financial accounts variants, as the variables will be functions of structural parameters of demand and supply and marginal cost curves.

The Household

The household is assumed as previously to diversify its real assets into financial assets: deposits with the two banks and banknotes. The quantity of the latter is given. To keep the model as simple as possible, the deposit supply of the household is assumed to be proportional to the interest rate offered by banks (*b* being a positive constant):

$$D^S = bi \tag{13.1}$$

Households / Investors			
Real Assets	$E - D_1 - D_2 - B$	Household Equity	E
Deposits Bank 1	D_1		
Deposits Bank 2	D_2		
Banknotes	B		

Corporates			
Real assets	$L_1 + L_2$	Credits from banks	$L_1 + L_2$

Bank 1			
Lending to corporates	L_1	Household deposits	D_1
Deposits with CB	CBD_1	Credit from central bank	CBB_1
Interbank credit	Y	Interbank credit	0

Bank 2			
Lending to corporates	L_2	Household deposits	D_2
Deposits with CB	CBD_2	Credit from central bank	CBB_2
Interbank credit	0	Interbank credit	Y

Central Bank			
Credit to bank	$CBB_1 + CBB_2$	Banknotes	B
		Deposits of banks	$CBD_1 + CBD_2$

Fig. 13.1. A financial account representation to model the cost of interbank markets and central bank intermediation on the borrowing conditions of corporates

This reflects the opportunity costs of giving up real assets (beyond the ones given up to be able to hold banknotes). Inverted, one obtains the marginal valuation, or opportunity cost, curve of deposit holdings of the household:

$$MV_{HH}(D) = D / b \tag{13.2}$$

Total deposits of households with banks are split up into deposits with the two banks respectively, i.e. $D = D_1 + D_2$; the split will be explained when presenting the banking system.

Corporates

The demand for loans by corporates is assumed to be analogously simple (*R* and *d* being two positive constants):

$$L^D = R - di \tag{13.3}$$

Again, one may invert this to obtain a marginal valuation curve:

$$MV_{CORP}(L) = (R - L)/d \tag{13.4}$$

The total loan volume is split between the two banks, whereby the split will result from the relative competitive advantages of the two banks: $L = L_1 + L_2$. Assuming for a moment that we would be in a 'zero transaction cost world' in which intermediation is costless, we could simply set demand equal to supply to obtain:

$$i^* = (R - B)/(b + d) \text{ and } D^* = L^* - B = b(B - R)/(b + d) \tag{13.5}$$

With positive intermediation costs, the outcome is slightly more complicated, and will be case dependent. As the initial amount (value) of real assets in the economy is equal to the household equity E, and since this amount always remains the same, and since only households and the corporates will hold real assets, the real assets of the corporate $L_1 + L_2$ will have to be equal to the households' financial assets, i.e. to $D_1 + D_2 + B$.

The Banks

It is assumed that banks have (potentially) three types of assets: loans to corporates (L), interbank loans (Y), and deposits with the central bank (CBD). They also have (potentially) three types of liabilities: deposits from households (D); interbank liabilities (Y); recourse to a central bank borrowing facility (CBB; the maturity of which is not relevant in the present model, i.e. it does not matter if we have in mind an overnight facility, or open market operations at a longer maturity applying the fixed-rate full allotment procedure). Financial intermediation is costly and it is assumed that banks incur costs both when collecting deposits and when granting loans. The marginal cost functions of the two banks differ and are given by: $c_j^D = k_j D_j; c_j^L = p_j L_j$, where c_j^D is the marginal cost function of bank *j* in collecting deposits, and c_j^L is the marginal cost function of bank *j* in providing loans to corporates, with k_j, p_j (j = 1, 2) being positive constants. Assuming fully competitive bank behaviour, the deposit and loan provision volumes of the banks will maximize social welfare gains from financial intermediation. This assumes, in principle, that marginal costs of deposit collection and marginal costs of loan provision are in equilibrium, equal across banks. This will, however, hold only under certain circumstances. *Before* bringing the central bank and the interbank market into the picture, the problem is thus to maximize social welfare by choosing D_1, D_2, L_1, L_2 (with $D_1 = L_1$ and $D_2 = L_2$, and $D_1, D_2, L_1, L_2 > 0$). The assumption of an interbank market makes it possible to soften the constraint $D_1 = L_1$ and $D_2 = L_2$ into $D_1 + D_2 = L_1 + L_2$. At the same time, we need to make an assumption on interbank transaction costs, and deduct them from total welfare gains. Call

Y the interbank lending volume from Bank 1 to Bank 2 (if Bank 2 is the net lender, then Y is negative). Assume that marginal interbank lending costs are constant, namely C_{MM}. Hence, total costs of interbank trading will be $C_{MM}Y$.

The Central Bank

The demand of households for banknotes is assumed to be exogenous. The borrowing of banks from the central bank matching the amount of banknotes will further modify the constraints inherent in the balance sheets of the economic actors. In fact, if the banking system has a liquidity deficit vis-à-vis the central bank (and there is no deposit facility, or no reason to use it), then the constraint $D_1 + D_2 = L_1 + L_2$ is now replaced by $D_1 + D_2 + CBB_1 + CBB_2 = L_1 + L_2$. Moreover, $CBB_1 + CBB_2 = B$. It is implied that loans are always equal to the sum of deposits collected and banknotes in circulation: $L = D + B$. If the central bank offers both a borrowing facility and a deposit facility, but at different rates, there can be cases, as we will see, of one bank depositing with the central bank and one borrowing from the central bank.

The Equilibrium

The equilibrium financial intermediation, i.e. the level of deposits, loans, and respective interest rates (and hence the spread between the two) will be determined by the intersection of the gross demand curve for intermediation and the supply curve of such services. The gross *demand* curve is exogenous to the financial sector, and rather simply established. We assume that loan demand is in any case strong enough to support some extent of intermediation including deposit collection from households. The *gross rent* from deposit–loan intermediation corresponds to the difference in the two marginal valuation curves:

$$MV_{corp}\ L\ - MV_{HH}\ D = \frac{R-L}{d} - \frac{D}{b} = \frac{R-\ D+B}{d} - \frac{D}{b}$$
$$= \frac{R-B}{d} - \frac{b+d}{db} D \qquad (13.6)$$

The *supply* curve of intermediation services, i.e. the *marginal cost curve* of the (competitive) banking system taking into account the central bank issuance of banknotes and possible intermediation through standing facilities, is slightly more complex as we obtain a linear marginal cost curve with two kinks. The intermediation supply curve is characterized by proposition 1 in Bindseil and Jablecki (2011a), and proposition 2 in this paper states that there is a unique financial intermediation equilibrium which fully characterizes the financial accounts. It is important to note that in the model with two banks either interbank intermediation or central bank intermediation exists, but not both (even with two banks, equilibria with both forms of intermediation could be obtained if one assumed increasing, instead of constant marginal costs of interbank intermediation).

The total marginal cost curve of intermediation is to be understood as follows and is characterized by three segments.

First segment and first kink point: Comparative advantages of banks on both sides of their balance sheet can be fully reaped thanks to some *relative* central bank interbank intermediation. In this segment, the comparative advantages of banks in deposit collection and loan provision can be fully realized in the sense that both types of marginal costs are in equilibrium equal across banks (i.e. $c_1^D = c_2^D; c_1^L = c_1^L$). The costless bridge between the banks that allows this condition to be maintained until the first kink point is the *allocation of central bank funding between the two banks*, i.e. the two banks will share the central bank borrowing in such a way as to maintain equality of marginal costs across banks on both sides of the balance sheets. This implies that the bank with a comparative advantage in deposit collection will borrow a lower share from the central bank than the one with a comparative advantage in loan provision. It may be noted that if a costless interbank intermediation technology is available, then the total marginal cost curve of the provision of banking services continues as in the first segment and no kinks ever appear. Such a costless technology is either given by a perfectly efficient interbank market ($C_{MM} = 0$), or by a zero-width standing facilities corridor ($C_{COR} = 0$). The implied interbank lending volumes or the implied double-sided recourse to the two standing facilities can be easily calculated following the approach above for the splitting of the central bank borrowing. As shown in proposition 1 of Bindseil and Jablecki (2011b), kink point 1 is characterized as follows

$$K1 = (D^{K1}, c^{T,K1}) = \left(\frac{p_2(k_{1_1} + k_2)}{p_1 k_2 - p_2 k_1} B, p_2 k_2 \frac{p_1 + k_1}{p_1 k_2 - p_2 k_1} B \right) \quad (13.7)$$

And from D = 0 to the first kink point, the marginal cost curve of intermediation is:

$$c^{T,0->K1} = \frac{p_1 p_2}{p_1 + p_2} B + \left(\frac{k_1 k_2}{k_1 + k_2} + \frac{p_1 p_2}{p_1 + p_2} \right) D \quad (13.8)$$

Second segment and second kink point: Growing divergence of marginal cost until interbank intermediation sets in. Once the split of the total liquidity deficit of the banking system vis-à-vis the central bank has been used up as a bridge to ensure equality of marginal cost, the banking businesses of the two banks will grow for a while independently—and this makes up the second linear segment of the total marginal cost curve. Independent growth means that additional loans provided by Bank 1 are financed precisely by additional deposit collection of Bank 1, and additional loans extended by Bank 2 are financed precisely by additional deposits collected by Bank 2. This will lead immediately to a growing divergence of marginal costs across banks on both sides of their balance sheets and will continue *until the difference in the marginal costs justifies interbank intermediation*, which itself is costly (C_{MM}). For instance, bid–ask spreads in the short-term unsecured interbank market are at the order of magnitude of 5–10 basis points in normal times, and much higher in crisis times (and even prohibitive for many banks). Efficient extension of bank intermediation with two banks having to expand their business separately needs to follow the condition of equality of total marginal cost across banks. The split in the total growth of bank intermediation needs to be inversely proportional to the marginal cost growth, such that total marginal costs stay equal across banks. Kink point 2 is characterized as follows:

$$K2 = (D^{K2}, c^{T,K2}) = \left(D^{K1} + C_{MM} \frac{k_1 + p_1 + k_2 + p_2}{p_1 k_2 - p_2 k_1}, c^{T,K1} + C_{MM} \frac{(p_1 + k_1)(k_2 + p_2)}{p_1 k_2 - p_2 k_1} \right) \tag{13.9}$$

And from K1 to K2 the marginal cost curve of intermediation is:

$$c^{T,K1->K2} = c^{T,K1} + \left(\frac{(k_1 + p_1)(k_2 + p_2)}{k_1 + k_2 + p_1 + p_2} \right)(D - D^{K1}) \tag{13.10}$$

Third segment: Growing interbank trading (or absolute intermediation) to keep the difference of marginal cost across banks equal to interbank intermediation costs. At kink point 2, defined in the proposition above, interbank trading sets in because the divergence of marginal costs across banks for the two banking activities are as high as the transaction costs. Growth of the four activities (deposit collection and loan provision of each bank) will be again inversely proportional to the growth of marginal cost, and differences between marginal costs across banks will stay at the same level—namely, marginal interbank intermediation costs (transaction costs). The total marginal cost of bank intermediation grows again at the speed of segment 1 of the intermediation supply curve. The marginal cost curve of intermediation will thus be:

$$c^{T,K2\to\infty} = c^{T,K2} + \left(\frac{k_1 k_2}{k_1 + k_2} + \frac{p_1 p_2}{p_1 + p_2} \right)(D - D^{K2}) \tag{13.11}$$

It can also be shown that if the intersection of the demand and supply curves of financial intermediation is in the third segment total interbank trading will be:

$$Y = \left(\frac{k_2}{k_1 + k_2} + \frac{p_2}{p_1 + p_2} \right) (D - D^{K2}) \tag{13.12}$$

Otherwise interbank trading will be zero.

In normal times, when interbank markets are very efficient, and C_{MM} is close to zero, then obviously the second kink point is close to the first one, and at the limit (if $C_{MM} = 0$) the credit intermediation supply curve is one linear curve without kink. The buffering function provided by the differentiation of the recourse to the central bank is continued by the perfectly efficient interbank market. If the financial system enters a crisis situation, two model parameters are likely to change. First, C_{MM} increases, such that D^{K2} starts to distance itself more and more from D^{K1} and the intersection with the credit intermediation demand curve shifts up and to the left, indicating lower rents from financial intermediation. Second, the marginal cost curves of deposit collection of the two banks are likely to diverge more and more, with the cost of the stressed, reputation-damaged bank growing, and the cost of the safe haven bank declining. This will steepen the middle segment of the kinked curve, with a related impact on the intersection of the demand and supply curves for financial intermediation.

What is important to note is that in this model, there is *either* interbank trading *or* central bank intermediation, but never both (but possibly neither). If $C_{MM} < C_{COR}$, then there is no central bank intermediation, and if $C_{MM} > C_{COR}$, then there is no interbank market. Therefore, in a financial crisis: (i) one will observe at some stage a sudden switch of intermediation from the interbank market to the central bank; (ii) spreads between household deposit rates and corporate funding rates will increase; (iii) the quantity of financial intermediation will decline. The latter two have a real economic impact and will trigger recessionary dynamics. If the increase in C_{MM} and in the differences in marginal funding costs of banks is abrupt (as it likely to be in a financial crisis, as markets may break down from one moment to the next because of an adverse selection threshold being reached, or because of a bank run), then these crisis effects may also occur abruptly, with their impact on the real economy. The width of the standing facility corridor then suddenly switches from being an economically irrelevant parameter to being one of fundamental economic relevance. By lowering the width of the corridor, the central bank can in principle reverse the financial crisis effects on the real economy in the model. However, there are two important potential limitations to this: First, the central bank lending to the weak bank is limited by the collateral availability of the weak bank and the haircuts applied by the central bank. The central bank might address this partially by relaxing the collateral framework in a financial crisis.

Second, large-scale central bank intermediation may also be costly in itself to society. Normally, the market is expected to be superior in its allocation function, and the central bank should not play a larger than necessary role in financial intermediation as it has no competitive advantage in doing so.

Example

Consider now a concrete parameter specification and some comparative statistics of the model, which make it possible to obtain an idea of the impact of interbank market impairment on the capacity of the banking system to intermediate the real economy, and hence on the transmission of monetary policy, such as to be able also to identify the effectiveness of a narrowing of the corridor in order to counteract these effects. Table 13.1 provides the parameter specifications of five scenarios, as well as the model results in terms of financial intermediation equilibrium.

Scenario I: In this scenario the two banks are still relatively similar, in the sense that the only difference consists in the twice higher marginal cost of loan provision of Bank 1 compared to Bank 2. The overall efficiency of the banking system in intermediating is so high that the intersection of the supply and demand curves for financial intermediation is at a point in which the differentiated recourse of banks to the central bank ('relative' central bank intermediation) still equalizes marginal costs across banks, and therefore despite the low transaction costs in the interbank market (of 10 basis points), no interbank market activity takes place, i.e. the intersection of the two marginal cost curves is before the first kink of the intermediation supply curve. For assessing the transmission of monetary policy, the key model output in this case is a loan volume to corporates of 259 and a rate of bank loans to corporates of 4.82%.

Scenario II: Compared with scenario I, banks are now much more heterogeneous in their marginal costs of bank deposit collection and their marginal costs of loan provision, whereby for each bank, one of these costs is increased. Both changes may reflect a crisis environment: Higher marginal cost of deposit collection may reflect the cost for some banks in a crisis environment of combating, through additional marketing, nervousness of depositors who may doubt the soundness of the bank. Higher marginal cost of loan provision may reflect the extra costs, in a crisis environment, of assessing credit risks of corporates, or of finding corporates with assessable and satisfactory credit quality. At the same time, in scenario II, the cost of interbank intermediation (C_{MM}) is assumed to remain low, which implies that full use of interbank intermediation through money markets will be made to minimize the impact of the different comparative advantages of the two banks. In other words, the relative strengths of the two banks can be pooled effectively thanks to the still-available efficient interbank intermediation. In figure 13.2, these effects are visualized by the higher steepness of the first and last segment of the intermediation supply curve relative to

Table 13.1. Example from Bindseil and Jablecki (2011a)—model with five alternative specifications of financial intermediation parameters

Model parameters	I	II	III	IV	V
Household equity E	500	500	500	500	500
Household banknote demand B	100	100	100	100	100
Household preference parameter b	5000	5000	5000	5000	5000
Corporate technology parameter R	500	500	500	500	500
Corporate technology parameter d	5000	5000	5000	5000	5000
Marginal cost deposit collection Bank 1: k_1	0.010%	0.010%	0.010%	0.010%	0.010%
Marginal cost deposit collection Bank 2: k_2	0.010%	0.200%	0.200%	0.200%	0.200%
Marginal cost loan provision BANK 1: p_1	0.010%	0.020%	0.020%	0.020%	0.020%
Marginal cost loan provision BANK 2: p_2	0.005%	0.005%	0.005%	0.005%	0.005%
Interbank market transaction cost*: C_{MM}	0.10%	0.10%	0.50%	1.25%	2.00%
Width standing facilities corridor*: C_{COR}	2%	2%	2%	2%	2%
Resulting intermediation equilibrium					
Total intermediation volume D	159	141	135	125	120
Total loans to corporates	259	241	235	225	220
Interbank trading/CB intermediation	0	82	59	18	0
Deposit remuneration rate	3.18%	2.82%	2.70%	2.50%	2.40%
Corporate loan rate	4.82%	5.18%	5.30%	5.50%	5.60%
Cost of financial intermediation	1.64%	2.36%	2.60%	3.00%	3.20%

* In fact what matters for the intermediation equilibrium is min(CMM, CCOR), and not the respective levels of the two rates looked at separately.

scenario I (lower efficiency of the aggregate banking system because of increase of marginal cost parameters), and the short intermediate segment of this curve, the shortness resulting from the low interbank intermediation cost. The interbank market is active and the volume of loans from bank 1 to bank 2 is 82. For assessing the transmission of monetary policy, one may note that relative to scenario I, the corporate loan volume has declined from 259 to 241 and the interest rate applied on bank loans to corporates has risen from 4.82% to 5.18%. The effective monetary conditions (i.e. what is effectively transmitted to the real economy) have tightened due to the lowered efficiency of financial intermediation. If the central bank has not reached the zero lower bound to nominal interest rates, it may want to react accordingly by modifying the level of its operational target rate.

Scenarios III–V each assume an increase of interbank transaction costs C_{MM}, namely from the initial 10 basis points to 50, 125, and 200 basis points.

The effect is that the intermediate segment of the financial intermediation supply curve gradually lengthens, and as this part is the steepest amongst the three segments, the third segment is also gradually shifted upwards in parallel. The intersection of the gross marginal rent curve and the marginal cost curves of intermediation gradually shifts up and to the left, indicating that loan volumes decline and interest rates charged on corporate loans increase further. Note that under scenario V, the intersection of the gross marginal rent and the marginal cost of intermediation curves is in the intermediate segment of the latter curve. This also explains why interbank market volumes are again zero (although for different reasons than in scenario I).

The scenarios can also be re-interpreted to understand the effects of a narrowing of the standing facilities corridor by the central bank in case of highly impaired interbank markets. Assume that interbank markets are totally broken in the sense that the interbank transaction costs are above 2%, i.e. in any case higher than the corridor of standing facilities set by the central bank. Then, in the model, it is the central bank that would be used as interbank intermediary, and the scenarios II–V can be interpreted as reflecting different widths of the standing facilities corridor (under the non-existence of interbank markets). Thus, by narrowing the corridor to 1.25%, 0.50%, 0.10%, the central bank can support the effectiveness of the banking system as financial intermediary through 'absolute' central bank intermediation, and restore the corporate loan volumes and rates of the chosen scenario. It can thereby achieve more accommodating monetary conditions through this non-standard monetary policy tool.

Figure 13.2 illustrates further the financial intermediation equilibrium under the five parameter scenarios. The curve 'gross marginal rent' is the

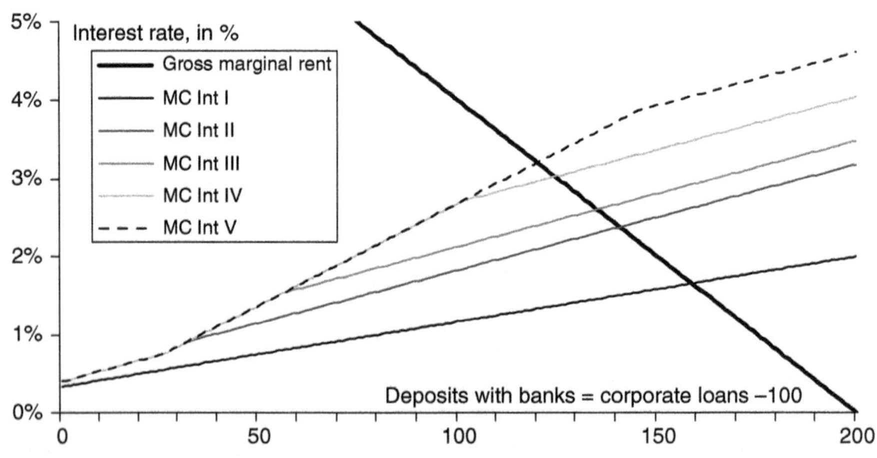

Fig. 13.2. Demand and supply of intermediation services under different scenarios of table 13.1

marginal rent that could be generated with a perfect, i.e. costless, financial intermediation between the household and the corporate sector. The curve 'MC Int I' is the marginal cost curve of financial intermediation under the parameter specifications of scenario I in table 13.1, and so on.

13.2 ADJUSTING CREDIT OPEN MARKET OPERATIONS

Lengthening of Maturity of Credit OMOs

Many central banks implemented a lengthening of the maturity of their credit open market operations during the crisis. For example the ECB had offered up to three-month credit operations between 1999 and 2007. It started to offer six-month operations in April 2008 (ECB press release of 28 March 2008), twelve-month operations in June 2009 (ECB press release of 7 May 2009), and three-year operations in December 2011 (ECB Press release of 8 December 2011).

Banks may consider a sequence of short-term borrowings from the central bank as inferior, from a liquidity risk perspective, to one longer-term borrowing operation. Consider three reasons for this: (i) Banks could perceive as uncertain the conditions under which central banks will provide short-term funding in the future (rates, access conditions, etc.). (ii) Even if the central bank commits to keep conditions for short-term access stable, e.g. it commits to full allotment at a given rate for its short-term operations for the next twelve months, banks may, as a matter of principle, find revolving short-term central bank refinancing less certain than twelve-month refinancing. (iii) Banks may be subject to some liquidity regulation, which treats longer-term refinancing from the central bank more favourably.

Taking an economic perspective, in a crisis the lowering of asset liquidity will make maturity transformation by banks more difficult, and lengthening of the central bank credit operations, together with a commitment not to tighten collateral rules, can reduce the deleveraging pressure resulting from this (or prevent an acute bank run).

Change of Auction Procedure for Credit Open Market Operations: Fixed-rate Full Allotment

The pros and cons of different central bank auction procedures is a science on its own (see for instance Ayuso and Repullo, 2003; Välimäki, 2003; or

Bindseil, 2005b). During the financial crisis, 'fixed rate full allotment' (FRFA) operations have been offered by a number of central banks, notably by the European Central Bank between October 2008 and at least June 2015. In principle, the *advantages* of this tender procedure, in particular during a crisis, are the following:

(i) It is even more automatic than the variable-rate tender with pre-announced volume. This is per se a positive feature, as automatism means simplicity and transparency and hence fewer potential mistakes by the central bank and the banks.

(ii) In a liquidity crisis, the reduction of banks' uncertainty about the results of the tender assuages liquidity risk.

(iii) Aggressive bidding in variable-rate tenders is avoided and with it high and more volatile marginal interest rates, which could imply an undesired stance of monetary policy (and unintended signals).

(iv) The central bank no longer needs to estimate which allotment amount would ensure that market rates remain close to target rates. Carrying out fixed-rate full allotment tenders is equivalent to setting standing facilities rates at the level of the target rate, with the only difference that an open market operation is not continuously open. This should bring short-term rates to the level of the fixed tender rates.

(v) The fact that open market operations resemble standing facilities underlines the commitment of the central bank to achieve its target rate in the market.

The *disadvantages* of the fixed-rate full allotment tender seem to be less relevant during a crisis:

(i) This tender modality has sometimes been criticized for introducing a random element into total allotment volumes as total bids of banks would not necessarily sum up to an appropriate aggregate amount corresponding to the liquidity needs of the banking system, also because of asymmetric information between the central bank and market participants (as mentioned in section 4.3). However, in an asymmetric corridor approach with structural reliance on one standing facility (see section 4.1), as practised e.g. in the US, UK, and euro area during 2010–2013, this is not an issue.

(ii) Fixed-rate full allotment tenders could crowd out the interbank market as they are so convenient for banks. While this may be a problem in normal times, in acute crisis times this seems to be a secondary issue.

(iii) For operations maturing beyond the subsequent date in which the central bank's interest rate-setting committee meets, applying fixed-rate tenders can lead to perceived arbitrage opportunities and unstable bidding behaviour. If, however, central banks have anyway reached the zero lower bound and stay there for long, this is not an issue. Moreover, the European Central Bank, for example, solved this issue by indexing its long-term credit operations to the rate applied in the shortest maturity operations (of one week).

(iv) Supporters of monetarist monetary policy implementation ('verticalists' to use the term of Moore, 1988) will (mistakenly) say that fixed-rate tenders with full allotment are as problematic as standing facilities, as they give away control over the monetary base. However, in financial crisis and if central banks have reached the zero lower bound, worries about inflation risks due to an uncontrolled monetary base are typically not considered by practitioners as a key problem.

Widening the Set of Eligible Counterparties

When interbank markets break down, then the financial institutions which are not central bank counterparties, but which could normally manage their day-to-day funding needs through credit operations with banks, are in trouble. Allowing direct central bank access makes them independent from the functioning of interbank markets. This can be considered as a first step in the direction of direct central bank lending towards the real sector. If all intermediation breaks down, then the central bank could, in principle, take over all of the roles previously played by other financial intermediaries. Of course, this extreme case is unrealistic and has serious drawbacks, such as the need to establish relationships with, and accommodate the operational needs of, non-bank counterparties while continuing to prudently manage risks (vis-à-vis all sorts of creditors with regard to which the central bank has little natural expertise). Under normal circumstances, a decentralized financial system is far more efficient than a centralized one. In the less extreme variant, in which the central bank extends counterparty status from a narrow subset of banks (like e.g. primary dealers) to all banks with which it has anyway account relations, the benefits easily outweigh costs in a crisis situation.

'Funding for Lending' Schemes

The Bank of England established in 2012 its 'funding for lending' scheme (FLS), a sort of credit facility which aims specifically at incentivizing banks to provide more loans to the small and medium-sized enterprises and mortgage borrowers (see Bank of England, 2012b). The FLS of the Bank of England is in fact a securities lending programme (see section 12.5), but would work similarly if it was a credit facility. The FLS provides incentives to banks as 'it encourages them to supply more credit by making more and cheaper funding available if they lend more' (Bank of England, 2012b, 306). It foresees a simple linear formula which determines how the net lending by the bank in a certain period affects (i) the total maximum access of the bank to the facility, and (ii) the rate charged. The preliminary conclusion on the working of the scheme is that it 'appears to have contributed to lower bank funding costs. There are early indications that it has begun to flow through into credit conditions, including falls in loan rates' (p. 315). In April 2013, the FLS was extended by a further year. In a news release of 3 June 2013, the Bank of England notes that 'Funding costs have fallen significantly since the announcement of the FLS, and remain at low levels. There is evidence that rates have fallen on mortgages, unsecured personal loans, and loans to businesses of all sizes.'

The Bank of Japan also operates a lending scheme with partially similar motivation, the 'Loan support programme' (LSP), which started in 2010. According to an announcement of the Bank of Japan (on its website) of 20 December 2012, it is 'a program established on the Bank's balance sheet to provide loans made against pooled collateral with the aim of supporting private financial institutions' efforts in strengthening the foundations for economic growth and stimulating bank lending, hereinafter the same'. It was 'introduced as a temporary measure to make the effect of monetary easing permeate the entire economy, with a view to achieving price stability and thereby contributing to the sound development of the national economy'. The basic idea is that banks who fulfil certain criteria in terms of lending to the real economy obtain long-term credit at favourable conditions from the Bank of Japan. As Bank of Japan (2010) explains:

> When a financial institution wishes to obtain loans from the Bank through the fund-provisioning measure, after becoming an eligible counterparty the financial institution must submit a plan of its initiatives to help strengthen the foundations for economic growth (hereafter 'the plan') and its actual record of individual investment or lending, and receive the Bank's confirmation. . . To receive funds in the Bank's first loan disbursement through this measure, financial institutions were required to have an actual record of new investment or lending under the plan in the period between April and June 2010. Of those financial institutions that submitted their plans, 47 institutions wished to receive funds from the Bank's first loan disbursement and submitted actual records of individual investment or lending.' (Bank of Japan 2010, 8)

The effectiveness of funding for lending schemes as non-conventional monetary policy tool in impaired market conditions is difficult to assess. In principle, the objective of directly supporting a specific bank asset class and the associated real economic activity seems legitimate when financial markets and monetary policy transmission are impaired. At the same time, as for any other non-conventional, focused monetary policy operation, it is important to explain what the origin of the market failure is, and whether one could not consider measures that directly address the root cause of the market failure, instead of healing a symptom. The closer a measure is to the root cause, and the less the measure requires the central bank to take views on the allocation of funding to real activity is, the better. For example, the limited willingness of banks to extend credit to the real economy in 2012–2013 in the UK, the euro area, or in Japan likely relates to (i) risk aversion of banks in view of scarce economic capital and the desire of banks to deleverage; (ii) scarce regulatory capital and regulatory uncertainty; (iii) a lack of economic projects that convincingly break even, i.e. of borrowers with good credit quality; or (iv) funding uncertainty. Policy measures closer to the root cause would be (i) recapitalizing banks, if needed with public money (diluting the old shareholders); (ii) easing monetary conditions (e.g. through lowering short-term interest rates, etc); (iii) maintaining a broad central bank collateral set so that banks know that they can, in case capital and interbank markets freeze, rely at least temporarily on central bank credit. A narrow focus on specific types of bank assets bears additional risks of allocative distortions and burdensome administrative procedures to prevent misuse.

Possibly, the popularity of funding for lending schemes also results from the fact that they represent an unconventional measure that is good to sell to the general public and the entire political spectrum. While other non-conventional measures have been heavily criticized by the right and left as bailing out greedy bankers, expropriate savers (low interest policies, QE programmes that depress long-term rates), or undermine incentives for fiscal consolidation (the ECB's sovereign debt purchase programmes), measures that direct banks to support (for once!) the 'real' economy and employment tend to meet wide support. If the need for public support is a real constraint to central bank measures, then the relative drawbacks of a funding for lending scheme (relative to other, economically more straightforward non-conventional central bank measures) may be accepted.

13.3 OUTRIGHT PURCHASE PROGRAMMES

All major central banks at some stage of the crisis that started in August 2007 established outright purchase programmes for financial assets. The following seven objectives of such measures can be identified.

(1) Anti-deflationary threat to 'purchase all real assets in the world'
(2) Creating excess reserves and relying on the money multiplier to generate monetary extension
(3) Bringing long-term risk-free yields down

(4) Compressing credit and liquidity spreads
(5) Taking risks into the central bank balance sheet and away from the banks, thereby easing capital constraints of banks
(6) Substituting illiquid with liquid assets in banks' balance sheets and thereby easing funding liquidity constraints of banks
(7) Directly supporting the funding liquidity of the issuing credit institutions or the real sector

All of these objectives relate to monetary policy. Functions (6) and (7) can also be understood as lender of last resort policies. Objectives (2) and (3) can be reached with purchases of risk free assets (normally sovereign bonds). Objectives (1) and (4) to (7) can be achieved only through purchases of credit-risky and/or relatively illiquid assets.

Outright purchases of assets as financial crisis central bank measures have always been more controversially debated than central bank credit provision against collateral. Already Wirth (1883, 528), a German economist and journalist, takes, on the grounds of moral hazard concerns, a clear position against asset purchases as central bank crisis measures (author's translation):

> The committee for emergency matters was able to stay away from one danger we had particularly warned it about: the outright purchases of securities. The most extensive secured lending, the most liberal discounting, even the provision of loans against collateral involving commercial goods are not as problematic as the purchase of securities. We must not recommend a medication of which the excessive consumption had itself caused the disease. Through outright purchases, one removes the responsibility of speculators, and one offers them the chance to restart playing the same game. The reasons for the crisis are not removed by that, the liquidation is only postponed to eventually return in an even more threatening form. After a while, it will appear that even this tool no longer works. In contrast, through collateralized lending, one achieves the strictly necessary, the confidence crisis and thereby the hoarding of cash is attenuated... Even the most liberal collateralized lending and discounting maintain that speculators are forced to put their things in order.

In 2013, critical views on outright purchase programmes by the ECB even made it to the German constitutional court for a two-day hearing on 10 and 11 June (see e.g. Schachtschneider, 2012, for one of the constitutional complaints against the ECB's 'outright monetary transaction' programme).

The rest of this section will not attempt to provide a comprehensive model of the effectiveness of asset purchase programmes, but will simply describe somewhat more the seven motivations behind asset purchase programmes. Harrison (2012), Curdia and Woodford (2011), Gertler and Karadi (2013), and Brunnermeier and Sannikov (2013), amongst others, provide state of the art macroeconomic models for analysing asset purchase programmes as a monetary policy tool.

(1) Anti-Deflationary Threat to 'Purchase All Real Assets in the World'

Besides hyperinflation, the biggest trauma to the monetary theorist *and* the monetary practitioner is the deflationary trap, as experienced to some extent by Japan since the bursting of its asset price bubble in the early 1990s, and as feared during 2002–2003 and again ten years later also in the western hemisphere (the basic problem of the zero lower bound was explained in chapter 3 and section 11.8). An escape seems however to relate to the central bank's ability in principle to purchase all assets of the world with the money that it can issue without constraints, in particular if the purchasing power of its currency seems to be ever-increasing. At some stage, when the central bank launches such a universal purchase programme, the other economic agents will become less willing to sell all their assets (including equity, commodities, etc.), they will require higher prices, and hence the purchasing power of the currency will fall. This will be anticipated, and a credible announcement of intention to purchase huge amounts of assets could immediately defeat deflationary pressures.

(2) Creating Excess Reserves and Waiting for the Money Multiplier to Generate Monetary Extension

Large-scale outright purchase programmes imply that large parts of the banking system end in a liquidity surplus position towards the central bank, such as happened in the US, the UK, and Japan from 2009 to 2013. This may be at least a welcome side-product of asset purchase programmes as it facilitates central bank liquidity management and the control of the overnight rate, and as a situation of general excess reserves may support the perception of financial stability.

Beyond these objectives, excess reserves targets play a role in the 'money supply' approach to monetary policy implementation as summarized in section 3.3, and have been applied as monetary policy instrument at the zero lower bound in particular by the Bank of Japan. Excess reserves relative to required reserves can be injected into the banking system either via outright purchases or via collateralized lending operations, whereby the latter may reach its limits earlier as it is not obvious how to convince banks to participate in credit operations in which they obtain further reserves, if anyway there is a general excess of reserves. In contrast, the central bank can always purchase assets, even in a situation of huge excess reserves. Excess reserves targets played a relatively minor role in the crisis that started in August of 2007, but were a core tool in the Bank of Japan policies from 2001 to 2006, and reflect the logic of textbook monetary economics during most of the twentieth century. For example, following their money multiplier view of the world, Friedman and Schwartz (1963, 398–9) heavily criticized the Federal Reserve System, suggesting that it would have engineered the financial meltdown through liquidity absorption via open market operations:

> Suppose the system had...purchase[d]...government securities...Reserve purchases of $1 billion of government securities would have meant an increase of $1,330 million in high powered money. That sum would have provided the whole $720 million in currency withdrawn by the public and at the same time have enabled bank reserves to increase by $610 million...The increase in bank reserves would have permitted a multiple expansion in deposits instead of the multiple contraction that actually took place.

What Friedman and Schwartz had in mind is a quantitative (i.e. interest rate-free) monetary policy implementation, in which the transmission channel can be summarized as follows: 'additional open market operations => higher level of excess reserves => increase of monetary aggregates through the money multiplier => real effects on inflation and output' (see also section 3.3).

After the bursting of the stock market bubble in Japan at the beginning of the 1990s, a series of reductions of interest rates did not help to revive the economy and, eventually, the zero lower bound to the setting of the interest rate target prevented the implementation of an adequately loose monetary policy stance, while the price level started to fall year after year bringing about a positive real interest rate. A *Bank of Japan* press release on 19 March 2001 explained the solution chosen at that time as follows:

> The main operating target for money market operations be changed from the current uncollateralized overnight call rate to the outstanding balance of the current accounts at the Bank of Japan. Under the new procedures, the Bank provides ample liquidity. b) Duration of the new procedures: The new procedures for money market operations continue to be in place until the consumer price index (excluding perishables, on a nationwide statistics) registers stably a zero percent or an increase year on year. c) Increase in the current-account balance at the Bank of Japan and declines in interest rates. For the time being, the balance outstanding at the Bank's current accounts be increased to around 5 trillion yen, or 1 trillion yen increase from the average outstanding of 4 trillion yen in February 2001. As a consequence, it is anticipated that the uncollateralized overnight call rate will significantly decline from the current target level of 0.15 percent and stay close to zero percent under normal circumstances.

After March 2001, the Bank of Japan several times raised its excess reserves target. For instance, in the one-month reserve maintenance period ending in May 2002, actual current accounts of banks subject to reserve requirements amounted to 13.8 trillion yen, against reserve requirements of 4.5 trillion yen, implying average excess reserves of 9.3 billion yen. What may have convinced the Bank of Japan to adopt quantitative operational targets (years after these had been dismissed by most other central banks)? First, the key argument against quantitative operational targets, that they imply a loss of control and actually huge volatility of short-term interest rates, is no longer valid under the assumption that the market is anyway left with an excess of reserves that forces short-term rates to zero. Second, although it may be unclear how exactly an excess reserves target is supposed to help to come out of the deflationary trap, it at least seems unlikely to harm.

The Bank of Japan put renewed emphasis on this channel in the context of the 'quantitative and qualitative easing' programme launched in 2013. In a press release of 4 April 2013, the Bank of Japan announced its intention to 'double the monetary base' within two years, and that 'with a view to pursuing quantitative monetary easing, the main operating target for money market operations is changed from the uncollateralized overnight call rate to the monetary base'. Moreover, 'under this guideline, the monetary base—whose amount outstanding was 138 trillion yen at end-2012 is expected to reach 200 trillion yen at end-2013 and 270 trillion yen at end-2014'.

The US Fed and the ECB have not put any emphasis on this channel during the current crisis. The Chairman of the Federal Reserve, Bernanke, discussed explicitly this issue in a speech of 13 January 2009 ('The crisis and the policy response'):

> Credit Easing versus Quantitative Easing. The Federal Reserve's approach to supporting credit markets is conceptually distinct from quantitative easing (QE), the policy approach used by the Bank of Japan from 2001 to 2006. Our approach—which could be described as 'credit easing'—resembles quantitative easing in one respect: It involves an expansion of the central bank's balance sheet. However, in a pure QE regime, the focus of policy is the quantity of bank reserves, which are liabilities of the central bank; . . . the Federal Reserve's credit easing approach focuses on the mix of loans and securities that it holds and on how this composition of assets affects credit conditions for households and businesses. This difference does not reflect any doctrinal disagreement with the Japanese approach, but rather the differences in financial and economic conditions between the two episodes. In particular, credit spreads are much wider and credit markets more dysfunctional in the United States today than was the case during the Japanese experiment with quantitative easing. To stimulate aggregate demand in the current environment, the Federal Reserve must focus its policies on reducing those spreads and improving the functioning of private credit markets more generally.

Since the massive purchase of assets by the Federal Reserve during the crisis led to an increase of reserves, the Federal Reserve could have explained the motivation behind these measures also in terms of a money multiplier channel. If it did not, then it must be because it no longer believed in its relevance (even if the quotation above makes the point that the differences were not a matter of doctrine, but of the details of the crisis).

Finally, **the Bank of England** explained its quantitative easing programme during the crisis, and precisely in the first quarter of 2009, with an argumentation reminiscent of quantitative easing working via the liability side of the central bank balance sheet and via the money multiplier. However, the 'pumping money into the economy' framing of the outright purchase programme of the Bank of England was used essentially for the large public. In contrast, the working paper by the Bank of England staff members Joyce et al. (2010) analysing the effectiveness of the purchase programme is focused on the achieved reduction of long-term sovereign yields, and does not contain a single reference to an excess reserves or money multiplier channel. Joyce et al. (2011, 202) explain further, when reviewing the different channels of the Bank of England's QE approach:

> When assets are purchased from non-banks... the banking sector gains both new reserves at the Bank of England and a corresponding increase in customer deposits. A higher level of liquid assets could then encourage banks to extend more new loans than they otherwise would have done. But, given the strains in the financial system at the time and the resultant pressures on banks to reduce the size of their balance sheets, the MPC expected little impact through this channel.

(3) Bringing Long-Term Risk-Free Yields Down

Central banks normally target only the short end of the yield curve, i.e. overnight rates. However, central banks know that the transmission of monetary policy goes through longer-term rates, as most economic decisions (e.g. building a house or a new plant) depend on longer-term rates (see section 11.8). Longer-term rates reflect an average of expected short-term rates, plus a term premium (according to the expectations hypothesis of the term structure of interest rates). Besides forward guidance, the purchase of long-term sovereign bonds is the most common approach of central banks to flatten the yield curve and therefore ease monetary conditions further when short-term rates have reached the zero lower bound. The central bank may also buy long-term private bonds, which has, however, additional effects. Attempts of central banks to control longer-term rates have quite a history of ambiguous success. Especially from the 1930s to the 1950s, outright open market operations were considered useful because they would make it possible, through an adequate choice of the maturity of the paper bought/sold outright, to influence directly longer-term interest rates and, even more ambitiously, the overall shape of the yield curve (see e.g. Meulendyke, 1998).

Normally, one would expect that bringing down long-term risk free yields also shifts down credit-risky yields, assuming constant credit and liquidity spreads. To that extent, lower risk-free yields should benefit all indebted agents in the economy. Gagnon et al. (2010) explicitly discuss the transmission of this effect between the risk-free and the risky rates:

> These portfolio-balance effects should not only reduce longer-term yields on the assets being purchased, but also spill over into the yields on other assets. The reason is that investors view different assets as substitutes and, in response to changes in the relative rates of return, will attempt to buy more of the assets with higher relative returns. In this case, lower prospective returns on agency debt, agency MBS, and Treasury securities should cause investors to seek to shift some of their portfolios into other assets, such as corporate bonds and equities, and thus should bid up their prices. It is through the broad array of all asset prices that the LSAPs [large scale asset purchase programmes] would be expected to provide stimulus to economic activity.

(4) Compressing Credit and Liquidity Spreads

In a financial crisis, risky assets' prices may be unduly depressed due to asset fire sales and the absence of optimistic buyers looking for bargains. More generally, the usual arbitrage between asset classes may no longer work because of liquidity and capital constraints, systemic uncertainty, and self-fulfilling fears. In such an environment, the central bank can, through purchases of the unduly depressed assets, directly affect parts of the universe of yields relevant for monetary policy transmission, and thereby ease funding costs and constraints. Of course, central banks should not compress spreads below a 'reasonable' risk premium in view of the higher credit risk and lower liquidity of a security. Assessing what is an appropriate spread is of course challenging.

(5) Taking Risks into the Central Bank Balance Sheet and Easing Capital Constraints on Banks

The central bank may reduce total risk in banks' balance sheets by buying outright credit- and market-risky assets from them. Therefore, if banks feel constrained in terms of economic or regulatory capital, outright purchases by central banks may attenuate these constraints and thereby influence positively their lending and in this sense ease effective monetary conditions felt by the real sector. In deciding on asset purchases, the central bank should keep in mind that it is unlikely to be competitive in assessing complex credit-risky assets. Therefore, while accepting some credit risk, it may want to take it via relatively straightforward assets, such as corporate bonds, commercial paper, equity, conventional standard asset-backed securities (e.g. plain vanilla residential mortgage-backed securities), or covered bonds, and also diversify sufficiently. Rating thresholds should be set such as to reflect market (i.e. institutional investor) standards. While only the Bank of Japan is explicit on this channel with regard to its equity purchases, it is plausible that all private paper purchase programmes of central banks implicitly also consider this effect as relevant.

(6) Substituting Banks' Illiquid with Liquid Assets to Improve Funding Liquidity of Banks

Purchasing outright assets helps liquidity only if the assets purchased by the central bank were previously not accepted by it as collateral, or were only accepted with high haircuts. If the assets that replace the illiquid securities in the banks' balance sheets are treasury paper, maybe because the central bank has sold them when buying the private paper, then these could also be used to re-activate the interbank repo market, which, in a crisis, mainly relies on such securities.

(7) Directly Supporting the Funding Liquidity of the Issuing Credit Institutions or the Real Sector

By purchasing in the primary market bonds from issuers (unsecured bank bonds, covered bank bonds, corporate bonds, etc.), the central bank can support in the most direct and obvious way the funding liquidity of these institutions. The forced shrinking of bank balance sheets during financial crises leads to a general unwillingness of banks to enter new lending business or to purchase or trade or support with liquidity the issuance of risky private debt instruments. During the crisis that started in August 2007, many banks were said to 'have retrenched to a pure broker-style trading model, whereby they will only stand between buyers and sellers when they can match both sides exactly. This is because they no longer want to hold bonds, or much else on their trading books for any period, be it days or weeks... Banks are very constrained. They are no longer dealing in the market because they cannot afford to take even temporary positions' (*Financial Times*, 25 March 2009). In line with this, for example, BusinessEurope, Europe's biggest employers' group, issued a press statement on 18 March 2009 according to which 'Access to finance is a major concern of business today... G20 Central Banks should engage in the purchase of short-term debt instruments issued by non-financial corporations (e.g. commercial paper, certificate of deposits, etc....) in order to reduce the cost and restore access to financing for a broad range of companies.'

Central bank purchases of private paper, if done in the primary market, directly refinance the real sector and thus can, at least partially, offset the unwillingness of banks to provide their usual lending and liquidity services. Moreover, secondary market purchases can indirectly support primary markets. A general problem with the direct refinancing of the real sector is the limited central bank expertise in commercial banking. If banks no longer lend and the central bank has to take over this function, then the human expertise in banks on such credit business is idle, while the central bank lacks this expertise. A more efficient solution seems to be to get banks lending again to the real sector through some other means, namely by overcoming the liquidity and capital constraints that prevent them from continuing their normal lending business.

Finally, it may be noted that this argument can also be presented, in principle, within the LOLR logic applied in sections 11.3 and 12.4 to banks. The readiness of the central bank to conduct outright purchases of debt instruments issued by non-banks can make the difference for the issuer's ability to maintain stable funding, in as much as it can ensure the uniqueness of a no-run equilibrium for the deposits of a bank. If in good times (in terms of asset liquidity) the corporate and/or government sectors leveraged themselves extensively on the basis of the assumption that there would be no bad times, but the bad times materialize, then it is in the hand of the central bank to restore funding stability by switching to a more supportive stance in terms of possible debt purchases (similar to the option to lower haircuts on bank assets when used as central bank collateral). It is important to note that the LOLR role does not necessarily imply actual purchases, as the readiness to act as LOLR in itself ideally restores market access. As mentioned previously, at least De Grauwe (2011) and Buiter and Rahbari (2012a) argue that for Governments, such a lender of last resort can make the difference in terms of maintaining market access (see section 11.3).

The Size and Effectiveness of Asset Purchase Programmes with Regard to Purposes 3 and 4

Table 13.2 on the quantities of purchases of sovereign and private assets is an excerpt from Fawley and Neely (2013). It provides evidence that the Bank of Japan bought more financial assets relative to GDP than any other central bank, followed by the Band of England, the Fed, and, by far in the last place, the Eurosystem.

The *effectiveness* of asset purchase programmes to reduce risk-free yields and credit spreads was analysed for the UK by Joyce et al. (2010), and by D'Amico and King (2010) and Gagnon et al. (2010) for the US Fed. These studies confirm some permanent effect on long-term yields. Hamilton and Wu (2012) estimate the effects of LSAPs on long-term yields and find that purchases for USD 400 billion in long maturity bonds would imply a reduction in long-term

Table 13.2. Asset purchase programmes of four central banks—in absolute numbers (billions, local currency) and in parentheses in % of GDP

	Public asset purchases	Private asset purchases
US Fed	1567 (12%)	1585 (12%)
Bank of England	375 (26%)	4 (0.2%)
Eurosystem	220 (2.4%)	80** (0.9%)
Bank of Japan	175300 (34.9%)	11630 (2.3%)

* Including maturity extension **Corrected by the fact that the second covered bond purchase programme ended with EUR 20 billion purchases.
Source: Fawley and Neely (2013), Table 2.

yields of 13 basis points. A comprehensive overview of studies on the effectiveness of LSAPs to lower yields and spreads is provided by Kozicki et al. (2011), Table 1; see also International Monetary Fund (2013). Accordingly, the impact on longer-term yields of asset purchase programmes would have been from a few to up to 100 basis points, depending on the programme and the study.

13.4 DANGERS OF TOO ACCOMMODATING POLICIES

Chapter 16 will look at moral hazard issues relating to the LOLR function of the central bank. Here, some more general monetary and economic policy drawbacks of a too-supportive monetary policy stance in a financial crisis will be briefly discussed, following the BIS annual reports (Bank for International Settlements, 2012, 2013, chapter IV in each). The BIS elaborates on four dangers of a too accommodative policy (BIS, 2012, 42–5).

First, prolonged unusually accommodating monetary conditions could mask underlying balance sheet problems and reduce incentives to address them head-on. Necessary fiscal consolidation and structural reform to restore fiscal sustainability could be delayed. BIS (2012, 48) also argues that 'A vicious circle can develop, with a widening gap between what central banks are expected to deliver and what they can actually deliver,' and that there is a risk of 'growing political economy risks,' also since 'Central banks' balance sheet policies have blurred the line between monetary and fiscal policy.' Moreover (p. 42),

> Similarly, large-scale asset purchases and unconditional liquidity support together with very low interest rates can undermine the perceived need to deal with banks' impaired assets. Banks are indeed still struggling with the legacy of the global financial crisis and often depend heavily on central bank funding...And low

> interest rates reduce the opportunity cost of carrying non-performing loans and may lead banks to overestimate repayment capacity. All this could perpetuate weak balance sheets and lead to a misallocation of credit.

The latter argument seems to relate to the findings of Caballero et al. (2008), who argue that continued 'zombie lending' by banks to in principle insolvent companies prolonged the depression in Japan and lowered productivity growth.

Second, 'monetary easing may over time undermine banks' profitability. The level of short-term interest rates and the slope of the yield curve are both positively associated with banks' net interest income as a result of their positive effects on deposit margins and on the returns from maturity transformation, respectively'. Moreover, 'Low returns on fixed income assets also create difficulties for life insurance companies and pension funds'.

Third, 'low short- and long-term interest rates may create risks of renewed excessive risk-taking…low interest rates can over time foster the build-up of financial vulnerabilities by triggering a search for yield in unwelcome segments.' This conclusion is also drawn by Farhi and Tirole (2012, 64), who argue that 'Loose interest rate policies today increase the likelihood of future crises. First, they signal the central bank's willingness to accommodate maturity mismatches and deprive it of future credibility. Second, they stimulate new maturity mismatches through a price effect: they make short-term debt cheaper, encouraging maturity mismatches…'

Fourth, 'aggressive and protracted monetary accommodation may distort financial markets. Low interest rates and central bank balance sheet policy measures have changed the dynamics of overnight money markets, which may complicate the exit from monetary accommodation.'

These arguments seem to suggest that the eventual monetary policy objectives would provide quite some degrees of freedom, and that within those, the central banks would have chosen to be on the (unnecessarily) accommodating side, creating the above-mentioned risks. However, it could also be argued that if a deflationary environment persists, a Wicksellian central banker (see chapter 3) should see no other choice than trying with all means to be accommodating, as acting too little and too late may deepen the deflationary problem. The Wicksellian central banker would not accept that there are substantial degrees of freedom in choosing the stance of monetary policy, and would maintain that it was still in 2012 and 2013 the only adequate policy of the central banks in industrialized countries to maintain very accommodating policies. Therefore, for instance, the argument that the low-rate environment created by central banks would depress profitability of banks and insurance and pension funds would be invalidated: the real rates of return are given by the real economy, and there is no way for the central bank to affect positively real rates. The central bank can only help at preventing a deflation, which would be even more harmful for the entire financial sector and the real economy.

ANNEX: CENTRAL BANK BALANCE SHEETS DURING THE CRISIS

In figures 4.8, 4.9, and 7.1, pre-crisis balance sheets of the Bank of England, the US Fed, and the Eurosystem were presented. This annex provides balance sheets of the same central banks during the financial crisis. Two types of financial crisis central bank balance sheets may be distinguished.

Central Bank Balance Sheet Expansion due to Intermediation Between Banks, Reflecting the Lender of Last Resort Function of the Central Bank

The balance sheet of the Eurosystem during the entire financial crisis (from Lehman to end 2013) and the Fed and Bank of England balance sheets during around 6–12 months after Lehman were characterized by central bank intermediation between banks substituting for the broken interbank market. Banks with excess reserves were reluctant to lend to funding-stressed banks, so that the latter had to take correspondingly higher recourse to central bank funding. In particular in the case of the Eurosystem, the two-directional recourse of the banking system to the central bank took place first of all on the basis of the built-in flexibility of the system, relying on existing non-encumbered central bank-eligible collateral. In addition, most central banks supported their interbank intermediation function through active measures, such as a widening of the collateral set, or a more convenient format of the liquidity-providing operations (e.g. fixed-rate full allotment operation; extension of maturity) or a narrowing of the corridor set by standing facilities.

Figure 2.10 in chapter 2 already provided a Eurosystem balance sheet as of 24 February 2012, which showed a two-directional recourse to the central bank, lengthening the Eurosystem balance sheet by around EUR 700 billion. Figure 13A.1 presents the post-Lehman Eurosystem balance sheet as of 2 January 2009.

The balance sheet reveals that after Lehman, USD liquidity provision to Eurosystem counterparties played an important role (EUR 189 billion), refinanced by the Eurosystem through a swap facility with the US Fed (see chapter 17). The lengthening of the balance sheet due to central bank intermediation between banks is essentially reflected in the EUR 282 billion recourse to the deposit facility (it should be noted that required reserves were still at around EUR 200 billion in 2009, while in February 2012, as reflected in figure 2.10, they had been halved and stood at around EUR 100 billion).

Figure 13A.2 shows the Bank of England balance sheet on 2 January 2009. Like the Eurosystem, the Bank of England provided US dollars to its counterparties (for GBP 23 billion), and refinanced them through a swap with the Fed (see chapter 17). The extent of central bank intermediation can be measured broadly by the liquidity-absorbing operations of GBP 101 billion.

Finally, the Fed balance sheet of January 2009 provides a similar picture of central bank intermediation between banks, as shown in figure 13A.3.

Outright holdings of securities (at that time still only Treasuries) had actually been reduced relative to the pre-crisis level (see the Fed 2007 balance sheet shown in figure 7.1). Large additional liquidity injections did not only take the form of credit operations (in particular the term auction facility TAF, providing three-month funds against the wide collateral set of the discount window), but also of lending to special

Eurosystem, 2 January 2009 (in billion euro)			
Autonomous factors		**Autonomous factors**	
Net Foreign assets	392	Banknotes	764
Domestic investment assets	320	Government deposits	85
		Net other autonomous factors	216
Monetary policy operations			
USD providing operations	189	Liability to the US Fed	189
Outright holdings	0		
Short term credit operations	240	Liquidity absorbing operations	9
Longer term credit operations	617	Deposit facility	282
Borrowing facility	1	**Current accounts of banks**	**213**
Sum	**1758**	**Sum**	**1758**

Fig. 13A.1. Stylized Eurosystem balance sheet, 2 January 2009

Bank of England, 2 January 2009 (in billion GBP)			
Autonomous factors		**Autonomous factors**	
		Banknotes	45
		Net other autonomous factors	33
Monetary policy operations			
USD repos	23	Liabilities to US Fed	23
Domestic assets held outright	45		
Short term credit operations		Liquidity absorbing operations	101
Longer term credit operations	190		
Borrowing facility	0	**Current accounts of banks**	**56**
Sum	**258**	**Sum**	**258**

Fig. 13A.2. Bank of England balance sheet, 2 January 2009

Federal Reserve System, 2 January 2009 (in billion USD)			
Autonomous factors		**Autonomous factors**	
Net Foreign assets	38	Banknotes	848
Central bank liquidity swaps	538	Government deposits	63
Lending to specific institutions	408	**Other autonomous factors**	**216**
Monetary policy operations		**Monetary policy operations**	
Outright holdings	495	Reverse repo operations	89
Credit operations	444		
Borrowing facility (discount window)	139	**Deposits of banks**	**846**
Sum	**2062**	**Sum**	**2062**

Fig. 13A.3. US Fed Balance sheet, 2 January 2009

Bank of England, 2 January 2013 (in billion GBP)			
Autonomous factors		**Autonomous factors**	
		Banknotes	60
		Net other autonomous factors	76
Monetary policy operations			
Domestic assets held outright	404		
Short term credit operations			
Longer term credit operations	6		
Borrowing facility	0	**Current accounts of banks**	274
Sum	410	**Sum**	410

Fig. 13A.4. Bank of England Balance sheet, 2 January 2013, in billion of GBP
Source: Bank of England.

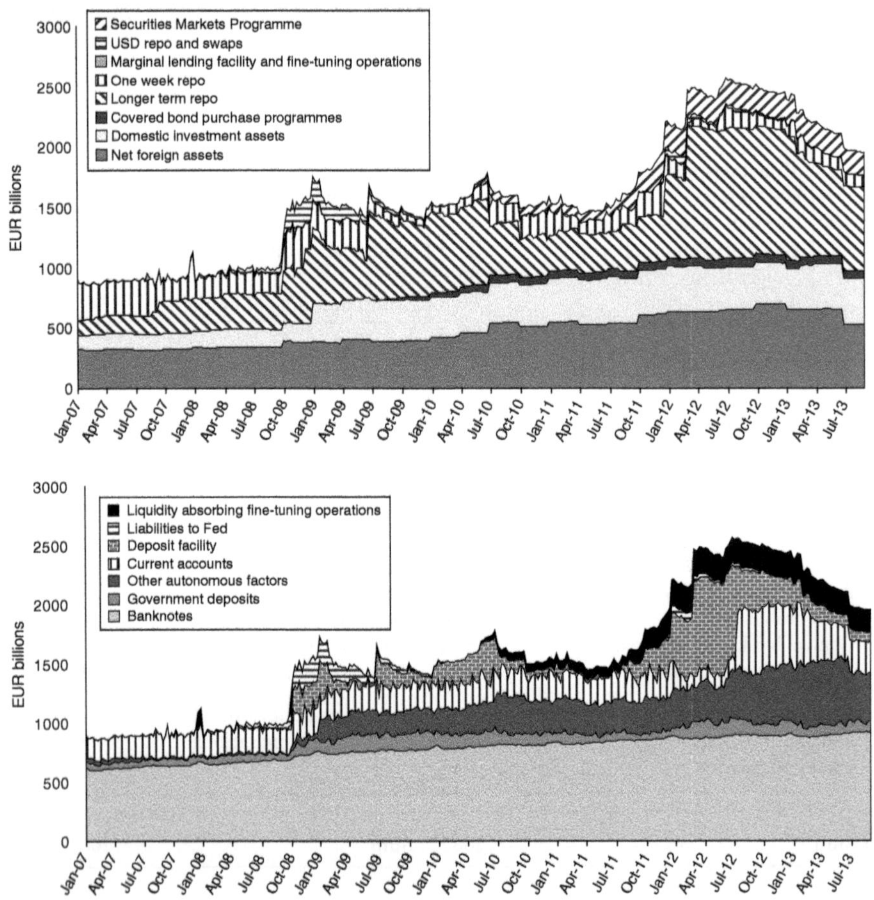

Fig. 13A.5. Evolution of assets and liabilities of the Eurosystem, January 2007–August 2013, in billion EUR
Source: ECB.

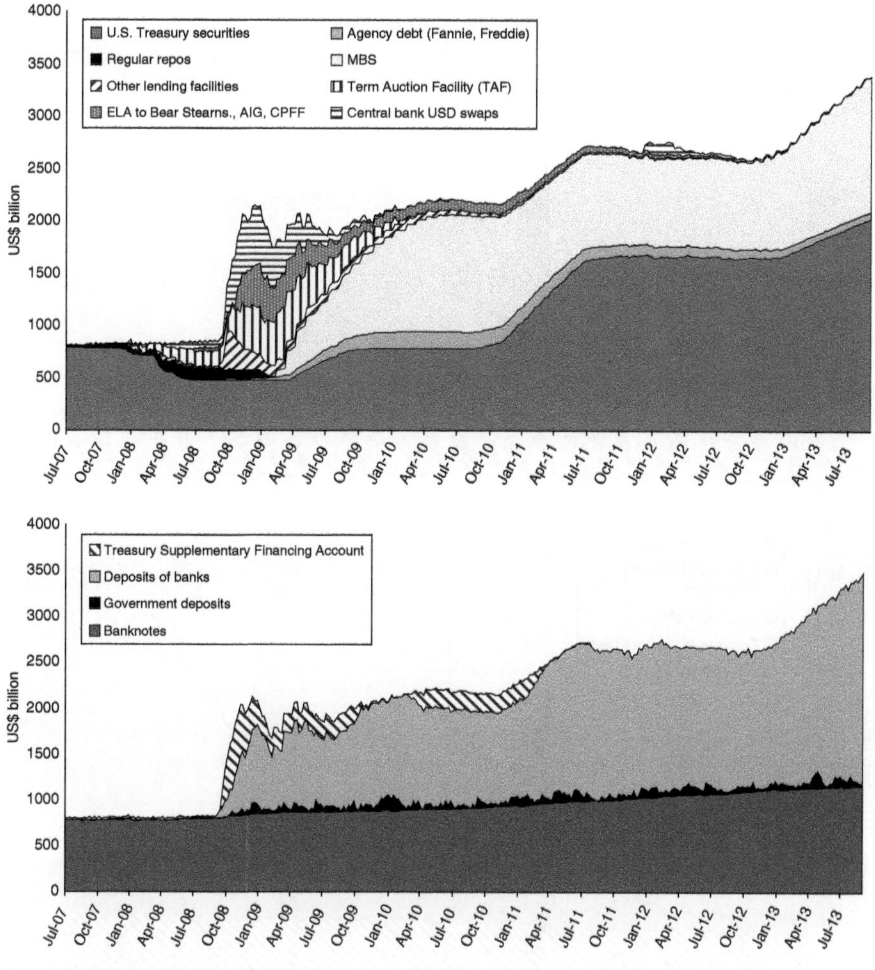

Fig. 13A.6. Evolution of the assets and liabilities of the US Fed, January 2007–August 2013, in billion USD

Source: Federal Reserve Board.

institutions such as AIG and relating to the resolution of Bear Stearns, and the USD provision to other central banks in the context of the swap operations.

Central Bank Balance Sheet Expansion due to Large-Scale Asset Purchase Programmes

The other type of central bank crisis balance sheets is that in which the lengthening is no longer driven by an impaired interbank market, but by large-scale asset purchase programmes of central banks. The central bank balance sheets of the Fed and the Bank of England take this shape from the second half of 2009 on. The US Fed balance sheet

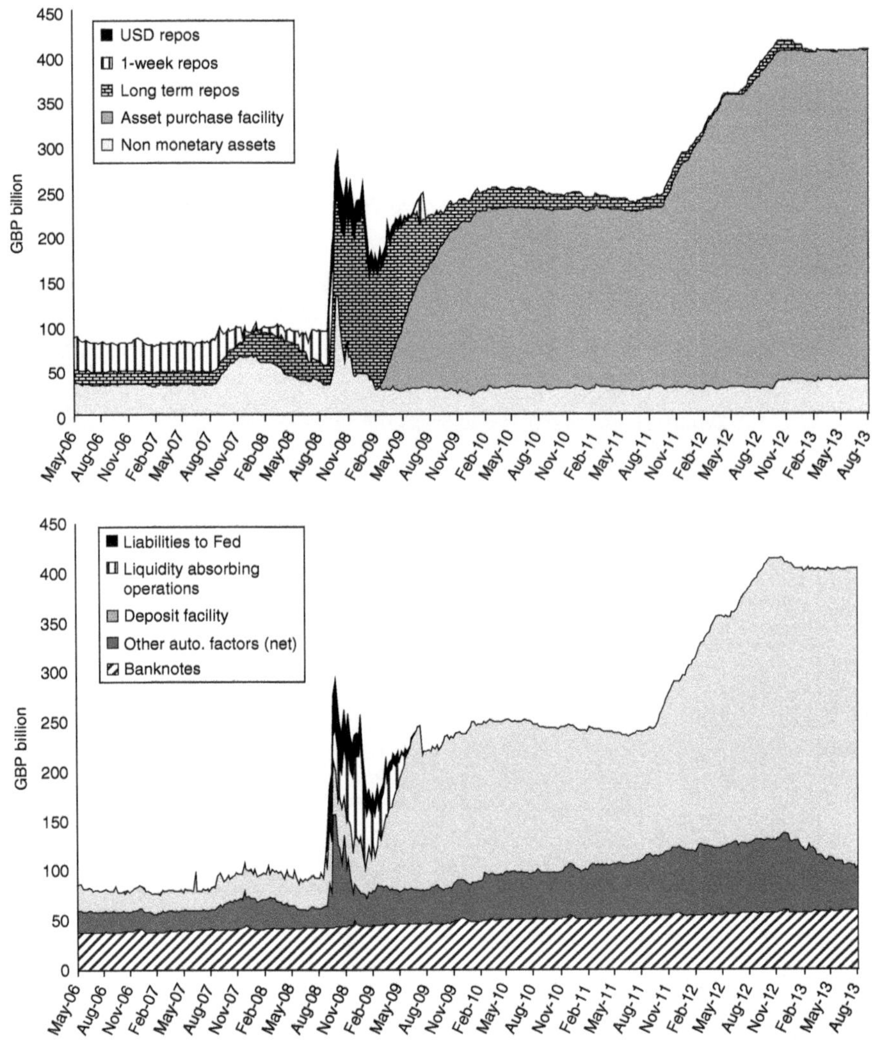

Fig. 13A.7. Evolution of assets and liabilities of the Bank of England, January 2007–August 2013, in billion GBP

Source: Bank of England.

as of 2 January 2013 was already provided in chapter 4 (figure 4.3) as an example of a monetary policy implementation approach based on a one-sided recourse to a standing facility. Figure 13A.4 shows the Bank of England balance sheet as of 2 January 2013.

The GBP 274 billion of current accounts broadly represent the lengthening of the central bank balance sheet due to the outright holdings totalling GBP 404 billion.

In Figures 13A.5, 13A.6, and 13A.7, time series of the evolution of assets and liabilities of these three central banks are shown for the period 1 January 2007 to mid-August 2013.

14

The Central Bank as Lender of Last Resort (LOLR)

14.1 THE NINETEENTH-CENTURY HERITAGE

During financial crises, not only does the monetary policy transmission mechanism get disrupted, implying that the central bank needs to adjust its policies to ensure that adequate monetary conditions continue to apply to the economy (chapters 12–13). In addition, the central bank is called upon to play a fundamental role in terms of providing liquidity support to banks in view of frozen asset, interbank, and capital markets, i.e. to act as 'lender of last resort' (LOLR). Obviously, the monetary policy and LOLR functions are closely interlinked, as a refusal by the central bank to act as LOLR will impair monetary policy transmission further. While the importance of this task was confirmed many times in history, it is still subject to various controversies.

As today's thinking on the LOLR function is still strongly inspired by nineteenth-century experience, and in particular Walter Bagehot's outstanding oeuvre *Lombard Street* of 1873, it is useful to start the discussion of the LOLR function by recalling some key historical statements (see e.g. Goodhart, 1999, for an overview of issues in modern interpretations of the nineteenth-century literature and Goodhart and Illing, 2002, for a collection of essential papers including more recent ones; see Rochet and Vives, 2004, for a recent model of the LOLR function).

Lend by every means consistent with the safety of the central bank. Jeremiah Harman, director of the Bank of England, in a hearing of the Lords' Committee in 1832 summarized the Bank's actions in the panic of 1825 as (found e.g. in Bagehot 1873, 204):

> We lent...by every possible means, and in modes that we never had adopted before; we took in stock of security, we purchased Exchequer bills, we made advances on Exchequer bills, we not only discounted outright, but we made advances on deposits of bills to an immense amount; in short, by every possible means consistent with the safety of the Bank;...seeing the dreadful state in which the public were, we rendered every assistance in our power.

First, it is useful to note that the statement is about extra liquidity injection into the financial system to the benefit of all banks under circumstances of a collective financial market liquidity crisis, not about emergency liquidity assistance to individual banks (as often wrongly assumed). Second, Harman explains the Bank of England's action as having been *creative and proactive*, i.e. the Bank innovated to find the best ways to support funding liquidity of financial institutions, the only constraint to creativity being the need to preserve the 'safety of the Bank'.

Inertia Principle. Bagehot (1873, 200) himself states this principle according to which the central bank should maintain its risk control framework inert, and accept not tightening it as a reaction to the deterioration of asset liquidity in a crisis situation:

> If it is known that the Bank of England is freely advancing on what in ordinary times is reckoned a good security and on what is then commonly pledged and easily convertible, the alarm of the solvent merchants and bankers will be stayed. But if securities, really good and usually convertible, are refused by the Bank, the alarm will not abate, the other loans made will fail in obtaining their end, and the panic will become worse and worse.

In contrast to Harman, Bagehot does not emphasize the proactive nature of the measures taken, but the fact that the central bank must remain 'inert' and not tighten its risk control framework (e.g. by restricting the set of eligible collateral for advances), such as other market players would do. While the emphasis is hence somewhat different, Bagehot can also be said to turn in this analysis around the duality of liquidity support and risk-taking.

Risk Endogeneity. Bagehot also provides an additional perspective on liquidity support and central bank risk-taking by arguing that supportive liquidity provision could be necessary *to minimize* the central bank's eventual own financial risks because such measures would be the only way to prevent a financial meltdown and accompanying losses for the central bank. Bagehot (1873, 201) explicitly writes:

> [M]aking no loans as we have seen will ruin it (Bank of England); making large loans and stopping, as we have also seen, will ruin it. The only safe plan for the Bank (of England) is the brave plan, to lend in a panic on every kind of current security, or every sort on which money is ordinarily and usually lent. This policy may not save the Bank; but if it do not, nothing will save it.

In other words, the riskiness of exposures would itself be endogenous to the central bank measures, and hence more liberal central bank policies could imply lower financial risk-taking than more conservative policies.

14.2 WHY SHOULD CENTRAL BANKS BE LENDER OF LAST RESORT?

In the following we distinguish six partially related reasons for the central bank to act as the lender of last resort in a financial crisis and to provide elastic credit, even if this leads to higher and more concentrated exposures. Justifying that the central bank should be ready to act as lender of last resort does not imply that there are no drawbacks to a too-supportive liquidity provision, such as e.g. to create moral hazard, to support businesses that should be stopped as they generate social losses ('zombie banks' to use the term of Caballero et al., 2008), or to prevent the necessary price adjustments in markets for certain assets. The trade-offs at stake will be discussed in more detail later.

1. Negative social externalities of funding liquidity stress and default due to illiquidity.[1] Negative externalities potentially justify the intervention of public authorities. As argued by Brunnermeier et al. (2009), the most important negative externality of bank default stems from the fire-sale spiral induced by liquidity problems of individual banks:

> In order to deal with such liquidity problems prior to failure, and in the course of liquidation after failure, the bank in difficulties will often be forced to sell assets (fire sales). But such sales will drive down the current market price of the same assets held on other banks' books, when these are valued on a mark-to-market basis... In short, there is an internal amplifying process (liquidity spirals) whereby a falling asset market leads banks, investment houses, etc., to make more sales (deleveraging), which further drives down asset prices and financial intermediaries' assessed profit and loss and balance sheet net worth.

By lending to banks against collateral and thereby eliminating the need for asset fire sales, the central bank can prevent the downward spiral and negative externalities of fire sales. Typically, central bank measures avoiding asset fire sales will help preserve solvency and reduce probabilities of default of counterparties and issuers. Asset fire sales are not the only form of negative externalities of bank funding stress and illiquidity-induced default that have been mentioned in the literature. Other forms of negative externalities are the spreading of depositors' panic in the form of a generalized bank run (such as observed in various countries in the early 1930s), and the generalized drying up of funding and market liquidity in the financial system as a consequence of hoarding driven by the experience that claims, including collateral, can get stuck in a default (see the various contagion channels of financial crises described in chapter 11). Generally, due to the systemic escalation inherent in most liquidity crises, it appears that many entities will find themselves to be (temporarily) illiquid even though they would in principle be solvent (i.e. if they survive the liquidity crisis without illiquidity-induced solvency damages). It is important to note in this context that it is lack of funding liquidity that typically triggers default, and not insolvency in the sense of negative capital. Solvency is an opaque concept and there is a significant grey area in which

[1] Chapman et al. (2010, 3) also allude to this argument, as well as to arguments 2, 3, and 6 below.

there is often no objective way to be certain about any indebted economic agent's solvency. Illiquidity is very concrete, being defined as the inability to meet a payment obligation.

2. Multiple equilibria in terms of banks' funding stability, with the ability of the central bank to support the prevalence of a unique stable funding equilibrium. As illustrated in sections 11.3 and 12.4, in case of a sudden non-anticipated deterioration of asset liquidity, a bank funding structure that was previously stable can suddenly be destabilized and suffer from multiple equilibria in which a bank run with implied bank default could occur at any time. The central bank can, by enhancing its LOLR role (for instance by increasing the eligible collateral set), counterbalance the drop of asset liquidity such that a unique stable funding equilibrium continues to prevail (see Bindseil, 2013). The challenge for the central bank and regulator is to ensure that banks do not factor in this support in advance, since otherwise banks may stretch their liquidity structure even more and may force the central bank to be even more supportive, etc. This argument for acting as LOLR is not identical to the externality argument, as it applies at the single-bank level without any externalities.

3. Central banks have been endowed with the monopoly and freedom to issue the legal tender, i.e. central bank money. Therefore, they are never threatened by illiquidity in their own currency and it seems only natural that, in case of a liquidity crisis when all agents attach a high price to liquidity, the central bank remains more willing than others to hold (as collateral or outright) assets which are less liquid (see also Armantier et al., 2008, 5). This argument does not rely on the existence of negative externalities. Even if the central bank were a purely profit-oriented enterprise, its exemption from liquidity stress should make it ready to take over illiquid assets in a crisis. Typically, asset prices will tend to recover after an acute liquidity crisis, and therefore the central bank may generate extraordinary profits (see Filardo, 2011, for an analysis of negative asset price bubbles during financial crisis; see also figure 11.12 in section 11.6 on the development of ABS prices in the US between 2006 and 2012; also note the extraordinary profits by the Fed in 2011 and 2012). After the crisis, liquidity operations can be wound down and the balance sheet size of the central bank can return to normal levels, so as not to crowd out financial intermediation or fuel the build-up of inflationary pressure. The fact that bank and corporate defaults are costly in themselves even without externalities, as they destroy organizational capital and normally block the efficient use of the companies' resources at least for a while, should also be seen in this context. If a bank or a corporate is threatened by illiquidity (and associated default) in a financial crisis, and if in the case of default the (presumably positive) organizational capital would be destroyed, then saving this capital is part of the 'rent' that can be achieved through cooperation between the liquidity-stressed economic

agent and the one that has unlimited liquidity. It is important to repeat that preventing costs of default in this sense through central bank liquidity does *not* invoke negative externalities, market failures, and the public nature of the central bank.

4. Haircuts are a powerful risk mitigation tool if credit risk is asymmetric and the collateral provider (repo borrower) is more credit-risky than the cash investor (repo lender). The power of haircuts is limited if cash-taker and cash-lender are equally credit-risky, since although haircuts protect the cash provider, they expose the cash-taker to unsecured credit risk which increases with the haircut level (Ewerhart and Tapking, 2008). Anecdotal evidence suggests that haircuts applied in repos between banks of similar credit quality tend to be rather low, while haircuts applied to other market participants, for example hedge funds, tend to be higher. Thus, banks would never question haircuts imposed by the central bank (repo lender), because the central bank cannot default.

5. The central bank may have superior knowledge on the state of stressed banks compared with other market participants, and may have special legal privileges in recovering claims (beyond collateralization). The first may relate to its information rights and practice as banking supervisor, and the fact that as a public entity, information access of the central bank does not need to be constrained. In contrast, if a competitor or a vulture fund were candidates for providing emergency lending, it is difficult to imagine that they could easily be given full access to all relevant information.[2] This is particularly relevant when decisions need to be taken in a very short time period. Moreover, the central bank, as public entity entrusted with special public functions and legal privileges, may be able to secure its claims resulting from LOLR operations more effectively than a private, ordinary lender.

[2] Armantier et al. (2008) and Acharya et al. (2012) also mention this argument. According to Armantier et al. (2008, 5): 'the Federal Reserve systematically monitors banks' financial health as part of its normal supervisory duties. The Fed is informed of the "CAMELS" rating of all depository institutions, even the ones for which it is not the primary supervisor. By limiting term lending to banks with CAMELS ratings of 1 to 3—the highest credit quality and the fewest supervisory concerns—the Fed can be reasonably confident of a borrower's ability to repay. In fact, recently issued CAMELS ratings have been shown to be a useful predictor of defaults. Under normal conditions, the supervisory information obtained by the Federal Reserve may be a less reliable signal of a firm's financial health than the information possessed by the firm's private counterparties, since banks monitor one another when engaged in a lending relationship. However, in crisis conditions, knowledge of a bank's supervisory rating may be more informative about basic creditworthiness than market insight because activity is typically reduced to very low levels and prices are often extremely volatile.' The LOLR model of Acharya et al. (2012, 186) relies on this idea in the sense that 'such a role requires the central bank to either be better than outside markets at extending loans to needy banks or be ready to incur losses. The former situation is more likely if the central bank also has a supervisory role allowing it to improve its ability to monitor its loans to needy banks. In particular, supervision ex ante does not reduce the incidence of the central bank making loans ex post, but makes such intervention credible, thereby improving the allocation of liquidity.'

6. Risk endogeneity. As Bagehot noted, the central bank might actually avoid losses by being supportive, while if it were restrictive (in the way of a granular player that wants to protect itself through a tightening of risk control measures), it might actually increase its expected loss because of the systemic role central bank lending plays in a crisis.

14.3 CENTRAL BANK INERTIA AND BEYOND

The simple system of accounts with two banks as used previously (see figure 2.5 in section 2.2), makes it possible to capture the interaction between central bank operations and banks' funding liquidity in a financial crisis. The lender of last resort (LOLR) function of the central bank gets activated automatically in a financial crisis as funding starts to become unstable and to dry up for some indebted institutions, and the banking system uses automatically the leeway it has with regard to the recourse to central bank credit. In this sense, central bank inertia already allows for some potentially substantial recourse to the LOLR. Also, risk-taking by the central bank changes automatically in such a context. The risk increase is driven by a number of factors as explained below, of which the last two have a representation in a financial account system such as the one in figure 2.5.

First, probabilities of default of central bank counterparties and issuers of debt instruments used as collateral increase. As illustrated e.g. by Standard & Poors (2009), investment-grade debtors (i.e. at least BBB-rated debtors) experience no default at all in good years (e.g. in 1992–1994, 1996, 2004, 2006, 2007 not even one single BBB-rated debtor defaulted). In contrast, during bad years even higher-rated companies default. For instance, in 2008 the default frequency for both AA- and A-rated debtors was 0.38%. Moreover, the correlation risks between central bank counterparties and collateral credit quality increase during a financial crisis. Generally, systemic crises create high correlation between debtors because common risk factors (instead of idiosyncratic risk factors) become predominant. Therefore, the likelihood of the worst case scenario for a repo operation, namely a simultaneous default of both the counterparty and the collateral issuer, increases significantly (e.g. if the issuer and counterparty have a 10 basis points probability of default, which is a good assumption for A-rated names, then the double default probability is 0.01 basis points in case of no correlation, while it is 10 basis points in case of perfect correlation, i.e. a difference of a factor of 1,000).

Second, asset price volatility increases, so the likelihood increases that after a counterparty default, a collateral value deterioration materializes, that exceeds the haircut.

Third, central bank lending shifts from good to less good counterparties and concentration tends to increase, a phenomenon we called 'relative' central bank intermediation. During financial crises, weaker banks tend to lose both capital and interbank market access and in addition may be subject to deposit outflows (as captured by the shocks k and y in figure 2.5). If assets are illiquid (which they tend to be in particular during a financial crisis) and therefore asset fire sales are problematic (as they imply losses), the central bank becomes the only source available to close the increasing funding gaps. At the same time, good names will tend to have inflows of funds, and can correspondingly reduce their reliance on the central bank.

Fourth, central bank balance sheets may lengthen for two reasons:

- Central banks start at some stage to take over the role of intermediary of the financial system in an *absolute* sense ('absolute' central bank intermediation). This occurs, to speak in terms of the stylized financial accounts model of figure 2.5, when the shock $k + y$ reaches a certain level, namely if $k + y > B/2 + d/2$. Then bank 1 is over-liquid and deposits its excess money with the central bank.
- *The central bank balance sheet may also lengthen due to a flight of households out of bank deposits into banknotes* (as happened to Northern Rock in 2007 or in the early 1930s). This is reflected in the shock d in the system of financial accounts shown in figure 2.5.

The automatic provision of funding support to the stressed bank is limited by the eligibility of the bank's assets as central bank collateral, and by the haircuts the central bank applies.

Going beyond inertia, the central bank can extend its LOLR function to the banking system in a crisis through a number of *active* measures, which may be grouped as follows:

(1) Measures which increase the borrowing potential of stressed banks towards the central bank. This requires an extension of eligible collateral, which can be engineered in two variants.

   a. Extending collateral eligibility in general (i.e. towards all banks). This can be done by a lowering of haircuts, or an extension of collateral eligibility (see Markets Committee, 2013), of which the latter is more common. It should be noted that typically, eligible collateral values have a natural tendency to shrink in a financial crisis due to lower valuation, and eligibility losses or automatic haircut increases due to deteriorating credit quality.

   b. Extending collateral eligibility bilaterally in the form of emergency liquidity assistance (ELA), as discussed in section 14.4.

(2) Offering a securities lending programme (see section 12.5).

(3) Outright purchases of securities to support the funding liquidity of banks and other stressed entities. This was discussed in more detail in section 13.3 under reason (7) for outright purchase programmes.

(4) Measures that extend the set of entities to which the central bank can lend directly. For example, the Fed decided in 2007 to provide emergency liquidity assistance (ELA) to the American International Group, which is the largest insurance company of the US.

(5) Measures which reactivate market access of stressed banks, such as for instance guaranteeing deposits or interbank credit—typically less of a central bank, but more of a state task. The option to recapitalize banks with public funds is also typically a Government, and not a central bank task.

(6) Finally, the central bank can make borrowing from it more reliable and more convenient, e.g. by switching the tender procedure for credit operations from a variable-rate auction to a fixed-rate full allotment procedure.

The idea is that by applying these tools, i.e. by going beyond inertia, the central bank can reduce the funding liquidity stress on banks, and thereby moderate or stop a financial crisis or prevent it from breaking out, such that banks do not stop lending to the real economy, preventing also the negative feedback loops summarized in figure 11.13 to gain momentum. In the words of the President of the Federal Reserve, Bernanke (speech, 'The Crisis and the Policy Response', 13 January 2009):

> Liquidity provision by the central bank reduces systemic risk by assuring market participants that, should short-term investors begin to lose confidence, financial institutions will be able to meet the resulting demands for cash without resorting to potentially destabilizing fire sales of assets. Moreover, backstopping the liquidity needs of financial institutions reduces funding stresses and, all else equal, should increase the willingness of those institutions to lend and make markets.

14.4 EMERGENCY LIQUIDITY ASSISTANCE AS SPECIAL TYPE OF LOLR

Above, two forms of LOLR were introduced in more detail, namely (i) tolerating the recourse of banks to the built-in elasticity of the central bank's credit framework; (ii) making actively more convenient the recourse of banks to this framework (e.g. widening collateral set; moving from variable-rate tenders to fixed-rate full allotment in credit operations, etc.). Now we turn to LOLR to help *individual* banks through what is called by the ECB, the Bank of England,

and the Bank of Canada '*Emergency Liquidity Assistance*' (ELA), i.e. provision of special central bank credit to a single bank at a higher interest rate against collateral that is normally not eligible, and often also against a Government guarantee protecting the central bank's exposure.

Table 14.1 compares normal central bank credit provision with ELA across a number of dimensions.

In fact a few central banks tried to design an at least partially rule-based ELA framework and published its main design features (for Canada see Daniel et al., 2004; for Hong Kong see Hong Kong Monetary Authority, 2011). The approach of the Hong Kong Monetary Authority (HKMA) seems to be the most transparent and rule-based of all central bank ELA approaches, and it is therefore interesting to look closer at it. The aims of ELA for the HKMA (2011, 1) are 'to prevent illiquidity from precipitating a situation of insolvency, and to prevent the contagion effect of bank runs'. The HKMA defines clear preconditions for ELA (p. 3):

(i) 'the judgment of the HKMA that the failure of a troubled institution, if it is deprived of liquidity assistance, would damage the stability of the exchange rate, monetary or financial systems (i.e. systemic risk)'. This condition clearly distinguishes ELA from normal central bank credit as ELA would only be provided if preventing damages to others. This also creates 'constructive ambiguity' for banks regarding whether they would receive ELA, and hence prevents banks from factoring in the availability of ELA *ex ante* when choosing their level of liquidity risk-taking.

(ii) 'The institution has a sufficient margin of solvency.' It is moreover specified that 'As a measure of whether an institution has a sufficient margin of solvency, the HKMA will generally require the institution to demonstrate that it maintains a capital adequacy ratio of at least 6% after making adjustment for any additional provisions that might be necessary.' It may be argued that to start with, a lack of solvency does not necessarily appear to be a reason to not provide ELA, since a bank may lack solvency but still (a) negative externalities of a default can be huge; (b) the bank may have a sound business model in the sense that if it continues to operate, it contributes positively to society and generates a positive profit stream. However, the solvency criterion has the merit of putting the responsibility on checking (a) and (b) onto the Government, which will have to decide whether it is ready to inject (if no other sources are available) the necessary capital into the bank. The mandate of the central bank would be unduly stretched if it had to take such difficult decisions.

(iii) 'the LOLR support will be adequately collateralized'. This criterion again protects the central bank and makes it unlikely that it will face a loss through ELA operations. A loss would mean an unwarranted re-allocation of resources within society which the central bank has no legitimacy to decide upon. Again

Table 14.1 Comparing regular central bank credit provision with emergency liquidity assistance (ELA)

	Normal central bank credit	ELA
Rules versus discretion	Rule based, i.e. within a well-defined and well-known framework	At the discretion of the central bank; no pre-commitment, normally no rules; 'Constructive ambiguity'
Interest rate	At or close to target policy rate (exception: borrowing facility in corridor system)	At penalty level (beyond level of standard borrowing facility)
Number of banks	All eligible counterparties	Normally to a single bank, sometimes to several banks individually in parallel
Collateral	Normal pre-defined central bank collateral set	Other bank assets, in principle everything that can be pledged; often complemented by a sovereign guarantee
Central bank counterparty monitoring/ conditionality	No special monitoring of counterparties when they take recourse to central bank credit; no conditionality	Only in the context of a special counterparty status and enhanced monitoring and conditionality
Stigmatization	Normally no stigma (as long as recourse is not too disproportionate)	Stigmatized as considered to reflect more serious problems of the relevant bank
Duration	No particular provisions against roll-over across time	Normally only short-term

it could be argued that even in case of a lack of collateral, negative externalities of default could be large, and the bank could be expected to achieve positive performance in the future. Then, again, the collateral criterion serves the purpose of ensuring that the Government judges on these two points, and if it concludes positively (i.e. the bank should be saved through ELA despite a lack of collateral), it should be the responsibility of the Government to close the collateral gap in one way or another (for example by guaranteeing the exposure of the central bank).

(iv) 'the institution has sought other reasonably available sources of funding before seeking LOLR assistance' and 'the shareholder controllers of the institution have made all reasonable efforts to provide liquidity and/or capital support as a demonstration of their own commitment'. These criteria stress that ELA is really the absolute last avenue a bank should consider to prevent illiquidity.

(v) 'there is no prima facie evidence that the management is not fit and proper, or that the liquidity problem is due to fraud' and 'the institution must be prepared to take appropriate remedial action to deal with its liquidity problems'. These criteria give the central bank power to impose management changes and other (painful) measures on the banks, making it more likely that impediments to future profitability can be removed, and creating strong disincentives to banks to rely *ex ante* on the possibility of ELA.

HKMA (2011) also contains specifications on the eligible collateral set for ELA (investment grade securities and mortgage portfolios are mentioned, including a haircut schedule). One could ask (not specifically in the case of the HKMA) why not include the ELA collateral set directly in the set of eligible collateral for normal central bank credit operations? One reason could be to maintain constructive ambiguity regarding the maximum central bank credit volume, i.e. with regard to the part that would be based on ELA collateral. Not pre-committing to make one part of the collateral set eligible could prevent banks from factoring in this further potential liquidity support and from stretching accordingly the liquidity structure of their balance sheet. Second, in normal times, it could seem inefficient to foresee the permanent eligibility of less liquid collateral, as such collateral is typically more special and information-intensive and requires more extensive and costly due diligence work regarding valuation and credit quality assessment. Third, if less illiquid assets (i.e. those typically activated as ELA collateral) would be permanently eligible, they would probably be the first ones to be used with the central bank, i.e. the scope for adverse selection in collateral use would be unnecessarily enlarged.

HKMA (2011) also limits duration of ELA (30 days with possibility of *one* 30-day roll-over). With regard to the interest rate to be charged, no figure is mentioned, but it is specified that 'The interest rate charged on LOLR support would be at a rate which is sufficient to maintain incentives for good management but not at a level which would defeat the purpose of the facility i.e. to prevent illiquidity from precipitating insolvency'. HKMA (2011) sets maximum amounts for ELA, namely an absolute maximum of HK$10 billion and in addition a relative cap:

> an institution which meets the minimum pre-conditions for LOLR support (i.e., a capital adequacy ratio of 6%) would be able to obtain liquidity support up to a maximum of 100% of its capital base. An institution, which can maintain a capital ratio above its statutory minimum, would be able to obtain liquidity support up to a maximum of 200% of its capital base. In either case, the HKMA would retain the discretion to lend less than the maximum.

The Bank of England has also moved recently towards more transparency in its ELA (and LOLR) framework. The 'Discount Window Facility' (Bank of England, 2013, 12–13) is a rather rule-based individual emergency lending facility[3] in which access conditions (in particular the collateral set and pricing) are known in advance. Interestingly, the pricing of recourse to the facility increases with the size of the recourse.

The majority of central banks deliberately choose to be less transparent on their ELA framework. It could for instance be argued that by specifying limits and collateral criteria *ex ante*, the central bank may bind itself unduly, such as to weaken its ability to preserve financial stability, or may invite banks to factor in support. The European Central Bank (2007, 80) has remained more general and explains the following with regard to its ELA framework[4]:

> One of the specific tools available to central banks in a crisis situation is the provision of emergency liquidity assistance (ELA) to individual credit institutions against adequate collateral. Generally, this tool consists of providing liquidity support in exceptional circumstances to a temporarily illiquid credit institution which cannot obtain liquidity through either the market or participation in monetary policy operations. This exceptional and temporary liquidity provision should respect the prohibition of monetary financing embodied in the Treaty establishing the European Community and the associated EU Council Regulation. A credit institution cannot, however, assume automatic access to central bank liquidity. As a central banking function, the provision of ELA is within the discretion of the national central bank, which will consider the relevant factors that may justify the access to this lending of last resort. Specifically, the provision of ELA may be justified to prevent or mitigate potential systemic effects on financial institutions...

In any case, no central bank pre-commits to ELA (i.e. neither those that outline their ELA framework and the limits to it, like the HKMA, nor the majority which do not provide *ex ante* specifications). The view is shared that pre-commitment would make banks factor in support, and accordingly they would choose (absent liquidity regulation) a more stretched liquidity structure of their balance sheet, which would make the actual reliance on ELA more likely. Central banks want to prevent this by keeping uncertainty.

Manna (2009) provides an overview of a number of concrete ELA cases (including the Swedish banking crisis of the 1990s, the case of Austrian Bawag in 2006, Northern Rock in 2007, Bear Stearns in 2008). Plenderleith (2012) is a detailed report on the Bank of England's ELA operations to HBOS and Royal Bank of Scotland in 2008–2009. The emergency lending operations of the Fed to American International Group (AIG) are described and motivated for example in Kohn (2009). Other cases on which information has been published relate to the German Hypo Real Estate and the Belgian Fortis group

[3] Actually the Bank of England's discount window facility could be regarded as being in between a central bank standing facility and ELA.

[4] In an announcement on 17 October 2013 ('ELA procedures'), the ECB, however, provided additional, in particular procedural information on ELA in the euro area.

Bank 2			
Credit to corporates	(D + B)/2	Deposits	D/2 − k
		Central bank monetary policy credit	(D + B)(1 − h)/2
		ELA	B/2 + k − (D + B)(1 − h)/2

Fig. 14.1. Bank 2 from figure 12.2 if the bank has run out of eligible collateral and receives ELA

(both 2009). According to publications of the relevant central banks, end 2011 ELA provided by the central banks of Greece, Ireland, Cyprus, Belgium, and France stood at around EUR 52, 42, 4, 6, and 19 billion, respectively. At end 2013, numbers had dropped significantly in most of these countries.

While there are substantial differences between ELA and normal central bank credit, as summarized in the table above, it may be noted that the financial accounts representation of ELA is identical to that of 'normal' central bank credit. If one distinguishes the two types of central bank credit in bank balance sheets, then the borderline between the two is collateral availability. Starting from e.g. the financial accounts of bank 2 in figure 12.2, and assuming that the bank has indeed run out of eligible standard collateral, the financial accounts with differentiation between the two forms of central bank credit take the form shown in figure 14.1.

Total central bank credit is B/2 + k, and the part of that which is normal central bank monetary policy credit is simply given by collateral availability. As central banks should be protected against credit risk also for ELA operations, this exposure is often secured by an extra Government guarantee.

15

LOLR and Central Bank Risk-Taking

15.1 EXOGENOUS RISK

In a financial crisis, banks are suddenly under both liquidity and solvency stress, and their individual optimization leads them to restrict lending and risk-taking vis-à-vis clients and other market participants, which may trigger a vicious downward spiral towards a socially suboptimal hoarding and default equilibrium. As shown in the previous section, the central bank has a number of tools to support the funding liquidity of banks in a crisis in a decisive way. But what about Harman's 'safety' of the central bank? How should risk management aspects be reflected by the central bank when deciding to support the liquidity of banks? What increase in its total risk should the central bank tolerate? Four different basic answers have been given to this question.

(a) **Inertia principle.** According to this principle, the central bank should essentially continue unchanged in terms of collateral acceptance when a crisis breaks out (see the relevant Bagehot statement quoted in section 14.1). Beyond the general arguments in favour of central banks providing funding liquidity to banks in a crisis, three arguments in favour of inertia per se may be brought forward. First, only central bank inertia ensures that banks can really plan well for the case of a crisis. The possibility that the central bank would take more constraining risk control measures or would reduce collateral eligibility in a crisis situation would make planning of banks much more difficult (including liquidity stress-testing). Second, the central bank is unlikely to be able to re-assess the complex trade-off between optimal financial risk management and optimal contribution to financial stability in the heat of a crisis, since both sides are difficult to quantify even in normal stable conditions. Therefore, ideally, it should design a risk control framework in normal times with which it would also feel comfortable in a financial crisis. Third, *ex ante* equivalence between (i) a series of consecutive short-term refinancing operations and (ii) longer-term central bank refinancing operations requires full trust of the banks in central bank inertia with regard to all access conditions to refinancing.

(b) **Active additional risk taking.** This approach has been advocated for example by Buiter and Sibert (2007): 'Dealing with a liquidity crisis and credit crunch is hard. Inevitably, it exposes the central bank to significant financial and reputational risk. The central banks will be asked to take credit risk (of unknown) magnitude onto their balance sheets and they will have to make explicit judgments about the creditworthiness of various counterparties. But without taking these risks the central banks will be financially and reputationally safe, but poor servants of the public interest.' The main argument for active extra risk-taking seems to be that the marginal social returns of risk-taking by the central bank increase substantially during a crisis.

(c) **Only the brave plan is the safe plan.** This view, which emphasizes risk endogeneity, is also based on Bagehot (see section 14.1). According to this view, the central bank should take supportive measures during a crisis not only for policy reasons, but also because this strategy would reduce (and not increase) the financial risks of the central bank.

(d) **Ensure above all credit-risk protection.** According to this view, the central bank should protect itself—not on the liquidity side, where it is, in contrast to all other banks, not threatened, but on the side of credit risk. This view emphasizes that the central bank is not the best credit-risk manager and it is not in its mandate to take large amounts of credit risk. Hence, when a crisis breaks out and central bank financial risk-taking tends to increase steeply, the central bank should take additional risk control measures to limit this increase.

A Conceptual Model

The following conceptual model aims at capturing the four different views summarized above more precisely.

Let L be *a variable that captures the funding liquidity of banks.* L depends both on the state of the financial system (functioning interbank markets, household deposit volatility) and on central bank operations and the central bank collateral framework. The measure L could be specified for instance as the average of individual banks' probabilities of remaining liquid.

Let R be *the total risk taking of the central bank*, as captured through some risk measure such as expected loss, value-at-risk, or expected shortfall. In practice, the risk measure should contain market risk and credit risk.

Let the framework $F = \{F_1, F_2, \ldots F_n\}$ be the vector of n parameters *describing the liquidity supply and collateral framework of the central bank.* Elements could be, for instance, the collateral set; the haircuts on the various collateral types; the propensity of the central bank to purchase outright different types of assets if needed; the maturity spectrum of open market operations, etc. The elements of the vector are defined such that *liquidity support increases with the value of the respective parameter*. Assume that before the crisis, the array of measures is F^0. It is useful to establish as benchmarks the two extreme frameworks in terms of central bank liquidity supportiveness.

- **Most supportive framework:** accept all assets of banks as collateral at fair values (net book values for assets held to maturity), thus allowing banks to finance all their assets with the central bank, if desired. Such an approach would provide confidence to the markets in the sense that all market participants would know that no solvent counterparty could ever default for liquidity reasons, as any liquidity outflow could be compensated by an increased recourse to central bank funding. It should be noted that what we call here the most supportive framework would still rely on two fundamental risk management principles: (i) that the collateral should be accepted at adequate valuations, reflecting at least an unbiased medium- to long-term fair value; (ii) that counterparties should be solvent in the sense of having positive capital. The only reason for a bank to default under the loosest framework would be the supervisory withdrawal of the banking licence due to violation of capital adequacy. If collateral was valued correctly, and if the bank's licence is withdrawn by the banking supervisor immediately when capital falls beyond the required level, but is still positive, then normally the central bank should not make any losses.[1]
- **Tightest framework:** the central bank implements monetary policy only against risk-free assets, such as T-bills, assuming a AAA-rated sovereign debt. It largely covers its asset side through outright holdings of the risk-free asset. The central bank may conduct at the margin some repos against risk-free assets, but in a bilateral way in which it chooses its counterparties and always goes for the most secure ones. In this framework, banks have no discretionary access to the central bank at all to close possible funding gaps.

Let the *state of the financial system* be captured in a variable Ω. In fact, this variable could also be perceived as an array, containing elements such as the

[1] The loosest reasonable framework described above should not be confused with a framework without any collateral constraints, i.e. one in which the central bank would provide unsecured lending without limits. In that case, market control would be removed completely. A 'mad' bank could buy in one day all outstanding financial assets. There would be no guarantee of economically rational behaviour—extreme leveraging and risk-taking would be possible (and likely if the bank has nothing to lose because capital is depleted anyway). Incentives to lie to supervisors to delay the point of licence withdrawal would be strong. The central bank liquidity supply would likely be extremely concentrated on weak banks. The central bank's risk-taking would be enormous and would depend fully on how early the supervisor withdraws banking licences. Eventually, the value of the currency and price stability would be jeopardized under such an extreme approach.

functioning of the interbank market, the level of capital buffers of banks, the stability of funding sources, etc. For the sake of simplicity, Ω is treated here as a single parameter. The crisis parameter Ω is defined in such a way that the more impaired the financial system is, the higher the value of Ω.

Now consider how the variables interact. For each combination of a framework F and crisis intensity Ω, the measures L and R take certain values: $R = R(F,\Omega)$, with R increasing in Ω and *normally* in each of the parameters captured in the array F (the important exception will be illustrated in the next section, and corresponds to the Bagehot insight that only the 'brave' plan may be the 'safe' plan for the central bank). Furthermore $L = L(F,\Omega)$ with L increasing in F and decreasing in Ω.

Moreover, *policy makers have preferences* with regard to providing liquidity services and taking risk on the central bank balance sheet. Assume that W() is total welfare, and at the same time the preference function of the central bankers, and $W = W(R,L)$ with W() decreasing in R, and increasing in L.

For every crisis, and for every intensity of the crisis, the optimal specification of the array F will normally be different, and will also be different from the pre-crisis array F. Denote by Ω_0 the pre-crisis level of Ω, and by Ω_1 its level in a crisis. Also denote with $F^*(\Omega)$ the framework that is optimal for a specific value of the variable Ω, given the preferences of the central bank.

The inertia principle could be interpreted in this setting as saying that $F^*(\Omega_0) = F^*(\Omega_1)$. In practice, however, this is not what was observed during the crisis, as central banks typically undertook changes of their frameworks in both directions. The optimality of a widening of the collateral set for instance would mean that for the relevant element i of the array F, $F_i^*(\Omega_0) < F_i^*(\Omega_1)$, i.e. the central bank would choose more 'liberal' parameters of its liquidity provision measures in the crisis. But one could observe also cases in which $F_j^*(\Omega_0) > F_j^*(\Omega_1)$, and thus restrictive measures were taken in the crisis. For instance, the European Central Bank announced on 4 September 2008 that it would increase the collateral haircut on a number of assets. Also, it announced on 15 January 2009 that it would no longer accept certain types of ABS (e.g. multiple-layer CDOs).

The choice of F, R, L, and W can also be illustrated as follows. For every level of risk-taking R, one can achieve a maximum value of L by choosing the efficient combination of values of the array F (and vice versa). Amongst all pairs on the efficient frontier, the pair chosen eventually will depend on the preferences of the central bank decision-makers and will be the one where the possibility set is tangent to an indifference curve between providing liquidity support to banks and taking risks on the central bank balance sheet. While the optimal central bank risk taking probably always increases when the financial system deteriorates, i.e. $dR^*/d\Omega > 0$ it is less clear whether $R(F^*(\Omega_1),\Omega_1) > R(F^*(\Omega_0),\Omega_1)$, i.e. whether the measures taken as a reaction to the crisis will increase or decrease total risk-taking relative to inertia (in which case the risk measures are those prevailing before the crisis). Similar considerations apply to the liquidity comfort of the banking system: while a liquidity crisis will always worsen the funding liquidity of banks, $dL^*/d\Omega < 0$, it is less clear whether $L(F^*(\Omega_1),\Omega_1) > L(F^*(\Omega_0),\Omega_1)$. According to Buiter and Sibert (2007), these two inequalities should certainly hold. In any case, it is important to note that the point $(R(F^*(\Omega_0),\Omega_1),L(F^*(\Omega_0),\Omega_1))$ will rarely be on the efficient frontier, i.e. not adjusting any measures (= showing full inertia) will rarely be optimal.

This is further illustrated in Figure 15.1. To simplify notation in the figure, $(R(F^*(\Omega_0),\Omega_1),L(F^*(\Omega_0),\Omega_1))$ is written as $RL(F^*(\Omega_0),\Omega_1)$, etc. The chart shows four possibilities of where the (R,L) combinations could be in the case of the central bank remaining inert in a crisis. In all cases $R(F^*(\Omega_0),\Omega_1) > R(F^*(\Omega_0),\Omega_0)$ and $L(F^*(\Omega_0),\Omega_1) < L(F^*(\Omega_0),\Omega_0)$, meaning that, in crisis conditions, both the liquidity situation of banks and the risk of the central bank worsen if the central bank does maintain its framework F unchanged.

However, the four cases are different in terms of what the adjustments of the central bank framework to the crisis environment imply for R and L. The four cases reflect the four views that were mentioned at the beginning of this section.

(a) Inertia principle being optimal: $RL(F^*(\Omega_0),\Omega_1) = RL(F^*(\Omega_1),\Omega_1)$ and in fact no adjustments would be needed. This is a special case that in fact has limited likelihood and plausibility in practice.
(b) F should be adjusted in such a way as to lead to an increase in central bank risk-taking and liquidity comfort of banks (Buiter and Sibert, 2007).
(c) F should be adjusted such as to support the liquidity situation of banks, which at the same time leads to a decrease in central bank risk-taking (only the brave plan is the safe plan).
(d) F should be adjusted so as to lead to both a decrease in central bank risk-taking and a reduced liquidity comfort for banks (ensure above all risk protection).

15.2 ENDOGENOUS RISK

The Standard Case of Exogenous Risk

First, consider the standard case of *exogenous* risks, i.e. a normal shape of the relationship between risk control measures and risk-taking as it will be relevant for any granular (or 'atomistic') lender, i.e. a lender whose decisions do not matter for the rest of the system because he is so small. Assume for example that a granular investor invests his cash in revolving one-month repo

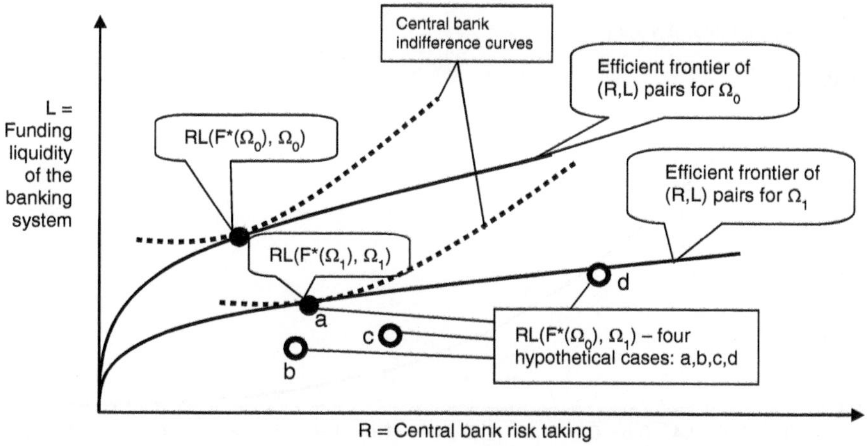

Fig. 15.1. Liquidity support and central bank risk-taking: efficient frontier, central bank preferences, and optima in stable times and in a financial crisis

operations with German Government bonds as collateral. Assume that daily margin calls are undertaken, but that in case of counterparty default, it takes one week to liquidate the bonds and that the one-week price change of the bills is N(0,1%). We can now consider different risk measures (i.e. metrics) conditional on counterparty default as a function of the haircut h imposed by the investor. Useful risk measures include (i) the probability of a loss; (ii) the expected loss; (iii) the value at risk; (iv) the expected shortfall (see e.g. Hull, 2012 for definitions of these risk measures). Note that in case of an increase of value of the bonds, i.e. a profit in liquidation, this profit has to be handed back to the insolvency administrator (i.e. there is never an upside). It is easy to show that each of these risk measures is a monotonously declining function in the haircut h. For example, figure 15.2 plots the first measure, the probability of a loss, which, as a function of the haircut, is simply given in this case by 1 – Φ(h%), whereby Φ() is the cumulative Gaussian distribution.

Risk Endogeneity in the Bank Run Game

Now a special case of an upwards-sloping risk function (i.e. central bank risks *increase* in the central bank collateral haircut) will be derived. Recall one more time the stylized bank balance sheet to illustrate the bank run problem in the most simple way. Figure 15.3 is identical to figure 12.7.

Suppose again that we are first in 'good' times in the sense that the mostly liquid assets are indeed fully liquid (and in fact no one has in mind that they could turn illiquid). The bank can generate a maximum liquidity in case of

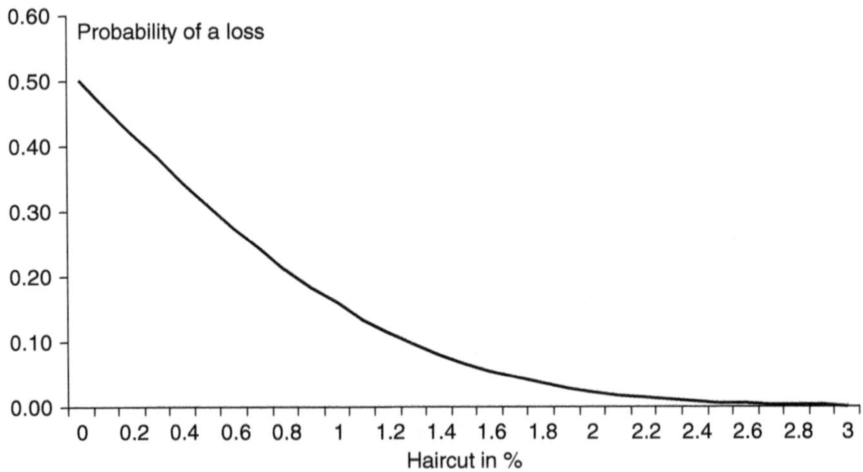

Fig. 15.2. Risk as a function of haircut—standard downward slope

Assets		Liabilities	
Liquid assets	$\Lambda(2 + E)$	Depositor 1	1
Mostly liquid assets	$\Pi(2 + E)$	Depositor 2	1
Non-liquid assets	$(1 - \Pi - \Lambda)(2 + E)$	Central bank credit	0
		Equity	E

Fig. 15.3. Another bank threatened by a bank run

a run of $L = (\Lambda + \Pi)(2 + E) + (1 - h)(1 - \Lambda - \Pi)(2 + E)$, and a single no-run deposit equilibrium exists if $(\Lambda + \Pi)(2 + E) + (1 - h)(1 - \Lambda - \Pi)(2 + E) \geq 1$ and $E \geq 0$. Assume moreover that the cost of default would be $C > E$.

As an example, choose the following parameter values: $\Lambda = 0$; $\Pi = 0.4$, $h = 0.6$, $E = 0$, and $C = 1.5$. The condition for a stable funding equilibrium is fulfilled since total liquidity buffers are 0.8 + 0.48 = 1.28. Now assume that the financial system enters a crisis and that the mostly liquid assets are in fact no longer liquid. Liquidity buffers of the bank fall to 0.8, and the single no-run equilibrium no longer prevails. Instead, the bank now faces two equilibria, including an inferior one in which a run occurs, the bank defaults, the default cost C materializes, and the remaining asset value is distributed across claimants. In case the run materializes, assets lose 75% of their value, and therefore also the haircut of the central bank of 0.6 is insufficient to fully protect it. At default, the central bank had an exposure of 0.8 (that was when the bank ran out of collateral), and all of the banks' assets were pledged to the central bank as collateral. The central bank will therefore have a recovery ratio of 0.5/0.8,

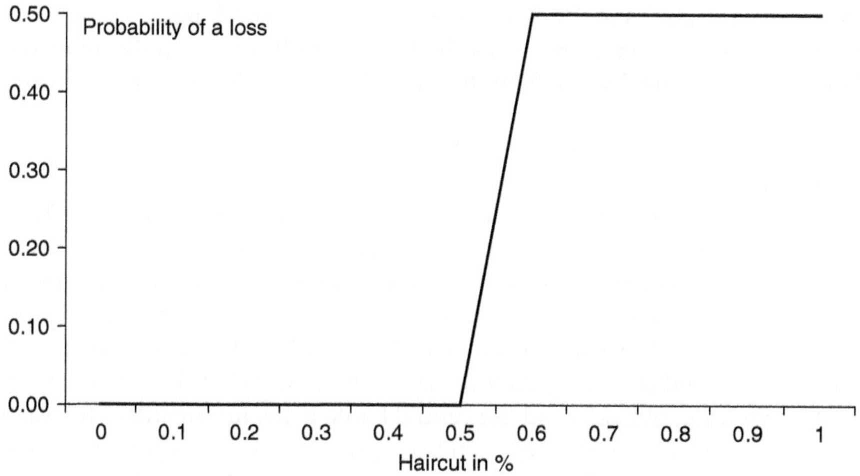

Fig. 15.4. Central bank risk as a function of central bank haircut—an example of an upwards sloping curve

while the remaining deposits will have a recovery ratio of zero (with these losses having possible further contagion effects for the rest of the economy).

The central bank could have prevented this from materializing by reducing its haircut from 0.6 to 0.5. Then, liquidity buffers of banks would have remained sufficient to prevent a bank run from constituting an equilibrium. Figure 15.4 shows the resulting loss probability function applicable in a financial crisis environment. It is assumed that in case of two equilibria, the one with a run materializes with a 50% probability.

Of course, this is a very simplistic case in which a specific parameter constellation drove the result to obtain a vindication of Bagehot's 'only the brave plan is the safe plan'. It is a partial model that omits various effects. The more sophisticated model in the following section will allow for partially more differentiated conclusions.

Risk Endogeneity and Economic Performance (Bindseil and Jablecki, 2013)

The model presented in this section, proposed in Bindseil and Jablecki (2013), formalizes the idea of endogeneity of risks in relation to central bank risk control measures. It builds on the financial accounts representation introduced earlier, but innovates in the following sense: (i) households also hold equity, and all private sector firms (banks and corporates) have capital buffers; (ii) there are two distinct corporates and each bank finances exactly one corporate; (iii) asset shocks drive solvency changes; (iv) liquidity shocks are correlated with solvency shocks as the household has some noisy information on solvency shocks; (v) illiquidity can trigger default; (vi) corporates and banks are liquidated once default occurs, and losses are attributed to the central bank and the household, whereby it matters that the central bank credit is collateralized.

At the outset, households are endowed with real assets E (equity). They invest these real assets partially in corporate equity P and bank equity Q, and also exchange another part of their real assets into financial assets, namely banknotes B and bank deposits D (assumed to be divided equally between Bank 1 and Bank 2). Corporates finance their projects by bank loans (equal to D + B + Q) and the equity endowment from households (P). The financial sector, consisting of banks and the central bank, is the intermediary between households and corporates (apart from equity stakes in corporates). First, it offers deposits D to households and invests them in loans offered to corporates. Second, the banking sector is still an intermediary to the operation between the households and the central bank with respect to the issuance of banknotes B. Banks use banknotes to purchase real assets from households, which they sell on to corporates who finance them through a loan from the bank. Thus, total funding, and hence total assets held by banks amount to B + D + Q.

The resulting financial structure of the economy is presented in figure 15.5. For the sake of simplicity, we do not present here the case of one bank becoming over-liquid due to deposit inflows, nor do we present the asset value shocks as the latter do not themselves trigger default (and also since their cascading through the financial accounts is relatively complex to present; see the annex of Bindseil and Jablecki, 2013). Relative to Bindseil and Jablecki (2013), the model is simplified to have only one type of liquidity shock (the deposit shift shock k, and no aggregate shock from deposits into banknotes).

When a bank defaults, which happens if the deposit outflows go so far as to exhaust the central bank collateral buffer, this has some assumed direct costs. In the model, these costs materialize in the following concrete way: if the bank defaults, the corporate that the bank was lending to also defaults as the bank is no longer able to roll over its credit, and other banks cannot take over quickly enough because they cannot easily assess the quality and solvency of the corporate enterprise. When the corporate defaults, there is economic damage because its management is changed, assets have to be sold at distressed prices, and there is a period of legal uncertainty and implied inertia, etc. The damage is simply captured in the model in the form of a one-off shrinkage of the value of the real assets of the corporate. The cost of default is one key parameter of the model that can be chosen. This makes it possible to assess the consequences of varying default costs across the business/financial cycle on optimal central bank collateral policies.

Households			
Real Assets	E − D − B − Q − P	Household Equity	E
Deposits Bank 1	D/2 + k		
Deposits Bank 2	D/2 − k		
Bank equity	Q		
Corporate equity	P		
Banknotes	B		

Corporate 1			
Real assets	(D + B + P + Q)/2	Credits from banks	(D + B + Q)/2
		Corporate Equity	P/2

Corporate 2			
Real assets	(D + B + P + Q)/2	Credits from banks	(D + B + Q)/2
		Corporate Equity	P/2

Bank 1			
Lending to corp 1	(D + B + Q)/2	Household deposits	D/2 + k
		Credit from central bank	B/2 − k
		Bank Equity	Q/2

Bank 2			
Lending to corp 2	(D + B + Q)/2	Household deposits	D/2 − k
		Credit from central bank	B/2 + k
		Bank Equity	Q/2

Central Bank			
Credit operations	B	Banknotes	B
		Equity	0

Fig. 15.5. A variant of the financial accounts to model risk endogeneity (Bindseil and Jablecki, 2013)

If, thanks to the central bank's elastic liquidity provision, defaults of institutions facing deposit outflows are prevented, then this may be good since it ensures uninterrupted operation of business projects, and avoidance of the cost of default. However, it can also be bad since banks and corporates may default for good reasons—investors may have withdrawn funding as they receive signals on solvency problems relating to bad management. In that case, preventing illiquidity through central bank credit may allow bad projects to continue longer than necessary, and to continue wasting social wealth. It may sometimes be better for society to discontinue a project through default and go through the one-off cost of reorganization, but then to allow again for a more productive use of the freed-up resources. The central bank in the model is assumed to have no particular information on solvency of banks and corporates, i.e. it does not even receive noisy signals, such as investors do. The central bank, however, can aim at providing liquidity to banks, i.e. set through haircuts limits to such provision, in a way that achieves the optimum with regard to minimizing the expected costs across two possible errors: Error 1, letting a bank default for liquidity reasons although it was viable in the sense that there was no reason to expect that it would produce losses in the future; Error 2, preventing, through extensive liquidity provision, the default of a bank which is not sound and is expected to generate future losses if it is not wound down. In the model, the unique parameter of the central bank to achieve the optimum is the haircut it imposes on collateral. The optimum haircut will depend on the information content of liquidity shocks with regard to individual banks' solvency/efficiency problems, and on the cost of default. The model is concretely specified through the following sequence of events. All random variables are, for simplicity, assumed to follow a normal distribution with expected value of zero.

Period 1:

(1) Solvency shocks:

η_1 = asset value shock affecting the assets held by corporate 1
η_2 = asset value shock affecting the assets held by corporate 2

(2) Liquidity shocks:

$k = \theta + (\eta_1 - \eta_2)$ = deposit shift shock out of bank 2 into bank 1, with θ being an independent random variable

(3) The funding liquidity shocks force banks to adjust (increase or decrease) their borrowing from the central bank. It is assumed that the banks pre-deposit all their assets with the central bank as collateral. Recourse to the CB cannot exceed available collateral after haircuts. The level of haircuts is h, so that the potential borrowing from the central bank is limited to $(1 - h)(B + D + Q)/2$.

(4) If a bank hits its central bank collateral constraint, it defaults. This has two implications. First, the corporate defaults as it depended on the bank (one may interpret this as the realization of a credit crunch). This is assumed to cause a negative effect on the corporate asset value, namely a damage to corporate asset value of x. On that basis, the values of the corporate liabilities can be established (on the basis of the juniority of equity relative to debt). Second, bankruptcy proceedings are initiated and banks' solvency is evaluated, whereby the value of remaining bank assets is divided between the creditors—the central bank and the households. First, the central bank will liquidate its collateral (in fact, by assumption, all assets of the bank), and the remaining asset value is

then divided *pari passu* between the central bank (as far as it still has claims after the liquidation of collateral) and the household (see the annex to Bindseil and Jablecki, 2013).

Period 2:

(5) Banks and corporates that have not defaulted continue to operate, and it is assumed that the idiosyncratic real asset shock of period 1 repeats itself precisely. This reflects an assumed *persistence of economic performance*. Corporates that default are subject to a new draw of the idiosyncratic shock, which reflects the fact that they have received new management and have been reorganized.

(6) Social welfare is measured at the end of period 2 in the form of the value of the real assets in the economy (equal to the equity of households).

Economic performance (i.e. the value of real assets at the end of period 2) will be driven by the relation between costs of default and the positive expected value of reoccurring asset value shocks of surviving companies. Bindseil and Jablecki (2013) analyse the impact of varying the different exogenous model parameters on the optimal central bank haircut policy, i.e. on the optimal limits to central bank lending (for the real asset values at end of period 2 an analytical solution is provided, while for central bank expected losses, results are obtained through simulations). Here only two parameter variations will be considered, as indicated in Table 15.1. To fully specify the model, the initial stocks in the financial accounts need to be quantified. The initial endowment of real assets (household equity) is assumed to be fixed (at E = 200) and divided between real assets (100) and the following financial assets: banknotes (B = 40), deposits (D = 54), and equity stakes in corporates (P = 4) and banks (Q = 2), whereby these different equity levels reflect the fact that banks are typically more leveraged than corporates. These structural parameters are also relevant as they imply that the banking system has an initial liquidity deficit

Table 15.1. Assumed parameter values for calculating impact of haircuts on welfare and central bank expected losses

	Parameter variation I (V in Bindseil and Jablecki, 2013)	Parameter variation II (VI in Bindseil and Jablecki, 2013)
$\sigma_{\eta 1} = \sigma_{\eta 2}$	2	2
σ_{θ}	0/1/4	1
σ	1	1
X (default cost)	1	0/1/15/25

Source: Bindseil and Jablecki (2013).

towards the central bank of 40 (20 per bank) and total bank assets of 100 (i.e. there are no real assets left directly with the household). This implies that the haircut level imposed by the central bank must never exceed 60%. With this level, the banks default when they are hit by the slightest negative liquidity shock (i.e. the probability that a bank defaults in period 2 is one).

The parameter σ_ε (noise in deposit shift shocks) is inversely related to the information content of liquidity shocks with regard to firm-specific asset value shocks. Figure 15.6 provides, for different haircut levels between 0 and 60%, the expected real economic asset values at end of period 2 (measuring economic efficiency) and expected central bank losses. First, the figure reveals for all values of σ_ε the existence of an interior optimum of haircuts with regard to economic efficiency, and a monotonously downward sloping central bank expected loss curve (i.e. the latter reveals that, in the words of Bagehot, an intermediately 'brave' plan is optimal for society, but is not the 'safest' plan from the perspective of the central bank). The figure also reveals that the higher the information content of liquidity shocks with regard to firm-specific asset value shocks (i.e. the lower the noise in deposit shocks), (i) the higher the maximum expected end-of-period-2 asset values (economic efficiency), which is driven by the fact that the selection mechanism to filter out bad performers through illiquidity-induced default works obviously best if the information content of liquidity shocks with regard to economic performance is high; (ii) the higher the optimum haircut. This is explained by the fact that if liquidity shocks contain a lot of information, then it is good to map negative shocks rather systematically into defaults, such as to stop projects with presumably poor performance. Interestingly, expected central bank losses are hardly affected by varying this parameter. This is due to the fact that the key loss driver—i.e. volatility of asset value shocks—remains unchanged and the cost of default ($x = 1$) can still most of the time be absorbed by corporate and bank equity.

Specification II investigates the impact of the cost of default on both economic efficiency and central bank losses. Economic efficiency and expected central bank loss functions are derived for four different levels of the cost of default, which increases in steps from 0 to 1 (corresponding to a loss given default of 4%, i.e. LGD = 4%), to 15 (LGD = 60%) and 25 (LGD = 100%). Figure 15.7 reveals various cases in terms of shapes of the curves and optima. For zero costs of default, the optimal haircut level is 60% (such that the slightest negative liquidity shock triggers default), and the central bank expected loss curve is monotonously downward sloping. This is intuitive as more restrictive haircuts ensure that more unsound business projects can be filtered out and wound down without costs, leading to higher expected asset value growth rates in period 2. As default costs increase, however, efficiency gains from stopping loss-making businesses are offset by the cost of restructuring and the efficiency curve first becomes hump-shaped ($x = 1$) and eventually a

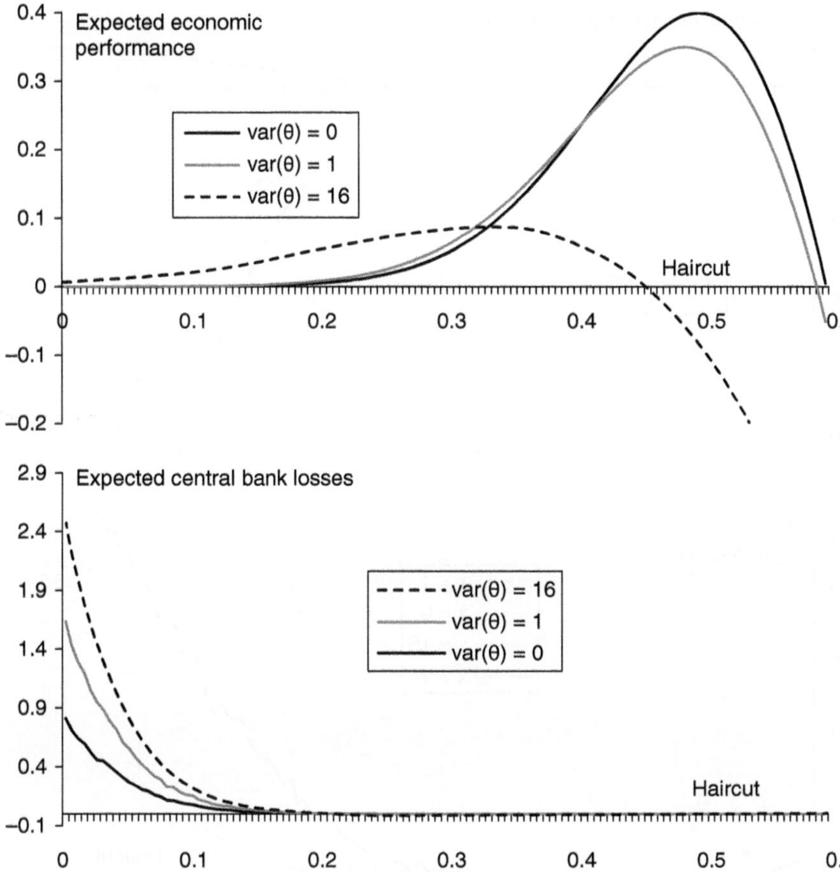

Fig. 15.6. Economic performance and expected central bank losses as a function of central bank collateral haircuts, for different levels of noise in deposit shift shocks
Source: Bindseil and Jablecki (2013).

monotonously decreasing one (x = 15; 25) as the high cost of default outweighs positive effects of discontinuing bad investments. Turning to central bank risk-taking, the figure (bottom panel) shows that when x = 0, expected losses decrease monotonously with the degree of restrictiveness of the haircut policy. Intuitively, the zero cost of default reflects a resilience of the financial system which can always reorganize without disruptions. Therefore, the system can cope even with a very conservative framework without being systemically destabilized. In such an environment, the central bank's risk management can in fact be approached similarly to that of a typical granular player on the market, so that increasing haircuts allows it to effectively mitigate credit risk without influencing financial stability. However, when LGD is 60% or higher,

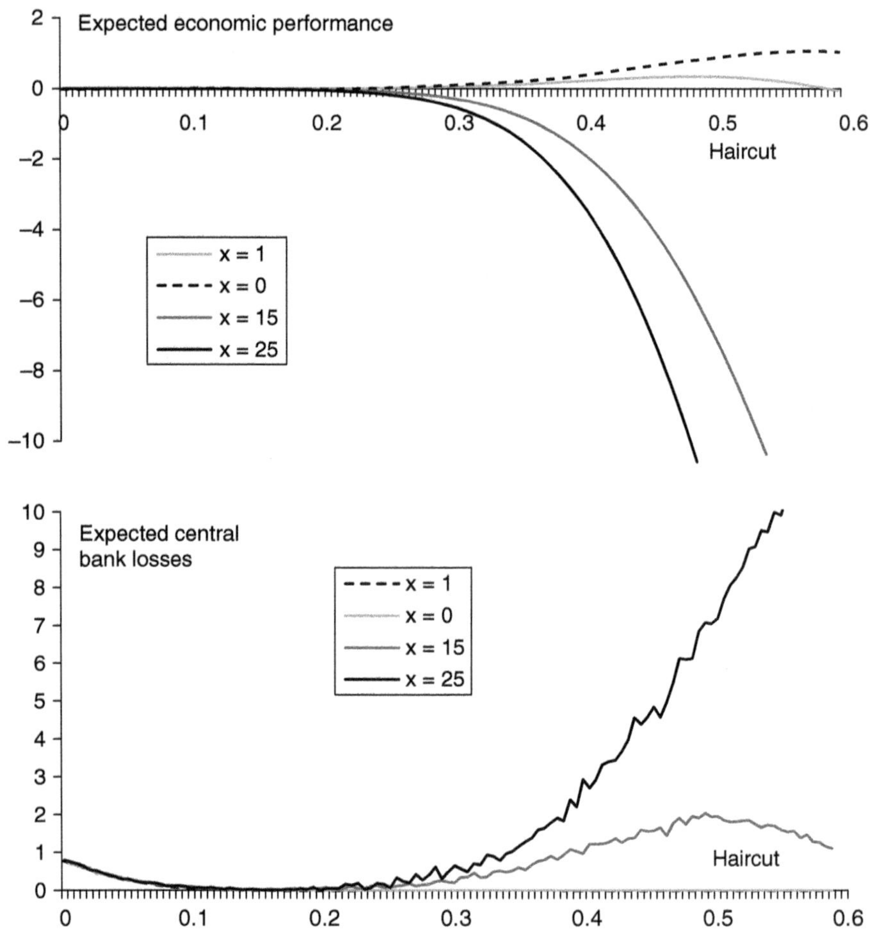

Fig. 15.7. Economic performance and expected central bank losses as a function of central bank collateral haircuts, for different levels of default costs

Source: Bindseil and Jablecki (2013).

the central bank expected loss curve changes from monotonously decreasing to a 'U'-shaped one, whereby expected losses fall as the central bank moves from a very liberal framework (h = 0%) to a moderate one (h = 30%; 40%), but pick up again once that point is surpassed. As the cost of default increases to 25, in which case reorganization entails almost total destruction of corporate assets (e.g. selling highly sophisticated machinery as scrap metal), the losses expected in the most restrictive framework skyrocket.

In sum, the model shows that economic performance and central bank risk-taking are in many cases non-monotonous functions of haircuts, and even if the functions are monotonous, they can be either upward- or downward-sloping. This means that depending on the haircut level and on economic circumstances, increasing haircuts can either increase or decrease economic performance. More surprisingly, in stressed market conditions, characterized by, say, high negative externalities of default, central bank losses can sometimes increase with the level of haircuts. Hence, loosening the collateral framework can be consistent with protecting the balance sheet of the central bank, as already implied by Bagehot's dictum that only the 'brave' plan of the central bank is the 'safe' plan. This is a specific consequence of a more general insight that financial sector risk tends to be endogenous with respect to the central bank's emergency liquidity support.

Going beyond model specification, this phenomenon can be illustrated by the following mechanism: if the funding stress of banks, together with other macroeconomic factors, leads to a continued credit crunch and economic downwards spiral affecting collateral values, counterparties' solvency will deteriorate over time and default probabilities will increase, eventually increasing also central bank risk-taking. To the extent that the central bank's LOLR operations manage to overcome the negative feedback loops characteristic of a systemic financial turmoil, then they should also reduce the central bank's long-term risk exposure. The model also makes it possible to explain why the major central banks have, over the course of the recent crisis, aimed at increasing the total post-haircut amount of collateral relative to the total balance sheet length of the banking system (Brunnermeier et al., 2009). Indeed, this result is precisely replicated in the model, which shows that under parameter changes that are consistent with a financial crisis, i.e. when costs of default increase and liquidity shocks become more erratic and carry less information on solvency, the central bank should increase the total post-haircut amount of collateral.

16

LOLR, Moral Hazard, and Liquidity Regulation

16.1 MORAL HAZARD AND NEGATIVE EXTERNALITIES OF INADEQUATE BANK LIQUIDITY MANAGEMENT

Moral Hazard and Externalities

Moral hazard is normally understood as deliberate decision-making of economic agents that is good for themselves, but suboptimal for society. An early use of the term 'moral hazard' in economics is by K. Arrow (1963, 961) to describe the problem of incentives of insured agents as their choices have an externality on the insurance provider, and hence the agent may choose the wrong effort level from the perspective of society:

> The outbreak of fire in one's house or business may be largely uncontrollable by the individual, but the probability of fire is somewhat influenced by carelessness, and of course arson is a possibility, if an extreme one. Similarly, in medical policies the cost of medical care is not completely determined by the illness suffered by the individual but depends on the choice of a doctor and his willingness to use medical services. It is frequently observed that widespread medical insurance increases the demand for medical care.

Already Arrow notes the difficulties of finding good solutions to the moral hazard problem. Moral hazard has been modelled formally in particular in the Principal–Agent literature (e.g. Holmstrom, 1979). Dowd (2009) discusses moral hazard in relation to the latest financial crisis. The issue of an undue maturity mismatch in bank balance sheets and insufficient liquidity buffers as one form of moral hazard is analysed for instance in the models of Acharya and Viswanathan (2011), Diamond and Rajan (2012), and Farhi and Tirole (2012).

The concept of moral hazard is closely linked to that of negative externalities, in the sense that the incentives for moral hazard originate from the externality of decisions on other agents. Indeed, after the large-scale lender of last resort (LOLR) role of central banks in 2007 and 2008, regulators, central banks, and the public appeared dissatisfied with the behaviour of financial institutions which provoked the crisis. Out of moral hazard, some bankers had taken risky decisions to maximize their income while taking into account that they would not have to bear the possible downside.

Brunnermeier et al. (2009, 20) note that to justify regulation,

> one must argue from a social welfare perspective that financial institutions over-expose themselves to the risk of getting caught in a liquidity spiral by holding highly levered positions with excessive maturity-mismatches. We argue that this is indeed the case due to the following two risk-spillover externalities...: a) Fire-sale externalities; b) Interconnectedness externalities. The fire-sale externality arises since each individual financial institution does not take into account the price impact its own fire-sales will have on asset prices in a possible future liquidity crunch. Hence, fire-sales by some institutions spillover, and adversely affect the balance sheet of others, causing a negative externality...It is arguably the main rationale for bank regulation.

It is also one of the rationales for central banks acting as lender of last resort, as argued in chapter 14. If the central bank's role of acting as lender of last resort to prevent asset fire sales were a perfect solution to the externality, no additional regulation would be needed. So why be dissatisfied with such a pure lender of last resort solution? Three reasons can be identified: (i) banks will tend to factor in *ex ante* the central bank's readiness to act as LOLR and will tend to take even bigger liquidity risks (see also the next paragraph); (ii) LOLR eliminates at least temporarily the market mechanism in terms of credit allocation, and the central bank in fact has no particular expertise in credit allocation; (iii) a liquidity crisis, even if countered by the central bank through non-conventional measures and elastic lending, will still lead to significant distortions of the transmission mechanism and to recessionary dynamics, which will lead to a failure to reach the socially optimal levels of price stability, growth, and full employment. If these limitations in the effectiveness of the central banks' LOLR function are accepted, then negative externalities of excessive leverage and poor liquidity risk management remain, even if the central bank is the best possible LOLR.

The Lender of Last Resort Function as *Origin* of Moral Hazard

It is a widespread view that supportive central bank LOLR policies are in fact a source of moral hazard as they prevent those financial institutions which run into liquidity problems because of insufficient *ex ante* liquidity risk management from having to pay the price of default for it (and the implied wiping out of equity holders and loss of employment for management). In other words, the concern is not only that some negative externalities of liquidity-stressed banks remain despite the existence of a LOLR, but that the LOLR weakens even more the non-externalized consequence of insufficient risk management as compared to the negative externalities, so that at the end, liquidity-risk management is even less prudent because of the existence of LOLR and society will overall be potentially worse off. For instance Clews et al. (2010, 294) develop this thinking:

> Central banks typically provide liquidity insurance to the banking system. When designing their liquidity insurance facilities, central banks—like any insurance provider—have concerns over 'moral hazard'. Moral hazard in this context refers to the risk that the availability of liquidity insurance induces banks to take on more risk than they otherwise would. A simple incentive arises because liquid assets such as reserves yield less than illiquid long-term loans and hence self-insurance is costly. Given that central banks can create reserves at effectively zero cost to themselves, it could be argued that it does not matter if banks take on more liquidity risk. That line of reasoning fails to take account, however, of the intimate relationship between banks' liquidity risk and their solvency.

Diamond and Rajan (2012, 554) also argue in that way:

> Unconstrained public intervention, however, undermines the discipline induced by private contracts. Banker rent extraction is usually limited by the banker's fear that he will precipitate runs if he takes too much. When the authorities are willing to intervene to prevent runs, they exacerbate ex post bank rent extraction. Ex ante, competitive banks will compensate by making even larger promises to households, making the system even more rigid, and sometimes even exceeding the authorities' ability to save the system. We show unconstrained intervention will make the system worse off.

Farhi and Tirole (2012, 64) also note that supportive central bank crisis policies 'increase the likelihood of future crisis' and 'encourage maturity mismatches'.

To address moral hazard caused by the LOLR function, two complementary approaches can be considered. First, *ex ante* liquidity regulation can constrain banks in stretching their liquidity structure unduly, even in anticipation of LOLR support in case of a crisis. This will be the subject of the next section. Second, the LOLR function can be designed in a way that it provides incentives against relying unduly on it. Clews et al. (2010, 294) consider the following options in this respect:

- **Lend only to solvent banks.** Clews et al. note that it is not always easy for the central bank to distinguish between solvency and liquidity problems (as confirmed by the bank run model introduced in section 11.3).
- **Provide liquidity insurance at a cost,** namely 'by charging higher interest rates for high usage of liquidity facilities or for accepting lower-quality collateral'.

- **Set higher haircuts on collateral than what would be strictly necessary from the risk management perspective.**

Clews et al. conclude that the second approach would be the most effective way to reduce moral hazard. However, they also note the drawback that 'to the extent that, in some conditions, these interest rates could influence market interest rates, the central bank may induce unwanted changes in the monetary policy stance'. Taking up these ideas, section 16.3 will propose a simple over-proportionality surcharge framework which may be an effective tool to reduce moral hazard concerns, while at the same time not giving up the advantages of being able to rely on the central bank as liquidity-unconstrained agent. The specifications of ELA as chosen for instance by the Hong Kong Monetary Authority (2011) also seem to address moral hazard (see section 14.4).

Bank of England (2013, 5) announces a more rule-based and less penalizing Bank of England LOLR framework, to become effective in 2014, noting that in view of other (new) tools, such as liquidity regulation, the monetary policy implementation framework 'no longer has to shoulder as much of the burden of tackling moral hazard'.

Moral Hazard and Central Bank Risk Management Relating to the Lender of Last Resort

It could be argued that as long as central banks do not make losses, moral hazard must also be contained since no wealth is eventually redistributed in a disorderly way. This would make the measurement of moral hazard and of the effectiveness of its control more concrete, as risk management and realizing losses are well-established disciplines of bank management and financial reporting. Such an approach would support the appropriateness of the central bank acting as lender of last resort, in particular in cases where a liquidity crisis leads to a systemic downward spiral in which eventual mean reversion of asset prices is plausible *ex ante*, such that the unique features of central banks (e.g. not being liquidity-constrained) make it logical that the central bank temporarily plays an exceptional role as lender to the financial system. This argumentation is complicated, though not invalidated, by the fact that in a financial crisis risk parameters of the financial system (e.g. probabilities of default of banks) are endogenous to central bank decisions.

16.2 LIQUIDITY REGULATION

In the *ex post* analysis of the 2007–2009 financial crisis in regulatory circles, the inadequacy of liquidity risk management of many financial firms was identified as one of the critical issues (Basel Committee on Banking Supervision, 2013). In reaction, to raise the standards of the liquidity risk management and supervisory practices, the Basel Committee updated their 'Principles for sound liquidity risk management and supervision' in 2008 (Basel Committee, 2008). In addition, to strengthen the resilience of international banks to liquidity shocks and to further harmonize liquidity risk supervision, the G20 requested the Basel Committee to define a liquidity risk framework that would promote stronger liquidity buffers at financial institutions. The liquidity risk framework has been issued, as part of the Basel III regulatory reform package, on 16 December 2010 (Basel Committee, 2010), and has been further adjusted afterwards (Basel Committee, 2013).

The Liquidity Coverage Ratio (LCR), being the first Basel III liquidity regulation to be implemented, has as its purpose to establish a minimum level of high-quality liquid assets to allow banks to withstand an acute stress scenario lasting one month. The stress scenario is a regulatorily defined stress composed of 'a conservative bank level and plausible severe system wide shock' and defines the potential net cash drain in a comprehensive manner. For instance, margin requirements from derivative transactions and liquidity support to conduits through committed facilities are also captured. The liquidity buffer thus has to enable the firm to survive through a cash-flow drain that results from a stress lasting one month. By requesting the liquidity buffer to consist of high-quality liquid assets, which provide relatively low yields, the measure internalizes the liquidity risks from the activities of the banks, as holding the high-quality liquid assets is costly to the bank. The LCR measure makes a comparison between the liquidity buffer and the net cash outflow over a thirty-day period and is precisely defined as the following ratio (HQLA are the 'high quality liquid assets'):

$$\text{LCR} = \text{HQLA} / 30 \text{ days' net cash outflow} \tag{16.1}$$

The LCR standard requires that the ratio is at least 100%. Basel Committee (2010) defined two categories of liquid assets. Level 1 liquid assets are mainly composed of cash and central bank reserves and government and public sector entity debt qualifying for the 0% risk weight under the Basel II standardized approach. The qualifying assets are subject to general additional criteria of being traded in large, deep, and active repo or cash markets, having a proven record of a reliable source of liquidity even during stressed conditions, and the assets cannot be an obligation of a financial institution. The level 2 liquid assets mainly consist of government and public sector entity debt qualifying for the 20% risk weight under Basel II and high-quality corporate and covered bonds. The corporate and covered bonds cannot be issued by a financial institution or by the bank itself and must have at least a AA credit rating assigned. The level 2 assets can comprise no more than 40% of the liquidity buffer. A 15% haircut has to be applied to the market value of the level 2 liquid assets. This definition of liquid assets, which constitute the liquidity buffer, results from the purpose of limiting the set of assets to those assets that most likely will allow banks to generate liquidity during a period of stress (e.g. through repo markets). This relates to a basic notion of the regulation that the firm has to rely on its own capacities to raise necessary funding. The definition of the HQLA set was broadened further in Basel Committee (2013).

An Example of how Liquidity Regulation Can Work

In section 12.4, it was shown that in a liquidity crisis, a decrease of central bank collateral haircuts can sustain the stability of short-term funding of banks and prevent the economic damage and negative externalities resulting from a bank run with the associated forced asset liquidation and bank defaults. However, as noted by a number of authors (e.g. Chapman et al., 2010, Acharya and Viswanathan, 2011, and Farhi and Tirole, 2012) such supportive central bank measures invite banks *ex ante* to stretch their leverage and maturity mismatches even further in anticipation of the supportive policies, possibly forcing the central bank in the next crisis to be even more accommodating, etc. If the central bank cannot prevent this form of moral hazard, liquidity regulation becomes an essential tool to achieve a stable financial system. Consider one more time the basic case of a bank with two depositors, as shown in figure 16.1.

Suppose again first that we are in 'good' times in the sense that the mostly liquid assets are indeed fully liquid (and in fact no-one has in mind that they could turn illiquid). The central bank applies a collateral haircut of h and the bank can thus generate a maximum liquidity in case of a run of $L = (\Lambda + \Pi)(2 + E) + (1 - h)(1 - \Lambda - \Pi)(2 + E)$, and a single no-run deposit equilibrium exists if $(\Lambda + \Pi)(2 + E) + (1 - h)(1 - \Lambda - \Pi)(2 + E) \geq 1$ and $E \geq 0$. Assume moreover that the cost of default would be $C > E$.

As shown previously, the minimum equity needed is $E^* = 1/(1 - h + h(\Lambda + \Pi)) - 2$, and, assuming that $i_E > i_A > i_D$ (these are the remuneration rates of bank equity, bank assets, and bank deposits, respectively), the banks will choose in

Assets		Liabilities	
Liquid assets	$\Lambda(2 + E)$	Depositor 1	1
Mostly liquid assets	$\Pi(2 + E)$	Depositor 2	1
Non-liquid assets	$(1 - \Pi - \Lambda)(2 + E)$	Central bank credit	0
		Equity	E

Fig. 16.1. Another bank threatened by a bank run

competitive equilibrium this minimum equity, i.e. they will go exactly to the limit of what is sustainable.

Assume now that every year with a probability of 1/100, an exogenous event materializes which leads to a bad state in which asset liquidity deteriorates in the sense that the mostly liquid assets migrate from a state of being liquid to one of being illiquid. Consider three cases: myopic banks, banks with foresight, and banks with foresight but causing externalities.

Myopic Banks

If banks are myopic and just do not think about bad states, they will in any case choose E^*. Then a switch to the bad state leads to a change of the strategic depositor game from the single no-run equilibrium to the one with two equilibria, with one being inferior and leading to bank default.

Liquidity regulation could solve the issue by imposing a minimum share of equity E', which is in this case equivalent to a minimum share of long-term funding, being equal to $E' = 1/(1 - h + h\Lambda) - 2$. Imposing E' is equivalent in our simple setting to (i) imposing a ratio of long-term funding to total assets of $E'/(E' + 1 + 1)$, or (ii) imposing a ratio of liquid assets (in normal times) to short-term funding (similar to the Basle III LCR) of $\Lambda(2 + E')/2$. Any of these regulations impose that in the crisis year of probability 1/100, the single no-run equilibrium is sustained. Whether such regulation makes sense is another question, as it may well be that the social cost of always satisfying E' exceeds the costs of having a bank run once every hundred years.

Banks with Foresight

The bank could itself come to the conclusion that it is optimal to hold E' and to avoid the damage that materializes under E^* on average once in a hundred years. This will depend on the default-related damage C in comparison with the extra cost of equity. Assume the following concrete example: $\Lambda = 0.1$; $\Pi = 0.1$, $h = 0.8$, such that $E^* = 1/(1 - 0.8 + 0.16) - 2 = 0.78$ and $E' = 1/(1 - 0.8 + 0.08) - 2 = 1.6$. Assume now that the cost of equity is i_E, the cost of deposits is 2%, and the remuneration of assets is 7%. Also assume that the cost of default is $C = (2 + E)/2$ (i.e. half of the asset value is destroyed). We can now compare the two strategies of the bank to hold E and E'.

Under strategy 1 the bank issues equity $E^* = 0.78$. In good years (99 out of 100 years on average), the bank will generate a profit of $2.78 * 7\% - 2 * 2\% - 0.78 * i_E = 0.17 - 0.78 * i_E$. With 1% probability, the bank will instead lose $0.5 * 2.78$, i.e. the annualized cost of this is 0.0139. So the total average annual profit is $0.151 - 0.78 * i_E$.

Under strategy 2, the bank issues $E' = 1.6$. Every year, the bank generates a profit of $3.6 * 7\% - 2 * 2\% - 1.6 * i_E = 0.22 - 1.6 * i_E$. Which of the two strategies the bank will choose will thus depend on the cost of equity. Strategy 1 will be preferred if:

$$0.15 - 0.78 * i_E > 0.22 - 1.6 * i_E \Leftrightarrow i_E > 0.07/0.82 = 8.7\%$$

Banks with foresight but causing externalities

As long as there are no externalities of default, one should assume that the non-myopic bank's calculus leads to the social optimum. Only if there is an additional externality X that has to be added to the cost C, the social planner may come to different conclusions from the bank. Adding X, the annualized cost of financial turmoil under strategy 1 is 0.0139 + X * 0.01, and the total average annual social profit is 0.151 – X * 0.01 – 0.78 * i_E. The condition for the social planner to choose between E* and E′ is to choose E* if:

$$0.15 - X * 0.01 - 0.78\ i_E > 0.22 - 1.6 * i_E \Leftrightarrow i_E > 8.7\% + X * 0.01 \quad (16.2)$$

Liquidity regulation imposing E′ makes sense if $i_E < 8.7\% + X * 0.01$. It makes a difference if in addition banks would without regulation choose E* although socially E′ is optimal, i.e. if $i_E < 8.7\% + X * 0.01$ and if $i_E > 8.7\%$.

Beyond this very simple example, a number of model sophistications should be considered to allow for a more qualified analysis of regulation. For example Cifuentes et al. (2005) develop and simulate a model of the asset fire sale channel of systemic contagion. In their model, merits of liquidity regulation emerge because of a negative externality of asset fire sales. They also note that in some cases liquidity regulation cannot be substituted with capital adequacy regulation. Acharya and Viswanathan (2011) and Farhi and Tirole (2012) develop sophisticated equilibrium models in which regulation improves welfare by addressing moral hazard.

Arbitrage Problems between Liquidity Regulation and Central Bank Operations

In this subsection, a few examples of interaction between the new liquidity risk regulation and the central bank credit operations and collateral framework are provided. More specifically, it will be shown how interactions between both frameworks provide 'arbitraging' opportunities of the liquidity risk regulation, which can have detrimental effects for both monetary policy and the effectiveness of regulation. The analysis consists of some basic illustrative examples that show the impact of bank behaviour on the LCR and a 'distance to illiquidity' (DTI) measure. We define DTI as the total amount of short-term market funding evaporation that the bank can handle without fires sales of less liquid assets. If negative externalities of imprudent liquidity risk management is mainly associated with fire sales, then the DTI measure should be relevant for regulation. Consider as example the two bank balance sheets shown in Figure 16.2 (taken, as the subsequent examples, from Bindseil and Lamoot, 2011).

Assume that the central bank accepts corporate bonds at a haircut of 10% (down to a BBB- rating, such as applied by the ECB) and Government bonds at a zero haircut, but does not accept ABSs at all. Of the assets considered in the example, the liquidity regulation only defines (non-encumbered) Government bonds as liquid assets. Additionally, assume a regulatory 75% run-off factor for short-term unsecured funding. One can easily calculate that bank 1 fulfils the LCR (LCR = 1) with a DTI of 75, while the second bank fails to fulfil the LCR (LCR = 0) but is much better in terms of the DTI (at 175). This results from the fact that Bank 2 has an unused central bank borrowing potential of 175, and can therefore survive an outflow of its entire short-term market funding before having to rely on asset fire sales. In contrast, Bank 1 may have to engage in asset fire sales of its ABSs when its short-term funding outflows reach a certain level.

Regulatory arbitrage through absolute central bank intermediation. The example shown in figure 16.3 considers a bank funding central bank deposits of π through central bank borrowing backed by LCR illiquid assets.

With $\pi = 0$ the bank has an LCR of 0.7. Interestingly, though, it can increase its LCR by demanding extra cash from the central bank (in this example through a 3-month central bank repo transaction) and holding it as deposit with the central bank. The bank can increase its LCR linearly by 0.1 with each 20 of extra central bank funding it takes for depositing with the central bank. The attractiveness of doing so of course depends on how desperate the bank is in its search for ways to comply with the LCR, and what costs arise with this technique, as central banks normally apply an interest rate spread between lending operations and deposit collection (the cost of C_{COR} as introduced in

Bank 1			
Government bonds	125	Long term market funding	100
A-rated corporate bonds	0	Short term unsecured market funding	100
ABSs	125	Long term central bank funding	50

Bank 2			
Government bonds	0	Long term market funding	100
A-rated corporate bonds	250	Short term unsecured market funding	100
ABSs	0	Long term central bank funding	50

Fig. 16.2. Balance sheets of two banks

Bindseil and Lamoot, 2011.

Bank			
Government bonds	100	Long term market funding	20
A-rated corporate bonds	200	Short term unsecured market funding	200
Deposits with central bank	π	Long term central bank funding	$80 + \pi$

Fig. 16.3. Balance sheet of a bank that may borrow from and deposit with the central bank to improve liquidity ratios

Bank 1			
Government bonds	100	Long term market funding	20
A-rated corporate bonds	200	Short term unsecured market funding	$200 - \pi$
		Long term central bank borrowing	$80 + \pi$

Bank 2			
Government bonds	100	Long term market funding	170
A-rated corporate bonds	200	Short term market funding	$50 + \pi$
		Central bank borrowing 3M	$80 - \pi$

Fig. 16.4. Balance sheets of two banks

section 13.1). However, for banks in desperate need to reduce any LCR shortfall, these spreads will not be prohibitive. It should also be noted that the spread might not necessarily be detrimental to banks improving their LCR through increased recourse to the central bank, as an increase of borrowing by an LCR-constrained bank can also be achieved through *relative* central bank intermediation.

Regulatory arbitrage through relative central bank intermediation. Consider the case of the two bank balance sheets shown in figure 16.4.

Bank 1 is identical to the initial bank in the previous example, and thus, again, does achieve an LCR of only 0.7. Bank 2 is an exemplary bank with a high share of long-term funding which already initially fulfils the LCR with a value of 2.7. Bank 1 can actually achieve compliance with the LCR by crowding out bank 2 from central bank refinancing. This works at low cost for bank 1 if bank 2 has no problems refinancing in the market at short term, i.e. if it has an excellent credit rating and therefore is not constrained in its market funding (bank 2 may even be able to increase its *long-term* funding). Then, bank 1 can bid somewhat more aggressively in the (assumed) variable-rate tenders for three-month funds, and bank 2 will conclude that competing for central bank funding is not attractive under these circumstances, and will instead go to the market. In the example chosen, bank 1 crowds out bank 2 completely, and both banks will eventually achieve a compliant LCR. Initially, bank 1 has an LCR of 0.7 and bank 2 of 2.7. If bank 1 reduces its short-term market funding by $\pi = 80$ and increases its central bank three-month borrowing by the same amount, while bank 2 does the opposite, then bank 1 achieves an LCR of 1.1 and bank 2 of 1.0. The central bank will have seen the weighted average credit quality of its counterparties decrease, and its concentration risk increase. Also, the true liquidity situation of the banks has not really improved.

Bindseil and Lamoot (2011) provide a number of further similar examples in which inconsistencies between monetary policy implementation and liquidity regulation seem to lead to suboptimal outcomes. The 'arbitrage' opportunities of the liquidity risk regulation through central bank operations may undermine the effectiveness of the liquidity risk regulation and imply that the regulation's purpose of internalizing liquidity risks and building adequate autonomous liquidity buffers is not achieved. Even worse, to comply with the regulation, weaker banks will be incited to rely even *more* heavily on central bank funding, using illiquid collateral. This increases average counterparty risk, concentration risk, and overall financial risk taking of the central bank.

Three approaches can be considered on the part of central banks to make liquidity regulation and central bank operations more compatible. *First, central banks could tighten collateral eligibility.* Central banks accepting a wide collateral set, such as the Eurosystem, could reduce the acceptance of non-HQLA assets (such as ABS and credit claims), and the 'self-use' of collateral, i.e. the use as collateral of self-originated ABS and self-issued covered bonds. *Second, central banks could differentiate between liquid and non-liquid assets in their operations.* In chapter 9, a number of such differentiated pool approaches were presented. In general, the creation of separated collateral pools allows the central bank to apply various forms of discrimination against the less liquid collateral set, also in a way to limit the arbitraging of the differences between central bank operations and the new liquidity regulation. If this is one of the purposes of differentiated collateral sets, then of course, ideally, the sets could be more closely aligned with the sets established by regulators (level 1, level 2, non-liquid). *Third, central banks could strengthen financial disincentives against over-reliance on the central bank.* As shown, the availability of central bank collateral is in some sense equivalent to the availability of HQLA in Basel III liquidity regulation, namely to support the superior equilibrium in which depositors/creditors do not feel incentivized to 'run'. It was however also argued that reliance on central bank eligibility had the relative advantage of not constraining the business model of banks, as the holding of high-quality liquid assets could be considered to be useless from the perspective of the contributions of banks to society, which is to originate and manage information-intense and hence illiquid assets. It may thus be the ideal solution that central banks accept their role as lender of last resort, but ensure financial disincentives against this being unduly exploited. For instance, the International Monetary Fund has been using for a long time surcharges depending on proportionality of the loans relative to the country quotas for its various facilities (see e.g. IMF, 2008). Something similar could be developed for the reliance of banks on central banks. Such an approach is outlined in section 16.3.

Liquidity Regulation and the Control of the Overnight Interest Rate by the Central Bank

Bech and Keister (2012) analyse within a stochastic model and a standing facilities corridor framework the effect of the LCR on the demand for central bank credit and for reserves with the central bank, and hence on the resulting market equilibrium in the interbank money market, i.e. short-term interest rates. They conclude (p. 57) that the LCR (if constraining) may imply a need to adjust central bank operational frameworks, such as making the corridor asymmetric or targeting a term interest rate. Bech and Keister also note that central bank open market operations will themselves affect the LCR of the banking system (also depending on collateral types), and that this may shift the demand curve for the reserves. Bech and Keister (2012, 60) conclude:

> This analysis points to three basic conclusions. First, the LCR will not impair the ability of central banks to implement monetary policy, but the process by which they do so may change. Second, correctly anticipating an open market operation's effect on interest rates will require central banks to consider not only the size of the operation, but also the way the operation is structured and how it impacts on bank balance sheets. Finally, the LCR may increase the steepness of the very short end of the yield curve by introducing an additional premium for interbank loans that extend beyond 30 days.

16.3 A FRAMEWORK WITH FINANCIAL INCENTIVES AGAINST DISPROPORTIONAL RELIANCE ON THE CENTRAL BANK

To address moral hazard in the form of excessive reliance on central bank funding, the central bank can make banks subject to an interest rate surcharge depending on the over-proportionality of their central bank borrowing. 'Proportional' central bank borrowing may be defined in terms of the ratio of total central bank credit divided by the total aggregate assets of the banking system. The idea is far from new: Goldenweiser (1949, 47) reports that in 1919 some Federal Reserve Banks 'adopted systems of rates graduated in proportion to the amount borrowed by an individual bank'. Also the Bundesbank applied for many decades a proportionality-based limit system ('Rediskontkontingente') to the recourse of banks to its main credit facility.

A surcharge framework will be specified on the basis of the financial system shown in figure 16.5.

Let $L = L_1 + L_2$ be the total balance sheet length of the banking system. 'Proportionality' can be defined in the financial accounts in figure 16.5 as a certain borrowing from the central bank relative to total bank assets. Define as overall proportionality P:

$$P = B / L \tag{16.3}$$

Define as the individual banks' proportionality factors p_i:

$$p_i = B_i / L_i \tag{16.4}$$

Bank i borrows proportionally if $p_i = P$. The surcharge for bank i, defined as a nominal extra cost imposed on bank i for its over-proportional borrowing, can be given the following general form:

$$\kappa_i = f\left(P, p_i, B_i\right) \tag{16.5}$$

with always for $p_i \leq P$: $f(P, p_i B_i), = 0$ and for $p_i > P$: $f(P, p_i B_i) \geq 0$. The surcharge κ_i can be defined as an absolute cost. Normally, in view of different business models of banks and short-term liquidity shocks, the central bank should provide some buffer for over-proportionality before surcharges kick in. This also prevents normal fluctuations in the relative recourse of banks to central bank credit from leading easily to a built-in tightening of the monetary policy stance. If surcharges kicked in as soon as a bank is marginally over-proportional, then in principle half of the banking system would normally be subject to a surcharge at the margin, and hence the normal monetary policy operations rate would only apply to the other half.

Bank 1			
Lending to corporates	$L_1 = D_1 + B_1$	Household deposits Credit from central bank (CB_1)	D_1 B_1

Bank 2			
Lending to corporates	$L_2 = D_2 + B_2$	Household deposits Credit from central bank (CB_2)	D_2 B_2

Central Bank			
Credit operations	$B = B_1 + B_1$	Banknotes	B

Fig. 16.5. Financial accounts to illustrate framework for surcharges on over-proportional borrowing

The assessment of the single bank with regard to its proportionality could be done within an averaging period of e.g. one month. The proportionality factor P should be known to banks at the beginning of this averaging period, such that banks can optimize their funding also on its basis. Therefore the calculation of P would have to be based on a snapshot (or several snapshots over which an average is taken) one or two months before the start of the averaging period in which p_i is calculated.

Consider the following example. If B = 20 and L = 100, $B_1 = 5$, $B_2 = 15$, $D_1 = 45$ and $D_2 = 35$, then P = 0.2, $p_1 = 0.1$, $p_2 = 0.3$. Assume now that the surcharge function $\kappa_i = f(P, p_i, B_i)$ is defined as for $p_i \leq aP$: $\kappa_i = f(P, p_i, B_i) = 0$ and for $p_i > aP$: $\kappa_i = f(P, p_i, B_i) = b(p_i - aP)B_i$, with a and b constants and a ≥ 1 and b > 0. The parameters a and b can be set by the central bank and will depend on the objectives of the surcharge (see below). If for example a = 2 and b = 1%, then there is no surcharge under the financial accounts example above. If, however, a is decreased to 1.2 then the surcharge to be imposed on bank 2 is: $\kappa_2 = b(p_2 - aP)B_2 = 1\% * (0.3 - 0.24) * 15 = 0.009$.

The application of such a framework could allow some aspects of liquidity regulation to be rethought. It can provide incentives both against structural over-reliance on the central bank, and against counting on the central bank to provide a cost-free buffer against negative funding shocks. By choosing the parameters and the functional form of the surcharge function, the central bank can determine the strength and shape of these incentives. If the central bank wants in particular to prevent banks from relying *ex ante* excessively on the central bank as lender of last resort in crisis times, then probably both a and b should be relatively high. If, in contrast, the central bank is worried about structural reliance on over-proportionality, then a should be relatively lower but also b can be lower.

Figure 16.6 provides a further illustrative example for the case of a surcharge function $\kappa_i = f(P, p_i, B_i)$ with for $p_i \leq aP$: $\kappa_i = f(P, p_i, B_i) = 0$ and for $p_i > aP$: $\kappa_i = f(P, p_i, B_i) = b(p_i - aP)B_i$. Assume that the (continuous) banking population is initially $N(P,\sigma_p^2)$ distributed in terms of the ratio of central bank credit to bank assets, and that the absolute central bank reliance of each bank would be 100 ($B_i = 100$ for all i). To take an example assume P = 10% and $\sigma_p = 2\%$, i.e. on average banks refinance 10% of their operations through central bank credit, and the standard deviation across banks of this measure is two percentage points. The first surcharge framework sets a = 1.1 and b = 2%. This framework will be directly binding for a relevant share of banks, namely for $1 - \Phi((11\% - 10\%)/2\%) = 1 - \Phi(0.5) = 31\%$ of banks. The average surcharge that the entire banking system would have to pay would be 0.79%, which could be considered as measure of the tightening of the monetary policy stance from introducing the framework. Of course banks will react to the surcharge and those subject to it will try to obtain interbank funding from those banks not subject to it. This will lead to a reduction in the variance of the distribution

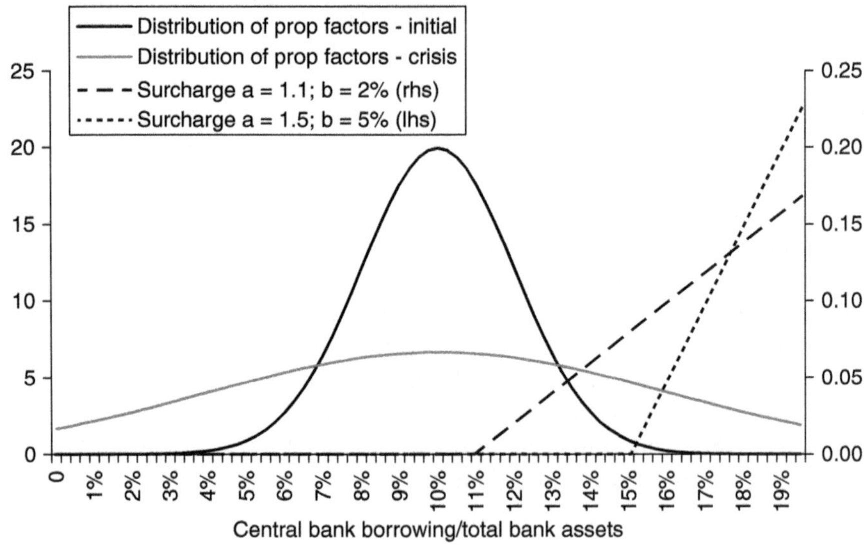

Fig. 16.6. Surcharges for over-proportional reliance on the central bank—an example with two specifications of the surcharge parameters

of the (central bank credit/bank asset) ratio across banks. The precise extent of this drop will depend on interbank market transaction costs and marginal costs of banks to access deposits and capital market funding. If we assume that after imposing the surcharge framework, σ_p would drop from 2% to 1%, then the average surcharge paid by the banking system would also decline, from 0.79% to 0.16%. To neutralize the tightening of the monetary policy stance resulting from the introduction of a surcharge framework, the central bank could adjust downward the level of its operational target variable (unless it has reached the zero lower bound).

Figure 16.6 also shows a second specification of a surcharge framework with a = 1.5 and b = 5%. This specification is not really binding for the assumed initial distribution of banks' recourse to the central bank and therefore seems to be conceived to provide disincentives against relying *in a crisis situation* excessively on the central bank. For instance, if in a crisis σ_p increases from 2% to 6%, then the average surcharge paid by the banking system to be paid under this parameter specification increases from 0.02% to 1.61%, and the 7% of banks relying most on the central bank will have to pay at least a surcharge of 10 percentage points on their central bank borrowing.

If an effective surcharge framework were in place, regulators could rely on liquidity measures, such as distance to illiquidity (DTI), which include the possibility of relying on central banks, but would require *capital charges* for the possible costs relating to surcharges in case a large over-proportional reliance on central bank funding should materialize. This approach would help regulators in addressing their concern about over-reliance of individual banks on central banks and would be in line with Bagehot's advice to 'lend freely, but at a high price' in a crisis.

An additional complementary measure, through which the central bank could address over-reliance via its operational framework, would be to *define cost-covering fees for the valuation and risk management of less liquid assets that are submitted to the central bank as collateral.* While it can be justified that central banks accept less liquid assets as collateral than the assets accepted in interbank repos (as the asymmetry of credit risk allows them to set relatively high haircuts and as central banks are not subject to liquidity risk), it will lead to distortions if the central bank did not perform a thorough risk and valuation analysis of these assets, or if it did do so, but without charging the banks submitting the collateral for that analysis.

Applying both surcharge components (over-proportionality surcharge and cost-based surcharge for the assessment and handling of illiquid collateral) with appropriate parameters could be effective to prevent undesired over-reliance, and supervisors should impose capital charges reflecting risks of prospective central bank reliance under contingency scenarios.

17

The International Lender of Last Resort

17.1 THE CASE OF A FIXED EXCHANGE RATE SYSTEM

So far, the financial system has been assumed to encompass only one currency and one central bank, and the LOLR function was also analysed from this perspective. With fixed exchange rate systems, dollarized economies, or in the case of international banks operating in multiple currencies, the central bank may be unable to provide LOLR services in the currency required by stressed domestic economic entities. This raises the question of the need and form of an international lender of last resort (ILOLR). As noted e.g. by Fischer (1999), the issues encountered in the optimal design of an international lender of last resort encompass those that arise in the case of a national lender of last resort (Calvo, 1988; Kaminsky and Reinhart, 1999; Obstfeld, 2009; Bindseil and Winkler, 2013). Like other episodes of financial turmoil, international liquidity crises can be managed by public authorities if sufficient systemic buffers are available to withstand liquidity shocks. Various dual liquidity crises in emerging markets during the 1990s involved countries that operated a fixed exchange rate, such as the Asian crisis countries. A fixed exchange rate implies that foreign exchange replaces banknotes as the 'safe haven' asset and that the central bank itself can become illiquid in the sense of being unable to maintain the currency peg to which it had committed (as seen e.g. in July 1931 in Germany).

International liquidity crises under a fixed exchange rate can be captured by broadening the previous financial accounts analysis to two countries: a safe haven country (country 1) and a financially distressed country (country 2). Each country has a banking sector and a central bank that issue deposits and banknotes to a single household/investor sector, as there is free capital mobility between the two countries. Moreover, the central bank balance sheets now must include foreign exchange reserves (FR_1, FR_2) as an asset. For the sake of simplicity, we limit ourselves here to a deposit shift shock k. When deposits are shifted from the country 2 bank to the country 1 bank, an FX spot transaction takes place as the two deposits are denominated in different currencies. For simplicity, we assume that the fixed exchange rate between the two currencies is 1. This, however, does not change the fact that we now have two currencies, and that to maintain equilibrium, the FX spot market must be balanced in terms of demand and supply. This will force central banks to 'intervene' in markets using their FX reserves, such as to just counterbalance the deposit shift-related FX flows emanating from the household. In an international context, the deposit shift k is in fact also a capital account flow (and if relating to fear of default, capital controls or devaluation, may be called 'capital flight').

Figure 17.1 shows the case in which central banks are not running out of foreign reserves, i.e. the deposit shift shock is lower than initial foreign reserves. Assume that country 1 is the US and country 2 is Panama, and that while both have foreign reserves, only Panama cares about defending the exchange rate. Deposit shift shocks are now named k^1, k^2, whereby the superscript is added to highlight that these are flows in different currencies (k^1 is a flow in currency 1, i.e. in the currency issued by central bank 1, etc.). That the exchange rate is equal to one implies that $k^1 = k^2$ and we could in principle also leave away the superscript. However, it makes it easier to check that indeed the currency market is in equilibrium in the sense that the sales and purchase flows in each currency match, such that the stability of the exchange rate is plausible. This is the case in figure 17.1. Indeed, the excess supply (demand) of currency 2 (1) created by the household through its deposit shift shock is exactly matched by demand (supply) by central bank 2.

Note that there is an initial claim of US banks towards Panama banks of ($FR_2 - FR_1$). This relates to how foreign reserves were initially built up by the central banks. One origin of central bank foreign reserves could be the accumulation of current account surpluses under fixed exchange rates (this can be modelled in the financial accounts by splitting up the households into one in each country and to have them exchange bank deposits against real goods—see annex A to this chapter). Here we assume instead that the foreign reserves were actively built up as follows: (i) CB of Panama approaches US bank in US and opens a US deposit account; (ii) CB of Panama (CBP) enters an FX cash transaction with the US bank: it gives 1 Panama dollar and obtains 1 USD; (iii) the 1 USD is credited on the CBP account with the US bank in the US; (iv) the 1 Panama dollar that the US bank obtains is credited on an account of the US bank with its correspondent bank in Panama; (v) as a result the US banking system has a 1 Panama dollar claim on the Panama banking system (while the Central Bank of Panama has a 1 USD claim against the US bank).

In principle, either of the two central banks can take over the role of compensating for the capital flows with its foreign reserves, and in fact if $k > 0$, central bank 1 is able without limits to compensate the flow, while central bank 2 can run out of foreign reserves. However, typically, large monetary areas (e.g. the US) do not target exchange rates, whereas small ones may peg their currency to a large neighbour (Panama to the US) but then will have to cope with maintaining the peg.

Households / Investors			
Real Assets	$E - D - B$	Household Equity	E
Banknotes 1	$B/2$		
Banknotes 2	$B/2$		
Deposits Bank 1	$D/2 + k^1$		
Deposits Bank 2	$D/2 - k^2$		

Corporate			
Real assets	$D + B$	Credits from banks	$D + B$

Bank 1 ('US bank')			
Lending to corporates	$(D + B)/2$	Household deposits / debt	$D/2 + k^1$
Claim towards banking system 2	$(FR_2 - FR_1)$	Foreign reserves of CB 2	$FR_2 - k^1$
		OMO credit CB 1	$B/2 - FR_1$

Bank 2 ('Panama bank')			
Lending to corporates	$(D + B)/2$	Household deposits	$D/2 - k^2$
		Foreign reserves CB 1	FR_1
		OMO credit CB 2	$B/2 - FR_2 + k^2$
		Liabilities towards banking system 2	$(FR_2 - FR_1)$

Central bank 1 ('Federal Reserve')			
OMO credit CB 1	$B/2 - FR_1$	Banknotes	$B/2$
Foreign reserves CB 1	FR_1		

Central bank 2 ('Central Bank of Panama')			
OMO credit CB 2	$B/2 - FR_2 + k^2$	Banknotes	$B/2$
Foreign reserves CB 2	$FR_2 - k^1$		

Fig. 17.1. A two countries fixed exchange rate regime

What if CB2 (the central bank of Panama) runs out of foreign reserves because $k > FR_2$? CB2 may obtain (indirectly) a loan from CB 1 (the US Federal Reserve) which allows it to intervene further to defend its currency. This generalized case is represented in figure 17.2.

If CB 1 is not ready to provide an inter-central bank loan in its currency, CB 2 will have difficulties defending its currency if k is large. In theory, private cross-border inflows from households could be secured by CB 2 raising the country 2 interest rate level, such as to partially reverse the deposit shift/capital flight shock k. However, such a policy approach implies that the interest

Bank 1			
Lending to corporates	$(D + B)/2$	Household deposits / debt	$D/2 + k^1$
Claim towards banking system 2	$(FR_2 - FR_1)$	Foreign Reserves CB 2	$\max(0, FR2 - k^1)$
		OMO credit CB 1	$B/2 - FR_1 - \max(0, - FR2 + k^1)$

Bank 2			
Lending to corporates	$(D + B)/2$	Household deposits	$D/2 - k^2$
		Foreign Reserves CB 1	FR_1
		OMO credit CB 2	$B/2 - FR_2 + k^2$
		Liabilities towards banking system 2	$(FR_2 - FR_1)$

Central bank 1 (Federal Reserve)			
OMO credit CB 1	$B/2 - FR_1 - \max(0, - FR2 + k^1)$	Banknotes	$B/2$
Foreign Reserves CB 1	FR_1		
Lending to CB 2	$\max(0, - FR_2 + k^1)$		

Central bank 2 (Panama)			
OMO credit CB 2	$B_2 - FR_2 + k^2$	Banknotes	$B/2$
Foreign Reserves CB 2	$\max(0, FR_2 - k^1)$	Borrowing from CB 1	$\max(0, -FR_2 + k^1)$

Fig. 17.2. A two countries fixed exchange rate regime with inter-central bank credit

rate is no longer used as an instrument to achieve price and output stability (Obstfeld et al., 2005). Most importantly, with rising interest rates, real economic activity is likely to decline, which reinforces doubts about the solvency of any borrower in the economy of country 2 and hence aggravates the liquidity crisis. Thus, under financial stress, interbank and capital markets typically are not a source of compensating flows. Instead, bad expectations can become self-fulfilling and CB 2 may eventually run out of foreign reserves.

The problem of foreign debt crises and its multiple equilibrium characteristics have been identified and modelled for a while (e.g. Calvo, 1988; Morris and Shin 1998; Calvo and Mendoza, 1999; Botman and Diks, 2005). The simplest way to capture the multiple equilibrium problem is in analogy to the simple bank run model introduced in section 11.3, assuming that the country's state sector (including the government and the central bank) has foreign debt (the case of fixed exchange rates is similar). Figure 17.3 shows the balance sheet of a state with foreign debt, in analogy to a bank balance sheet.

Similarly to the bank run problem as described in section 11.3, the question is whether in the strategic game played by the two short-term investors,

State A			
Assets	2 + E	Short term foreign debt – investor 1 Short term foreign debt – investor 2 Equity	1 1 E

Fig. 17.3. A state with foreign debt threatened by an investor strike

keeping deposits (or rolling over short-term debt) is better than withdrawing (not rolling over) regardless of what the other investor does. In particular, multiple equilibria arise if an investor is better off being the first one who withdraws, compared to the case where both investors withdraw simultaneously.[1] We had simplified the bank run problem to the maximum extent by distinguishing only perfectly liquid and completely illiquid assets (and an intermediary asset category which switched from one to the other depending on financial market conditions). In the case of speculative attacks on the state, it is useful to generalize by relying on a function f(x) from the state's assets ordered according to liquidity in [0,2 + E] into marginal liquidation costs within [0,1], whereby $f(0) = 0$ and $df(x)/dx \geq 0$. The following short-term sources of foreign currency are potentially available to a state:

- The state may have some cash reserve in foreign currency that can be used *without costs*; moreover, the state may have some regular inflows of foreign currency (e.g. relating to raw material exports) that are also available at no cost.
- The state may be able to generate short-term extra foreign currency by *selling to foreign investors state-owned companies, licences to exploit the natural resources of the country, or e.g. a harbour as a military base for a foreign power*. However, doing that very quickly and in stressed conditions implies the need to accept fire sale discounts and related costs eating up the country's equity (see Krugman, 2000).
- The state may impose an *extra wealth tax on the foreign currency holdings of citizens with domestic banks*. This is costly as it may be perceived as 'expropriation' by the state, undermines the trust of society in the state, and may lead to political instability and populist parties taking over.
- The state may *save on investments*, i.e. it may *stop infrastructure or education projects* (if those imply payments in foreign currency). Again this will be costly, as it will reduce the future growth potential of the economy.

[1] For a more general review of the particularities of sovereign default, see Buchheit et al. (2013).

In analogy to the simple two-depositors bank run model of section 11.3, it can be shown that a single no-run equilibrium of two investors can be maintained if the cumulative cost of generating enough cash for paying out one investor is less than E. On the basis of f(x), one can derive a function g(y) which describes the total cost g that arises for generating a total amount of cash y (see Bindseil, 2013), with $g(0) = 0$, $dg/dy > 0$. Then the condition for a no-run equilibrium is:

$$g(1) < E \tag{17.1}$$

This condition ensures that staying invested does not lead to losses even if the other investor runs and generates associated damages to the country. A country may feel it is in a comfortable situation in terms of fulfilling this condition, but may then be subject to a shock which, by destruction of equity, or by a steepening of the functions f(x) and g(y), may switch the situation into one with multiple equilibria, including the possibility of a run and the default of the country.

As mentioned above, one source of short-term foreign currency consists in receiving a loan from the foreign central bank (analogous to being able as a bank to access the central bank as lender of last resort). Returning to the notation of figure 17.2, access to an inter-central bank loan from CB 1 may be the only solution to avoid, after a negative shock hitting the country, a multiple-equilibrium situation and a devaluation (or default in foreign currency). Why might CB 1 be unwilling to provide an inter-central bank loan? Three reasons may be relevant:

- Lending to CB 2 could be perceived as macroeconomically destabilizing, e.g. by triggering inflationary pressures in the future.
- Lending to CB 2 might be considered to create moral hazard, i.e. the government of country 2 might reduce its own efforts to restore confidence.
- CB 1 may doubt the ability or willingness of CB 2 to pay back at maturity, i.e. it may have credit risk concerns. This fear may be particularly justified if, overall, country 2 is in a disastrous state and politically unstable.

The IMF, acting as an intermediary and as monitor of global economic and monetary conditions, and imposing programmes and conditionality whenever providing loans, can be interpreted as an institution established to address all three of these concerns (Fischer, 1999; Corsetti et al., 2006).

17.2 PROVISION OF FOREIGN CURRENCY BY CENTRAL BANKS TO DOMESTIC COUNTERPARTIES IN 2009–2013

Beyond the IMF and fixed exchange rate systems, it is noteworthy that in the current crisis, central banks developed a new form of mutual cooperation in view of foreign exchange funding stress of international banking groups. International banks typically do business in different currencies and are thus subject to liquidity shocks in these different currencies. At the same time, they may have collateral in different currencies and deposited in different regions of the world. Ideally, collateral could be used as one large pool when offsetting, by means of central bank funding, liquidity shocks arising in whatever currency. In normal practice, however, central banks tend to limit collateral eligibility to assets located in their own jurisdiction and denominated in their own currency and, in particular, to provide funding only in their own money. As long as foreign exchange swap markets function, global banking groups are able to swap currencies, such as to effectively manage one pool of collateral and cash (although regulatory and supervisory treatment of cross-border banking, as well as legal issues, will still lead to some fragmentation). Foreign exchange swaps are over-the-counter transactions consisting in a simultaneous purchase and sale of identical values of one currency for another, with two different value dates (normally a spot and a forward date). As many other over-the-counter contracts, they have zero value when agreed, i.e. specify cash flows which at prevailing market conditions have a zero net value for both parties. However, they become valuable during their lifetime (i.e. they get a 'replacement value') and thus create counterparty exposure as actual foreign exchange rates move away from the forward rate. The replacement value is normally collateralized to mitigate counterparty risk. Settlement risk has been an issue for a long time in FX markets, although settlement through CLS ('Continuous Link Settlement'), a global central-clearing counterparty for FX transactions, has largely addressed that in recent years. Nevertheless, residual counterparty risks remain in FX transactions, which explains why FX markets, and in particular FX swap markets, were impaired in several episodes within 2007–2013.

In a crisis, in which even the FX swap markets become less efficient (or break down: see Baba and Packer, 2009), central banks may help by providing themselves currency bridges to the market, extending their intermediation function from the domestic currency to foreign currencies and/or from domestic to foreign counterparties. There are two main techniques for central banks to do this: (i) provision of domestic liquidity against foreign currency-denominated collateral, possibly to banks domiciled in foreign jurisdictions;[2] (ii) lending foreign currency against domestic collateral to domestic banks. For the latter, the central bank must have available foreign currency, possibly in large

[2] The Basel Committee on Payment and Settlement Systems (CPSS) has undertaken substantial work on cross-border collateral arrangements between central banks (see e.g. CPSS, 2006), making a distinction between general cross-border arrangements and those to be activated during a financial crisis. Its 2006 report also discusses alternative models for the acceptance of foreign collateral and identifies the potential implications of a central bank's collateral policy for financial stability and competition.

amounts. These necessary FX resources could derive from the existing foreign reserves of the central bank. Alternatively, they could be obtained through a swap with the central bank issuing the needed currency, which is more efficient and may have higher credibility as it is potentially unlimited.

Similarly, like other LOLR functions of central banks, providing such currency bridges will be relevant for monetary conditions as it will reduce the perceived credit-riskiness of banks, and therefore improve their general access and costs of funding, and therefore the banks' willingness to lend. This is more important, the more banks have diversified their business across borders. Over the last decades, cross-border and cross-currency business has grown substantially, including through cross-border mergers.

In view of difficulties in late 2007 for non-US banks accessing USD funding with the usual efficiency though FX swap markets, key central banks announced on 12 December 2007 USD-providing operations as 'measures designed to address elevated pressures in short-term funding markets'. For example, the ECB announced that:

> The Governing Council of the ECB has decided to take joint action with the Federal Reserve by offering US dollar funding to Eurosystem counterparties. The Eurosystem shall conduct two US dollar liquidity-providing operations, in connection with the US dollar Term Auction Facility, against ECB-eligible collateral for a maturity of 28 and 35 days. The submission of bids will take place on 17 and 20 December 2007 for settlement on 20 and 27 December 2007, respectively.

The announcement was thus limited to two operations, and in terms of total volume. More regular operations were conducted later on, but in early 2010 they were discontinued in view of improved market conditions. They were reactivated again, and with the intensification of the sovereign debt crisis in the euro area, the USD-providing operations, including the reliance on swaps of central banks with the New York Fed, were extended and made more efficient and convenient. On 30 November 2011, the following 'coordinated central bank action to address pressures in global money markets' was announced (from ECB press release):

> The Bank of Canada, the Bank of England, the Bank of Japan, the European Central Bank, the Federal Reserve and the Swiss National Bank are today announcing coordinated actions to enhance their capacity to provide liquidity support to the global financial system. The purpose of these actions is to ease strains in financial markets and thereby mitigate the effects of such strains on the supply of credit to households and businesses and so help foster economic activity... These central banks have agreed to lower the pricing on the existing temporary US dollar liquidity swap arrangements by 50 basis points so that the new rate will be the US dollar Overnight Index Swap (OIS) rate plus 50 basis points... In addition, the Bank of England, the Bank of Japan, the European Central Bank, and the Swiss National Bank will continue to offer three-month tenders until further notice.

The pricing was made more favourable as stigmatization of the facility was considered a more important problem than moral hazard. The changes of November 2011 were considered a full success as they did not lead to a large recourse by euro area banks to the facilities, but to an improved market access, such that US funding issues were not a major problem any longer, despite the continuation and temporary intensification of the sovereign debt crisis. To that extent, the FX provision by major central banks on the basis of inter-central bank swaps appears as ideal type not only of effective international central bank cooperation, but also of the provision of backstop facilities that lead eventually to *less* and not to more central bank dependence of banks (in the sense of the bank-run model of sections 11.3 and 12.4 in which central bank access supports the unique no-run equilibrium).

Ben Bernanke summarized in 2008 the logic of the central bank FX swaps and foreign currency provision of central banks as follows (Speech delivered at the Fifth European Central Bank Central Banking Conference, *The Euro at Ten: Lessons and Challenges*, Frankfurt, Germany, 14 November 2008):

> Many financial institutions outside the United States, especially in Europe, had substantially increased their dollar investments in recent years, including loans to nonbanks and purchases of asset-backed securities issued by U.S. residents... This collaborative approach to the injection of liquidity reflects more than the global, multi-currency nature of funding difficulties. It also reflects the importance of relationships between central banks and the institutions they serve. Under swap agreements, the responsibility for allocating foreign-currency liquidity within a jurisdiction lies with the domestic central bank. This arrangement makes use of the fact that the domestic central bank is best positioned to understand the mechanics and special features of its own country's financial and payments systems and, because of its existing relationships with domestic financial institutions, can best assess the strength of each institution and its needs for foreign-currency liquidity. The domestic central bank is also typically best informed about the quality of the collateral offered by potential borrowers.

A detailed description of the operations is provided by Allen and Moessner (2010), Goldberg et al. (2010), Flemming and Klagge (2010), and Papadia (2013). Figure 17.4 shows the ECB provision of USD to its counterparties, including the second wave during 2012 in the context of the sovereign debt crisis, split up according to the maturities of the operations with banks.

A simple financial accounts representation of the foreign exchange swap operations between central banks and of the underlying liquidity problem is provided in figure 17.5. As the operations do not rely on foreign reserves, it is assumed below that none of the central banks involved has foreign reserves. The balance sheet of bank 2 ('European banks') is split into a USD part and a EUR part, and it is assumed that the liquidity outflows relate only to USD deposits. Before the outflows, the bank had funded its USD assets precisely with USD liabilities. As bank 2 is not a counterparty of the Fed (CB 1), it

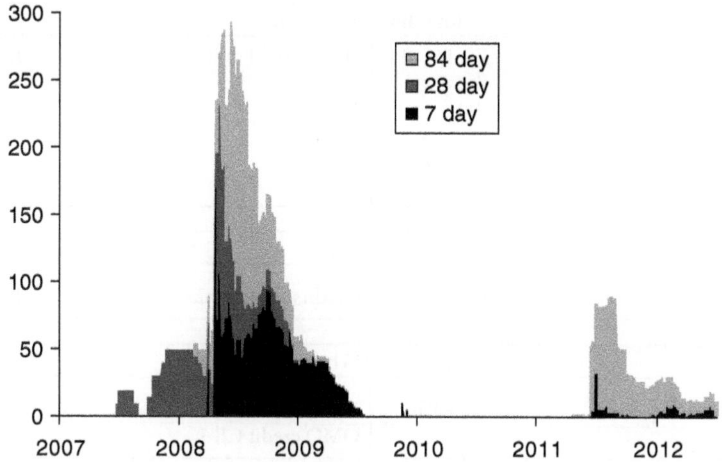

Fig. 17.4. ECB USD operations, according to maturities
Source: ECB.

has no access to the Fed's USD credit operations, so if it experiences a USD outflow, and also has no access to FX swap markets (because the market is impaired as a symptom of a financial crisis), its only chance to prevent default is to obtain some USD from its home central bank. It is assumed in figure 17.5 that bank 2's non-central bank funding, and the related assets, are half in USD and half in EUR.

ANNEX A: CURRENT ACCOUNT TRANSACTIONS AS ORIGIN OF FOREIGN RESERVES

In figure 17.1, it had been assumed that the foreign reserves of the two central banks had been built up through active purchases of central banks, and the banking systems had accepted having counterbalancing positions. In figure 17A.1, it is shown how the financial system would look if current account transactions are at the origin of the building up of foreign reserves. It is assumed that 'Panama' had current account surpluses of CUR relative to the US, and the central bank of Panama has accordingly built up foreign reserves (that could then serve to provide buffers against capital flight).

ANNEX B: TARGET2 BALANCES IN THE EURO AREA

A lot has been written on TARGET2 balances in the euro area (e.g. Sinn and Wollmershäuser, 2011; Bindseil and König, 2011, 2012; Buiter and Rabhari, 2012b; Merler and Pisani-Ferry, 2012; Cour-Thimann, 2013). The mechanics of TARGET2 balances are briefly presented in this annex to clarify again their nature. They should

Households / Investors			
Real Assets	E – D – B	Household Equity	E
Banknotes 1	B/2		
Banknotes 2	B/2		
USD Deposits Bank 1	D/2 + *k*		
USD Deposits Bank 2	D/4 – *k*		
EUR Deposits Bank 2	D/4		

Corporate			
Real assets	D + B	Credits from banks	D + B

Bank 1 ('US bank')			
Lending to corporates	(D + B)/2	Household deposits / debt	D/2 + **k**
		OMO credit CB 1	B/2 – **k**

Bank 2 ('European bank')			
USD lending to corporates	D/4	Household deposits in USD	D/4 – *k*
		Special USD borrowing from CB 2	k
EUR Lending to corporates	D/4 + B/2	Household deposits	D/4
		OMO credit CB 2	B/2

Central bank 1 ('Federal Reserve')			
OMO credit CB 1	B/2 – **k**	Banknotes	B/2
USD claim on CB 2	**k**		

Central bank 2 ('ECB')			
OMO credit CB 2	B/2	Banknotes	B/2
Special USD lending to bank 2	**k**	USD liability to CB 1	**k**

Fig. 17.5. USD liquidity provision to euro area banks by the ECB, relying on FX swap with the US Fed

not be regarded particularly as a phenomenon of the 'international' lender of last resort, but the debates surrounding them relate to the balance of payments of individual euro area countries, and thereby they relate to the issues touched upon in this chapter.

Figure 17B.1 captures two possible sources of TARGET2 balances in a monetary area—current account transactions ('CUR') and capital transactions ('CAP'). The household sector has been split into a country A and a country B household. Both households undertake capital flight (i.e. both the A-household and the B-household transfer deposits from the B-banking system to the A-banking system). In addition, household A sells a good (say, a used car) to household B, reflecting a current account transaction. The impact of both transactions on household deposits, central bank credit-taking by the two banking systems, and TARGET2 balances within the Eurosystem are of an identical nature, implying that it is not possible to identify the nature of TARGET2 balances in terms of type of balance-of-payment transaction from

Households / Investors Country 1 (US)			
Real Assets	(E – D – B)/2 + CUR	Household Equity	E/2
Banknotes 1	B/2		
Deposits Bank 1	D/2 – CUR		

Households / Investors Country 2 (Panama)			
Real Assets	(E – D – B)/2 – CUR	Household Equity	E/2
Banknotes 2	B/2		
Deposits Bank 1	D/2 + CUR		

Corporate			
Real assets	D + B	Credits from banks	D + B

Bank 1 (US)			
Lending to corporates	(D + B)/2	Household deposits / debt	D/2 – CUR
		Foreign reserves of CB 2	CUR
		OMO credit CB 1	B/2

Bank 2 (Panama)			
Lending to corporates	(D + B)/2	Household deposits	D/2 + CUR
		OMO credit CB 2	B/2 – CUR

Central bank 1 (US)			
OMO credit CB 1	B/2	Banknotes	B/2

Central bank 2 (Panama)			
OMO credit CB 2	B/2 – CUR	Banknotes	B/2
Foreign reserves CB 2	CUR		

Fig. 17A.1. A two-countries fixed exchange rate regime in which foreign reserves have resulted from a current account surplus

any position in the financial system (i.e. in the banking system or central banks). Only the balance-of-payment statistics are able to provide an answer to the question whether a change of TARGET2 balances is driven by current-account or capital-account transactions. The balance-of-payment statistics actually suggest that different cases have to be distinguished. In Ireland, the country with the highest-ever-reached TARGET2 to GDP ratio, current account imbalances played no role in driving TARGET2 balances. For most other TARGET2 liability countries, from an *ex post* perspective, one would probably agree that the large current-account deficits observed ever since the start of monetary union were an important element of the imbalances and distortions that led to the vulnerable situation in 2010/2011, which then led to the large-scale capital

Household A

Assets		Liabilities	
Deposits A-bank	D/4 + **CAP/2 + CUR**	Equity	E/2
Deposits B-bank	D/4 – **CAP/2**		
Banknotes	B/2		
Real assets	(E – D – B)/2 – **CUR**		

Household B

Assets		Liabilities	
Deposits A-bank	D/4 + **CAP/2**	Equity	E/2
Deposits B-bank	D/4 – **CAP/2 – CUR**		
Banknotes	B/2		
Real assets	(E – D – B)/2 + **CUR**		

Euro area corporate sector

Assets		Liabilities	
Real assets	D + B	Credit from banks	D + B

A bank

Assets		Liabilities	
Corp loans	(D + B)/2	Deposits	D/2 + **CAP + CUR**
		CB credit	B/2 – **CAP – CUR**

B bank

Assets		Liabilities	
Corp loans	(D + B)/2	Deposits	D/2 – **CAP – CUR**
		CB credit	B/2 + **CAP + CUR**

NCB A

Assets		Liabilities	
Credit to bank	B/2–**CAP–CUR**	Banknotes	B/2
T2 claims	**CAP + CUR**		

NCB B

Assets		Liabilities	
Credit to bank	B/2 + **CAP + CUR**	Banknotes	B/2
		T2Liabilities	**CAP + CUR**

ECB

Assets		Liabilities	
T2 claims	CAP + CUR	T2 Liabilities	CAP + CUR

Eurosystem = ECB + NCB A + NCB B

Assets		Liabilities	
Eurosystem credit	B	Banknotes	B

Fig. 17B.1. System of financial accounts to present TARGET2 balances

flight. In any case, even the finding that past current-account imbalances were part of the problem should not be considered equivalent with the conclusion that countries 'lived beyond their means'. For concluding this, the savings ratios should also be considered, and the savings ratio for e.g. Italy or Spain was not particularly low (e.g. much higher than those of the US or UK). Much of the inflows of funding and the associated current-account imbalances were investments. These investments in retrospect often did not have the productivity that was assumed *ex ante*.

In the accounts representation in figure 17B.1, it is assumed that the banking system A remains dependent on central bank funding. In case CUR + CAP exceeds the initial reliance of the banking system A on central bank credit, the banking system A will end in excess liquidity and hold a deposit with the central bank A. It should be noted that in any case the monetary base in country B shrinks, while it increases in country A. Central bank credit increases in country A and decreases in country B. Whether this is well summarized in statements such as 'In the periphery countries, the printing presses were overheating, and the core countries had to replace their printing presses with paper shredders' (Sinn and Wollmershäuser, 2011, 19) is a matter of taste.

18

Optimal Monetary Policy Operations in Crisis Times

In normal times and with well-developed money markets, monetary policy implementation is about steering the overnight interbank rate in the simplest and most efficient way. In contrast to what has sometimes been said, monetary policy implementation is not an 'art' under such conditions, but a relatively straightforward technical task not requiring any macroeconomic or monetary economics knowledge (reflecting the 'separation principle' introduced in chapter 1). If monetary policy implementation has been complex for many decades even when markets functioned well, this was mainly due to a (wrong) monetary policy transmission doctrine, which was considered to have implications for the appropriate way to implement monetary policy. More generally, one could diagnose in retrospect a lack of discipline and parsimony in the design and use of monetary policy instruments in normal times during the twentieth century.

In a financial crisis, instead, monetary policy implementation becomes not only an art, but one which implies considerable risks for the central bank. From a focus on one single variable (the overnight interbank rate), the set of target variables expands to a full variety of interest rates, since the usual arbitrage relationships between market interest rates break down. On one side, the central bank perceives the need to act directly on different rates (and quantities) in such circumstances. On the other side, the central bank is aware that identifying the appropriate level of spreads under such circumstances is very difficult. Hence, any central bank action will be subject to substantial uncertainty. However, not acting at all due to the underlying uncertainties is also not a solution, as this would likely lead to deflation and economic contraction. Moreover, the support of the funding liquidity of banks becomes a *leitmotiv* of monetary policy operations and framework decision of the central bank during a financial crisis. The existence of liquidity facilities with relevant accessibility thanks to a sufficient collateral basis (i) contributes to preserving market access; (ii) contributes to avoiding fire sale losses, excessive deleveraging, and the social costs of defaults of solvent but illiquid institutions; (iii) contributes to moderating the tightening of monetary conditions in an environment likely characterized by a very restrictive credit provision of banks to the real economy; (iv) risks creating moral hazard in different senses such as allowing the survival of insolvent or loss-making firms, or inviting in the future an even less prudent liquidity risk management policy by financial and non-financial institutions as the perception develops that the central bank will always help if needed; (v) risks leading to excessively centralized and hence inefficient decision-making on the allocation of funding, as central banks have no special expertise in the micro-allocation of credit to the economy.

How to strike the right balance between these various considerations is in practice a complicated matter, and the management of the financial crisis by central banks over the last years has provided various tentative lessons. One can aim at generalizing these lessons for the future handling of crises, although each crisis will be characterized by new elements. Also, views about the crisis and the measures taken by central banks and governments differ. For example, in the case of the euro area debt crisis, one camp (mainly represented in Germany) would continue to argue that the measures taken by the ECB were often not needed, only created moral hazard of Governments who relaxed their efforts whenever they felt that acute market pressure was receding, and were potentially inflationary in the long run. The other camp would consider that the ECB remained on the side of excessive prudence and that euro area governments opted for excessive austerity, both of which contributed to the long-term recession in the euro area. Moreover, the following list of lessons is somewhat eclectic and premature, reflecting the complexity of the matter, the diversity of topics, and our limited knowledge.

First, in a liquidity crisis, the central bank must give up the idea of a single operational target, as the normal relations between various interest rates are perturbed, and because funding availability to the real economy can no longer be taken for granted. Defining and implementing a monetary policy stance in a financial crisis is difficult and econometric models of the transmission mechanism are largely useless because of the unique nature of each financial crisis. In any case, the effects of a liquidity crisis on the availability of credit to the real economy should be taken into account in the setting of monetary policy in a crisis, so as to avoid allowing an economic downturn and the implied further deterioration of solvency of banks and corporates to further fuel the crisis and lead to an economic and financial downward spiral. The undesirability of hitting the zero lower bound to nominal interest rates should be considered in decision-making.

Second, and as being in fact well-known at least since Bagehot (1873), **elastic central bank backstops protecting banks against funding liquidity shocks** are essential in a financial crisis to break the vicious circles that may otherwise materialize, whereby maintaining or widening collateral availability is a key approach to maintain financial stability *ex ante* (preserve a no-run equilibrium) and *ex post* (prevent a run leading to widespread defaults). In acute stress situations, moral hazard considerations become less relevant because liquidity shocks tend to have less information content on solvency, and hence funding problems are less correlated to past wrong bank-specific management decisions. The existence of a central bank liquidity backstop in itself can contribute to reducing fears of depositors and investors, and can therefore ideally preserve market access and lead to a limited actual recourse to the backstops.

Third, central banks should be proactive and bold if needed to impress on the market their ability and willingness to provide whatever amount of liquidity is needed in an acute stress situation with self-fulfilling dynamics. Financial crises create multiple-equilibria issues, and the central bank with its unlimited resources is the institution that has the most power to contribute to preserving more favourable equilibria.

Fourth, liquidity support by the central bank must not undermine the incentives for banks, regulators, and the government to undertake the necessary clean-up of the banking system and if applicable fiscal reforms. Both liquidity support and these efforts by others are necessary conditions for minimizing the social welfare damage of a financial crisis, and one part cannot substitute for the other. The central bank must insist on this to the other parties, and make supportive liquidity policies conditional on their adequate efforts and contributions. Doing so should not be interpreted as a loss of central bank independence, but as an approach that ensures that the necessary conditions for successful central bank policies are met.

Fifth, central banks should rely on price disincentives against an undue over-reliance on central bank credit. A framework of surcharges on over-proportional reliance on central bank funding, and a cost recovery on due diligence work on non-liquid and difficult-to-evaluate collateral both contribute in this respect. Of course these costs should be known *ex ante* to the banks, i.e. they should not be announced only when a crisis materializes and when these costs become actually applicable. Also, possible stigma issues associated with surcharges should be taken into account and be reflected possibly in continuously increasing surcharges. Regulators should reflect such surcharges for excessive central bank reliance in capital surcharges (for liquidity management models that seem to risk ending with high central bank reliance and the associated costs).

Sixth, even in a financial crisis, the central bank should not save every financial institution from illiquidity-induced stress and even default, and the associated damage. Moral hazard can only partially be prevented through *ex ante* regulation and price disincentives. Eventually, it is a necessary part of the market mechanism that default can occur. In particular, institutions that have contributed to their problems through poor strategies, and that are not only the victim of an 'exogenous' financial crisis, should encounter limits of the official sector's willingness to rescue them. The ability of the central bank and the regulator to distinguish between the two sorts of financial institutions (those with self-made problems and those that can be regarded as essentially suffering from negative externalities originated by others) is crucial in this respect. In the case of doubt, it seems adequate to inflict losses on equity holders (up to wiping out equity) and top management (who would lose their positions). The tricky question is the treatment of uninsured depositors and senior bondholders. On the one hand, a policy of always rescuing those cannot be optimal as it will lead to moral hazard on the part of depositors and investors (as there would be no incentives to worry about credit risk inherent to bank bonds and deposits). On the other hand, bailing in uninsured depositors or senior bond holders in a crisis environment can destabilize funding for all other banks, and could thus be self-defeating.

Seventh, central banks must devote adequate resources to evaluating the particularly dependent counterparties and concentrated collateral exposures in financial crises, to be able to make adequate judgements on the merits of continued support and on the merits of non-conventional measures in general. Central banks must have built up in normal times the necessary knowledge of financial markets and institutions. At the same time, it is natural that the actual resources invested by central banks in the assessment of counterparties and collateral increase steeply during crises as the central bank gains an unprecedented role in the allocation of credit to the economy. The central bank has to make the best of this situation which contradicts the ideal of a decentralized market-based economy, and it can do so only if it combines high expertise with an adequate amount of resources devoted to its Herculean crisis management tasks.

Eighth, central banks must take into account in their crisis management that the **financial system and liquidity crises are global and encompass more than one currency**. This makes central bank cooperation in their lender of last resort role essential, such that indebted entities under funding stress can possibly get emergency liquidity in all relevant currencies (if it is deemed that they deserve to).

Ninth, central banks and banking regulators must avoid pro-cyclicality. An acute liquidity crisis is not the ideal moment to impose additional constraints and regulations. Public authorities must set in place regulations and disincentives against excessive reliance on central bank backstops *in normal or boom times*. To deliver maximum service to society, they must try hard to identify risks *ex ante* and to address them through regulation early and in good times, instead of doing so with a lag, being backward-looking and possibly pro-cyclical. Banking regulators must from the start consider all systemic consequences of new regulation, such as to be sufficiently sure that new regulation really makes the financial system more safe. For regulations imposing buffers, such as the Liquidity Cover Ratio, it is obviously important to allow for the use of the buffer in a financial crisis or a bank-specific stress scenario.

Tenth, central bank **outright purchase programmes** can have various good justifications. While they can be highly effective in stress situations as they demonstrate the ability of the central bank to impact on liquidity and asset prices in an in-principle unlimited way, they can also lead, more easily than collateralized central bank credit operations, to economic distortions and to moral hazard.

Eleventh, it may appear that **'exit' from non-conventional measures is more a question of will, than of technical ability** of central banks. Indeed, regardless of how the asset side of the central bank looks, and regardless of the amount of excess reserves, the central bank can always absorb reserves and restore the interest rate level that is appropriate from a monetary policy point of view. Of course, such a normalization of policies, if coming abruptly, might have strong consequences on long-term yields, asset prices, state funding costs, and on the profit or loss of banks and the central bank. The central bank will of course factor in the effects of exit on yields and on the transmission mechanism more generally when choosing the pace of exit and the related communication strategy. In view of the varying effects of exit on different stakeholders, and possible resulting political pressures, it is important that monetary policy remains the only needle in the compass of the central bank. This problem is not specific to the exit from non-standard measures, as central banks always need to show their focused commitment to their monetary policy mandates to preserve their credibility. If this is the attitude of central banks, then there is also no need to hesitate in undertaking non-conventional measures because of fears that the exit will be delayed due to political considerations.

Finally, what have we learnt about *the role of monetary policy operations in normal times to prevent the build-up of financial instability*? In particular, can the adequacy of the 2006 consensus on monetary policy implementation in normal times, including the strict application of the separation principle, be confirmed also from this perspective? This seems to be the case.[1] However, as mentioned, due attention should be paid to designing the central bank credit operations and collateral framework in normal times in a way that does not contribute to pro-cyclicality. Accordingly, access of banks to central bank credit should not be of extreme convenience and unlimited elasticity in normal times. If this is respected, there will also be less need to tighten access conditions in crisis times (more to the contrary, there should be scope to relax access if needed in crisis times). The use of macro-prudential measures can support the counter-cyclicality of policies further.

[1] Whether central bank interest rate policies can and should prevent the build-up of asset price bubbles is another issue (see e.g. Schularik and Taylor, 2012).

References

Acharya, V. V., D. Gale, and T. Yorulmazer (2011), 'Rollover risk and market freezes', *Journal of Finance*, 66, 1177–209.

Acharya V. V., D. Gromb and T. Yorulmazer (2012), 'Imperfect competition in the interbank market for liquidity as a rationale for central banking', *American Economic Journal: Macroeconomics*, 4, 184–217.

Acharya, V. V. and S. Viswanathan (2011), 'Leverage, moral hazard, and liquidity,' *Journal of Finance*, 66, 99–138.

Acharya, V. V. and T. Yorulmazer (2008), 'Information contagion and bank herding', *Journal of Money, Credit and Banking*, 40, 215–32.

Adrian, T. and H. S. Shin (2009), 'Liquidity and leverage', *Federal Reserve Bank of New York Staff Report*, No. 328.

Akerlof, G. (1970), 'The market for lemons: Quality uncertainty and the market mechanism', *Quarterly Journal of Economics*, 84, 488–500.

Allen, W. A. (2002): 'Bank of England open market operations: the introduction of a deposit facility for counterparties', *Bank for International Settlements Paper*, No. 12.

Allen, W. A. and R. Moessner (2010), 'Central bank co-operation and international liquidity in the financial crisis of 2008-9', *BIS Working Papers*, No. 310.

Allen, W. A. and R. Moessner (2013), 'The liquidity consequences of the euro area sovereign debt crisis', *BIS Working Papers*, No. 390.

Allen, L. and A. Saunders (1992), 'Bank window dressing: Theory and evidence', *Journal of Banking and Finance*, 16, 585–623.

Allenspach, N. (2009), 'Banking and transparency: Is more information always better?', *Swiss National Bank Working Papers*, 2009-11.

Anderson, L. C. (1969), 'Money market conditions as a guide for monetary management', in K. Brunner (ed.), *Targets and Indicators of Monetary Policy*, 66–83, San Francisco: Chandler Publishing Company.

Angeletos, G.-M., C. Hellwig, and A. Pavan (2006), 'Signalling in a global game: Coordination and policy traps', *Journal of Political Economy*, 114, 452–84.

Angelini, P. (2000), 'Are banks risk averse? Intraday timing of operations in the interbank market', *Journal of Money, Credit and Banking*, 32, 54–73.

Angelini, P. (2002), 'Liquidity and announcement effects in the euro area', *Banca d'Italia Temi di Discussione*, No. 451.

Armantier, O., E. Ghysels, A. Sarkar, and J. Shrader (2011), 'Stigma in financial markets: Evidence from liquidity auctions and discount window borrowing during the crisis', *Federal Reserve Bank of New York Staff Reports*, No. 483.

Armantier, O., S. Krieger, and J. McAndrews (2008), 'The Federal Reserve's Term Auction Facility', *Current Issues in Economics and Finance*, Federal Reserve Bank of New York, 14 (5), 2–11.

Arrow, K. A. (1963), 'Uncertainty and the welfare economics of medical care', *American Economic Review*, 53 (5), 941–73.

Ashcraft, A., N. Gârleanu, and L. H. Pedersen (2011), 'Two monetary tools: Interest rates and haircuts', in D. Acemoglu and M. Woodford (eds.), *NBER Macroeconomics Annual 2010*, Volume 25, 143–80, University of Chicago Press.

Association of British Insurers et al. (2010), *Securities lending: An introductory guide*, September 2010.

Axilrod, S. H. and D. E. Lindsey (1981), 'Federal Reserve System Implementation of monetary policy: Analytical foundations of the new approach', *American Economic Review*, 71, 246–52.

Ayuso, J. and Repullo, R. (2003), 'A model of the open market operations of the European Central Bank', *Economic Journal*, 113, 889–902.

Baba, N. and F. Packer (2009), 'From turmoil to crisis: Dislocations in the FX swap market before and after the failure of Lehman Brothers', *BIS Working Paper*, No. 285.

Bagehot, W. (1873), *Lombard Street: A Description of the Money Market*, H.S. King.

Baltensperger, E. (1982), 'Reserve requirements and economic stability', *Journal of Money, Credit and Banking*, 14, 205–15.

Bank of Canada (1995), 'A proposed framework for the implementation of monetary policy in the large value transfer system environment', Discussion paper I (November).

Bank of Canada (2010), 'A primer on the implementation of monetary policy in the LVTS Environment', Bank of Canada.

Bank of England (2008), 'The development of the Bank of England's market operations—A consultative paper by the Bank of England', October 2008.

Bank of England (2010), 'Bank of England market notice: sterling monetary framework—changes to the collateral concentration limit', 30 April 2010.

Bank of England (2012a), 'The framework for the Bank of England's operations in the sterling money markets', June 2012.

Bank of England (2012b), 'The funding for lending scheme', *Quarterly Bulletin*, 2012, Q4, 306–20.

Bank of England (2013), 'The Bank of England's Sterling monetary framework', Update of October 2013.

Bank for International Settlements (2012), *82nd Annual Report*, Basle, BIS.

Bank for International Settlements (2013), *83rd Annual Report*, Basle, BIS.

Bank of Japan (2010), 'Fund provisioning measure to support strengthening the foundations for economic growth', *Bank of Japan Review* (September 2010), 2010-E-5, 1–12.

Bartolini, L., G. Bertola, and A. Prati (2001), 'Banks' reserve management, transaction costs, and the timing of Federal Reserve interventions', *Journal of Banking and Finance*, 25, 1287–317.

Bartolini, L., G. Bertola, and A. Prati (2002), 'Day-to-day implementation of monetary policy and the volatility of the federal funds rate', *Journal of Money, Credit and Banking*, 34, 137–59.

Basel Committee on Banking Supervision (2008), 'Principles for sound liquidity risk management and supervision', Bank for International Settlements.

Basel Committee on Banking Supervision (2010), 'Basel III—international framework for liquidity risk measurement, standards and monitoring', Bank for International Settlements.

Basle Committee on Banking Supervision (2013), 'Basel III: The liquidity coverage ratio and liquidity risk monitoring tools', Bank for International Settlements.

Bech, M. and T. Keister (2012), 'Basel III—On the liquidity coverage ratio and monetary policy Implementation', *BIS Quarterly Review*, December 2012, 49–61.

Berentsen, A., A. Marchesiani, and C. J. Waller (2010), 'Channel systems: why is there a positive spread?', *IEW—Working Papers 517*, Institute for Empirical Research in Economics—IEW.

Berentsen, A. and C. Monnet (2008), 'Monetary policy in a channel system', *Journal of Monetary Economics*, 55, 1067–80.

Bernanke, B. S. (2010), 'Federal Reserve's exit strategy', Testimony before the Committee on Financial Services, U.S. House of Representatives, Washington, DC, 10 February 2010.

Bernanke, B. and M. Gertler (1989), 'Agency cost, net worth, and business fluctuations', *American Economic Review*, 79, 14–31.

Bernanke, B., M. Gertler, and S. Gilchrist (1996), 'The financial accelerator and the flight to quality', *The Review of Economics and Statistics*, 78, 1–15.

Bindseil, U. (2005a), *Monetary Policy Implementation*, Oxford University Press.

Bindseil, U. (2005b), 'Over- and underbidding in central bank open market operations conducted as fixed rate tender', *German Economic Review*, 6, 95–130.

Bindseil, U. (2013), 'Central bank collateral, asset fire sales, regulation and liquidity,' *ECB Working Paper Series*, No. 1612.

Bindseil, U., G. Camba-Mendez, A. Hirsch, and B. Weller (2006), 'Excess reserves and the implementation of monetary policy of the ECB', *Journal of Policy Modelling*, 28, 491–510.

Bindseil, U. and J. Jablecki (2011a), 'A structural model of central bank operations and bank intermediation', *ECB Working Paper*, No. 1312.

Bindseil, U. and J. Jablecki (2011b), 'The optimal width of the central bank standing facilities corridor and banks' day-to-day liquidity management', *ECB Working Paper*, No. 1350.

Bindseil, U. and J. Jablecki (2013), 'Central bank liquidity provision, risk taking and economic efficiency', *ECB Working Paper*, No. 1542.

Bindseil, U. and P. König (2011), 'The Economics of Target2 balances', *SFB 649 Discussion Paper*, No. 2011-35, Humboldt-Universität Berlin.

Bindseil, U. and P. König (2012), 'Target2 and the European debt crisis', *Kredit und Kapital*, 45, 135–72.

Bindseil, U. and J. Lamoot (2011), 'The Basel III framework for liquidity standards and monetary policy implementation', *SFB 649 Discussion Paper*, No. 2011-41, Humboldt-Universität Berlin.

Bindseil, U. and K. Nyborg (2008), 'Monetary policy implementation', in X. Freixas, P. Hartmann, and C. Mayer (eds.), *Handbook of European Financial Markets and Institutions*, 742–78, Oxford University Press.

Bindseil, U., K. Nyborg, and I. A. Strebulaev (2009), 'Repo auctions and the market for liquidity', *Journal of Money, Credit and Banking*, 41, 1391–421.

Bindseil, U. and F. Papadia (2006), 'Credit risk mitigation in central bank credit operations and effects on financial markets: the case of the Eurosystem', *ECB Occasional Paper*, No. 49.

Bindseil, U., B. Weller, and F. Würtz (2003), 'Central bank and commercial banks' liquidity management—what is the relationship?', *Economic Notes*, 32, 37–66.
Bindseil, U. and A. Winkler (2013), 'Dual liquidity crises—A financial accounts framework', *Review of International Economics*, 21, 151–63.
Blanchard, O., G. Dell'Ariccia, and P. Mauro (2010), 'Rethinking Macro Policy', *VoxEU.org*, 6 February 2010.
Bloomfield, A. I. (1959), 'Monetary policy under the gold standard: 1880–1914', Federal Reserve Bank of New York.
Board of Governors (1954/1974/1994), *The Federal Reserve System: Purposes and Functions*, Washington, DC: Board of Governors of the Federal Reserve System.
Bolton, P. and X. Freixas (2006), 'Corporate finance and the monetary transmission mechanism', *Review of Financial Studies*, 19, 829–70.
Borio, C. E. V. (1997), 'Monetary policy operating procedures in industrial countries', *BIS conference papers*, Vol. 3, 286–368, Bank of International Settlements.
Borio, C. E. V. (2001), 'A Hundred ways to skin a cat: Comparing monetary policy operating procedures in the United States, Japan and the Euro area', *BIS Paper*, No. 9.
Botman, D. P. J. and C. G. H. Diks (2005), 'The role of domestic and foreign investors in a simple model of speculative attacks', *IMF Working Paper*, WP/05/205.
Brousseau, V. and A. Manzanares (2005), 'A look at intraday frictions in the euro area overnight deposit market', *ECB Working Paper Series*, No. 439.
Brunnermeier, M., A. Crockett, C. Goodhart, A. D. Persaud, and H. Shin (2009), 'The fundamental principles of financial regulation', Geneva Reports on the World Economy 11, International Center for Monetary and Banking Studies.
Brunnermeier, M., T. M. Eisenbach, and Y. Samikov (2012), 'Macroeconomics with financial frictions', *NBER Working Paper*, No. 18102.
Brunnermeier, M. and Y. Sannikov (2013), 'The I theory of money', manuscript, Princeton University.
Buchheit, Lee C., A. Gelpern, M. Gulati, U. Panizza, B. Weder di Mauro, and J. Zettelmeyer (2013), *Revisiting Sovereign Bankruptcy*, Washington, DC: Committee on International Economic Policy and Reform, Brookings.
Buiter, W. and E. Rahbari (2012a), 'The ECB as lender of last resort for sovereigns in the euro area', *CEPR Discussion Paper*, No. 8974, Centre for Economic Policy Research.
Buiter, W. and E. Rahbari (2012b), 'TARGET2 redux: the simple accountancy and slightly more complex economics of Bundesbank loss exposure through the Eurosystem', *CEPR Discussion Paper*, No 9211, Centre for Economic Policy Research.
Buiter, W. and A. Sibert (2005), 'How the Eurosystem's treatment of collateral in its open market operations weakens fiscal discipline in the euro zone (and what to do about it)', *CEPR discussion paper*, No. 5387.
Buiter, W. and A. Sibert (2007), 'The central bank as market maker of last resort - I', <http://blogs.ft.com/maverecon/2007/08/the-central-banhtml/#axzz2wFuzNII6>.
Burgess, W. R. (1927), *The Reserve Banks and the Money Market*, Harper and Brothers.
Caballero, R. J., T. Hoshi, and A. K. Kashyap, (2008), 'Zombie lending and depressed restructuring in Japan', *American Economic Review*, 98, 1943–77.
Caballero, R. J. and A. Krishnamurthy (2008), 'Collective Risk Management in a Flight to Quality Episode', *Journal of Finance*, 63, 2195–230.

Cabrero, A., G. Camba-Mendez, A. Hirsch, and F. Nieto (2002), 'Modeling the daily banknotes in circulation in the context of the liquidity management of the European Central Bank', *ECB Working Paper Series*, No. 142.

Calvo, G. A. (1988), 'Servicing the public debt: the role of expectations', *American Economic Review*, 78, 647–61.

Calvo, G. A. and E. Mendoza (1999), 'Rational Herd Behavior and the Globalization of Securities Markets', *Journal of International Economics*, 51, 79–113.

Campbell, J. Y. (1987), 'Money announcements, the demand for bank reserves, and the behavior of the federal funds rate within the statement week', *Journal of Money, Credit and Banking*, 19, 56–67.

Chailloux, A., S. Gray, and R. McCaughrin (2008), 'Central bank collateral frameworks, principles and policies', *IMF Working Papers*, WP/08/222.

Chapman, J., J. Chiu, and M. Molico (2010), 'Central bank haircut policy', *Bank of Canada Working Paper*, 2010–23.

Chen, Y. (1999), 'Banking panics: the role of the first-come, first-served rule and information externalities', *Journal of Political Economy*, 107, 946–68.

Chen, Y, and I. Hasan (2006), 'The transparency of the banking industry and the efficiency of information-based bank runs', *Journal of Financial Intermediation*, 15, 307–31.

Cheun, S., I. von Köppen-Mertes, and B. Weller (2009), 'The Eurosystem collateral frameworks of the Eurosystem, the Federal Reserve and the Bank of England, and the financial market turmoil', *ECB Occasional Paper*, No. 107.

Cifuentes, R., G. Ferrucci, and H. Shin (2005), 'Liquidity Risk and Contagion', *Journal of the European Economic Association*, 3, 556–66.

Citi (2013), 'Financial conditions neutral, at best, on growth', *Euro Economics Weekly*, 7 June.

Clapham, J. (1944), *The Bank of England*, Cambridge: Cambridge University Press (2 vols.).

Clews, R. (2005), 'Implementing monetary policy: reforms to the Bank of England's operations in the money market', *Bank of England Quarterly Bulletin*, Q2, 211–20.

Clews, R., C. Salmon, and O. Weeken (2010), 'The Bank's money market framework', *Bank of England Quarterly Bulletin*, Q4, 291–301.

Clinton, K. (1997), 'Implementation of monetary policy in a regime with zero reserve requirements', *Bank of Canada Working Paper*, No. 97/8.

Clouse, J. A. and J. P. Dow (1999), 'Fixed costs and the behavior of the federal funds rate', *Journal of Banking and Finance*, 23, 1015–29.

Clouse, J. A. and D. W. Elmendorf (1997), 'Declining required reserves and the volatility of the federal funds rate', Working paper, Board of Governors of the Federal Reserve System.

Clouse, J., D. Henderson, A. Orphanides, D. Small, and P. Tinsley (1999), 'Monetary policy when the nominal short-term interest rate is zero', Working Paper, Board of Governors of the Federal Reserve System.

Coeuré, B. (2012), 'Challenges to the single monetary policy and the ECB's response', Speech held at the Institut d'études politiques, Paris, 20 September 2012.

Cole, H. L. and T. J Kehoe (2000), 'Self-fulfilling debt crisis', *Review of Economic Studies*, 67, 91–116.

Committee on Payment and Settlement Systems (2006), *Cross Border collateral arrangements*, CPSS Publications, No. 71.

Cook, T. C. and T. Hahn (1989), 'The effect of changes in the federal funds rate target on market interest rate in the 1970s', *Journal of Monetary Economics*, 24, 331–51.

Cooper, R. and T. W. Ross (1998), 'Bank runs: liquidity costs and investment distortions', *Journal of Monetary Economics*, 41, 27–38.

Corsetti, G., B. Guimarães, and N. Roubini (2006), 'International lending of last resort and moral hazard: A model of IMF's catalytic finance', *Journal of Monetary Economics*, 53, 441–71.

Cour-Thimann, P. (2013), 'Target balances and the crisis in the euro area', CESIFO Forum, Volume 14, Special Issue.

Cour-Thimann, P. and B. Winkler (2013), 'The ECB's non-standard monetary policy measures: the role of institutional factors and financial structure', *ECB Working Paper Series*, No. 1528.

Craig, B. and F. Fecht (2007), 'The Eurosystem money market auctions: A banking perspective', *Journal of Banking and Finance*, 31, 2925–44.

Crosbie, P. and J. Bohn (2003), 'Modelling Default Risk', Moody's KMV.

Cross, M., P. Fisher, and O. Weeken (2010), 'The Bank's balance sheet during the crisis', *Bank of England Quarterly Bulletin*, Q1, 34–42.

Curdia, V. and M. Woodford (2010), 'Credit spreads and monetary policy', *Journal of Money, Credit and Banking*, 42, 3–35.

Curdia, V. and M. Woodford (2011), 'The central bank balance sheet as an instrument of monetary policy', *Journal of Monetary Economics*, 58, 54–79.

D'Amico, S. and T. B. King (2010), 'Flow and stock effects of large-scale treasury purchases', *Finance and Economics Discussion Series*, No. 2010-52, Board of Governors of the Federal Reserve System.

Daniel, F, W. Engert, and D. MacLean (2004), 'The Bank of Canada as lender of last resort', *Bank of Canada Review*, Winter 2004–05, 3–16.

Davies, H. (1998), 'Averaging in a framework of zero reserve requirements: Implications for the operation of monetary policy', *Bank of England Working Paper Series*, No. 84.

Davydenko, S. A., I. A. Strebulaev, and X. Zhao (2012), 'A market-based study of the cost of default', *Review of Financial Studies*, 25, 2959–99.

De Grauwe, P. (2011), 'The European Central Bank: Lender of last resort in the Government bond markets?', *CESIFO Working Paper*, No. 3569.

Deutsche Bundesbank (1976), *Geld- und Bankwesen in Zahlen, 1876–1975*, Frankfurt am Main: Deutsche Bundesbank.

Deutsche Bundesbank (1982), 'Central bank money requirements of banks and liquidity policy measures of the Bundesbank', *Monthly Report of the Deutsche Bundesbank*, 34/4, 20–5.

Deutsche Bundesbank (1995), *The Monetary Policy of the Deutsche Bundesbank*, Frankfurt am Main.

Diamond, D. W. and P. H. Dybvig (1983), 'Bank Runs, Deposit Insurance and Liquidity', *Journal of Political Economy*, 91, 401–19.

Diamond, D. W. and R. G. Rajan (2012), 'Illiquid banks, financial stability, and interest rate policy', *Journal of Political Economy*, 120, 552–91.

Dow, J. P. (2001), 'The demand for excess reserves', *Southern Economic Journal*, 67, 685–700.

Dowd, K. (2009), 'Moral hazard and the financial crisis', *Cato Journal*, 29, 141–66.

Drehmann, M. and K. Nikolaou (2013), 'Funding liquidity risk: definition and measurement', *Journal of Banking and Finance*, 37, 2173–82.

Duarte, F. and T. M. Eisenbach (2013), 'Fire-sale spillovers and systemic risk', *Federal Reserve Bank of New York Staff Reports*, No. 645.

Ennis, H. and T. Keister (2006), 'Bank runs and investment decisions revisited', *Journal of Monetary Economics*, 53, 217–32.

European Central Bank (2004), 'Risk mitigation methods in Eurosystem credit operations', *Monthly Bulletin of the European Central Bank*, May 2004, 71–9.

European Central Bank (2005a), 'Initial experience with the changes to the Eurosystem's operational framework for monetary policy implementation', *ECB Monthly Bulletin*, February 2005, 65–71.

European Central Bank (2005b), 'A measure of the real cost of the external financing of euro area non-financial corporations', Box, *ECB Monthly Bulletin*, March 2005, 37–9.

European Central Bank (2007), 'The EU arrangements for financial crisis management', *ECB Monthly Bulletin*, February 2007, 73–85.

European Central Bank (2009), 'The external financing of households and non-financial corporations: A Comparison of the euro area and the United States', *ECB Monthly Bulletin*, April 2009, 69–84.

European Central Bank (2010), 'The ECB's response to the financial crisis', *ECB Monthly Bulletin*, October 2010, 59–74.

European Central Bank (2011a), 'The monetary policy of the ECB', Frankfurt am Main.

European Central Bank (2011b), 'The implementation of monetary policy in the euro area: General documentation on eurosystem monetary policy instruments and procedures', Frankfurt am Main.

European Central Bank (2012), 'Euro Money Market Survey', September 2012.

European Central Bank (2013a), 'The ECB collateral framework throughout the crisis', *ECB Monthly Bulletin*, July 2013, 71–86.

European Central Bank (2013b), 'Collateral eligibility requirements—a comparative study across specific frameworks', Special Report, European Central Bank.

European Central Bank (2013c), 'Survey on the access to finance of small and medium-sized enterprises in the euro area—October 2012 to March 2013', Frankfurt am Main.

European Central Bank (2013d), 'The euro area bank lending survey—1st quarter of 2013', Frankfurt am Main

Ewerhart, C., Cassola, N., and Valla, N. (2010), 'Declining valuations and equilibrium bidding in central bank refinancing operations', *International Journal of Industrial Organisation*, 28, 30–43.

Ewerhart, C. and Tapking, J. (2008), 'Repo markets, counterparty risk and the 2007/2008 liquidity crisis', *ECB Working Paper*, No. 909.

Farhi, E. and J. Tirole (2012), 'Collective moral hazard, maturity mismatch, and systemic bailouts', *American Economic Review*, 102, 60–93.

Fawley, B. W. and C. J. Neely (2013), 'Four stories of quantitative easing', *Federal Reserve Bank of St. Louis Review*, 95(1), 51–88.

Fecht, F., K. G. Nyborg, and J. Rocholl (2011), 'The price of liquidity: The effects of market conditions and bank characteristics', *Journal of Financial Economics*, 102, 355–62.

Federal Reserve Bank of New York (2000), 'Understanding open market operations', Federal Reserve Bank of New York.

Federal Reserve Bank of New York (2002), 'Domestic open market operations during 2001', Federal Reserve Bank of New York.

Federal Reserve System (2002), 'Alternative instruments for open market and discount window operations', *Federal Reserve System Study Group on Alternative Instruments for System Operations*, December 2002.

Feinman, J. (1993), 'Reserve requirements: History, current practice, and potential reform', *Federal Reserve Bulletin*, 79, 569–89.

Filardo, A. (2011), 'The impact of the international financial crisis on Asia and the Pacific: Highlighting monetary policy challenges from a negative asset price bubble perspective', *BIS Working Paper*, No. 356.

Filardo, A., M. Mohatny, and R. Moreno (2012), 'Central bank and government debt management: issues for monetary policy', *BIS Papers*, No. 67, 51–71.

Filardo, A. and J. Yetman (2012), 'The expansion of central bank balance sheets in emerging Asia: what are the risks?', *BIS Quarterly Review*, June 2012, 47–63.

Financial Stability Board (2012), 'Securities lending and repos: market overview and financial stability issues', *Interim Report*, 27 April 2012.

Fischer, S. (1999), 'On the need for an international lender of last resort', *Journal of Economic Perspectives*, 13, 85–104.

Flannery, M. J. (1996), 'Financial crises, payment system problems, and discount window lending', *Journal of Money, Credit and Banking*, 28, 804–24.

Flemming, M. J. and N. J. Klagge (2010), 'The Federal Reserve's foreign exchange swap lines', *Current Issues in Economics and Finance*, Federal Reserve Bank of New York, 16 (4).

Freeman, S. (1987), 'Reserve requirements and optimal seigniorage', *Journal of Monetary Economics*, 19, 307–14.

Freixas, X. and J.-C. Rochet (2008), *The Microeconomics of Banking*, 2nd edition, MIT Press.

Friedman, B. M. (2013), 'The simple analytics of monetary policy: a post-crisis approach', *NBER Working Paper Series, No. 18960.*

Friedman, M. (1960), *A Program for Monetary Stability*, Fordham University Press.

Friedman, M. (1982), 'Monetary policy: theory and practice', *Journal of Money, Credit and Banking*, 14, 98–118.

Friedman, M. and A. Schwartz (1963), *A Monetary History of the United States, 1867–1960*, Princeton University Press (for the National Bureau of Economic Research).

Fudenberg, D. and J. Tirole (1991), *Game Theory*, MIT Press.

Furfine, C. H. (2000), 'Interbank payments and the daily federal funds rate', *Journal of Monetary Economics*, 46, 535–53.

Furfine, C. (2002), 'The interbank market during a financial crisis', *European Economic Review*, 46, 809–20.

Gagnon, J., Raskin, M., Remache, J. and Sack, B. (2010), 'Large-scale asset purchases by the Federal Reserve: Did they work?', *Federal Reserve Bank of New York Staff Reports, No 441.*

Geanakoplos, J. (2009), 'Solving the present crisis and managing the leverage cycle', Cowles Foundation Discussion Paper, No. 1751.

Gertler, M. and P. Karadi (2011), 'A model of unconventional monetary policy', *Journal of Monetary Economics*, 58, 17–34.

Gertler, M. and P. Karadi (2013), 'QE 1 vs. 2 vs 3. . . . A framework for analysing Large Scale Asset Purchases as a monetary policy tool', *International Journal of Central Banking*, 9, 5–53.

Gertler, M. and N. Kiyotaki (2010), 'Financial intermediation and credit policy in business cycle analysis', in: B. Friedman and M. Woodford (eds.), *Handbook of Monetary Economics*, Volume 3, 547–99, Elsevier.

Glosten, L. R. and Milgrom, P.R. (1985), 'Bid, ask and transaction prices in a specialist market with heterogeneously informed traders', *Journal of Financial Economics*, 14, 71–100.

Glover, B. (2011), 'The expected costs of default', working paper, Carnegie Mellon University.

Godley, W. and M. Lavoie (2012), *Monetary Economics—An integrated approach to credit, money, income, production, and wealth*, Palgrave-Macmillan.

Goldberg, L. S., C. Kennedy, and J. Miu (2010), 'Central bank dollar swap lines and overseas dollar funding costs', *Staff report*, No. 429, Federal Reserve Bank of New York.

Goldenweiser, E. A. (1925), *The Federal Reserve System in Operation*, McGraw-Hill.

Goldenweiser, E. A. (1949), *Monetary Management*, Committee for Economic Development Research Study, McGraw-Hill.

Gonzalez, F. and Molitor, P. (2009), 'Risk mitigation measures and credit risk assessment in central bank policy operations', in U. Bindseil, F. Gonzalez, and E. Tabakis (eds.), *Risk Management for Central Banks and other Public investors*, Cambridge University Press.

González-Páramo, José Manuel (2011), 'The ECB's monetary policy during the crisis', Closing speech at the Tenth Economic Policy Conference, Málaga, 21 October 2011 (available on the ECB website).

Goodfriend, M., and M. Hargraves (1983), 'A historical assessment of the rationales and functions of reserve requirements', *Federal Reserve Bank of Richmond Economic Review*, March/April 1983, 3–21.

Goodhart, C. A. E. (1999), 'Myths about the lender of last resort', *International Finance*, 2, 339–60.

Goodhart, C. A. E. (2001), 'The endogeneity of money', in P. Arestis, M. Desai, and S. Dow (eds.), *Money, Macroeconomics and Keynes*, Routledge.

Goodhart, C. and G. Illing (eds.) (2002), *Financial Crises, Contagion, and the Lender of Last Resort—A Reader*, Oxford University Press.

Gray, S., P. Karam, V. Meeyam, and M. Stubbe (2013), 'Monetary issues in the Middle East and North Africa, A policy implementation handbook for central bankers', IMF, Washington, DC.

Green, R. (1987), 'Real bills doctrine', in *The New Palgrave: A Dictionary of Economics*, volume 4, Macmillan.

Guthrie, G., and J. Wright (2000), 'Open mouth operations', *Journal of Monetary Economics*, 46, 489–516.

Hakkio, C. S. and G. H. Sellon (2000), 'The discount window: time for reform?', *Federal Reserve Bank of Kansas City Economic Review*, 87/1, 57–63.

Hamilton, J. D. (1996), 'The daily market for federal funds', *Journal of Political Economy*, 104, 26–56.

Hamilton, J. D. and J. C. Wu (2012), 'The effectiveness of alternative monetary policy tools in a zero lower bound environment', *Journal of Money, Credit and Banking*, 44, Supplement, 3-46.

Hardy, D. (1996), 'Reserve requirements and monetary management: An introduction', *IMF Working Paper*, WP/93/35.

Harrison, R. (2012), 'Asset purchase policy at the effective lower bound for interest rates', *Bank of England Working Paper*, No. 444.

Hartmann, P., M. Manna, and A. Manzanares (2001), 'The microstructure of the euro money market', *Journal of International Money and Finance*, 20, 895–948.

Hatzius, J., P. Hooper, F. Mishkin, K. L. Schoenholtz, and M. Watson (2010), 'Financial conditions indicators: A fresh look at the financial crisis', working paper.

Heider, F., M. Hoerova, and C. Holthausen (2009), 'Liquidity hoarding and interbank market spreads—the role of counterparty risk', *ECB Working Paper Series*, No. 1126.

Heinemann, F. and G. Illing (2002), 'Speculative attacks: unique equilibrium and transparency', *Journal of International Economics*, 58, 429–50.

Heinemann, F., R. Nagel, and P. Ockenfels (2004), 'The theory of global games on test: experimental analysis of coordination games with public and private information', *Econometrica*, 72, 1583–99.

Ho, T. S. Y. and A. Saunders (1985), 'A micro model of the federal funds market', *Journal of Finance*, 15, 977–88.

Hoerova, M., and C. Monnet (2010), 'Central bank lending and money market discipline', Unpublished manuscript.

Hollo, D., M. Kremer, and M. Lo Duca (2012), 'CISS—A composite indicator of systemic stress in the financial system', *ECB Working Paper Series*, No. 1426.

Holmström, B. (1979), 'Moral hazard and observability', *Bell Journal of Economics*, 10, 74–91.

Holmström, B. and J. Tirole (1997), 'Financial intermediation, loanable funds, and the real sector', *Quarterly Journal of Economics*, 112, 663–91.

Holthausen, C., C. Monet, and F. Würtz (2008), 'Monetary policy without reserve requirements', mimeo.

Hong Kong Monetary Authority (2011), 'Policy statement on the role of the HKMA as lender of last resort', version of 1 August 2011; initially published in *Quarterly Bulletin*, 8/1999, 77–81.

Horrigan, B. R. (1988), 'Are reserve requirements relevant for economic stabilization?', *Journal of Monetary Economics*, 21, 97–105.

House of Commons (2008), *The Run on the Rock*, Report by the Treasury Committee of the House of Commons, London.

Huang, R. and L. Ratnovski (2011), 'The dark side of bank wholesale funding', *Journal of Financial Intermediation*, 20, 248–63.

Hull, J. (2012), *Risk Management and Financial Institutions*, Wiley Finance.

Illing, G. (2007), 'Financial stability and monetary policy—a framework', April 2007, CESIfo Working Paper, No. 1971.

International Monetary Fund (2008), *Global Financial Stability Report*, November 2008.

International Monetary Fund (2013), 'Unconventional monetary policies—recent experience and prospects', IMF background paper.

International Swaps and Derivatives Association (2013), *ISDA Margin Survey 2013*.

Jensen, M. C. and W. H. Meckling (1976), 'Theory of the firm: managerial behavior, agency costs and ownership', *Journal of Financial Economics*, 3, 305–60.

Jimenez, G., S. Ongena, J. Peydró-Alcalde, and J. Saurina (2012), 'Credit supply and monetary policy: Identifying the bank balance-sheet channel with loan applications', *American Economic Review*, 102, 2301–26.

Jobst, C. (2009), 'Market leader: the Austro-Hungarian Bank and the making of foreign exchange intervention, 1896–1913', *European Review of Economic History*, 13, 287–318.

Jørgensen, A. and L. Risbjerg (2012), 'Negative interest rates', *Monetary Review*, 3rd Quarter 2012, Part 1.

Joyce, M., A. Lasaosa, I. Stevens, and M. Tong (2010), 'The financial market impact of quantitative easing', *Bank of England Working Paper Series*, No 393.

Joyce, M., M. Tong, and R. Woods (2011), 'The United Kingdom's quantitative easing policy: design, operation and impact', *Bank of England Quarterly Bulletin*, 51 (3), 200–212.

Kaminsky, G. L., and C. M. Reinhart (1999), 'The two crises: the causes of banking and balance of payment problems', *American Economic Review*, 89, 473–500.

Kashyap, A. K., and J. C. Stein (2012), 'The optimal conduct of monetary policy with interest on reserves', *American Economic Journal: Macroeconomics*, 4, 266–82.

Keister, T., and J. McAndrews (2009), 'Why are banks holding so many excess reserves?' *Current Issues in Economics and Finance*, Federal Reserve Bank of New York, 15 (8), 1–10.

Keynes, J. M. (1930/1971), *A Treatise on Money*, volume 2: *The Applied Theory of Money*. Reprinted in *The Collected Works of John Maynard Keynes*, volume 6, Macmillan/Cambridge University Press.

Kindleberger, C. P. and R. Aliber (2005), *Manias, Panics and Crashes*, 5th edition, Wiley.

King, W. T. C. (1936), *History of the London Discount Market*, Frank Cass.

Kiyotaki, N. and J. Moore (1997), 'Credit cycles', *Journal of Political Economy*, 105, 2, 211–48.

Kohn, D. L. (2009), 'American International Group', Testimony before the Committee on Banking, Housing, and Urban Affairs, U.S. Senate, Washington, DC, 5 March 2009.

Kopecky, K. J. and A. L. Tucker (1993), 'Interest rate smoothness and the non-settling-day behavior of banks', *Journal of Economics and Business*, 45, 297–314.

Koulischer, F. and D. Struyven (2013), 'Central bank liquidity provision and collateral quality', unpublished paper, September 2013.

Kozicki, S., E. Santor, and L. Suchanek (2011), 'Unconventional monetary policy: The international experience with central bank asset purchases', *Bank of Canada Review*, Spring 2011, 13–25.

Krugman, P. (2000), 'Fire-sale FDI', in S. Edwards (ed.), *Capital Flows and the Emerging Economies: Theory, Evidence and Controversies*, 43–60, Chicago University Press.

Kuttner, K. N. and P. C. Mosser (2002), 'The monetary transmission mechanism: Some answers and further questions', *FRBNY Economic Policy Review*, Volume 8 (1),

Proceedings of a Conference Sponsored by the Federal Reserve Bank of New York, 5 and 6 April, 15–26.

Kyle, Albert S. (1985), 'Continuous auctions and insider trading', *Econometrica*, 53, 1315–36.

Laeven, L. and F. Valencia (2008), 'Systemic banking crises: A new database', *IMF Working Paper*, WP/08/224.

Laubach, T. and J. C. Williams (2001), 'Measuring the natural rate of interest', working paper, Board of Governors of the Federal Reserve System.

Laufenberg, D. E. (1976), 'Contemporaneous vs. lagged reserve accounting', *Journal of Money, Credit and Banking*, 8, 239–45.

Linzert, T., D. Nautz, and U. Bindseil (2007), 'The Longer term refinancing operations of the ECB', *Journal of Banking and Finance*, 31, 1521–43.

Linzert, T., D. Nautz, and J. Breitung (2006), 'Bidder behavior in central bank repo auctions: Evidence from the Bundesbank', *Journal of International Financial Markets, Institutions, and Money*, 16, 215–50.

Majnoni d'Intignano, G. (2013), 'Secured bank funding, credit supply, and unconventional monetary policies', Bank of Italy, unpublished working paper.

Manna, M. (2009), 'Emergency liquidity assistance at work: both words and deeds matter', *Studi e Note di Economia*, 16, 155–86.

Markets Committee (2009), *MC Compendium—Monetary policy frameworks and central bank market operations*, BIS Markets Committee, May 2009.

Markets Committee (2013), *Central bank collateral frameworks and practices*, Report by a Study Group chaired by Guy Debelle and established by the BIS Markets Committee.

McCallum, B. T. (1986), 'Some issues concerning interest rate pegging, price level determinacy, and the real bills doctrine', *Journal of Monetary Economics*, 17, 135–60.

Meigs, J. A. (1962), *Free Reserves and the Money Supply*, University of Chicago Press.

Meltzer, A. H. (2003), *A History of the Federal Reserve*, volume 1: *1913–1951*, University of Chicago Press.

Merler, S. and J. Pisani-Ferry (2012), 'Sudden stops in the euro area', Issue 2012/06, March, Bruegel Policy Contribution.

Merton, R. C. (1974), 'The pricing of corporate debt: the risk structure of interest rates', *Journal of Finance*, 29, 449–70.

Meulendyke, A.-M. (1998), *US Monetary Policy and Financial Markets*, Federal Reserve Bank of New York.

Mishkin, F. S. (1991), 'Asymmetric information and financial crises: a historical perspective', in R. G. Hubbard (ed.), *Financial Markets and Financial Crises*, 69–108, National Bureau of Economic Research.

Mishkin, F. (2004), *The Economics of Money, Banking and Financial Markets*, 7th edition, Addison-Wesley.

Mitlid, K., and M. Vesterlund (2001), 'Steering interest rates in monetary policy—How does it work?', *Sveriges Riksbank Quarterly Review*, 1, 19–41.

Moody's (2008), 'Corporate default and recovery rates, 1920–2007', Special comment, Moody's Investors Service.

Moore, Basil (1988), *Horizontalists and Verticalists: The Macroeconomics of Credit Money*, Oxford University Press.

Morris, S. and H. S. Shin (1998), 'Unique Equilibrium in a model of self-fulfilling currency attacks', *American Economic Review*, 88, 587–97.

Morris, S. and H. S. Shin (2001), 'The theory of global games', *Cowles Foundation Discussion Papers*, 1275R.

Morris, S. and H. S. Shin (2004), 'Liquidity black holes', *Review of Finance*, 8(1), 1–18.

Mourmouras, A. and S. Russel (1992), 'Optimal reserve requirements, deposit taxation, and the demand for Money', *Journal of Monetary Economics*, 30, 129–42.

Nautz, D. and J. Oechsler (2003), 'The repo auctions of the European Central Bank and the vanishing quota puzzle', *Scandinavian Journal of Economics*, 105, 207–20.

Nautz, D. and J. Scheithauer (2011), 'Monetary policy implementation and overnight rate persistence', *Journal of International Money and Finance*, 30, 1375–86.

Nyawata, O. (2012), 'Treasury bills and/or central bank bills for absorbing surplus liquidity: The main considerations', *IMF Working Paper*, WP/12/40.

Obstfeld, M. (2009), 'Lenders of last resort in a globalized economy', *CEPR Discussion Paper Series*, No. 7355.

Obstfeld, M., J. C. Shambaugh, and A. M. Taylor (2005), 'The trilemma in history: trade-offs among exchange rates, monetary policies, and capital mobility.' *Review of Economics and Statistics*, 87, 423–38.

Papadia, F. (2013), 'Central bank cooperation during the great recession', Bruegel Policy Contribution, Issue 2013/08, June.

Papadia, F. and T. Välimäki (2011), 'The functioning of the Eurosystem framework since 1999', in P. Mercier and F. Papadia (eds.), *The Concrete Euro—Implementing Monetary Policy in the Euro Area*, 215–342, Oxford University Press.

Perez Quiros, G. and H. Rodriguez (2006), 'The daily market for funds in Europe—has something changed with the EMU?', *Journal of Money Credit and Banking*, 38, 91–118.

Plenderleith, I. (2012), 'Review of the Bank of England's provision of emergency liquidity assistance in 2008-2009', *Report presented to the Court of the Bank of England*, October 2012.

Poole, W. (1970), 'Optimal choice of monetary policy instruments in a simple stochastic macro model', *Quarterly Journal of Economics*, 84, 197–216.

Priester, H. E. (1932), *Das Geheimnis des 13 Juli*, Berlin: Verlag von Georg Stilke.

Reichsbank (1910), *The Reichsbank 1876–1900*, trans. National Monetary Commission, Washington, DC: Government Printing Office.

Reinhart, C. M. and K. S. Rogoff (2009), *This Time is Different: Eight Centuries of Financial Folly*, Princeton University Press.

Richter, R. (1968), 'The banking system within macroeconomic theory', *German Economic Review*, 6, 273–93.

Richter, R. (1990), *Money: Lectures on the Basis of General Equilibrium Theory and the Economics of Institutions*, Berlin: Springer Verlag.

Ritz, Robert A. (2012), 'How do banks respond to increased funding uncertainty?', Working Paper, Faculty of Economics, Cambridge University.

Rochet, J.-C. and X. Vives (2004), 'Coordination failures and the lender of last resort: was Bagehot right after all?', *Journal of the European Economic Association*, 2, 1116–47.

Romer, D. (1985), 'Financial intermediation, reserve requirements, and inside money: a general equilibrium approach', *Journal of Monetary Economics*, 16, 175–94.

Rudebusch, G. (1995), 'Federal Reserve interest rate targeting, rational expectations, and the term structure', *Journal of Monetary Economics*, 35, 245–74.

Sayers, R. S. (1953), 'Open market operations in English central banking', *Schweizerische Zeitschrift für Volkswirtschaftslehre und Statistik*, 89, 389–98.

Schacht, H. (1927), *The Stabilization of the Mark*, Allen & Unwin.

Schachtschneider, K. A. (2012), 'Schriftsatz gegen die Staatsfinanzierung des ESZB und der EZB vom 13. November 2012', Text of constitutional complaint, as considered by German constitutional court in hearings on 10 and 11 June 2013.

Schmid, P. and H. Asche (1997), 'Monetary policy instruments and procedures in Germany: Evolution, deployment and effects', in BIS, *Monetary Policy Operating Procedures in Industrial Countries* (BIS Conference Papers iii), Basle: BIS.

Schmidt, S. and D. Nautz (2009), 'Monetary Policy Implementation and the federal funds rate', *Journal of Banking and Finance*, 33, 1274–84.

Schotter, A. and T. Yorulmazer (2009), 'On the severity of bank runs', *Journal of Financial Intermediation*, 18, 217–41.

Schularik, M., and A. M. Taylor (2012), 'Credit booms gone bust: monetary policy, leverage cycles and financial crises, 1870–2008', *American Economic Review*, 102, 1029–61.

Sellin, P. and P. Å. Sommar (2013), 'Operational frameworks for implementing monetary policy', forthcoming in *Quarterly Review of the Sveriges Riksbank.*

Shambaugh, J. (2012), 'The euro's three crises', *Brooking Papers on Economic Activity*, Spring 2012, 257–311.

Shin, H. S. (2009), 'Reflections on Northern Rock: The bank run that heralded the global financial crisis', *Journal of Economic Perspectives*, 23, 101–19.

Siegel, J. J. (1981). 'Bank reserves and financial stability', *Journal of Finance*, 34, 1073–84.

Singh, M. (2013), 'Collateral and monetary policy', *IMF Working Paper*, WP/13/186.

Sinn, H.-W. and T. Wollmershäuser (2011), 'Target loans, current account balances and capital flows: the ECB's rescue facility', *NBER Working Paper*, No. 17626.

Spindt, P. A. and J. R. Hoffmeister (1988), 'The micromechanics of the federal funds market: Implications for day-of-the-week effects in funds rate volatility', *Journal of Financial and Quantitative Analysis*, 23, 401–16.

Standard & Poors (2009), 'Annual global corporate default study and rating transitions', Ratings direct.

Stein, J. C. (1998), 'An adverse selection model of bank asset and liability management with implications for the transmission of monetary policy', *RAND Journal of Economics*, 29, 466–86.

Stevens, E. J. (1991), 'Is there a rationale for reserve requirements?', *Federal Reserve Bank of Cleveland Economic Review*, 27/4, 2–17.

Stiglitz, J. E. and Weiss, A. (1981), 'Credit rationing in markets with imperfect information', *American Economic Review*, 71, 393–410.

Stolper, G. (1940/1969), 'The German Economy', in Fritz K. Ringer (ed.), *The German Inflation of 1923*, Oxford University Press.

Strongin, S. (1995), 'The identification of monetary policy disturbances—explaining the liquidity puzzle', *Journal of Monetary Economics*, 35, 463–97.

Tabakis, E. and B. Weller (2009), 'Collateral and risk mitigation frameworks of central bank policy operations—a comparison across central banks', in U. Bindseil,

F. Gonzalez, and E. Tabakis (eds.), *Risk Management for Central Banks and Other Public Institutions*, 340–58, Cambridge University Press.

Tamagna, F. M. (1963), 'Processes and instruments of monetary policy: a comparative analysis', in F. M. Tamagna et al. (eds.), *Monetary Management*, 1–174, Prentice-Hall.

Taylor, J. B. (1993), 'Discretion versus policy rules in practice', *Carnegie-Rochester Conference Series on Public Policy*, 39, 195–214.

Thornton, H. (1802), *An Inquiry into the Nature and Effects of Paper Credit of Great Britain*, Reprint 1962, New York: Kelley.

Tobin, J. (1963), 'Commercial banks as creators of "money"', in Dean Carson (ed.), *Banking and Monetary Studies*, 408–19, for the Comptroller of the Currency, U.S. Treasury, Richard D. Irwin.

Tucker, P. (2004), 'Managing the central bank's balance sheet: where monetary policy meets financial stability', *Bank of England Quarterly Bulletin*, Autumn 2004, 359–82.

Välimäki, T. (1999), 'The overnight rate of interest under averaged reserve requirements', *Bank of Finland Discussion Papers*, 8/1999.

Välimäki, T. (2003), *Central Bank Tenders: Three Essays on Money Market Liquidity Auctions*, Bank of Finland Studies E:26.

Warburg, P. M. (1930), *The Federal Reserve System, its Origins and Growth* (2 vols.). Macmillan.

Whitesell, W. (2006), 'Interest-rate corridors and reserves', *Journal of Monetary Economics*, 53, 1177–95.

Wicker, E. (1996), *The Banking Panics of the Great Depression*, Cambridge University Press.

Wicksell, K. (1898/1936), *Interest and Prices: A Study of the Causes Regulating the Value of Money*, Macmillan, 1936. Translation of: *Geldzins und Güterpreise, Eine Studie ueber die den Tauschwert des Geldes bestimmende Ursachen*, Gustav Fischer, 1898.

Wirth, M. (1883), *Geschichte der Handelskrisen*, 3rd edition, J. D. Sauerländers Verlag.

Wood, E. (1939), *English Theories of Central Banking Control (1819–1858)*, Harvard University Press.

Woodford, M. (2003), *Interest and Prices: Foundations of a Theory of Monetary Policy*, Princeton University Press.

Woodford, M. (2010), 'Financial intermediation and macroeconomic analysis', *Journal of Economic Perspectives*, 24, 21–44.

Würtz, F. R. (2003), 'A comprehensive model of the euro overnight rate', *ECB Working Paper Series*, No. 207.

Index